BURN AFTER READING

A catalogue record for this book is available from the British Library.

First published in Great Britain in 2012 by:
Carpet Bombing Culture, imprint of Pro-actif Communications Ltd

Second edition

ISBN: 978-1-908211-06-4

email: books@carpetbombingculture.co.uk

WWW.CARPETBOMBINGCULTURE.CO.UK

BURN AFTER READING

RomanyWG

BURN AFTER READING

It's been forty years since the phenomena of Hip Hop Graffiti exploded out of Philadelphia and NYC, electrifying a generation of rebel youth across the world. Writing has evolved into a pulsating, living virus, infecting the cities and towns of every nation where you can buy or steal spray paints.

B.A.R. showcases the most recent phases of evolution in the form showing the hybridised, bastardised, mutant styles of today. Despite crackdowns in most major cities the culture lives on and it shows no sign of slowing down. Reinvigorated by the internet and cross fertilised with the newer 'street art' styles these collected images show how Graffiti 'pieces' have survived the backlash by migrating to semi legal spots and hidden away urban ruins where the writers can paint all day without fear.

B.A.R. is a vision of the world as if Graffiti were legal and free human expression ruled our visual landscape instead of advertising.

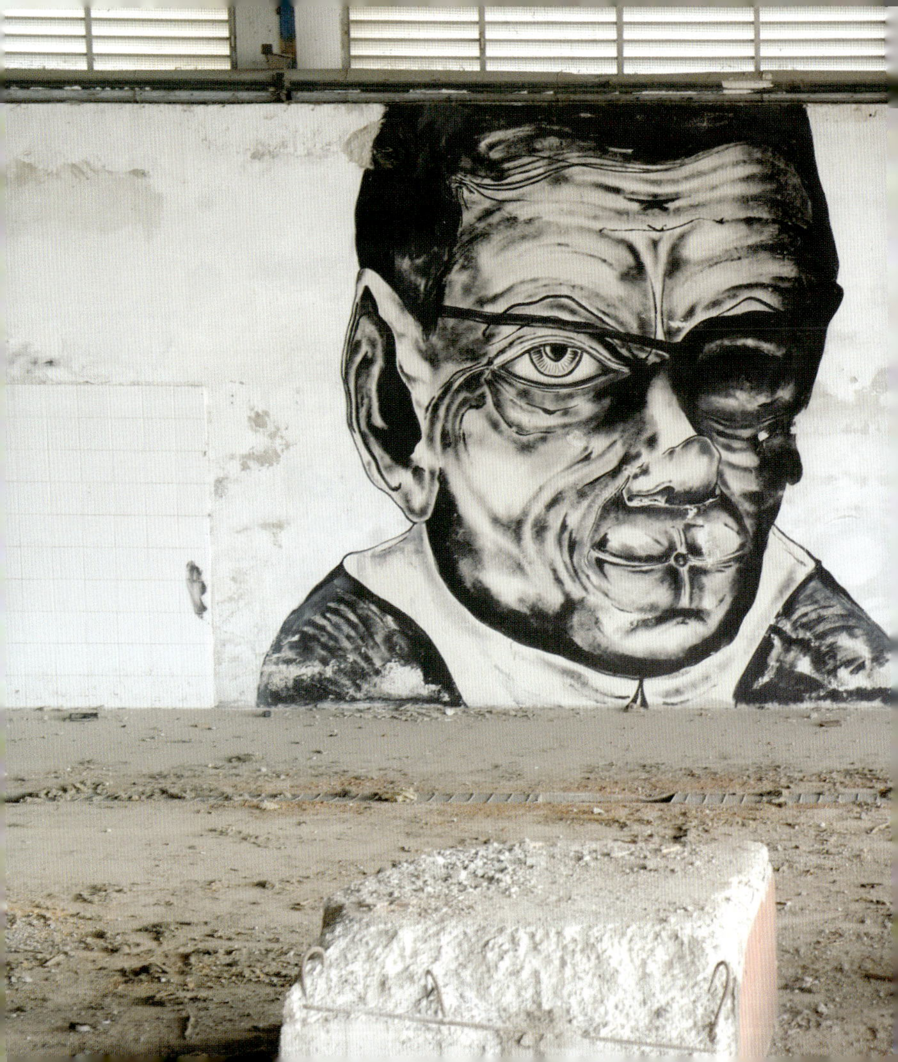

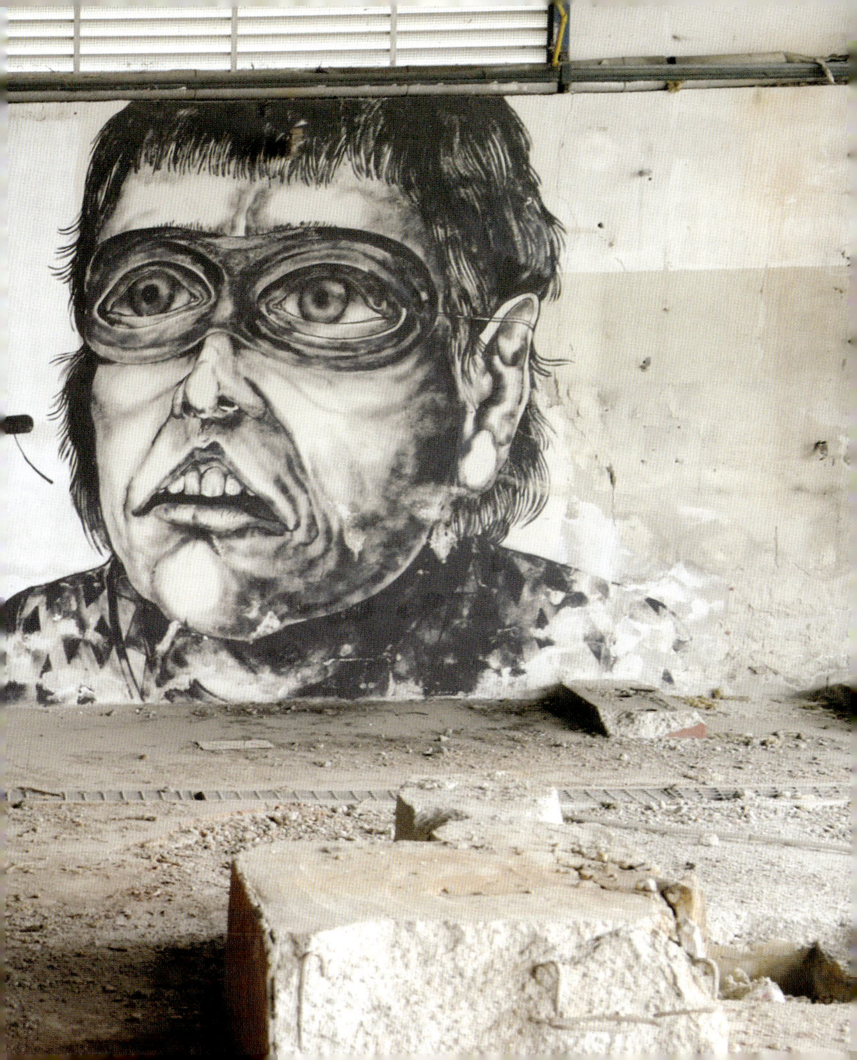

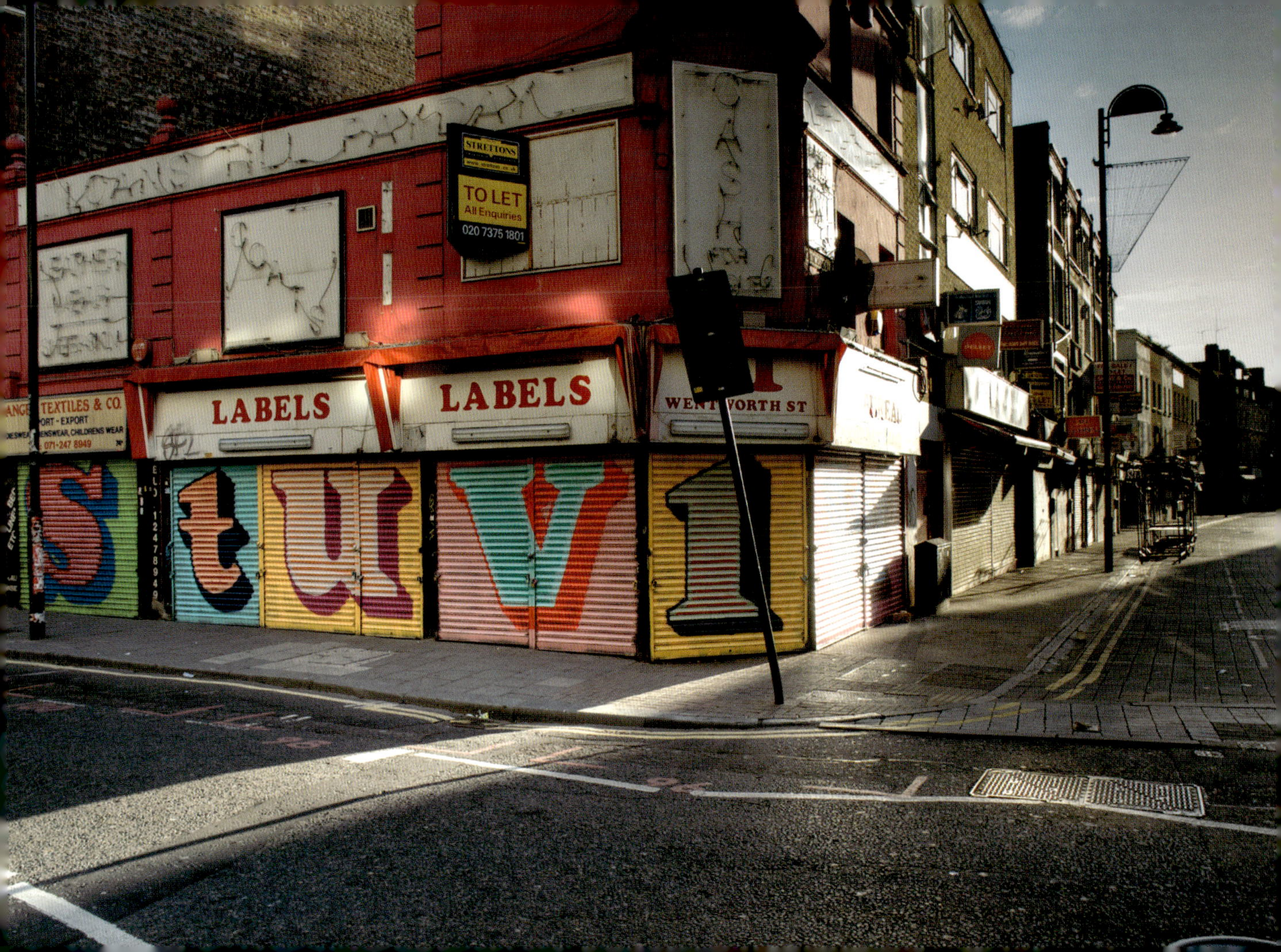
STRETTONS
TO LET
All Enquiries
020 7375 1801
TEXTILES & CO.
071-247 8949
LABELS
LABELS
WENTWORTH ST

[WO]MAN + CAN + WALL

The problem with the police these days is that they're too damn quick. There are over four million CCTV cameras in the UK. The logistics of painting on walls under these conditions have led to the dominance of the sticker, the stencil and the wheat paste. This is all well and good however the desire to paint on walls still burns in many a heart and for some, the artistry of working freehand is the whole point.

This folk mural-ism grown out of graffiti culture continues to thrive where it can, these days more often in legal initiatives or out in the urban ruins where a painter can take a full day at a wall.

It is 'folk' because it is still open, popular and democratic. It is not the practice of an art elite, nor the worthy 'public art' commissioned by council's and bestowed upon the plebs willy nilly. The work collected here still has the raw energy of it's illegal past.

There is powerful magic in painting like this. Unlike the agitprop political comedy of most stencil work, freehand painting offers a deeper, perhaps weirder look through the eyes of the artist. It is not shorthand for anything. It is what it is.

It is sometimes beautiful, sometimes ugly but always breathtaking in it's skill of execution. Although it may be unfashionable to say so – it's impressive at least in part because it's really bloody difficult to do it well. Sadly these murals take too long to create for the culture to proliferate. So, until the revolution of consciousness when our leaders will simultaneously attain enlightenment and shut the fuck up, budding muralists need to find legal walls.

Collected here are some of the best.

. . .Patrick Potter

I prefer to do my painting in abandoned houses or industrial sites . . . it's their ambiance . . . and because my art comes to life in these kind of places

LA MOUCHE

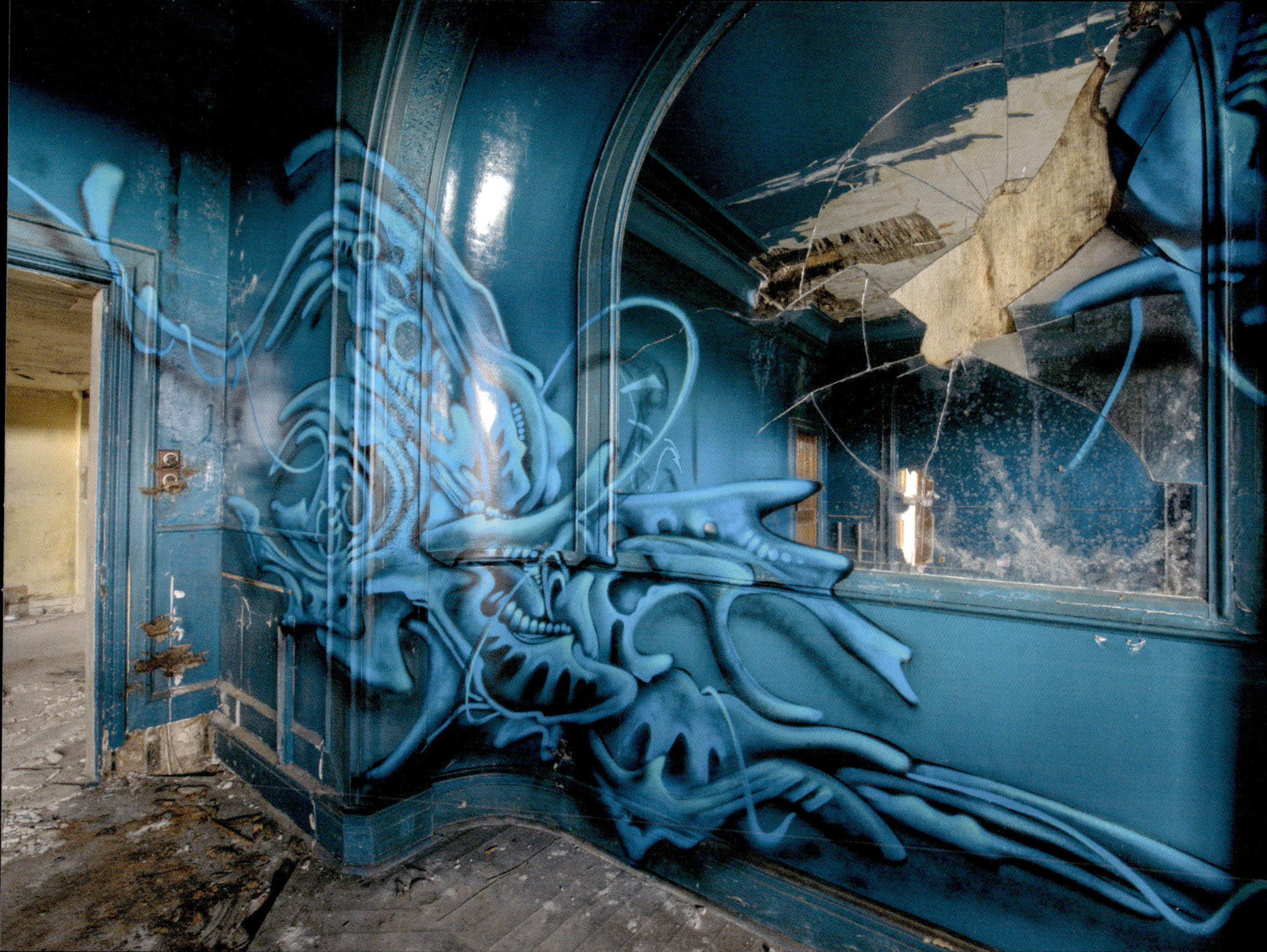

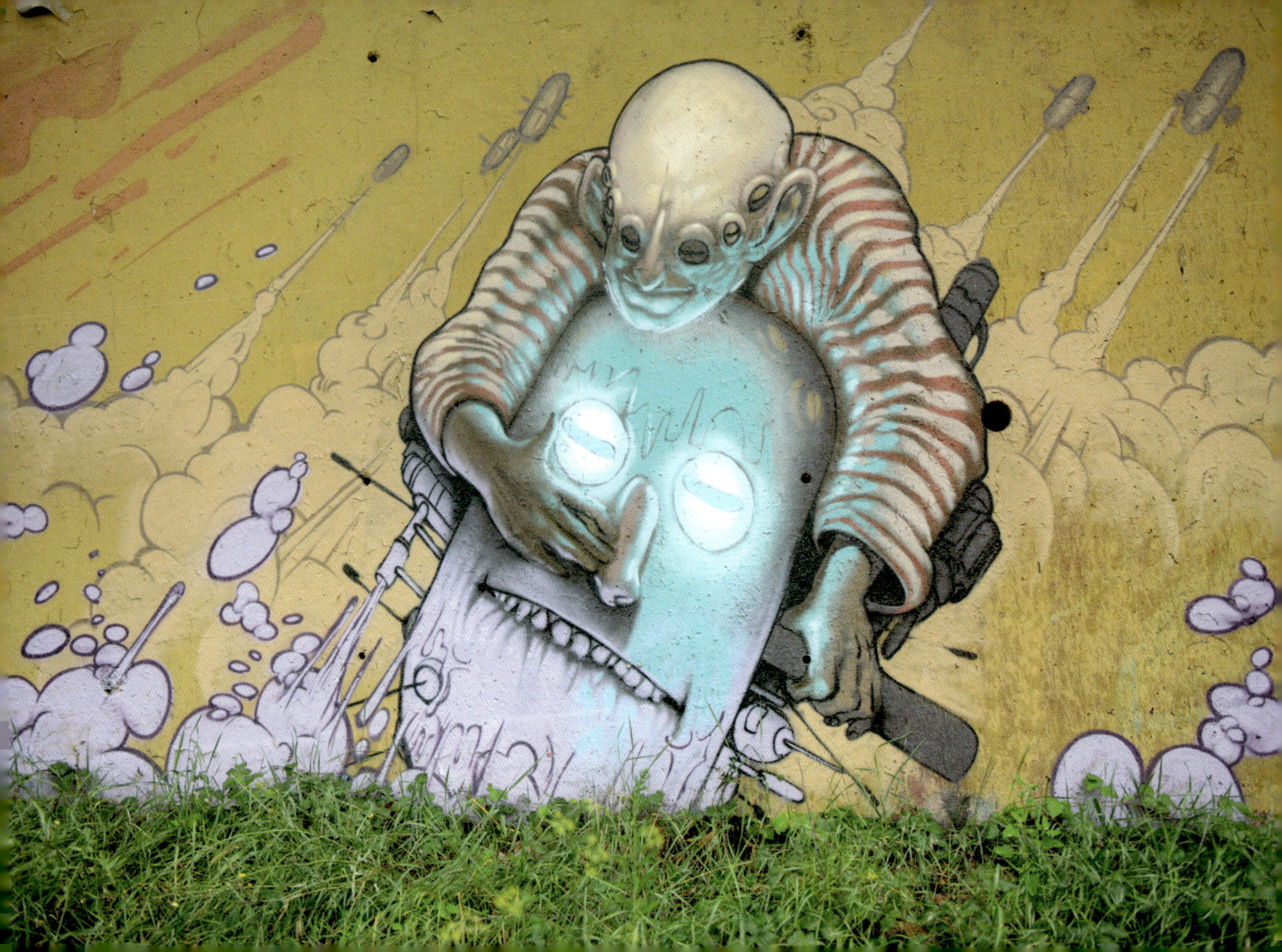

A SUPER CONDENSED HISTORY OF MODERN GRAFFITI IN CHUNKS

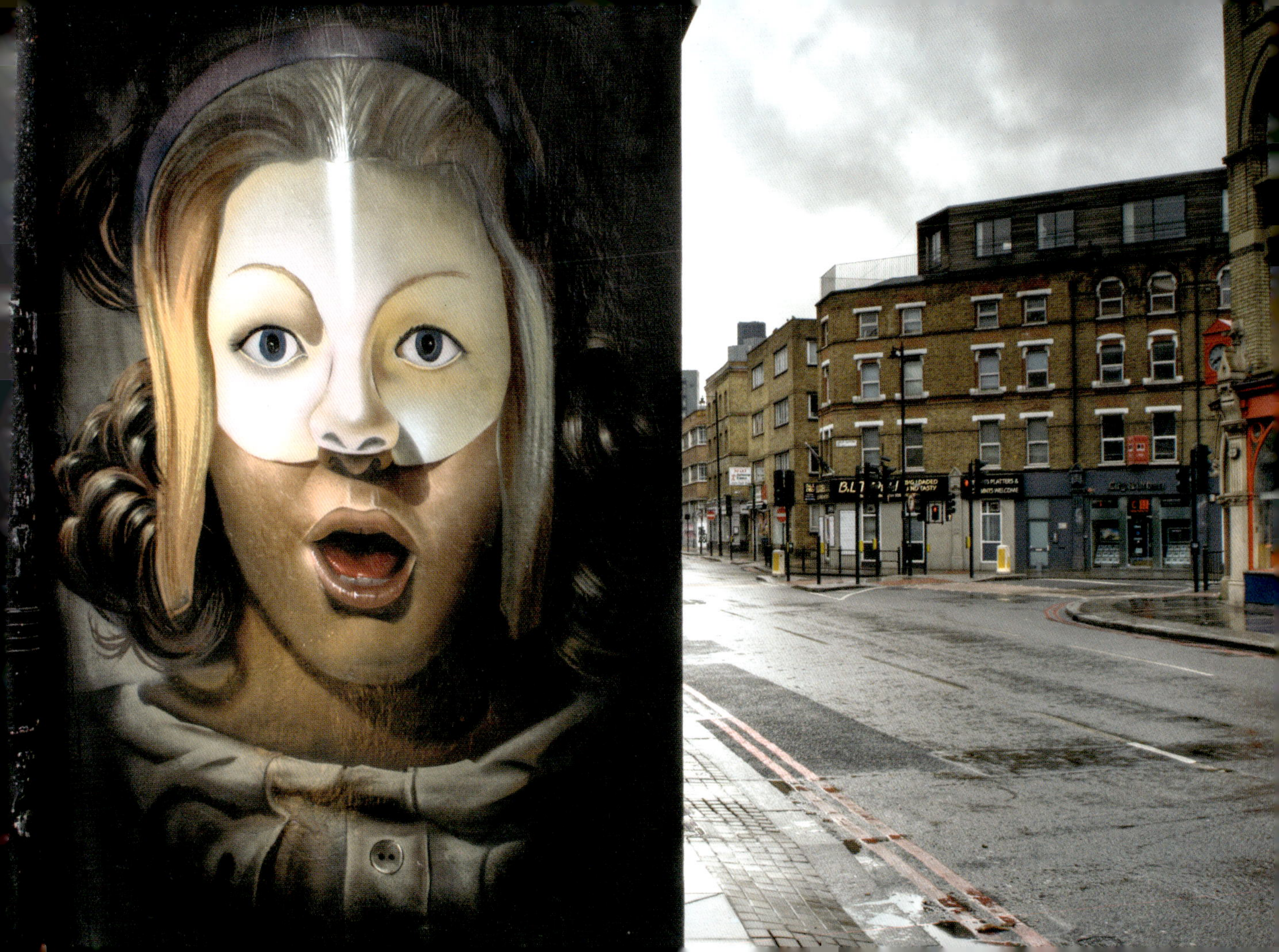

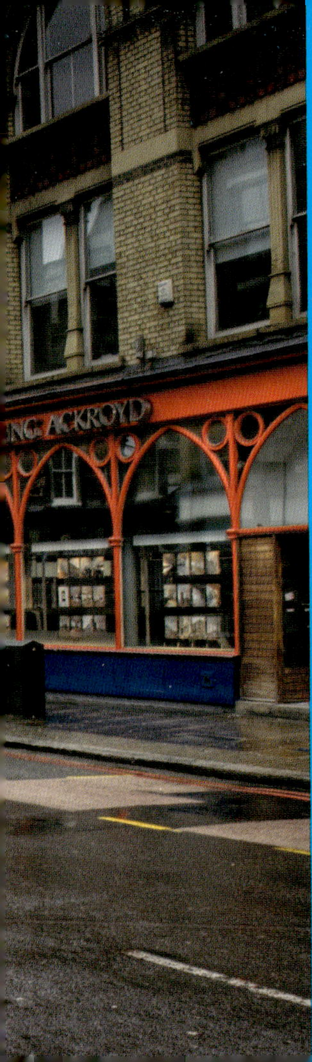

BROKE KIDS

UNDER PRESSURE

NYC 1972. Young men working dead end jobs, under pressure, no money, no time and nowhere safe to hide. Murderers walk the streets. Gangs control the barrios. The glamour of the high life is shoved in your face. But you ain't allowed in to Studio 54. You're just a schmuck. A low life kid. Well screw you NYC. I am somebody. This is my name. I'm going to write it till my fingers bleed.

TAKI 183 bought a permanent market. Travelling all over the city as a courier, he wrote his name on the subway trains. It became an obsession. He got himself so famous the papers interviewed him. All the other kids realised they could get famous too, all for the price of a pen.

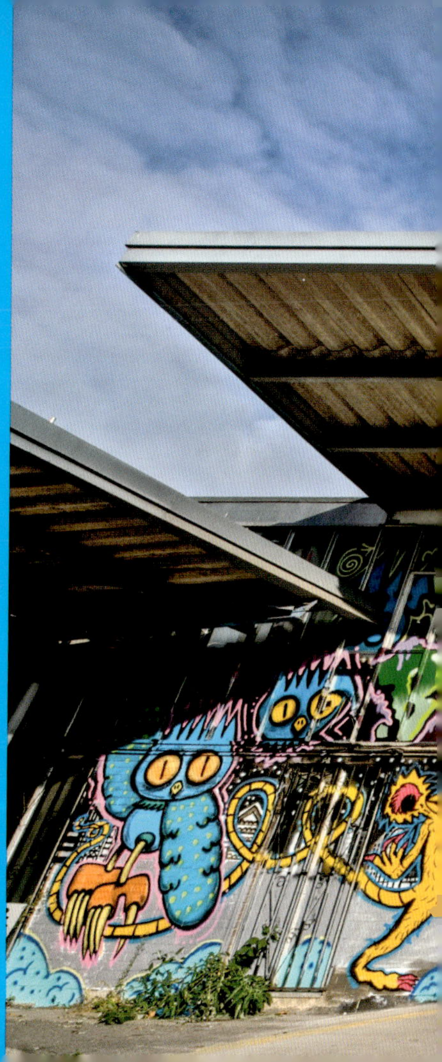

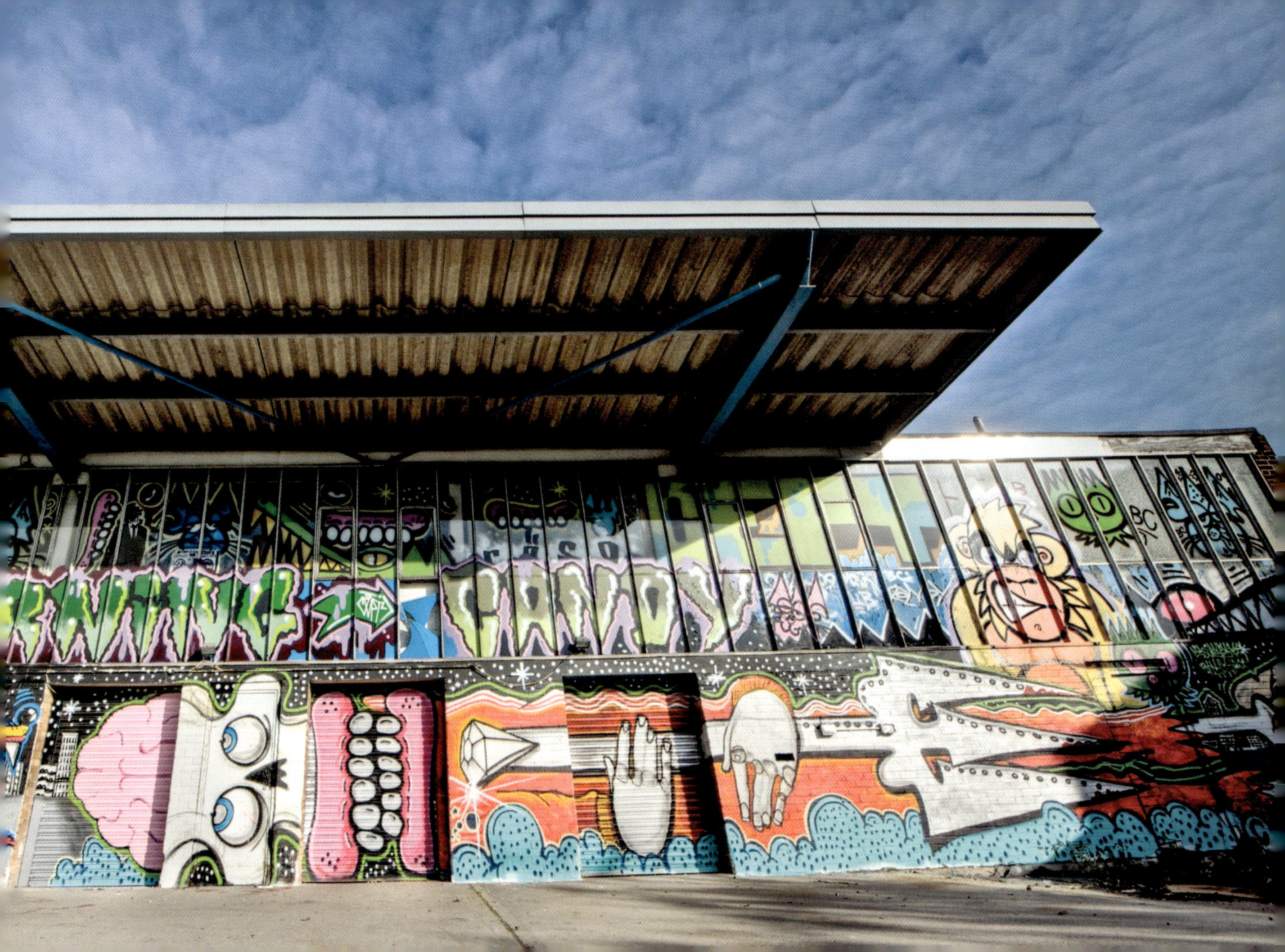

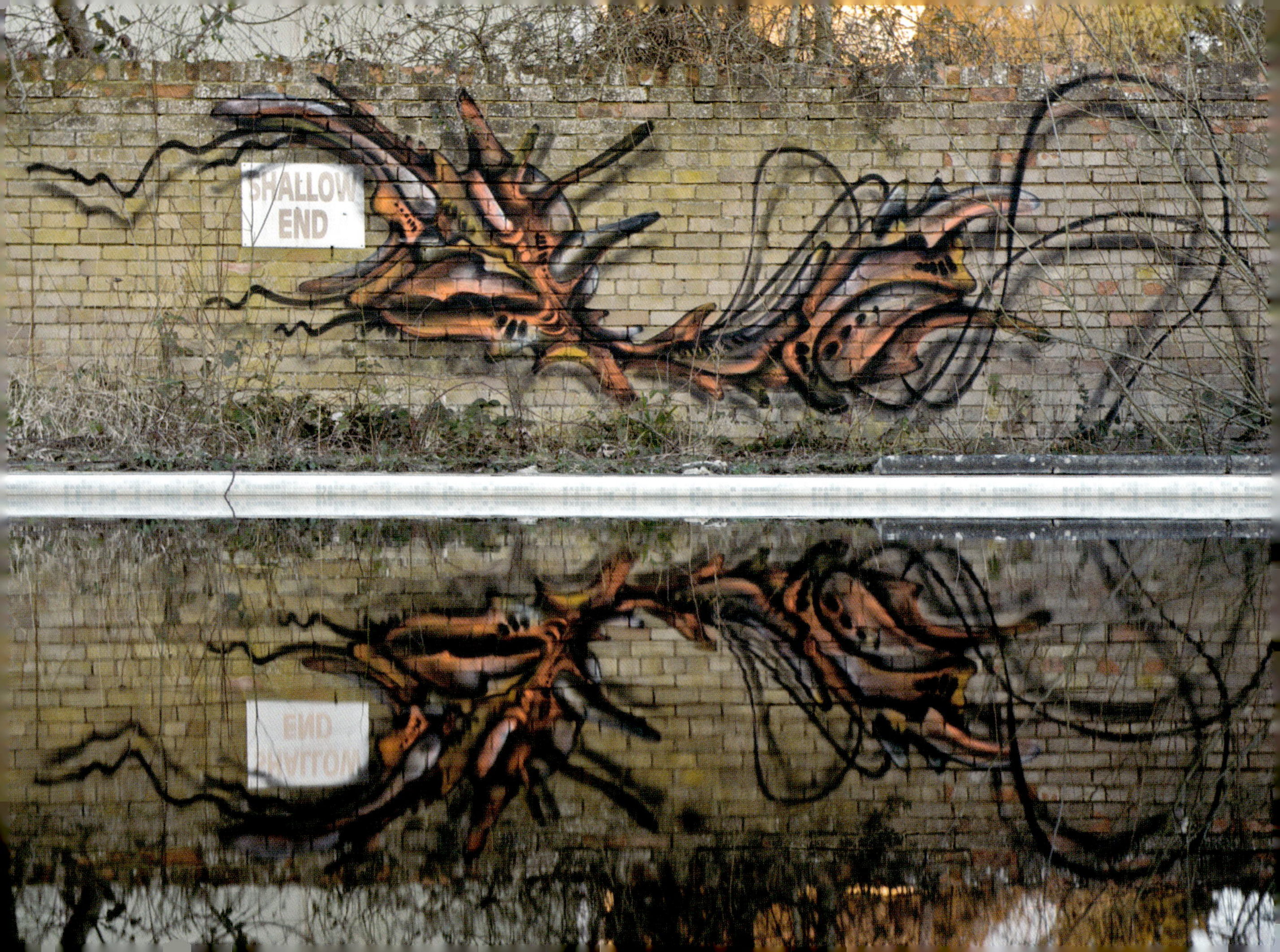
SHALLOW
END

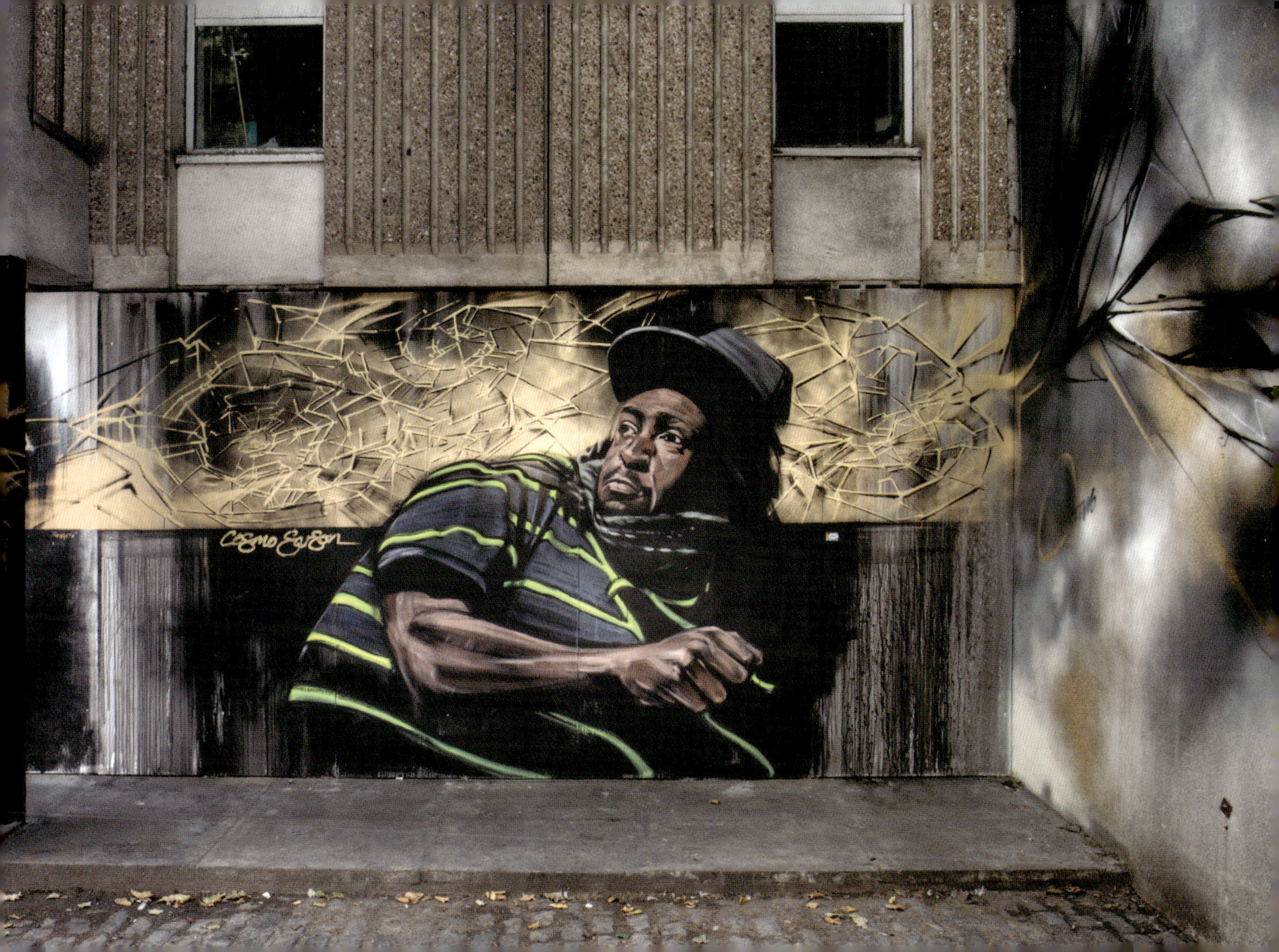

Working outside gives me a sense of freedom that a canvas bound for a gallery would never allow. Art should be like a dance in front of a surface, with paint brushes for hands. The bigger the surface, the more you can bug out - and once you're done bugging out, the work is on display (for free) to a 24-hour audience.

SICKBOY

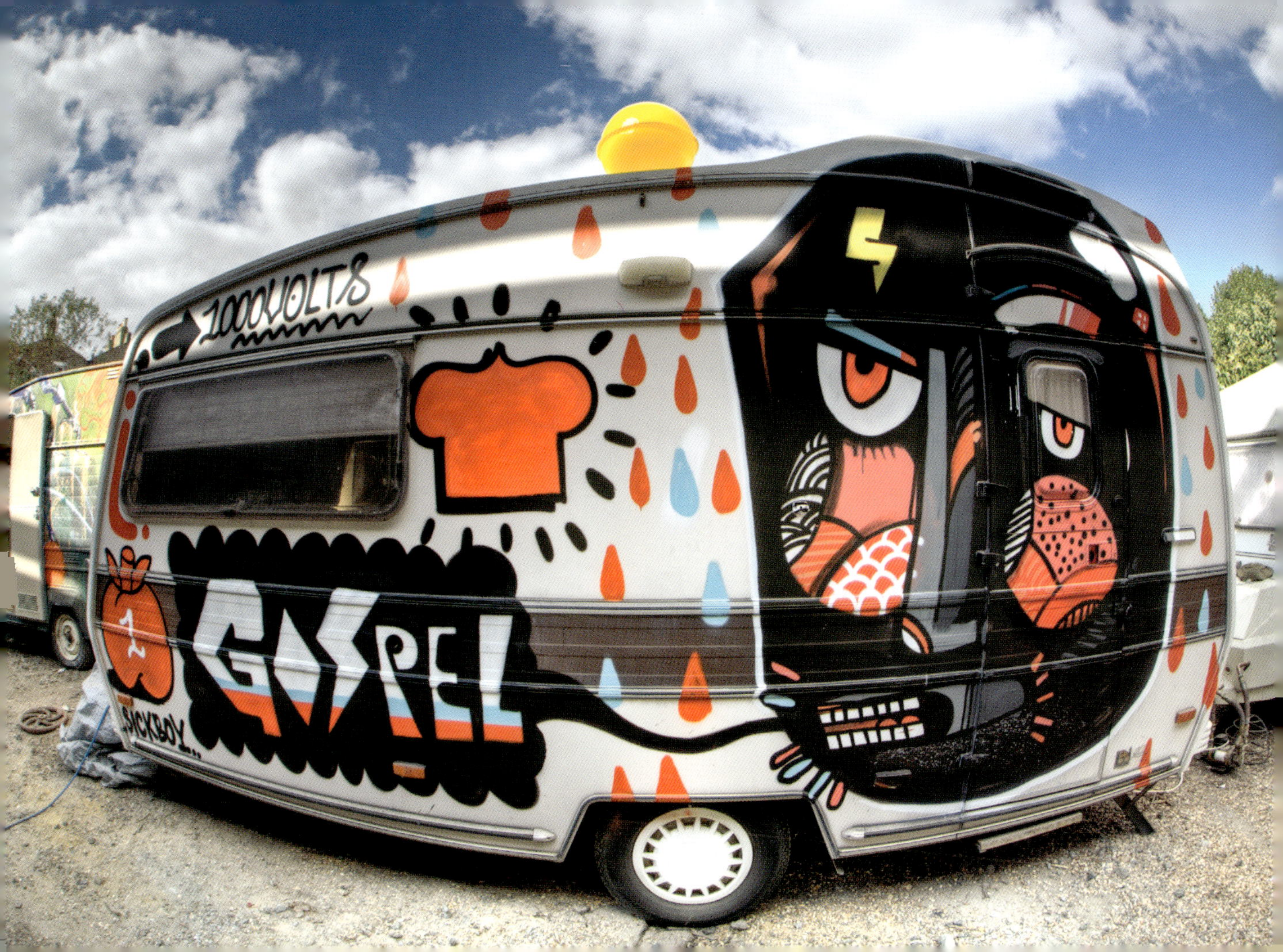
1000VOLTS
GOSPEL
SICKBOY

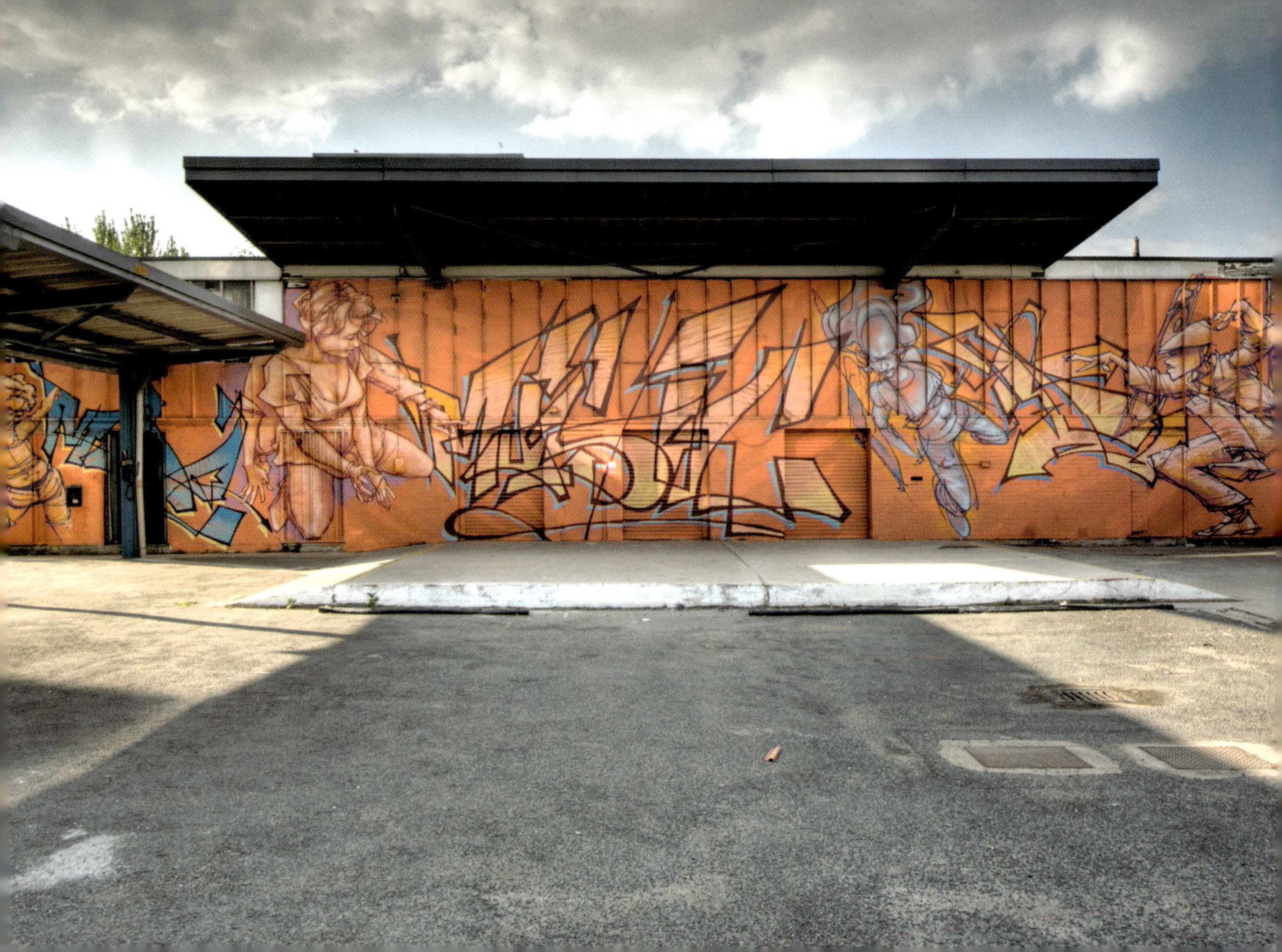

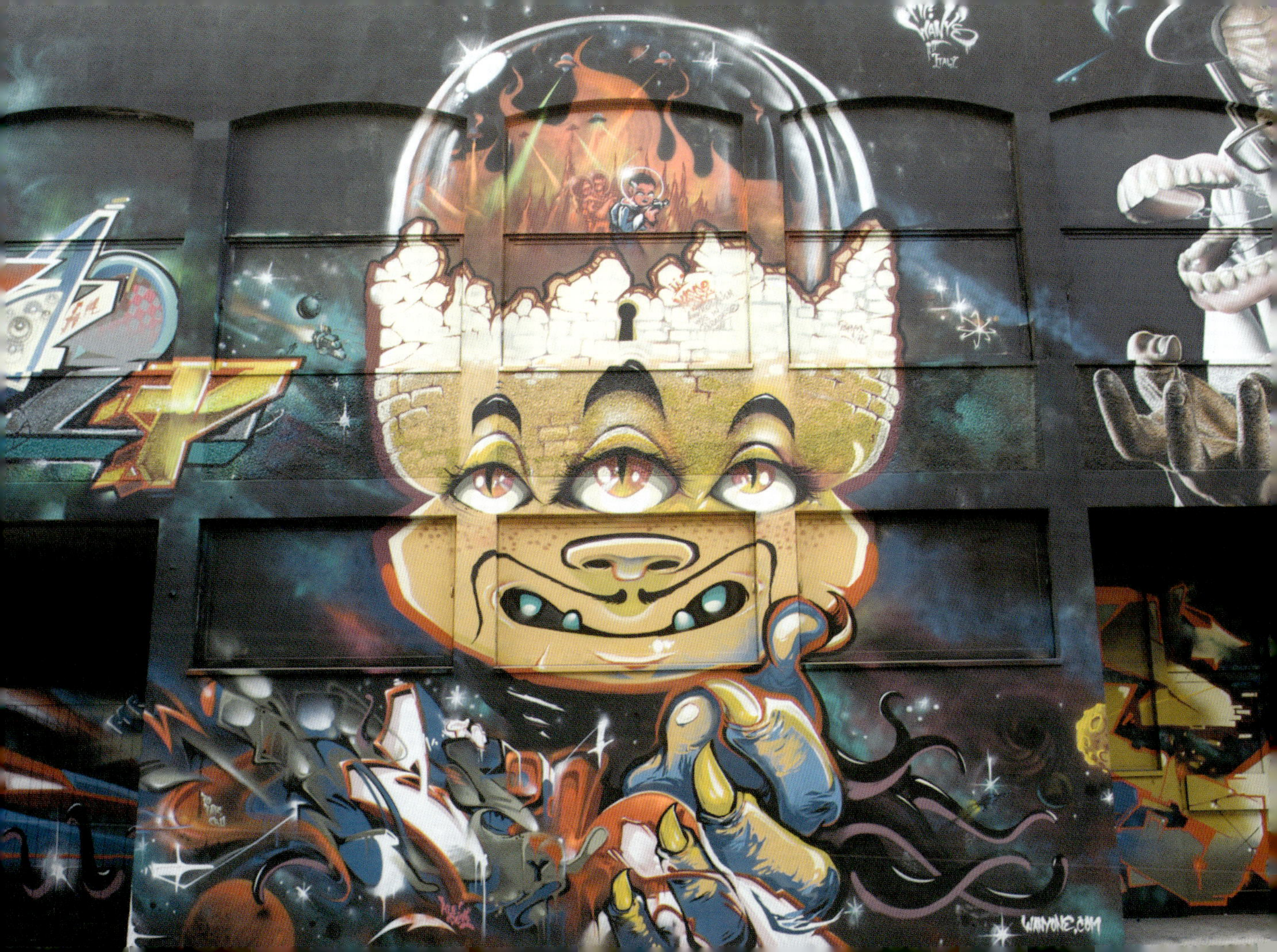
WANYONE.COM

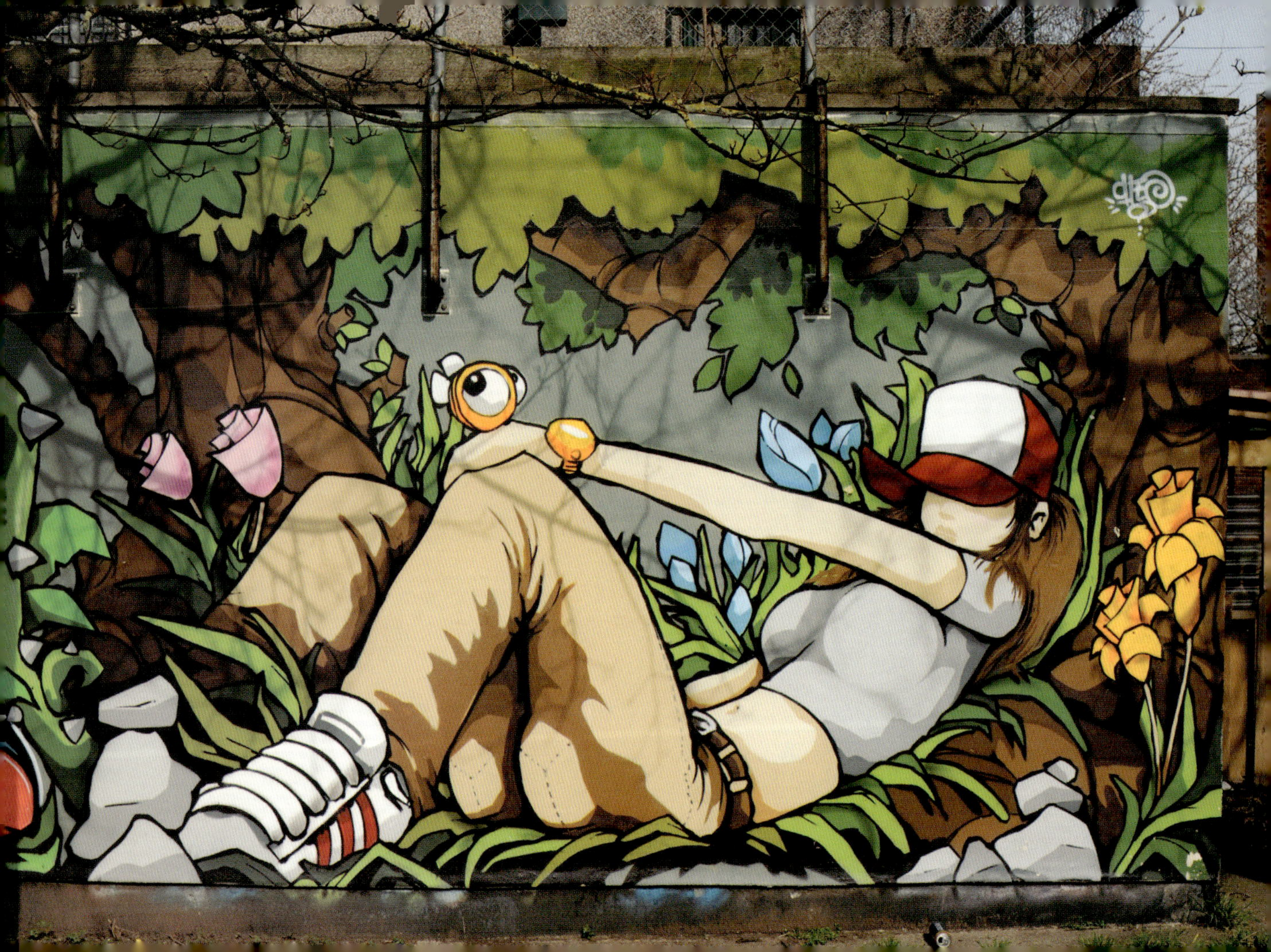

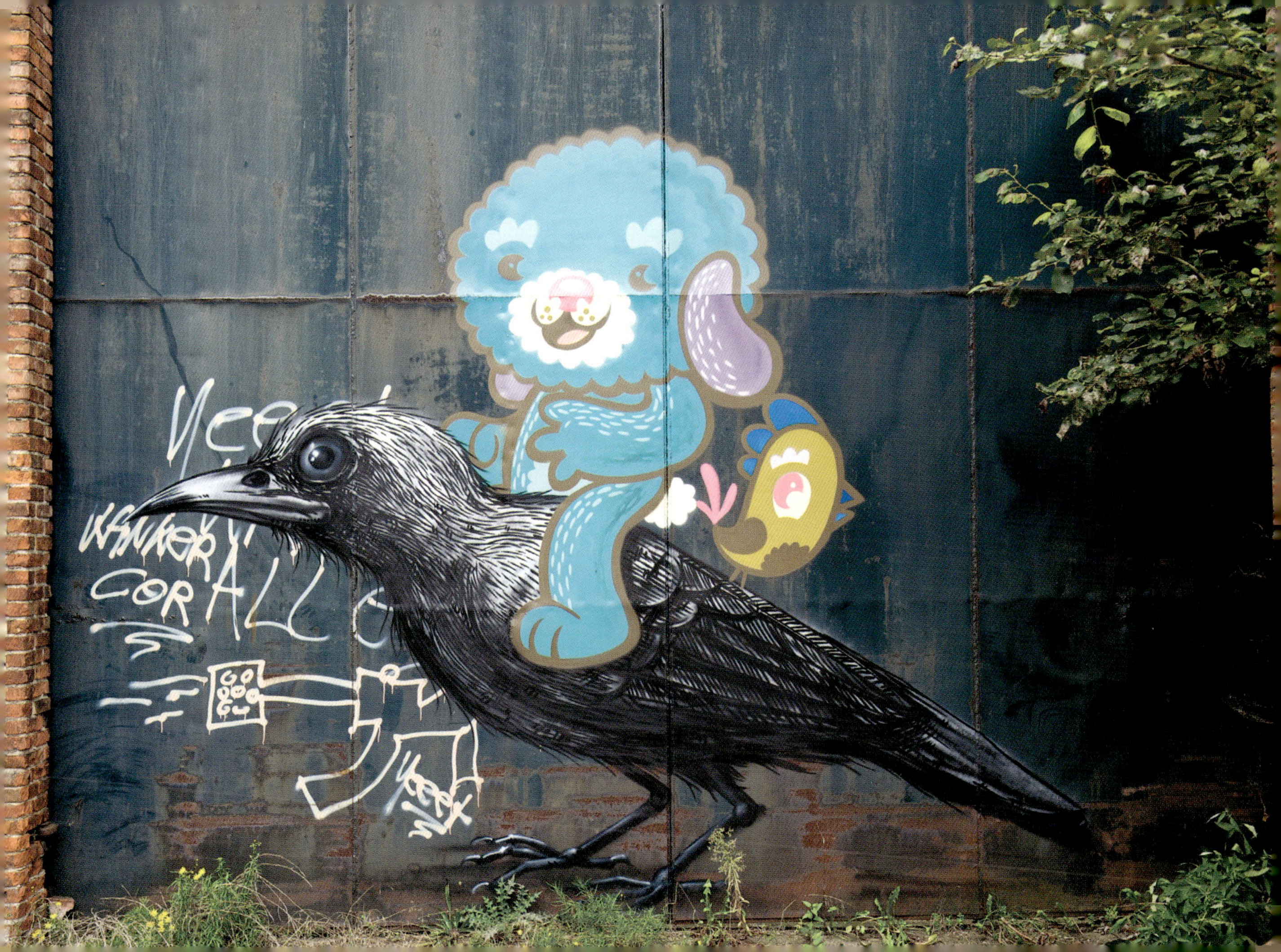

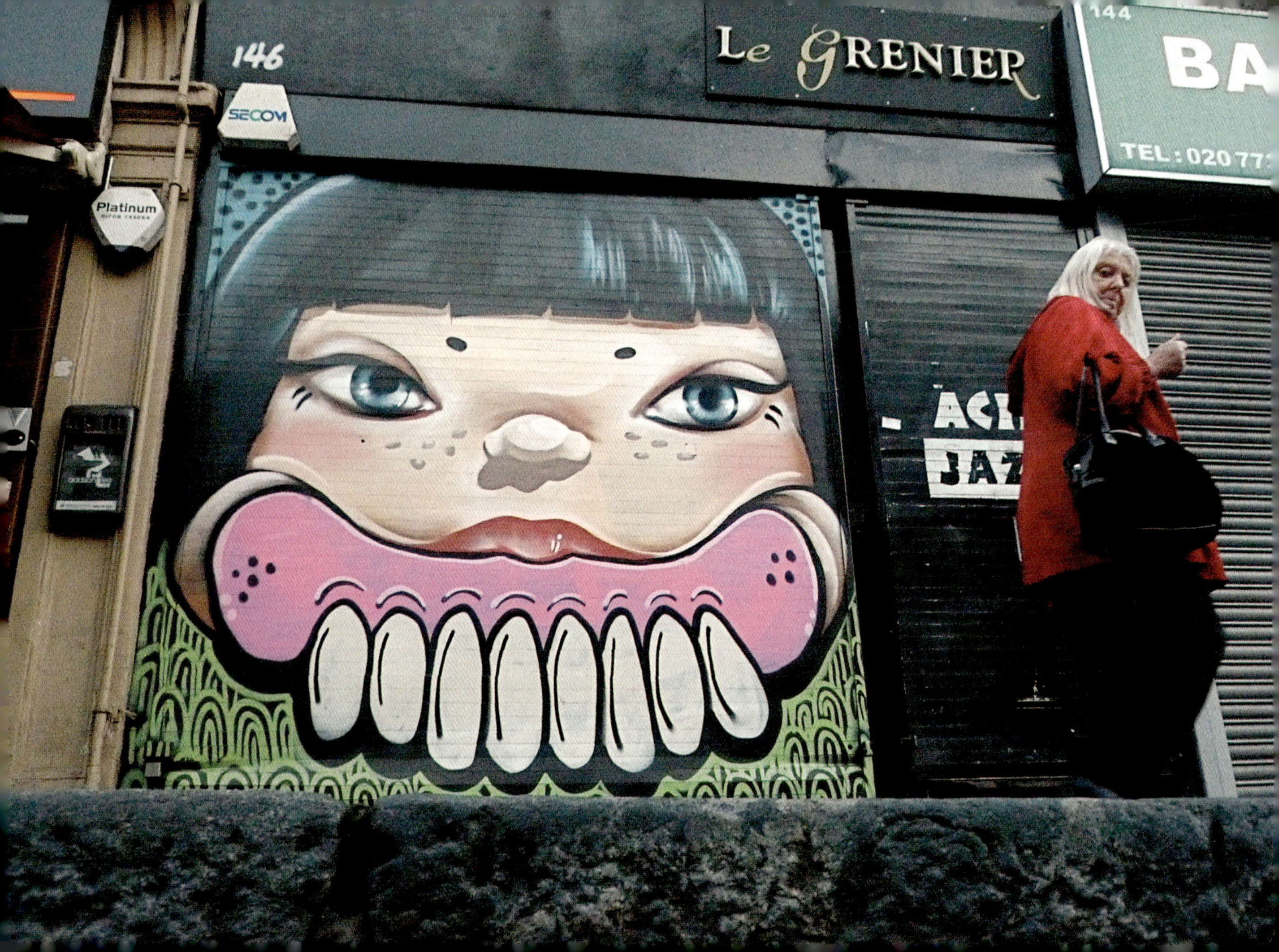

146
Le GRENIER
144
BA
TEL: 020 77
SECOM
Platinum

TOO MANY NAMES

The subway carriages of NYC filled up with names. Too many names. It got hard to get noticed. So the kids started to compete with each other. Trying to get more attention. Trying to be the king of the line.

They fought with numbers, putting more tags up than the others. Then they fought with size, putting bigger tags up. Then they fought with style. The style wars began.

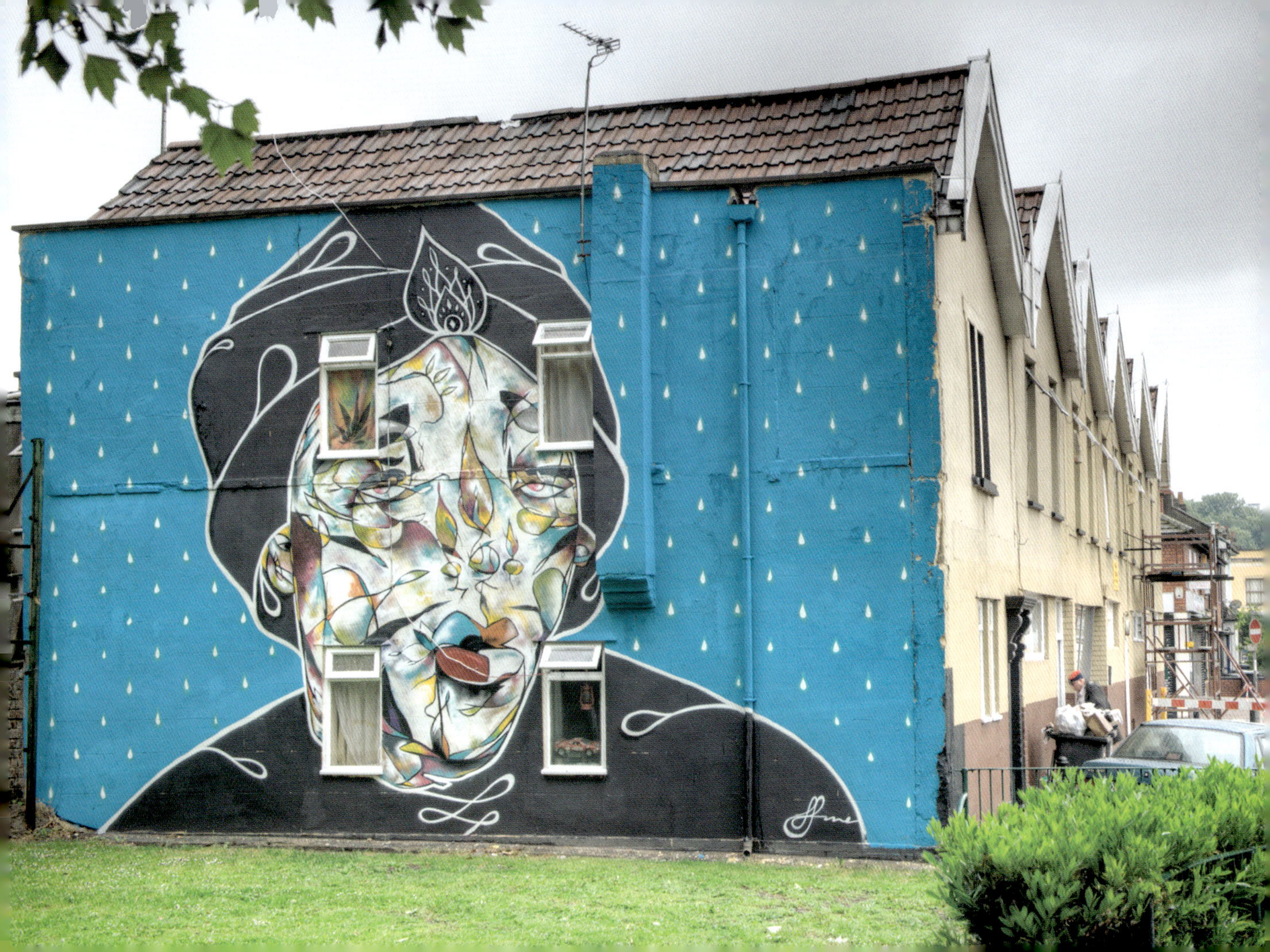

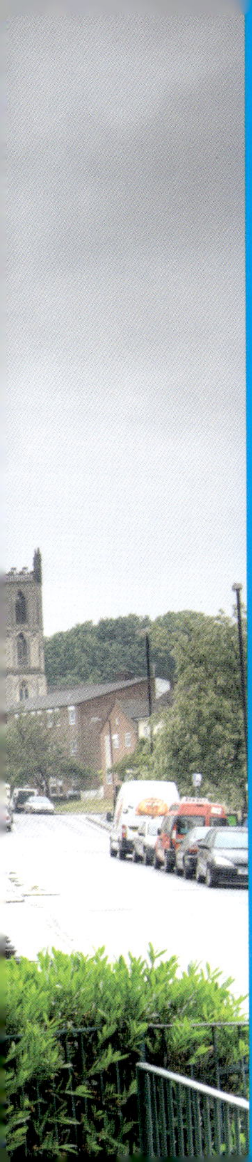

MOVING MASTERPIECES

NYC Subway Graffiti peaked in the late 1970's. The city was in chaos. Nobody cared about policing the train yards. The crews had free reign. They painted whole cars. This was a time of innovation. Writers peaked in their creativity, mixing up styles, adding characters and scenery. Always pushing to do something bigger, better and more original than their rival crews. Crews would meet at trackside benches to compare sketchbooks and watch their work roll by. For many, the ultimate expression of graffiti is still a moving train, broadcasting your name around the whole city.

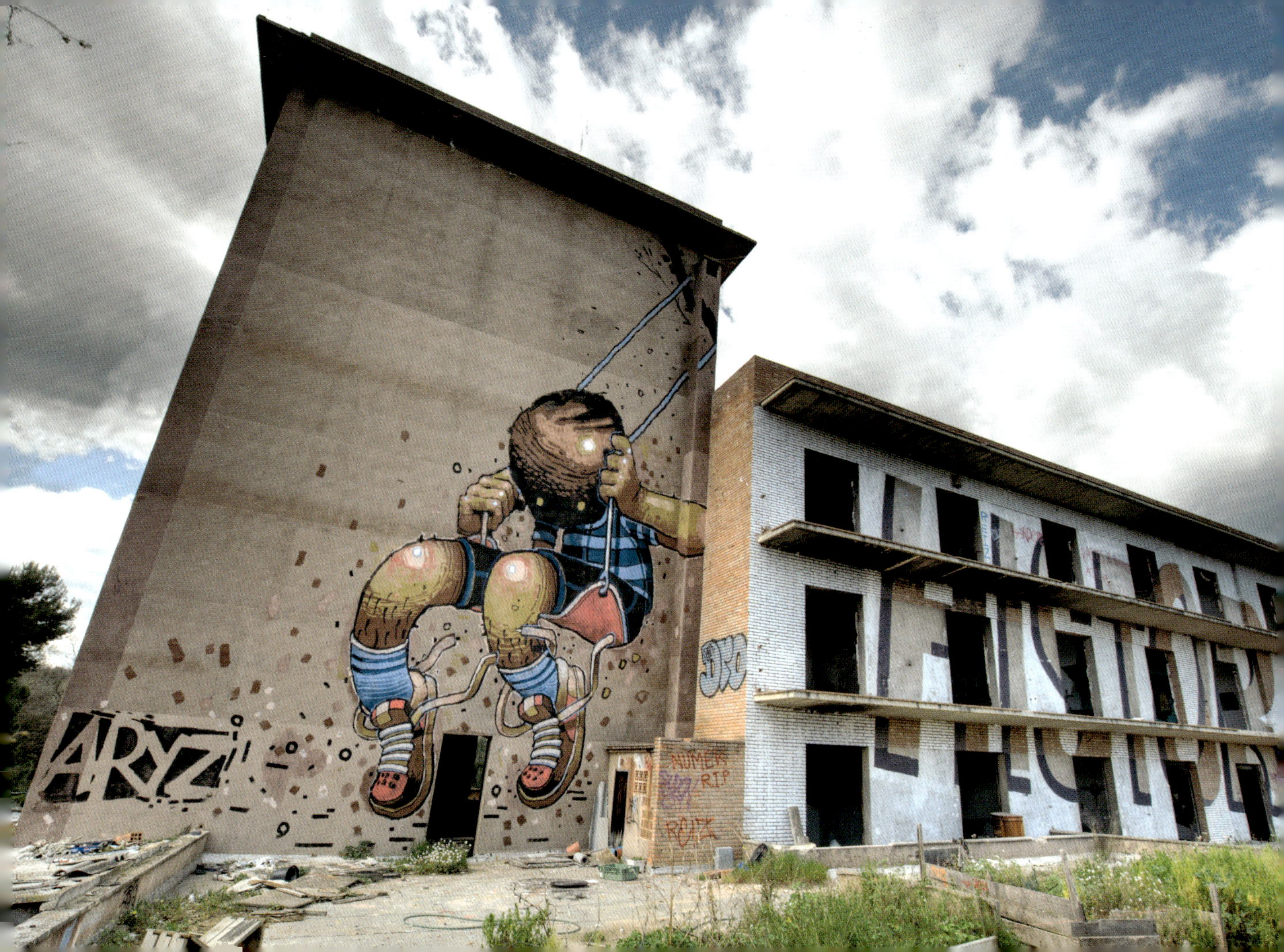
ARYZ
NUMER RIP
REIZ

COMING TO EUROPE

In 1979 an Italian art dealer called Claudio Bruni invited two NYC writers to do a gallery show in Rome. Fab 5 Freddy and Lee Quinones gave Europe her first taste of graffiti style. Other influences soon crossed the Atlantic. Blondie released 'the Rapture', the music video featured Graffiti. Then in 1983 Charlie Ahearn released the indy movie 'Wild Style'. That same year PBS released the documentary 'Style Wars'. European pioneers were inspired by these films as they were by early Hip Hop mix tapes. Graffiti took hold in the cities of Europe.

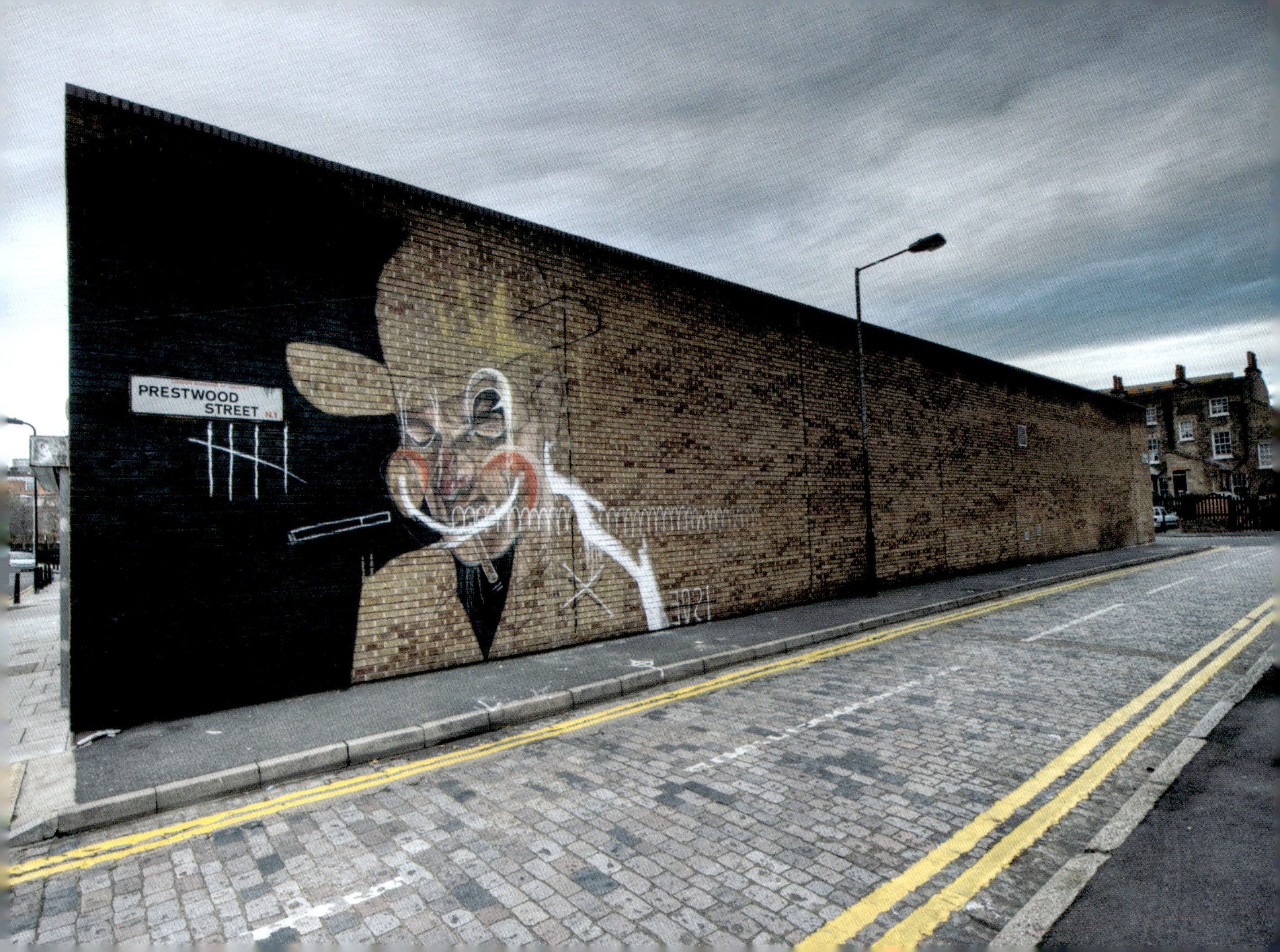
PRESTWOOD
STREET N.1

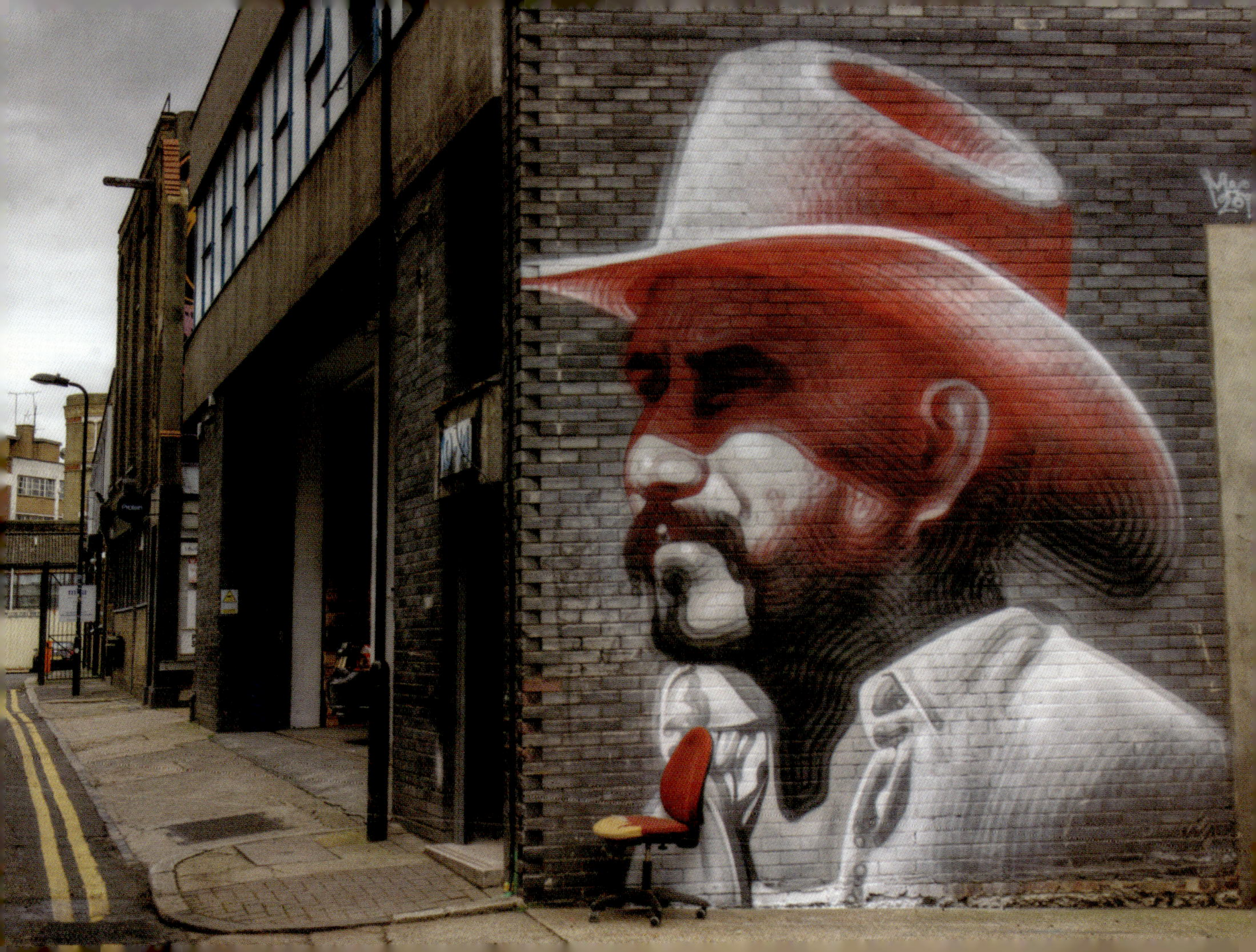

When I paint on the street, it's because I want to engage with the city I live in. Any time I'm painting on the street, it's as a participatory action, it is a response to the notion that I should be a vacant consumer, the property laws that are in place to benefit those who own said property, and the idea that I should abide in silence . . . ..

Or more likely, it's just me writing "I was 'ere" in expensive paint.

CYCLOPS

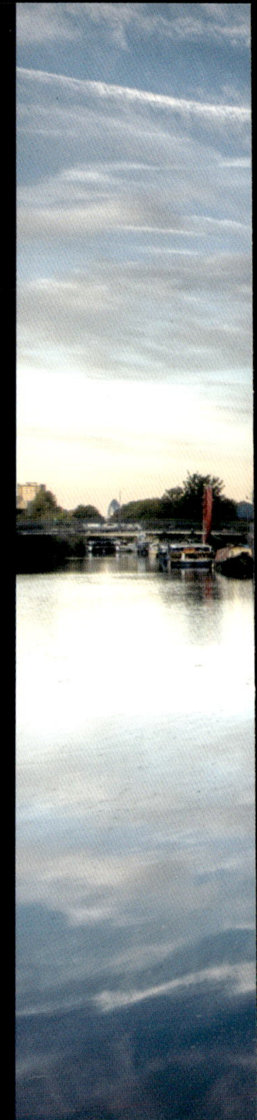

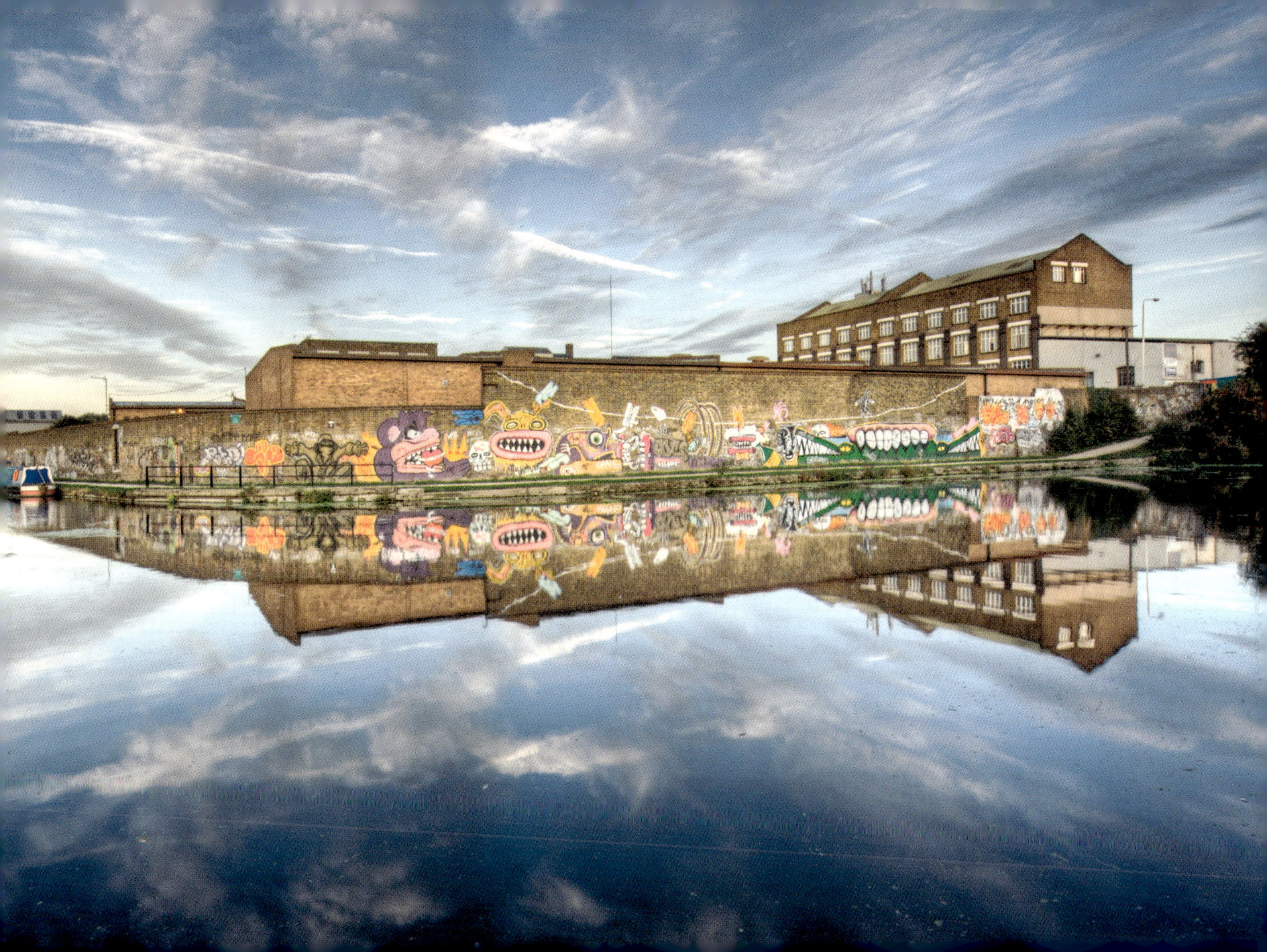

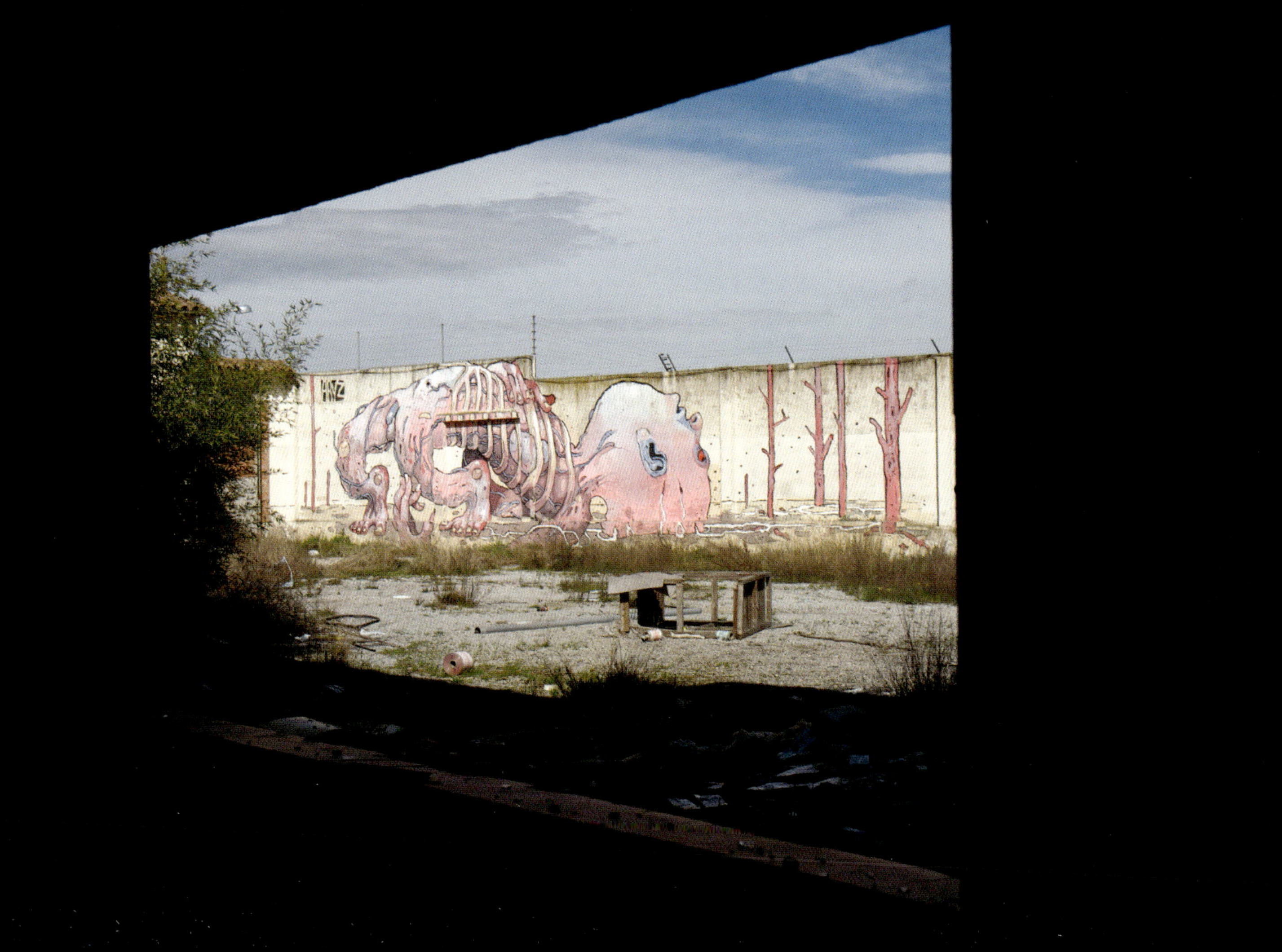

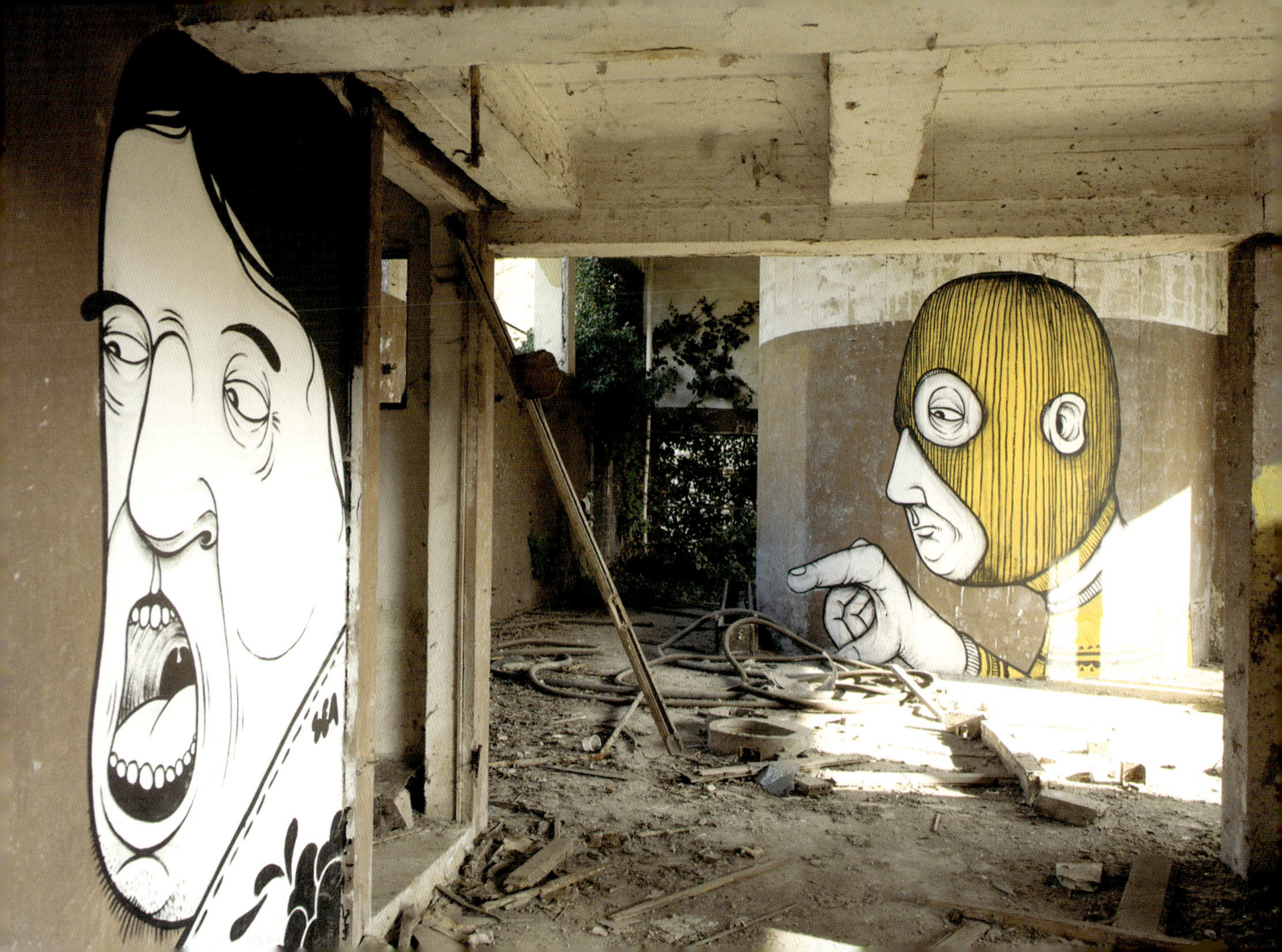

WRITING IS FIGHTING

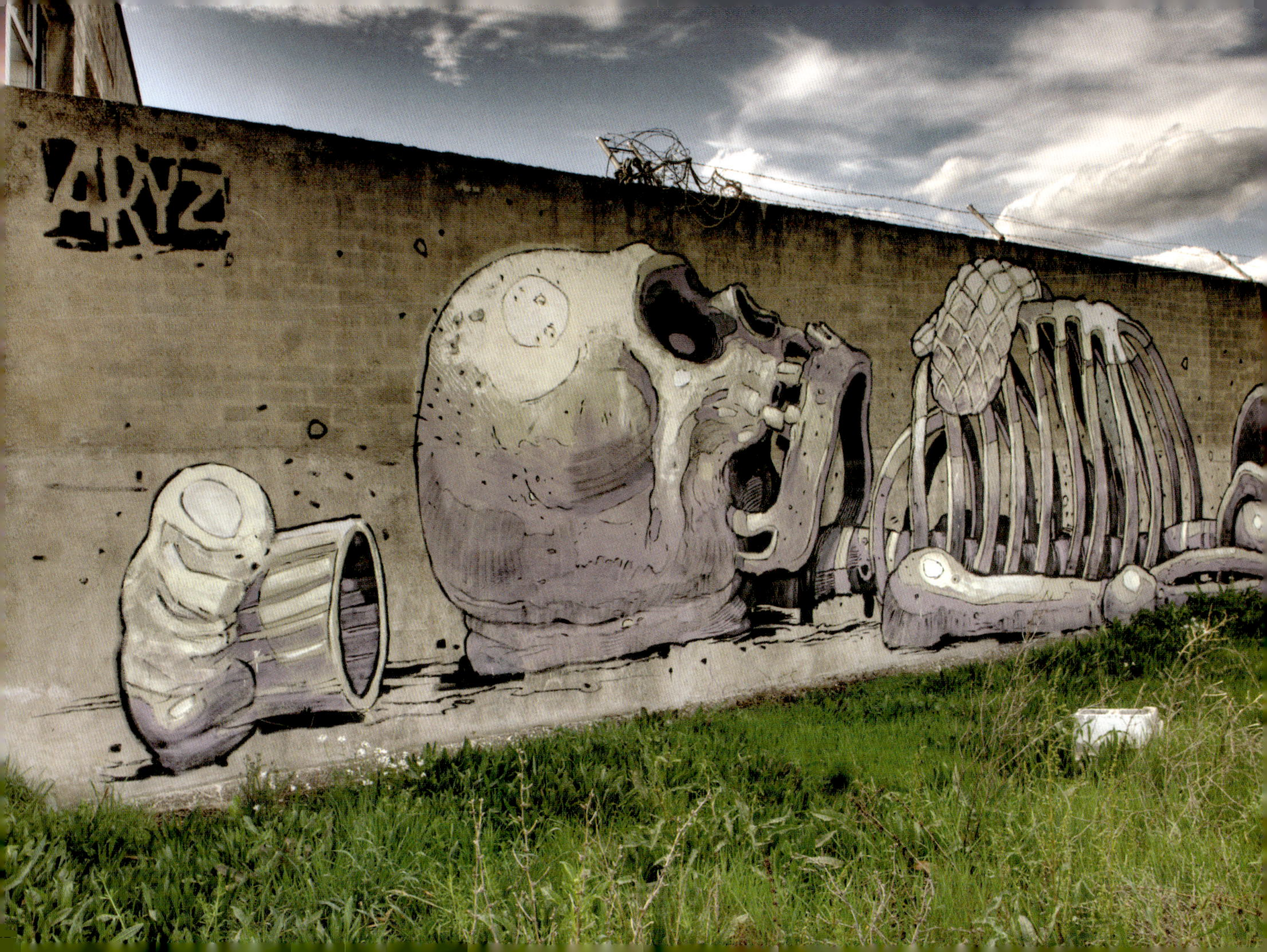
ARYZ

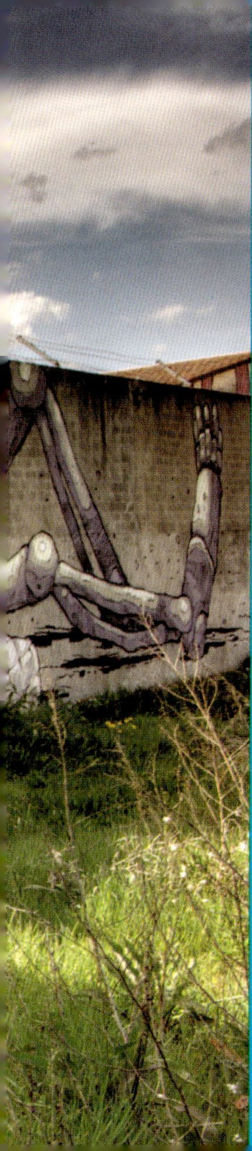

PAINTING THE TOWN

Graffiti writing is the revenge of the kids from the wrong side of the tracks. The big city is all about money. Everywhere you look people have it. Everybody seems to be loaded except you. All the messages scream luxury lifestyles and all the posh bars and restaurants don't want your kind coming in. Writing is a way of fighting back.

BLOOD SPORT

Long before the extreme sports channel, writers were risking their lives for the shits and giggles. So much blood, sweat and tears go into writing it's no wonder it demands respect. When you see those throw ups way up high it takes your breath away. Balls of steel. Something that college kids with stencils rarely understand.

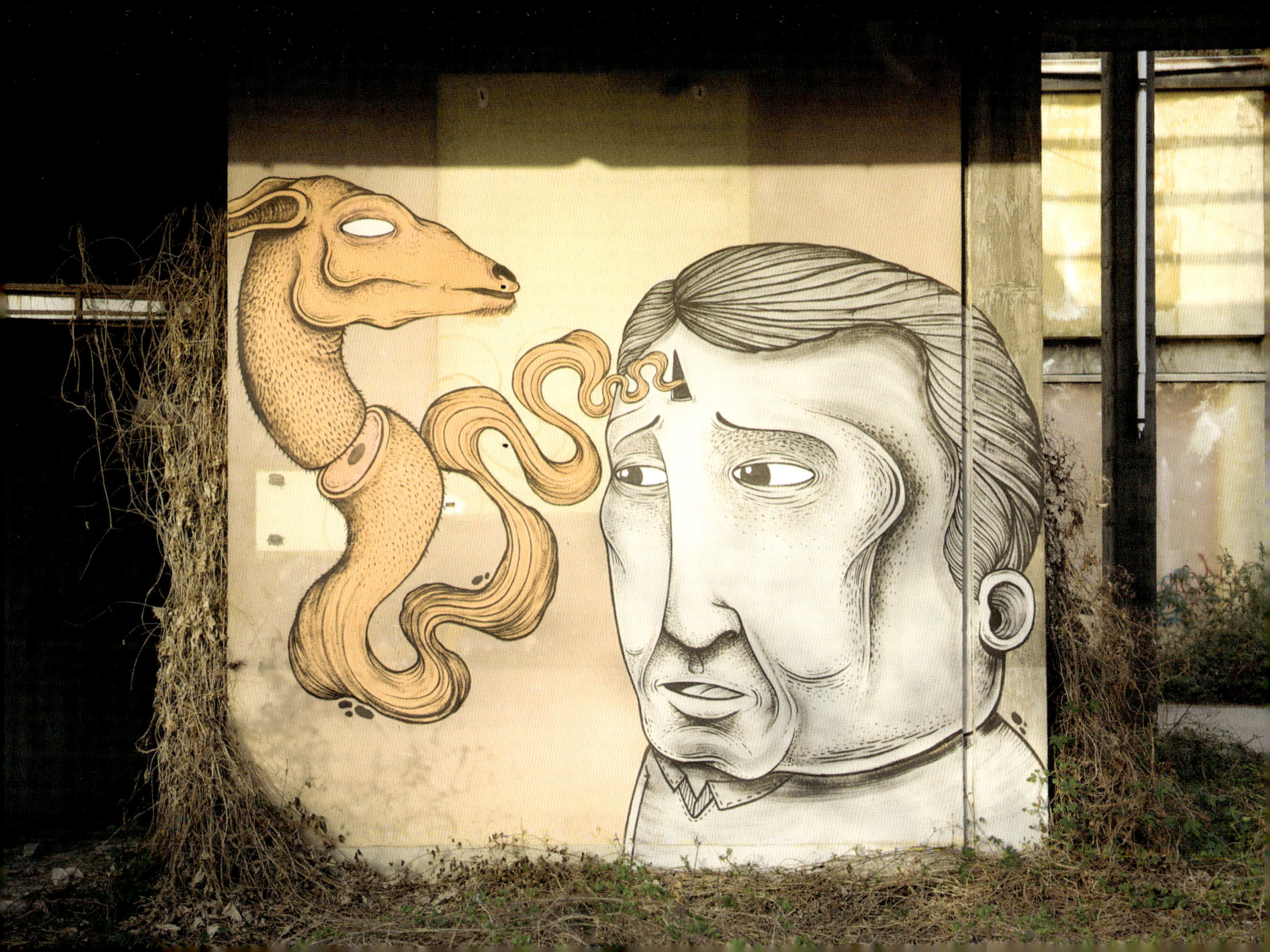

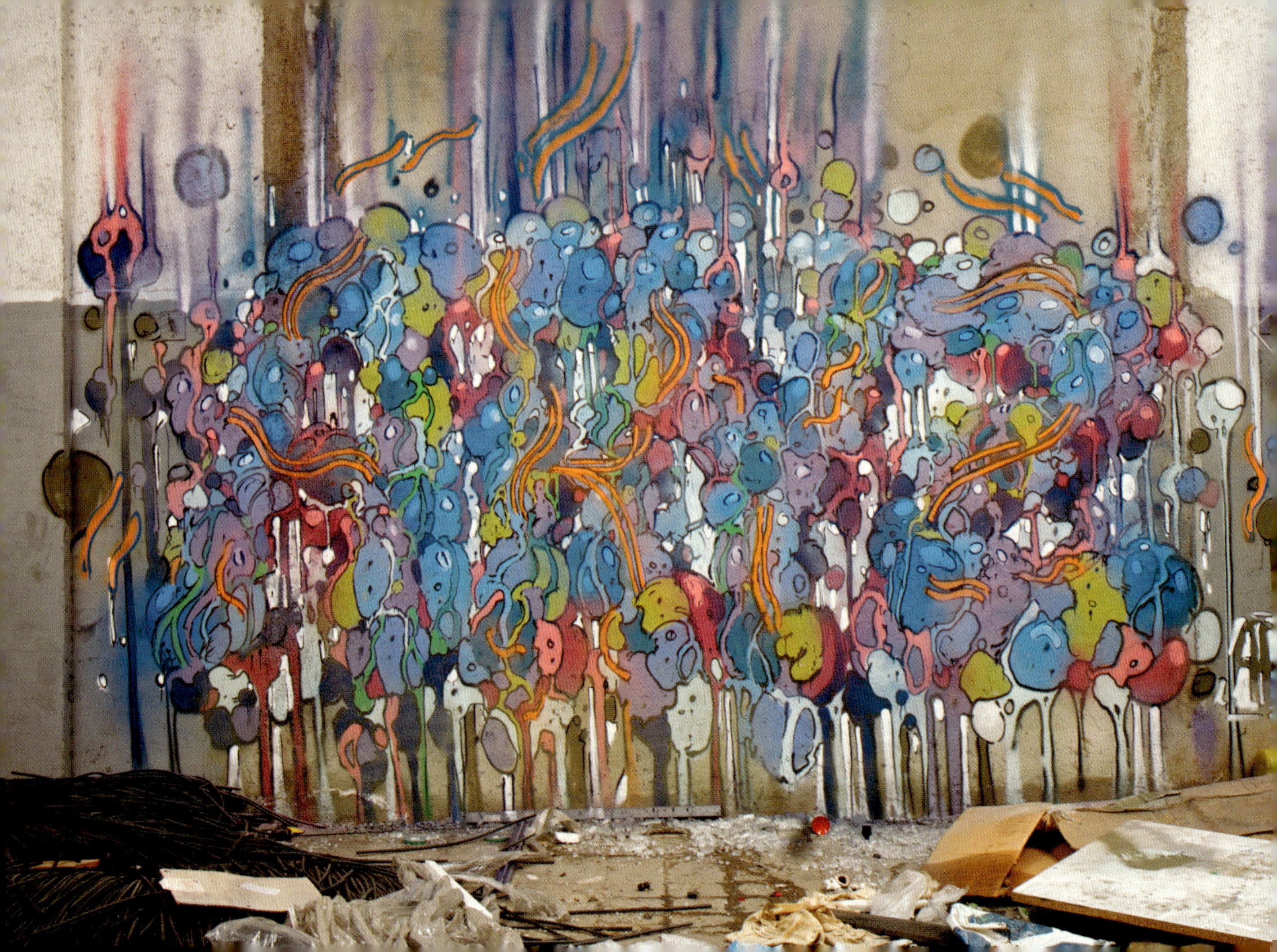

SECRET SOCIETY

Writing in a coded language that only the few understand, this is a cult, a secret society. The citizen wage slaves aren't meant to 'get it', the city fathers aren't supposed to like it, it isn't for you. It's for us. If you can't read the signs then it's your loss. This is one art form that doesn't give a flying duck about the audience. And that's good for you. You're getting spoilt.

MIRROR IMAGE

You do it with a Macbook. I do it with a spraycan. It's all in the game. The values of the graffiti culture are a mirror image of the advertising culture. Aggressive self promotion. Getting up everywhere all the time. Being unique and surprising. Making your own style. These are all things the marketing guys do every day. The difference is that the punks down the tracks with the aerosol are doing it for themselves, not some faceless corporate client trying to buy street cred. Which came first? The chicken or . . .?

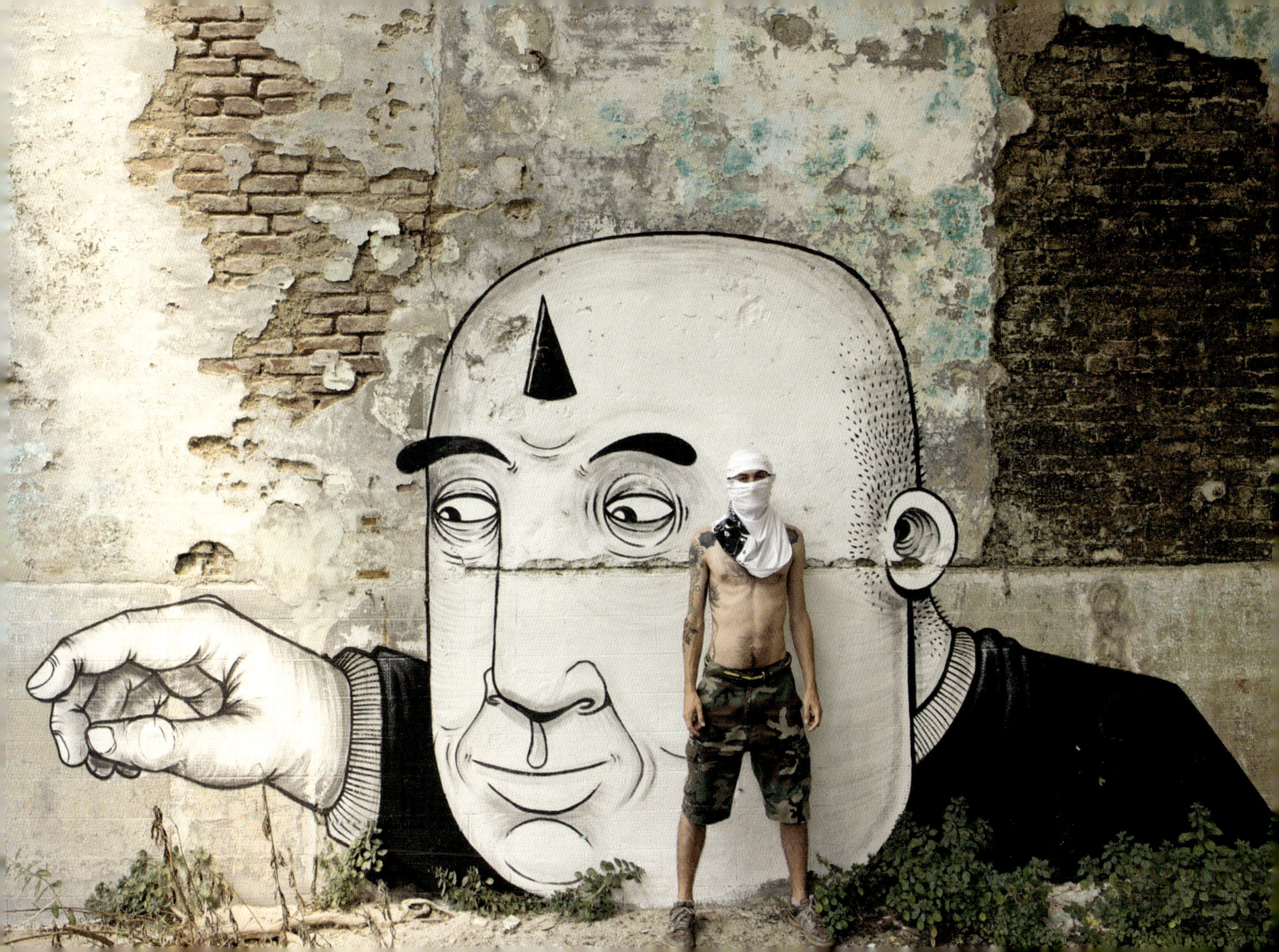

BIG PHAT NO

The graff style is a way of saying no to the life they have mapped out for you without your permission. I will not make 'good art'. I will not make 'proper art'. I will not 'play the game'. I will not play *your* game. I will play *mine* and if *you* want to catch up then *you* better chase me because I ain't interested in *your* world.

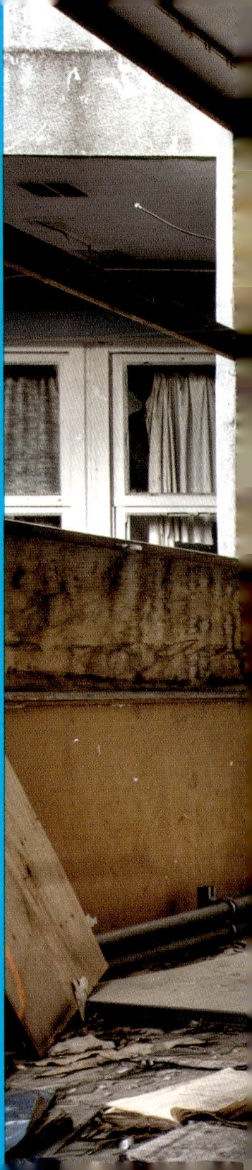

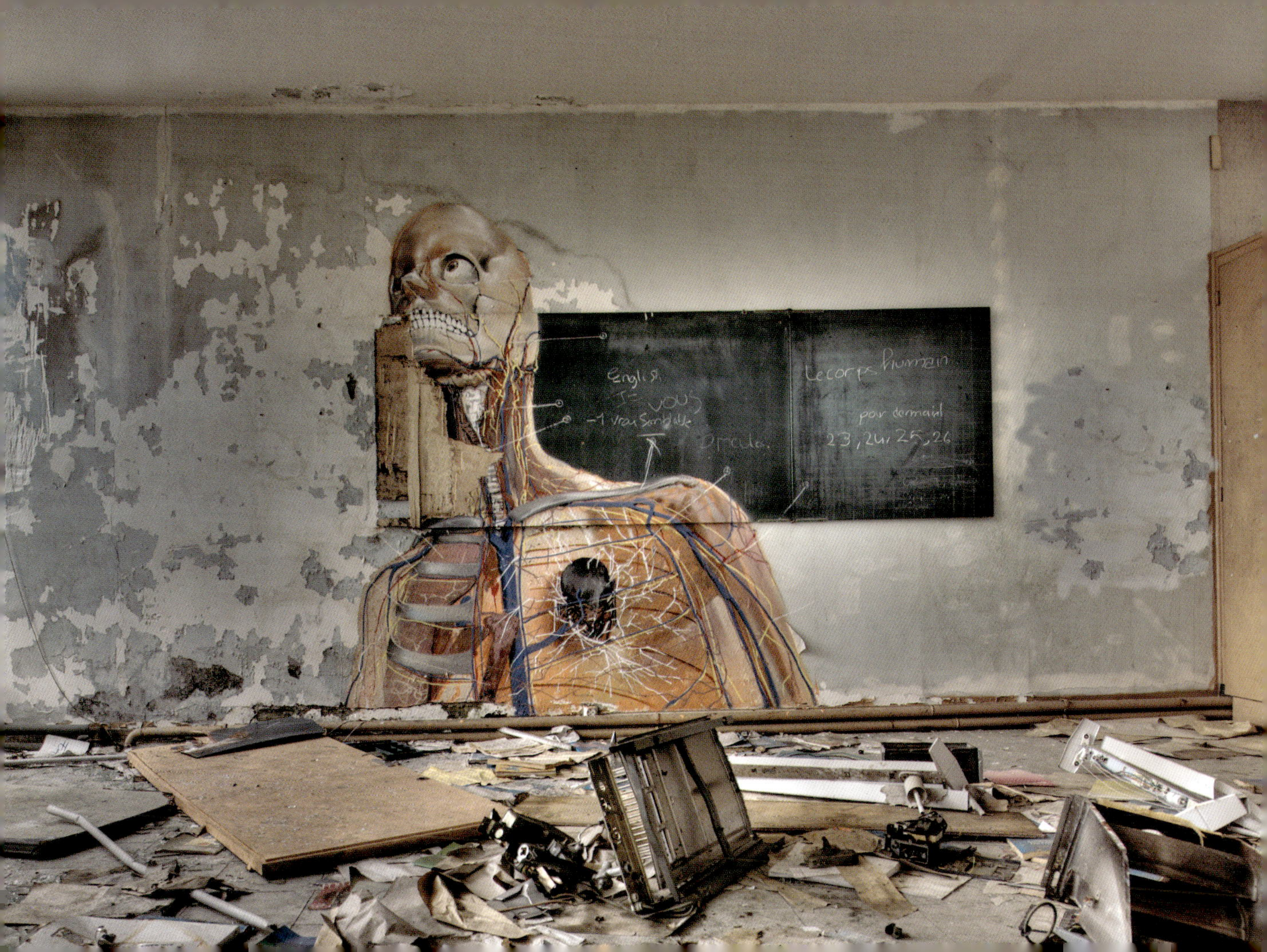
English
Je vous
Lecorps humain
por demain
23, 24, 25, 26

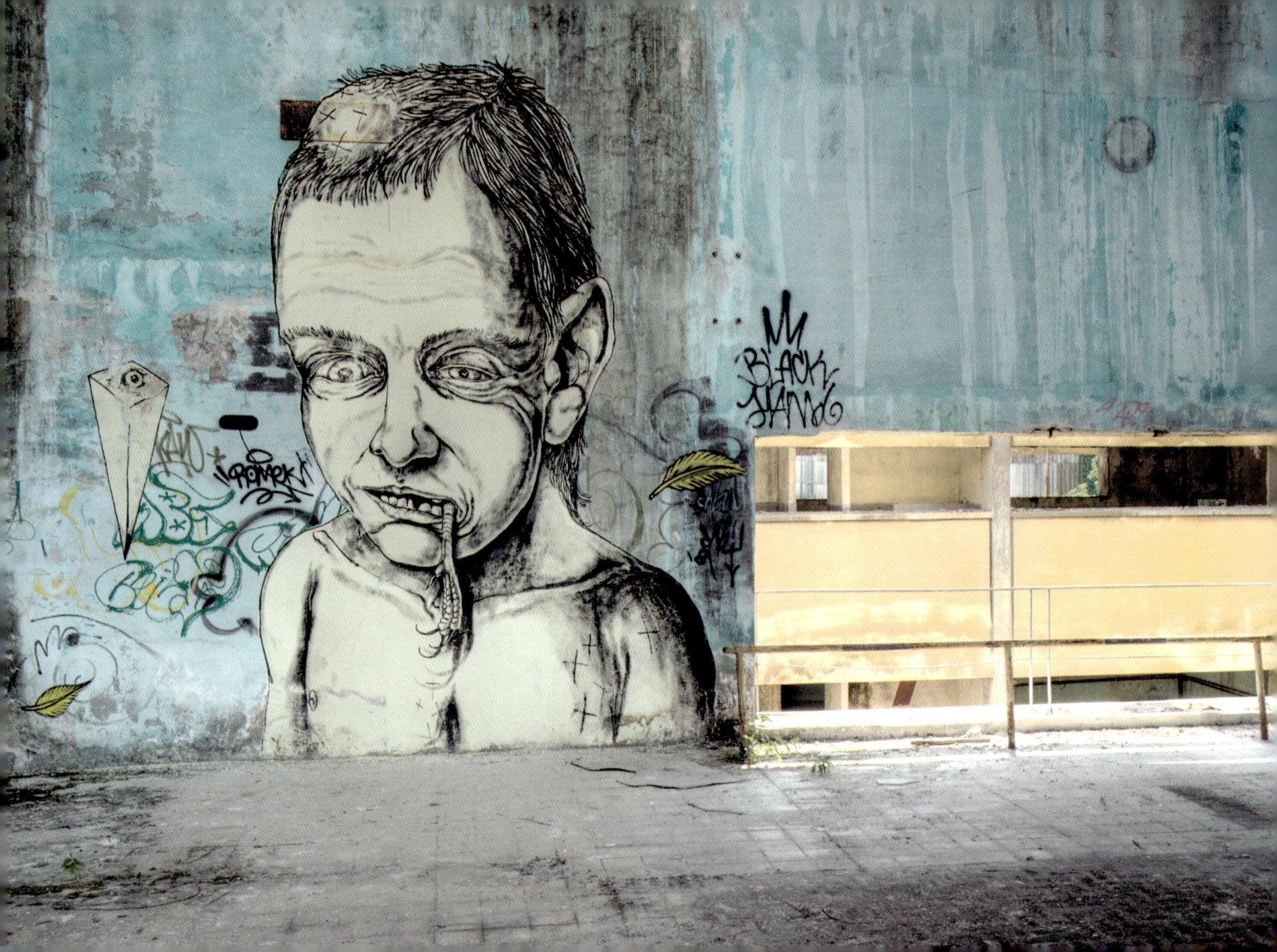
BLACK

BROKEN PLACES

In the broken places where the trash grows like plastic weeds around the rusted twists of metal and the crumbling walls, just off the main street, down an alley, where the kids go to pull buckets or hide from the streetlights, or just a quick piss, or a place to fight, settle scores or just hide. This is where the hissing is heard, where the aerosols sing like snakes. Places where the energetic hand of order cannot reach. And the only law is entropy.

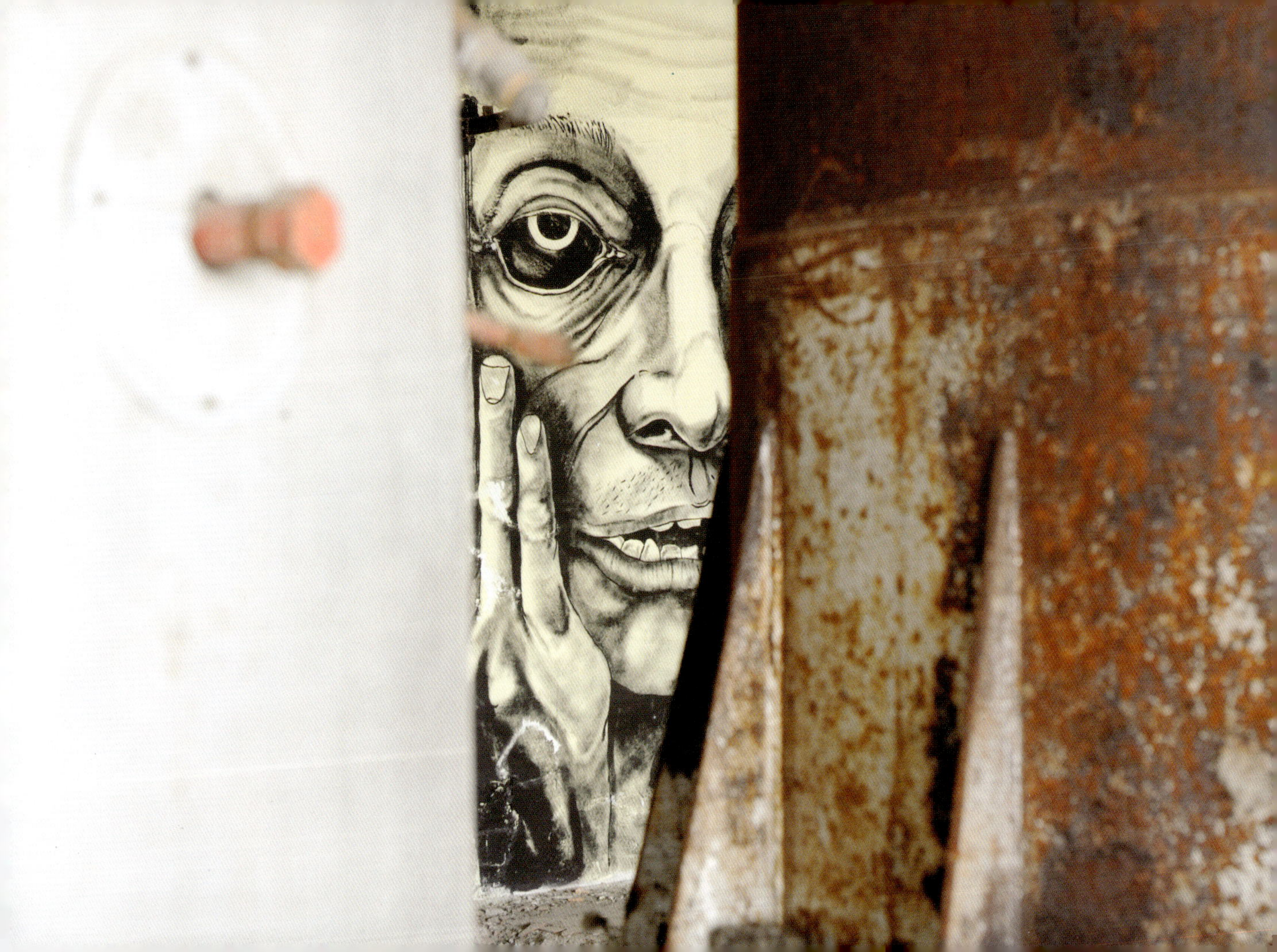

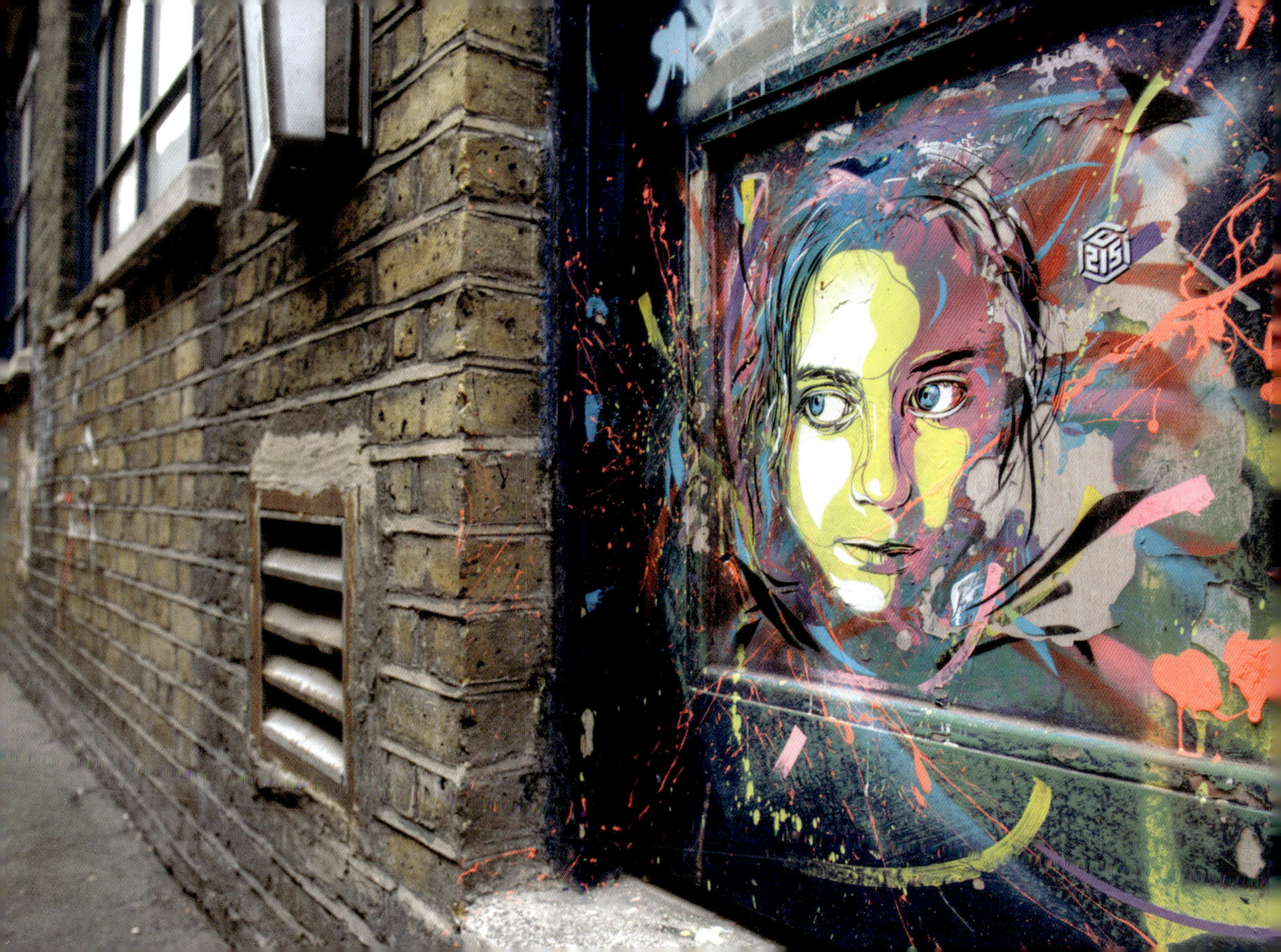

The Witch Trials

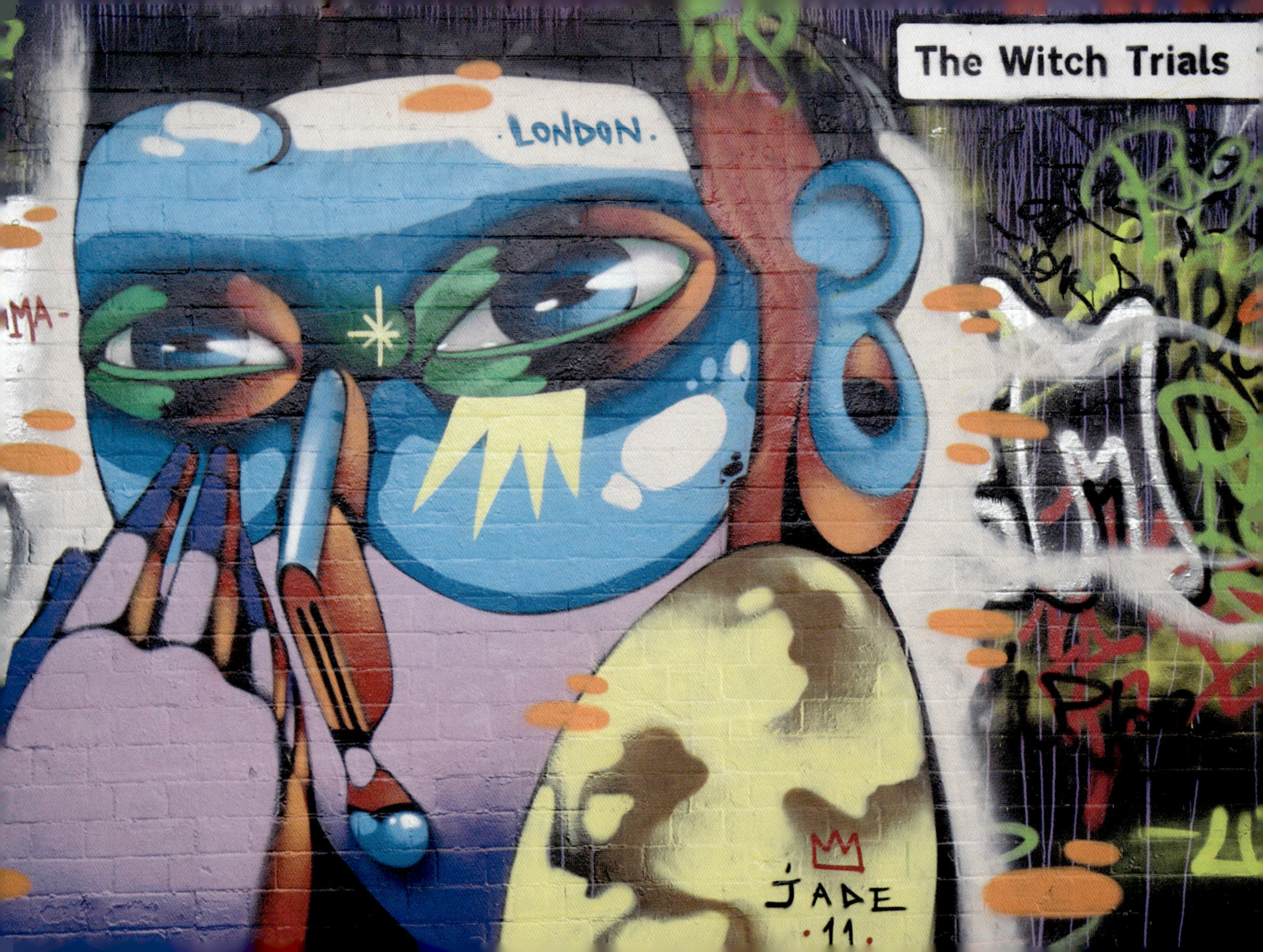

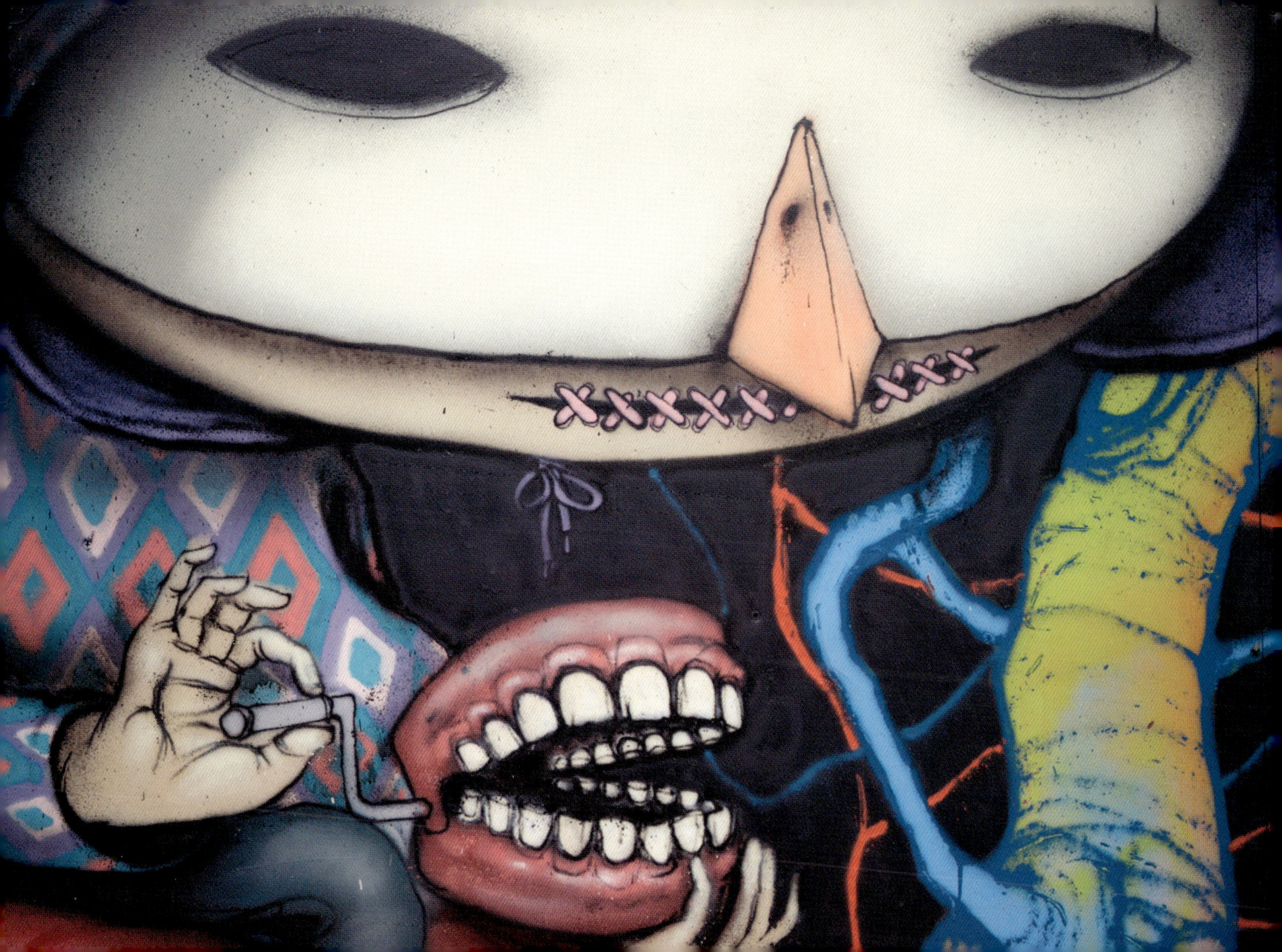

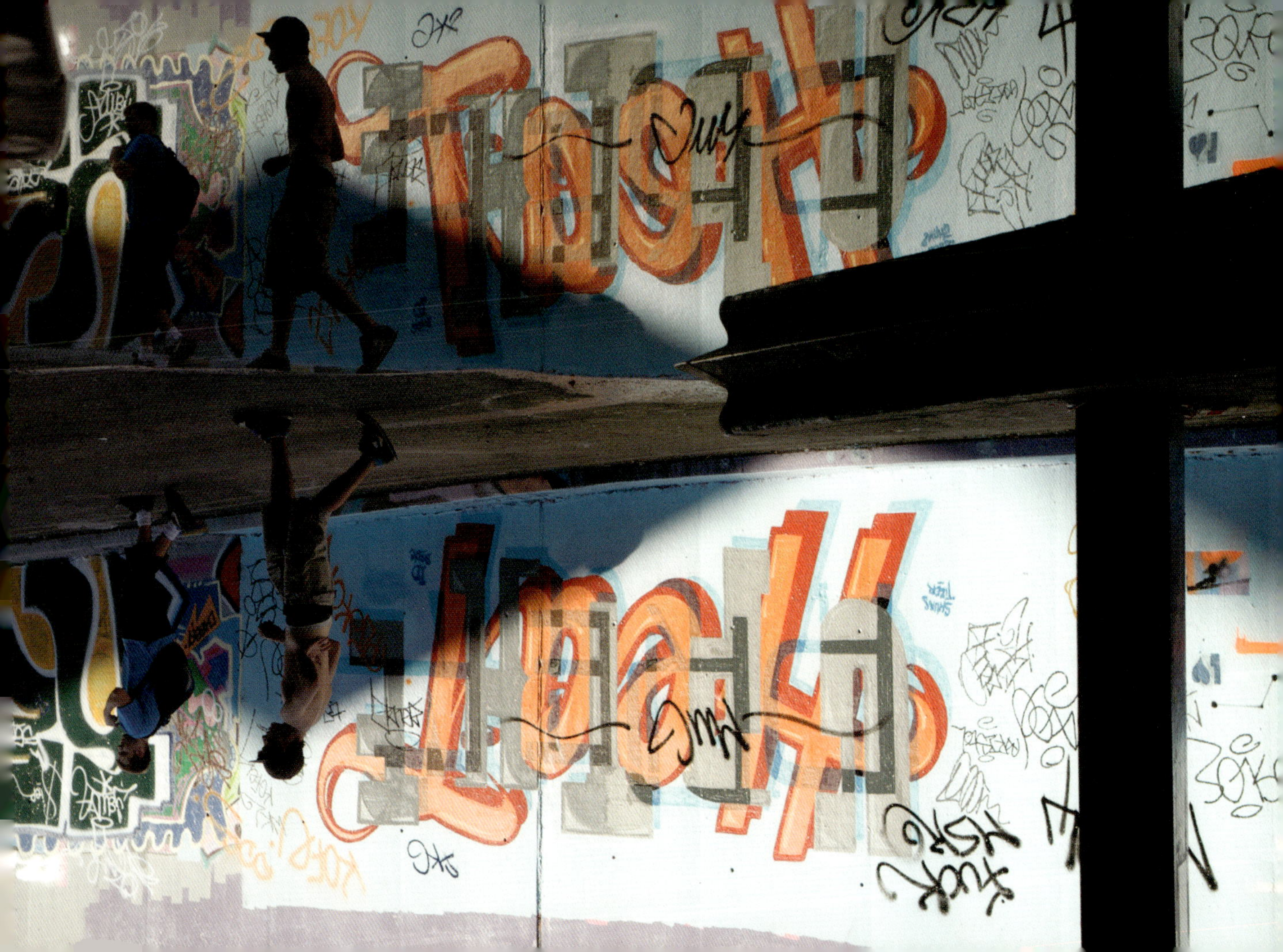

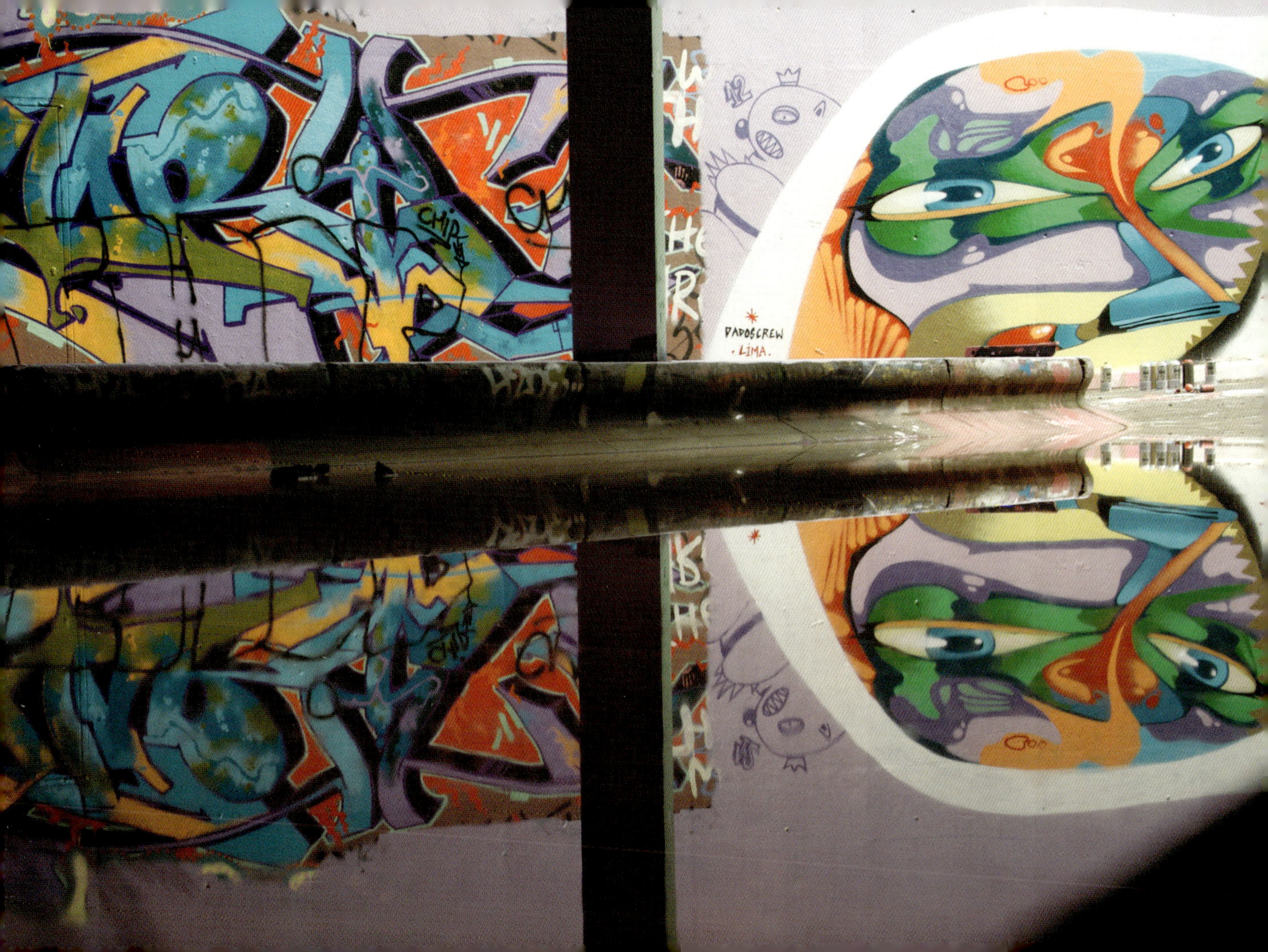
CHIP
DADOSCREW
LIMA

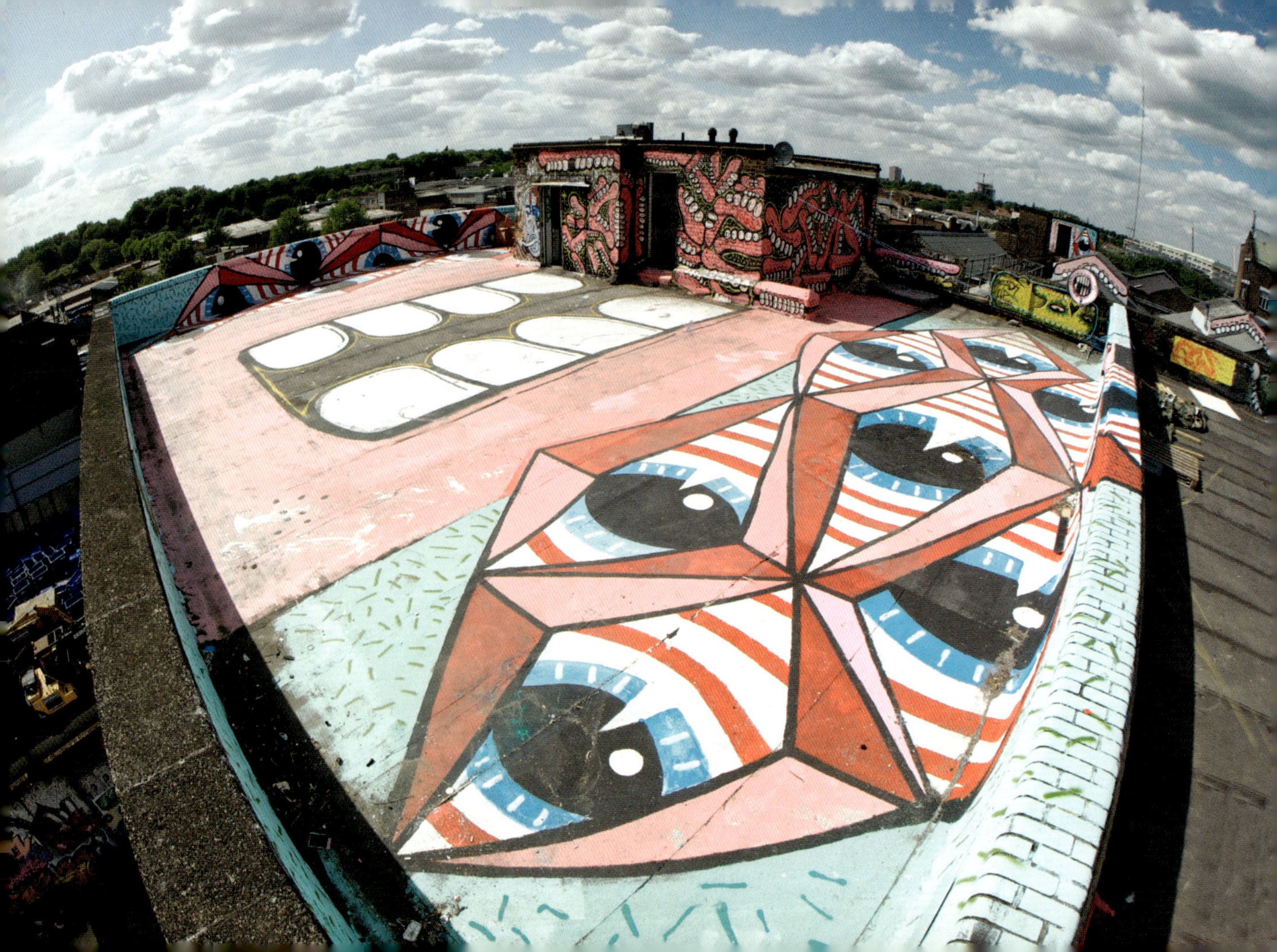

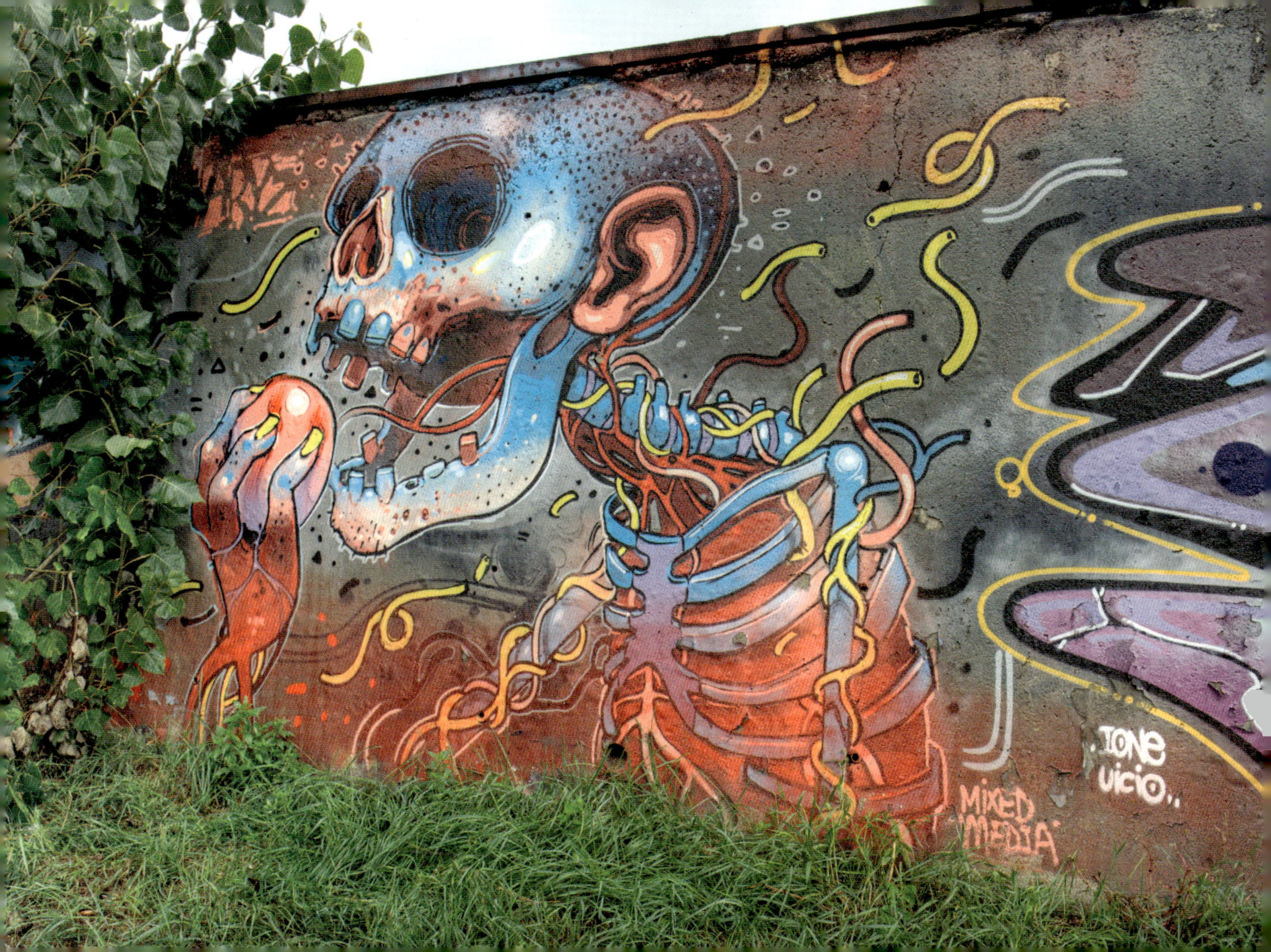
MIXED MEDIA
IONE
vicio..

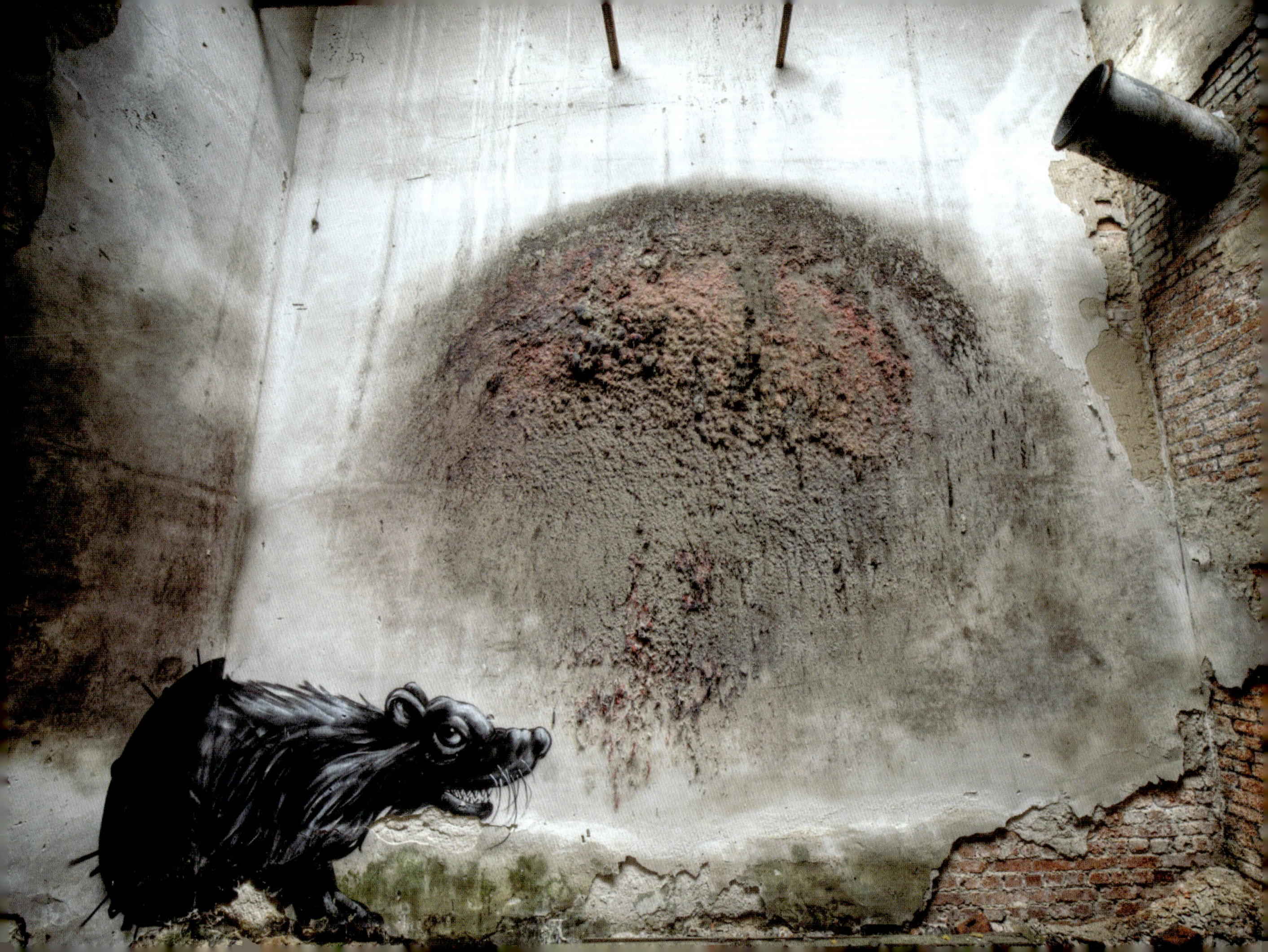

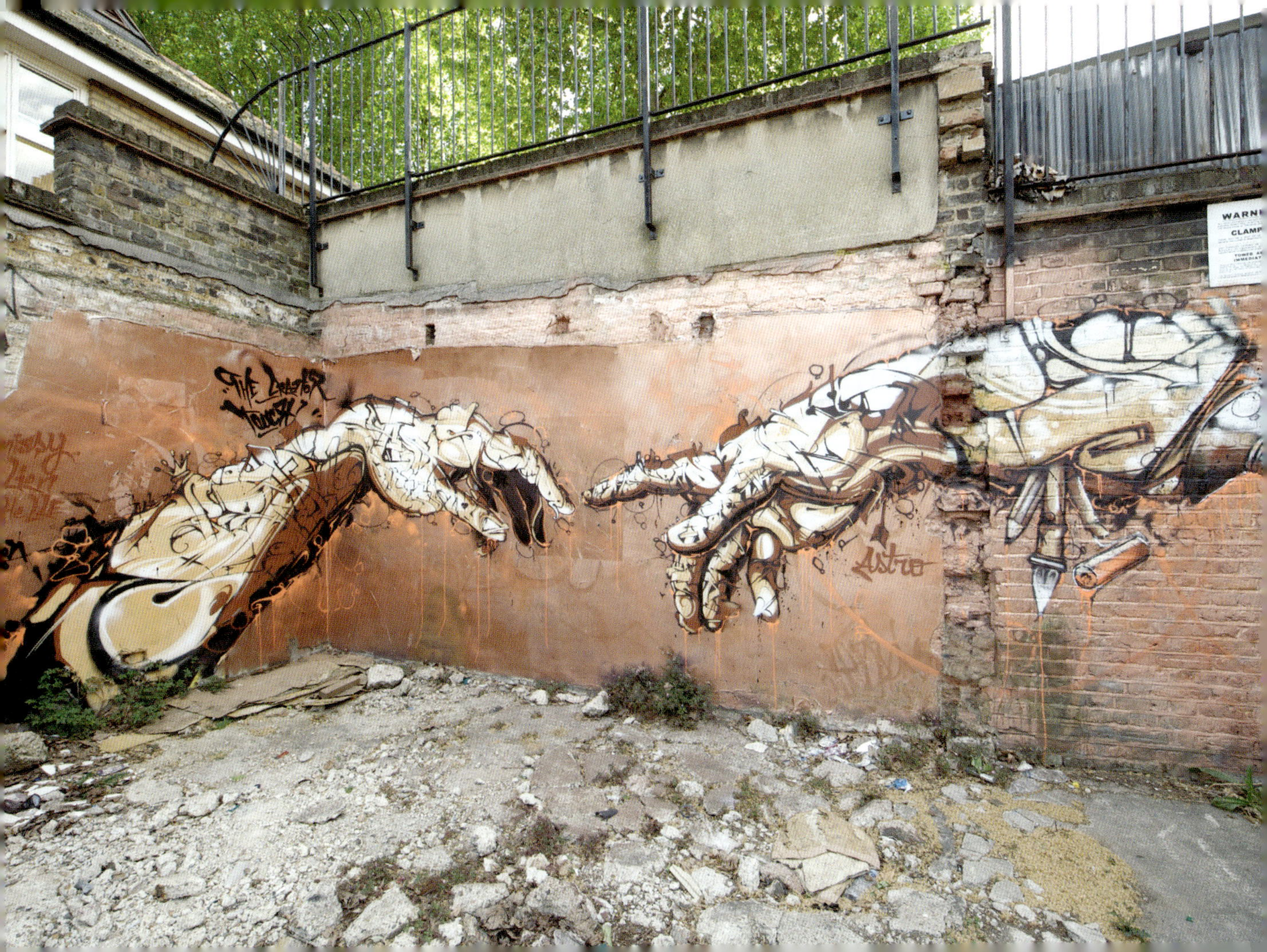
WARN
CLAMP
Astro

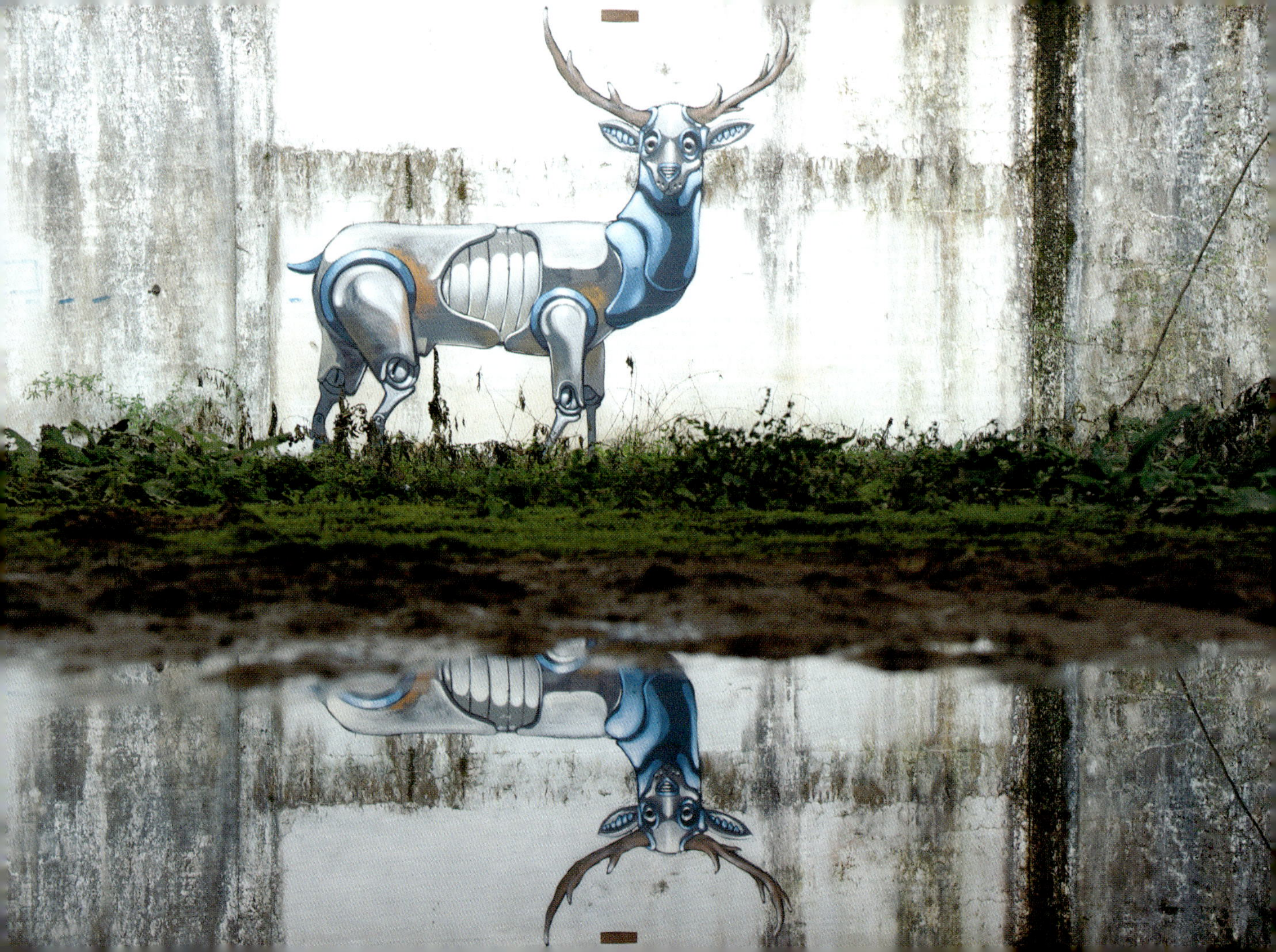

I paint on the street because the streets ask me to do it. All the places I have painted have a story behind them and each place and its surface have told me what I should paint there.

Painting on canvas or paper is much more difficult as it's so blank and white ... too much white for me.

When I start it's like play - but I soon discover my line of thinking - and my point of view.

PIXEL PANCHO

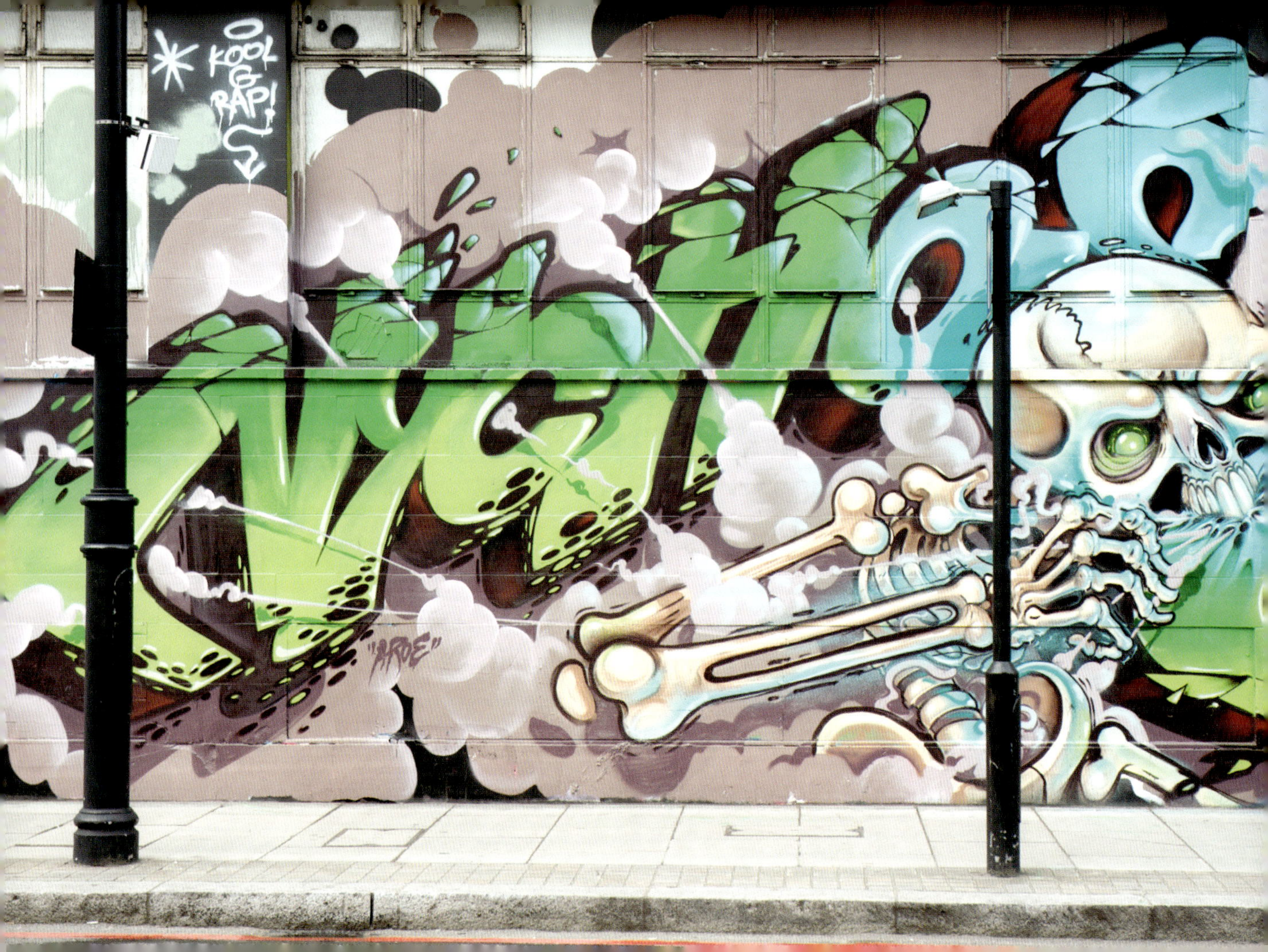
KOOL
G
RAP!
"AROE"

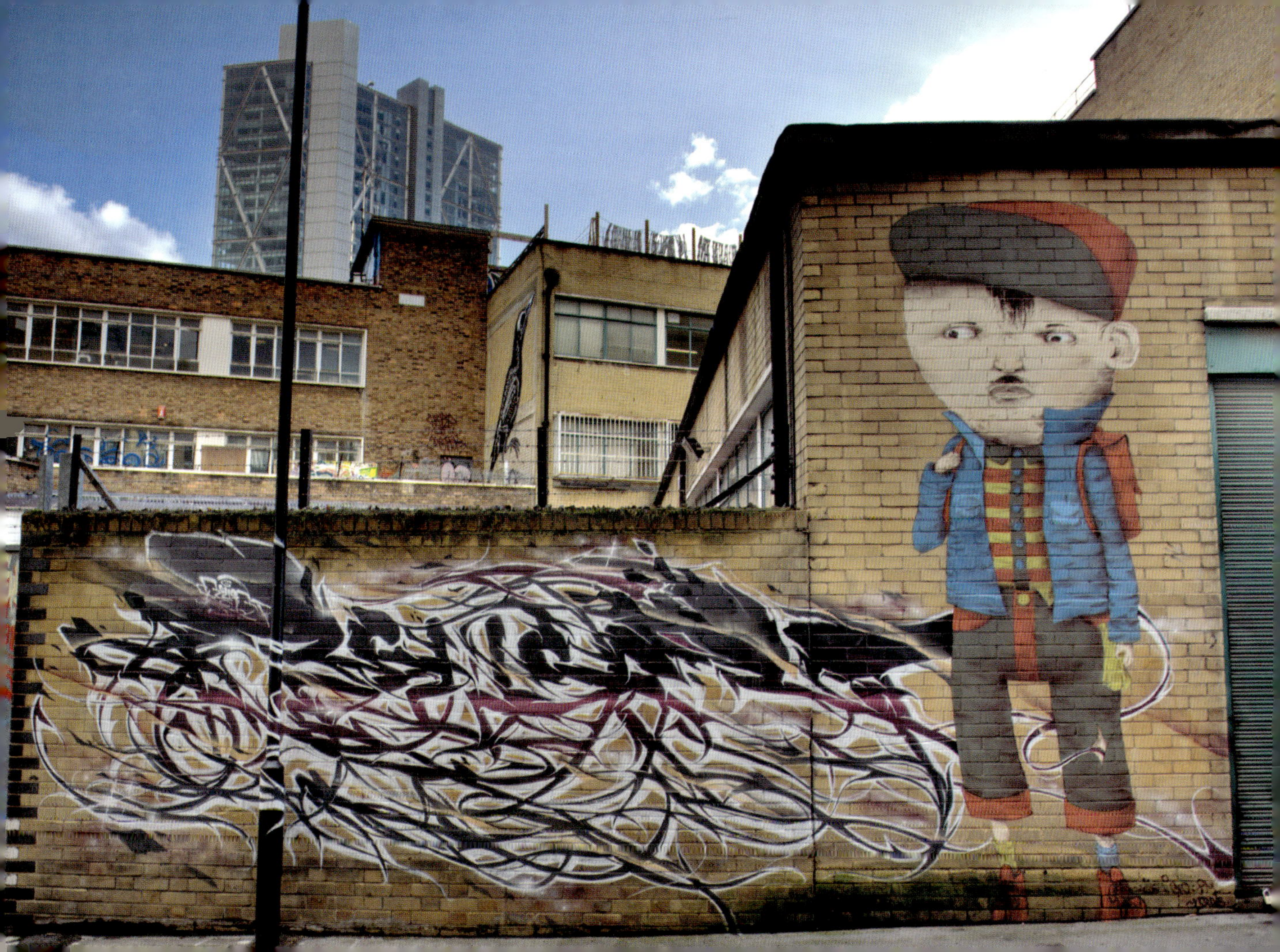

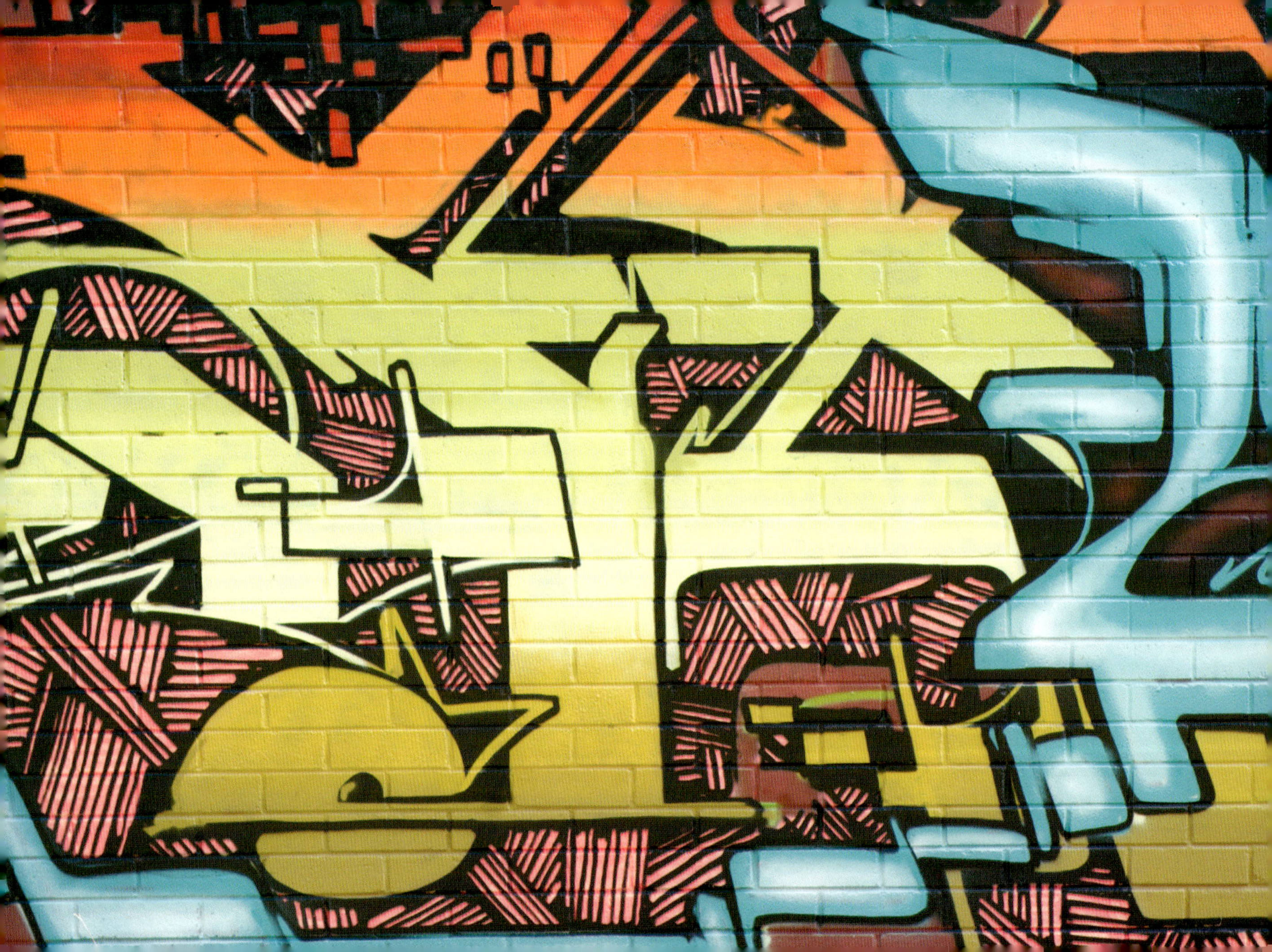

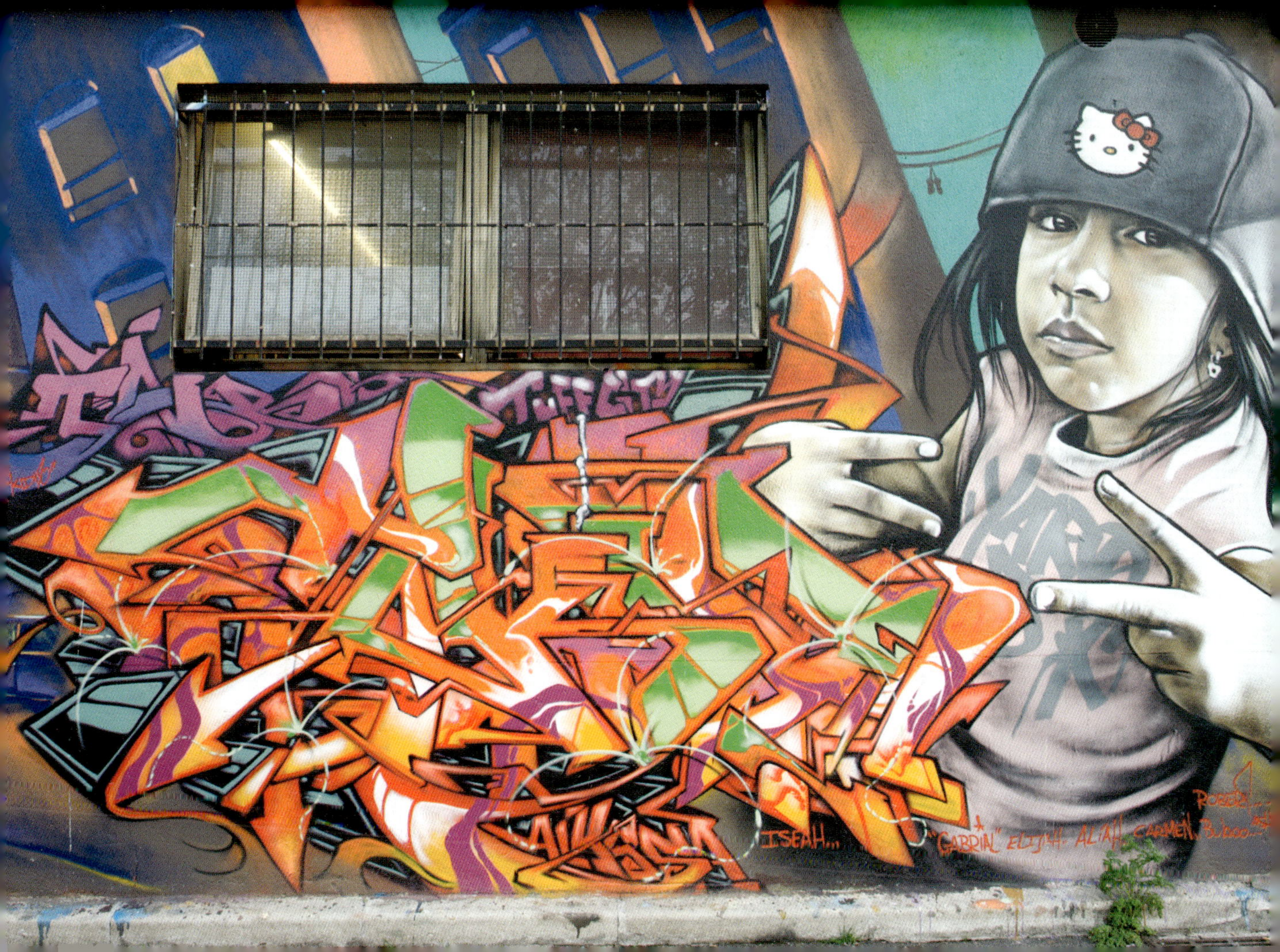
ISEAH...
"GABRIAL" ELIJAH. ALIAH. CARMEN. BUBOO...

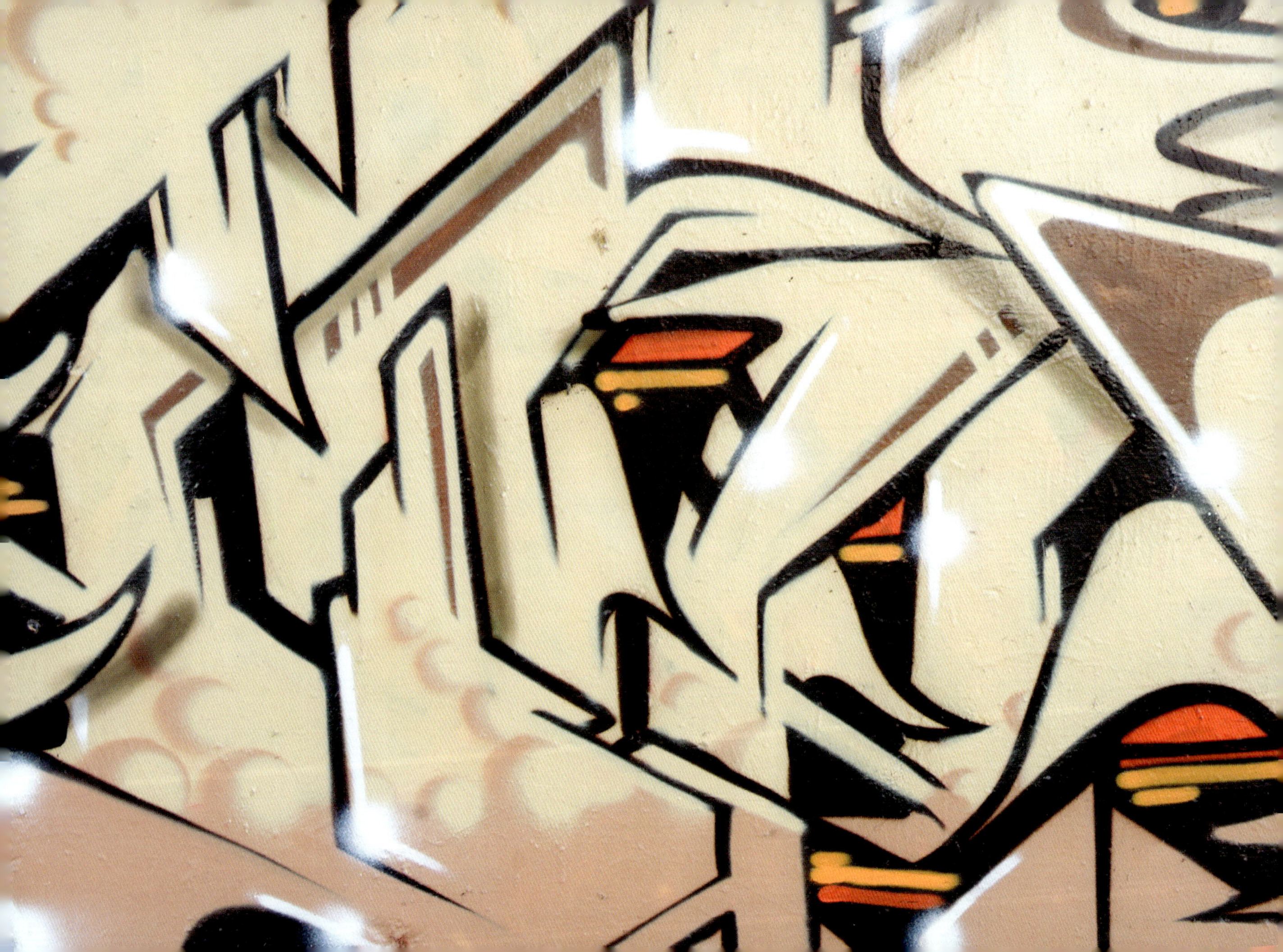

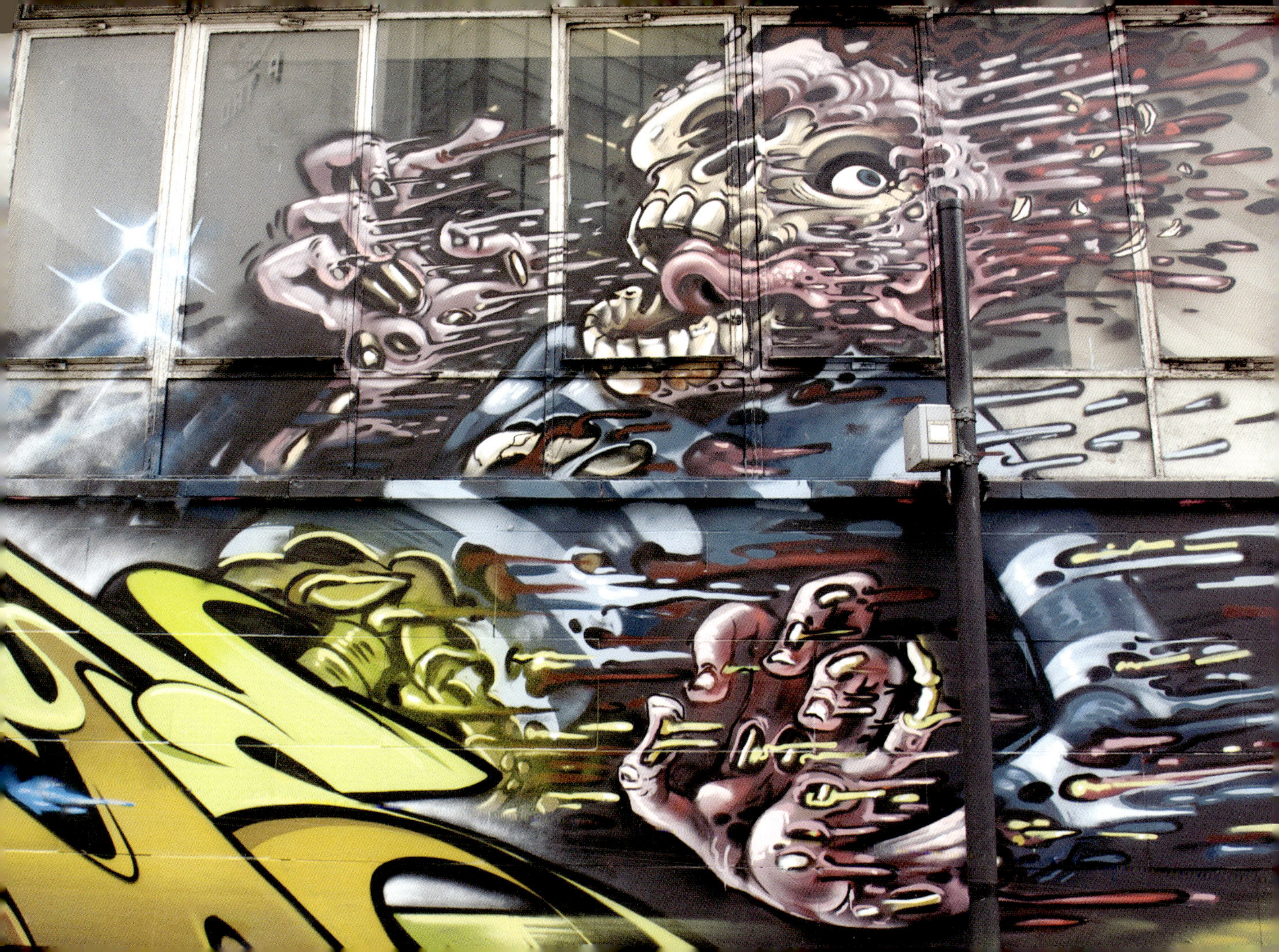

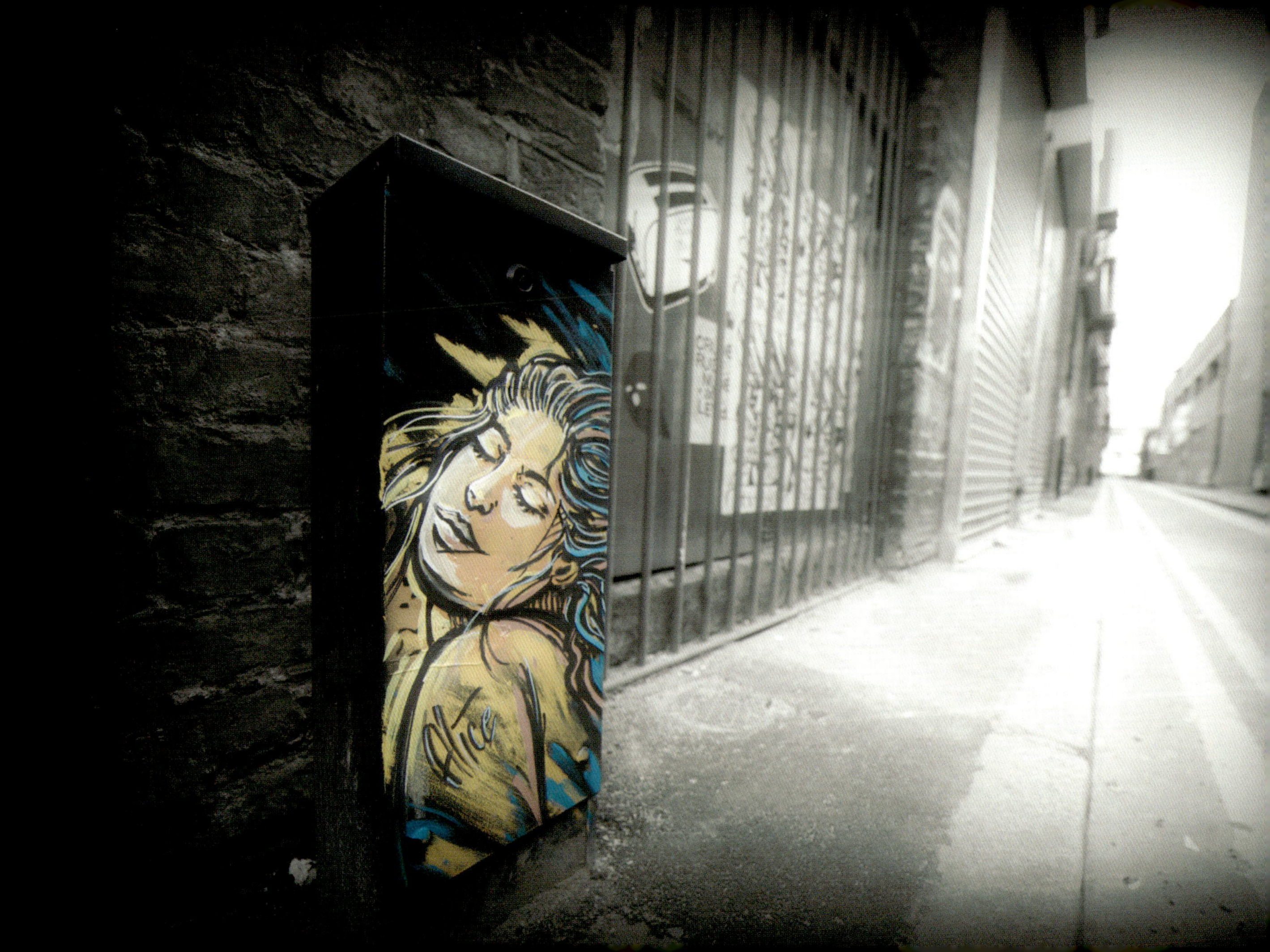
Alice

Painting on the street is a way to completely and freely express myself, without any constraints. When I paint in the studio I'm just with myself, it's an intimate and creative moment in which the goal is the artwork. In the streets there are many other factors, like the people, the adrenaline and the location, that make the act of painting "alive".

So, when I paint in the streets the final result, the artwork, becomes secondary . . . For me, the act of painting and what I feel when I'm painting are much more important. For me, doing art is the act of painting, the performance, rather than the artwork. Also, if I create something on canvas, the people coming to the exhibition are expecting to see art, they come for that. In the street, the viewer is not expecting to see art, so the impact the artwork has is unexpected and as such, I think, it's much more powerful.

ALICE

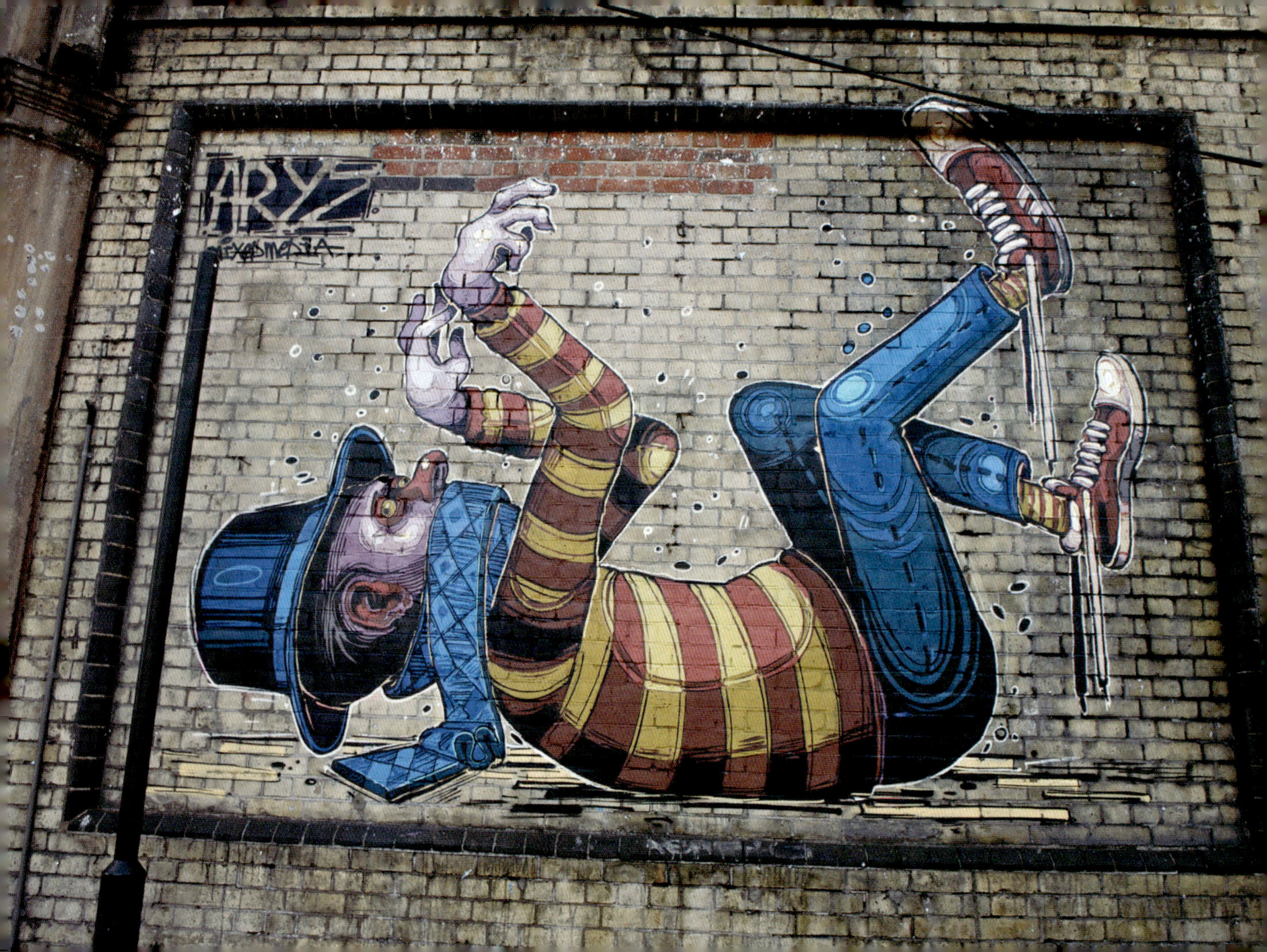
ARYZ

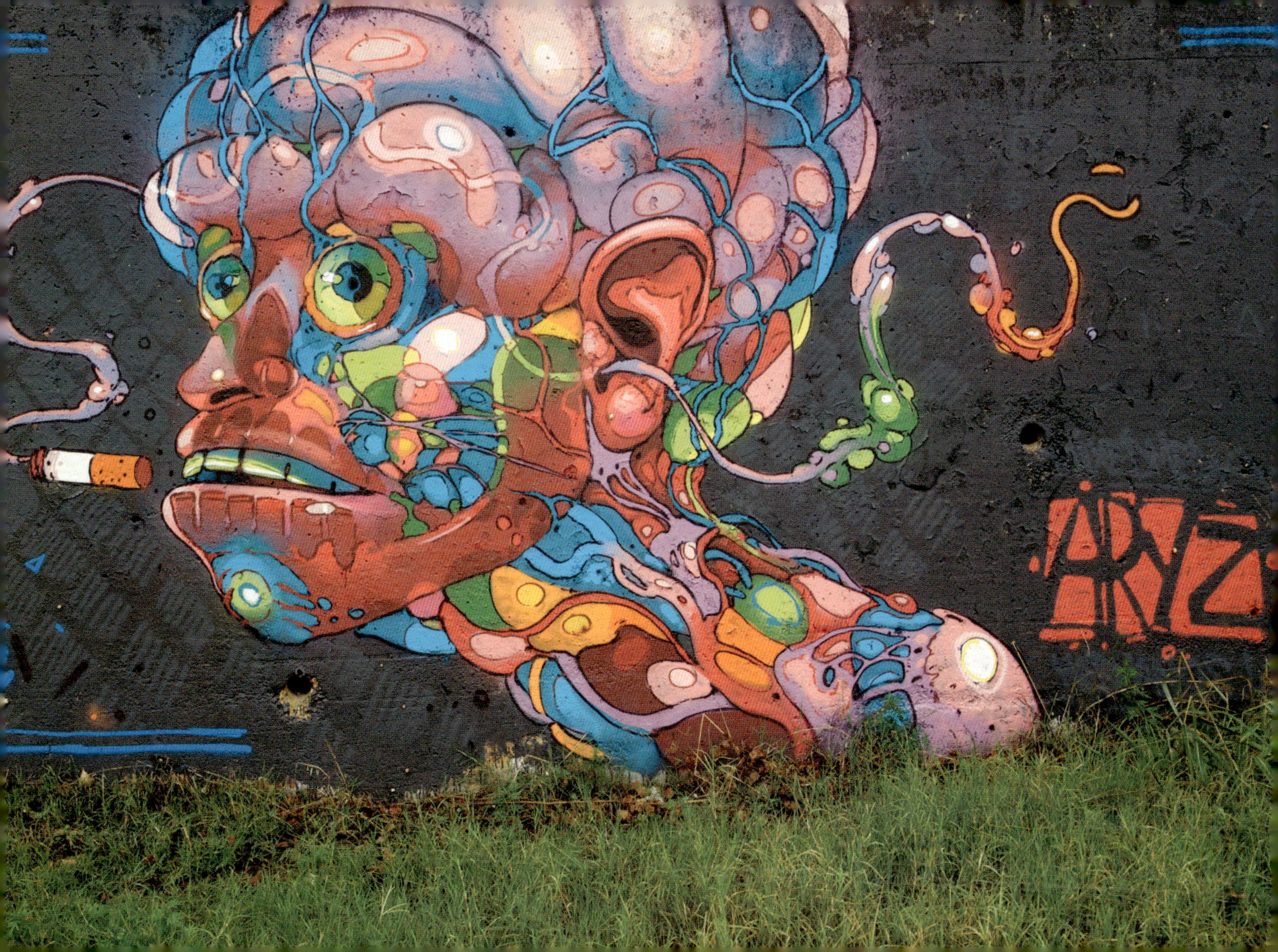

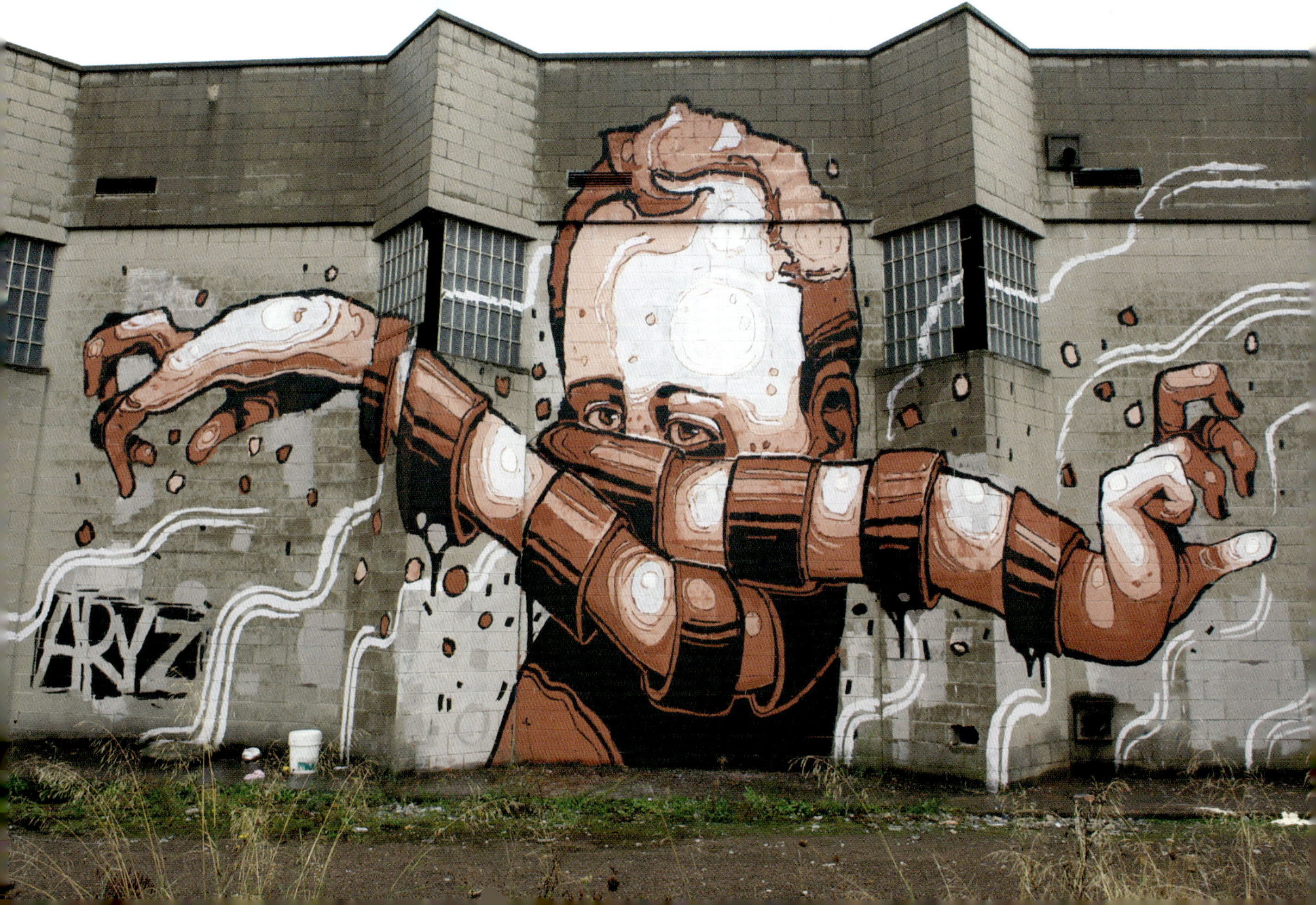
ARYZ

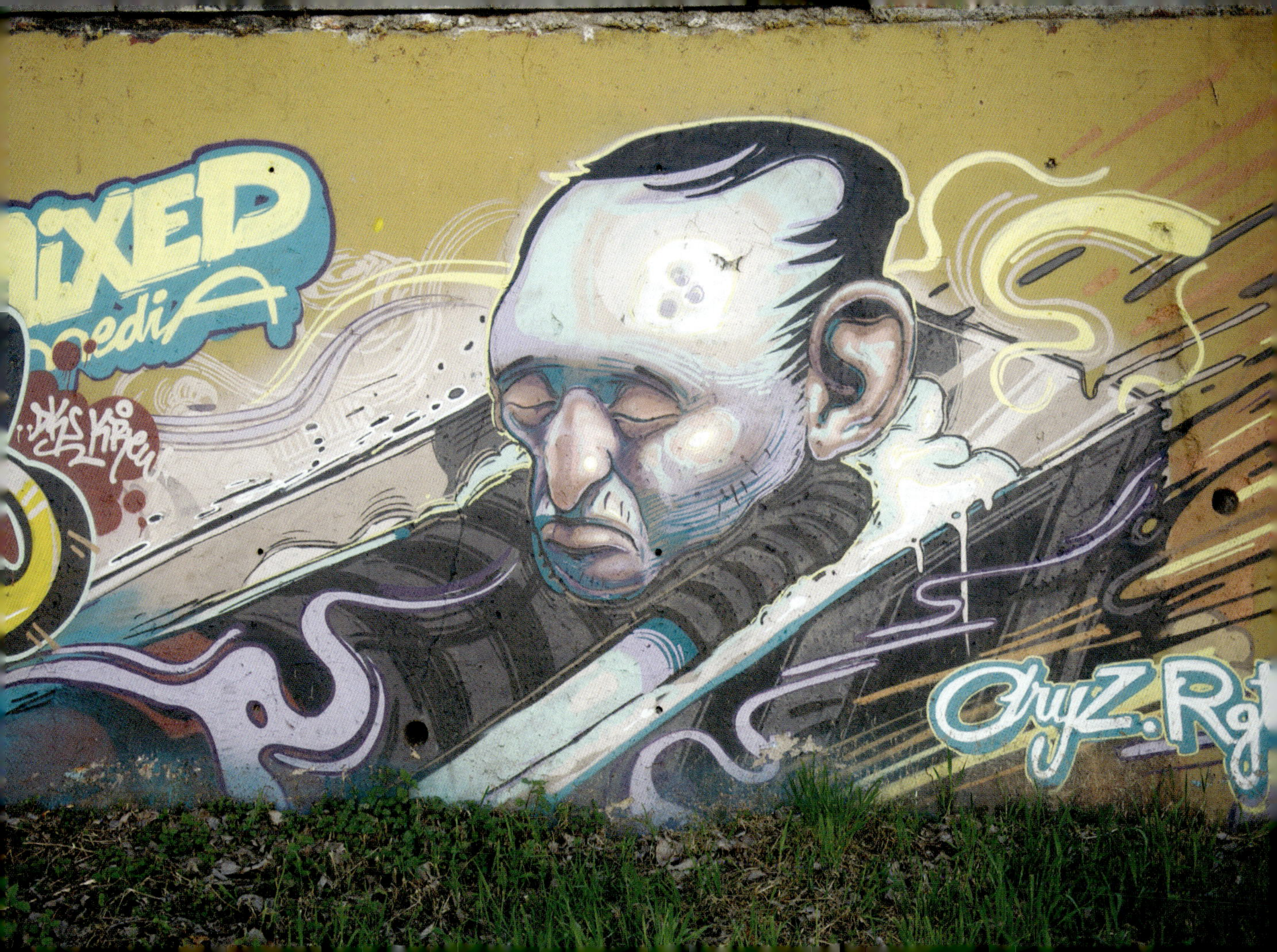

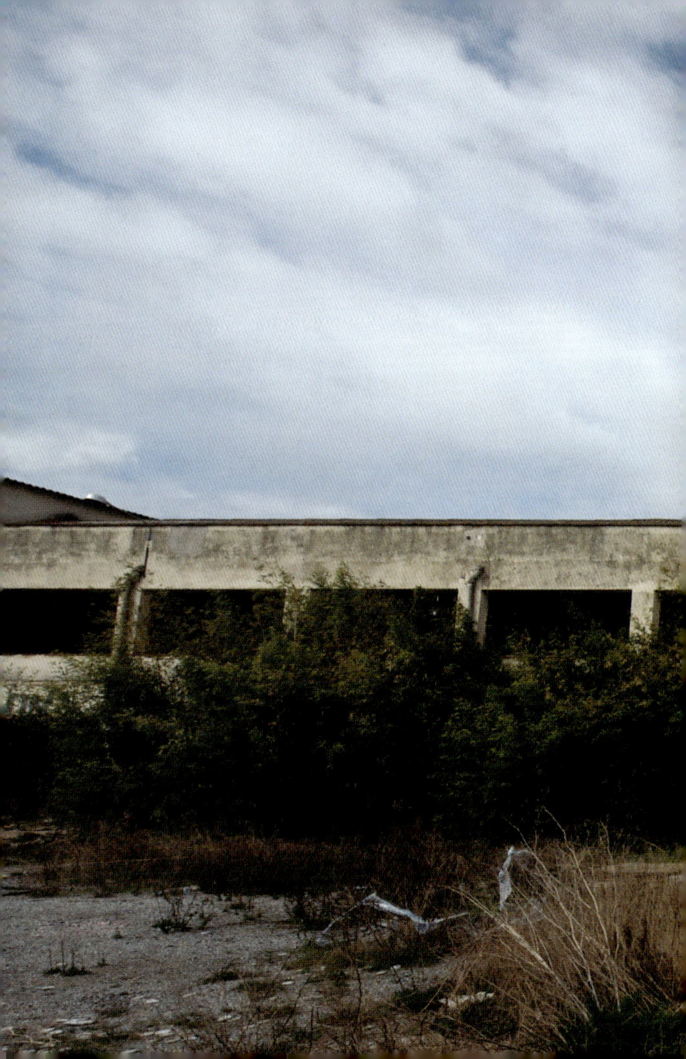

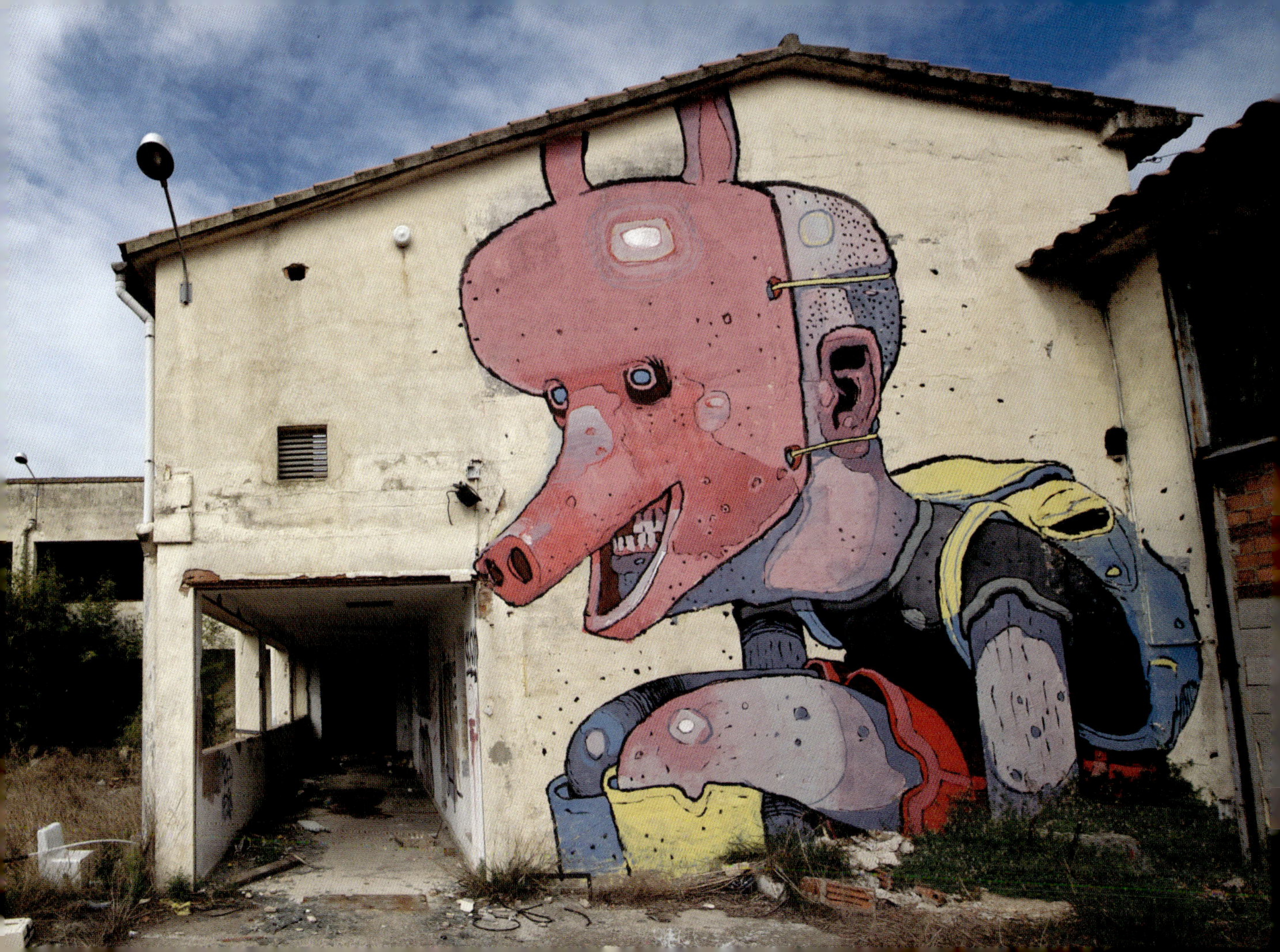

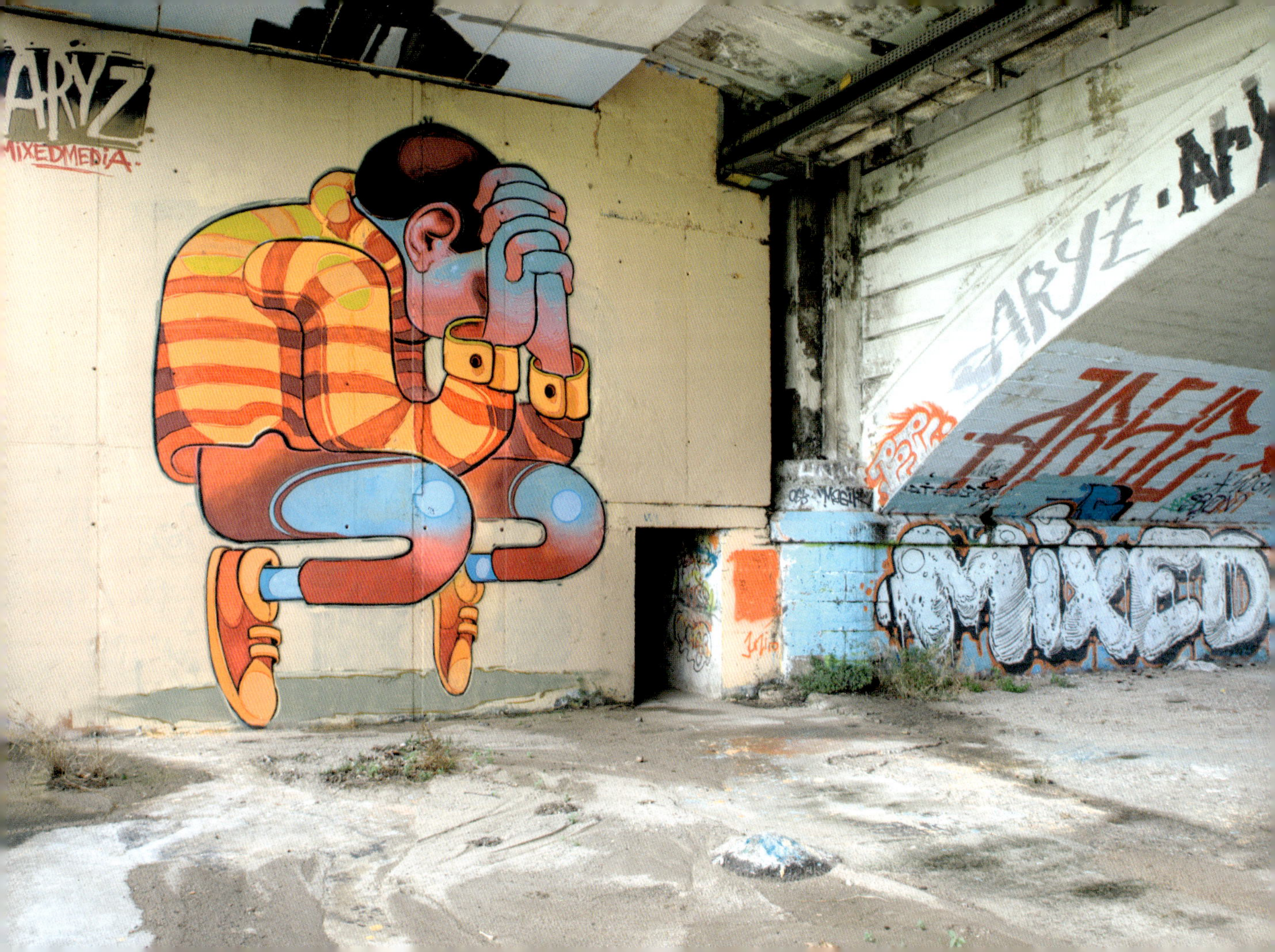
ARYZ
MIXEDMEDIA
ARYZ
MIXED

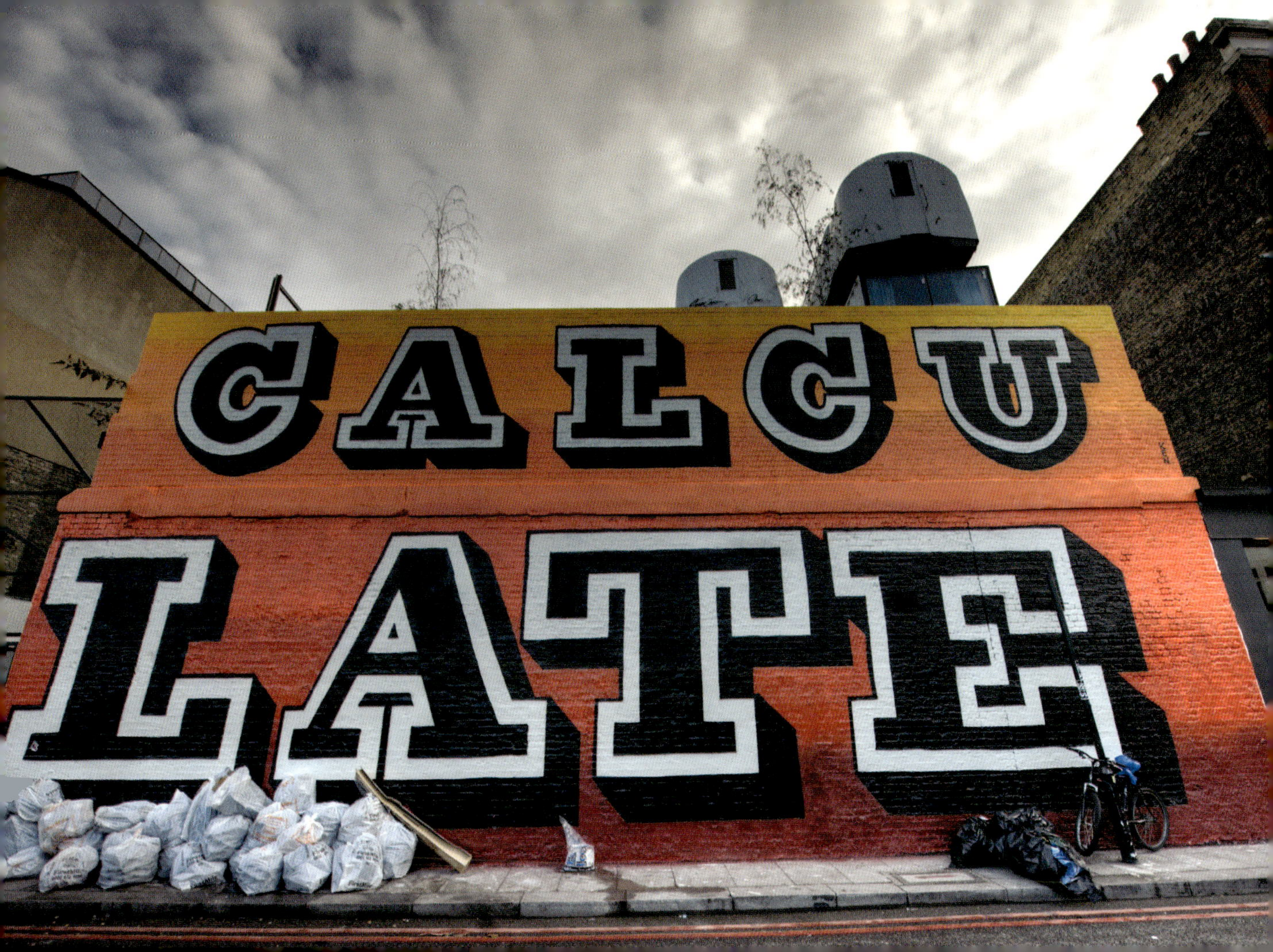
CALCU
LATE

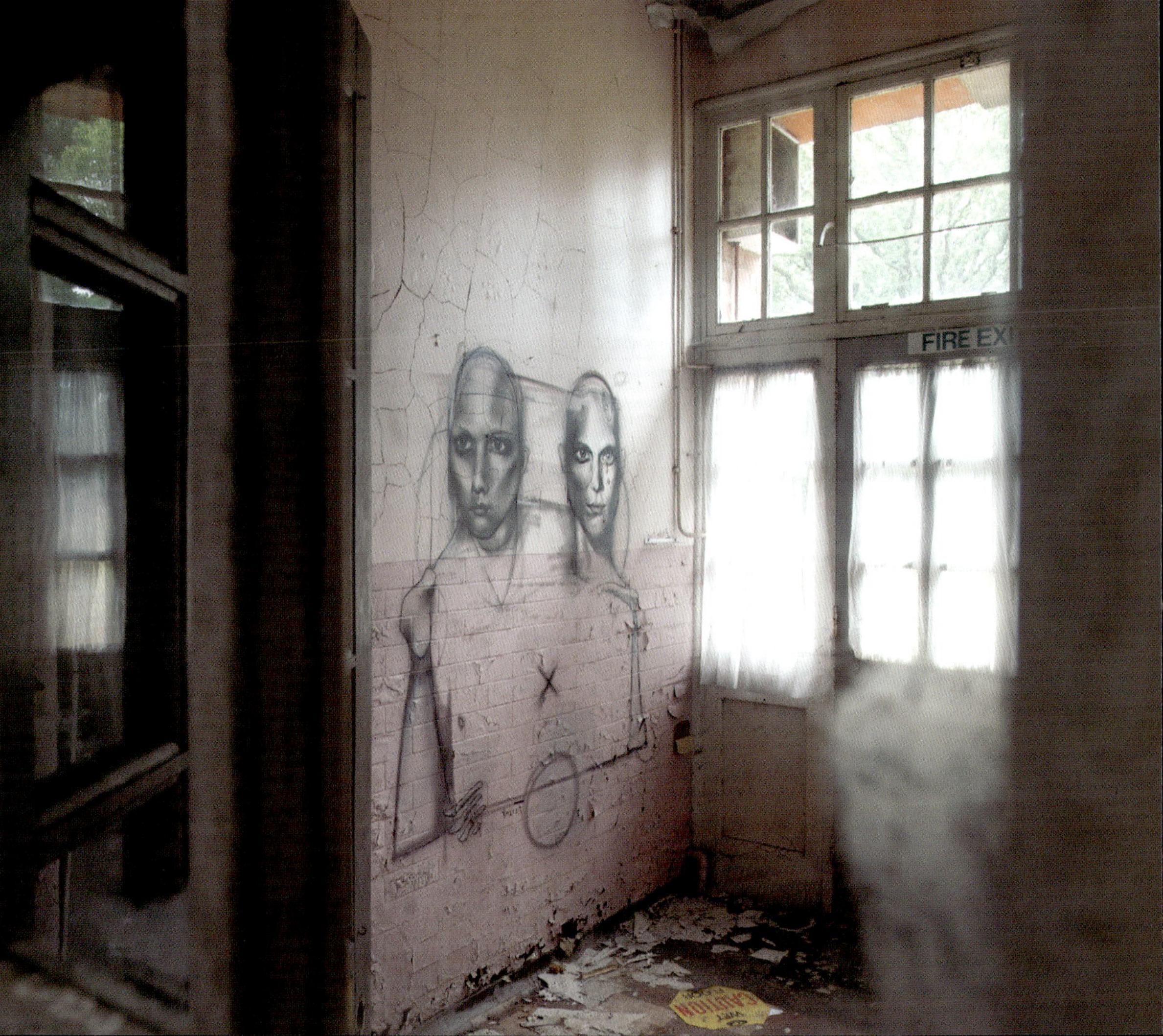
FIRE EXI

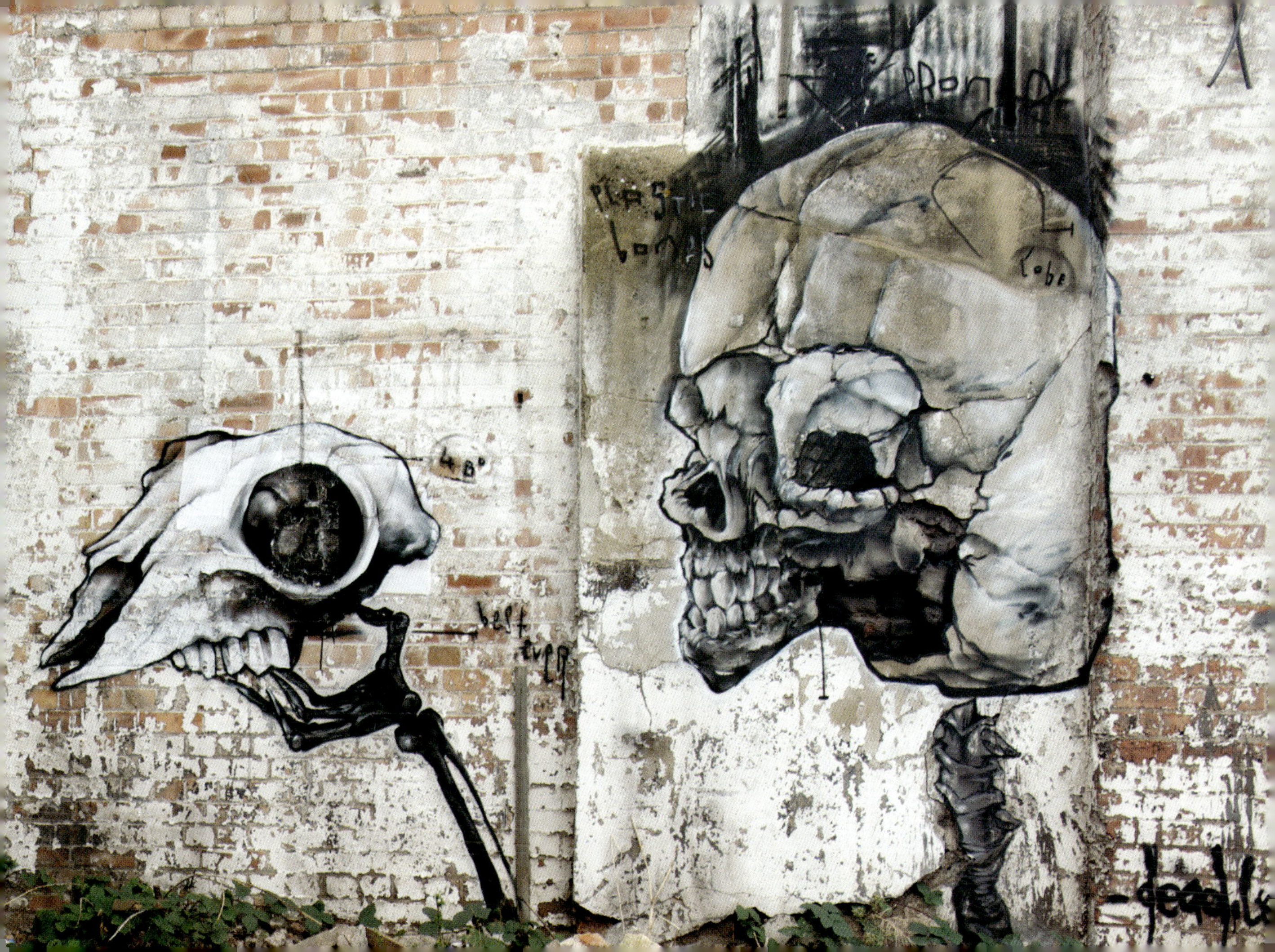
PLaStiC
bones
lobe
48°
best
ever

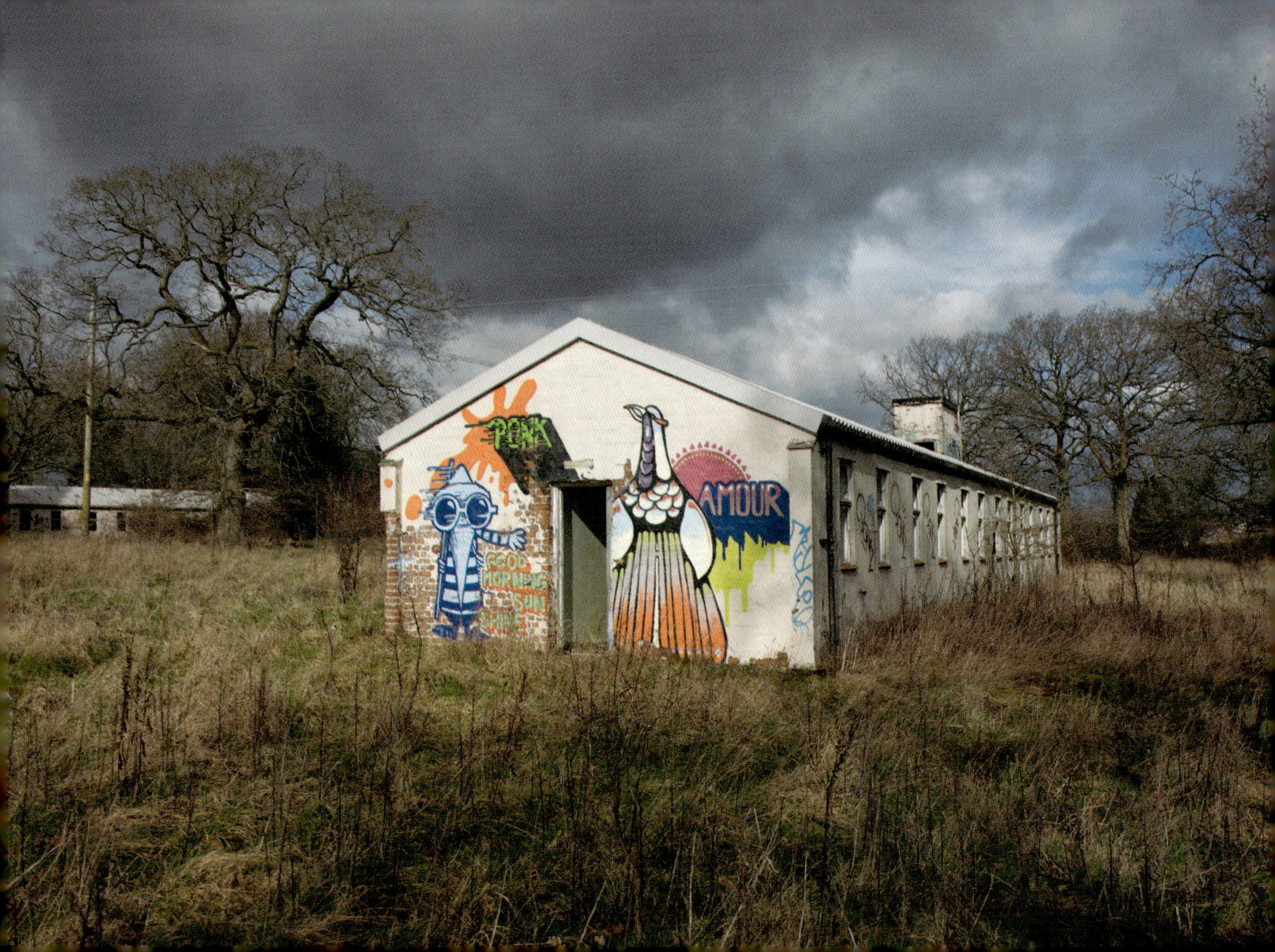
PONK
GOOD MORNING SUN SHINE
AMOUR

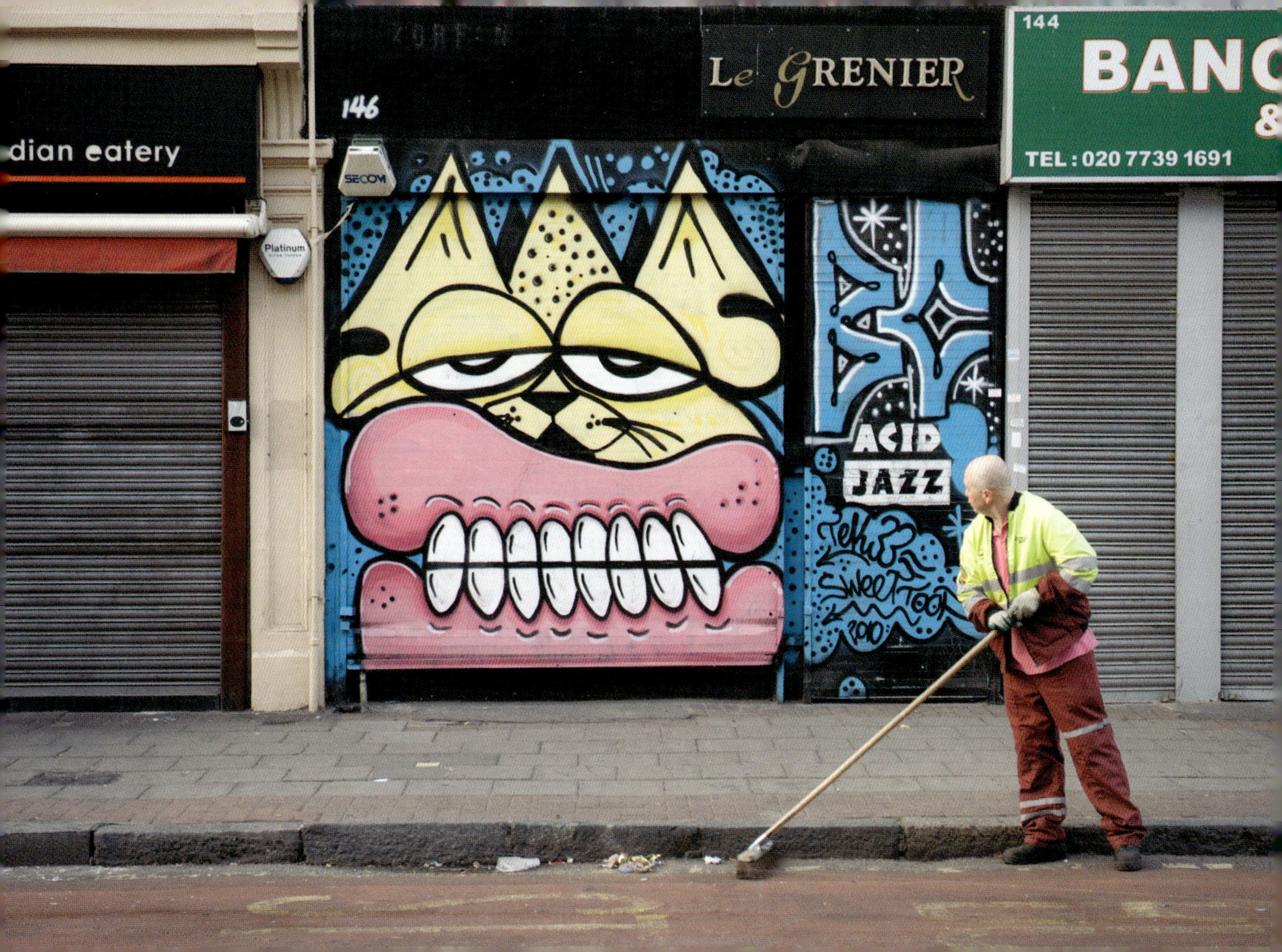
dian eatery
146
Le GRENIER
144
TEL : 020 7739 1691
SECOM
Platinum
ACID
JAZZ

The idea behind that wall was to create two separate worlds, one black and grey, filled with gloomy buildings and derelict walls and a more colorful one, populated with demons, herculean B.boys and Toxic trees. Coming from under the bowels of the earth, this strange bestiary is desperately trying to free itself from the dark forces by destroying anything standing in their way on the surface of the earth, one human spray-can at a time. On a less dramatic note, as true hip-hop heads, we also wanted to paint the world's largest Kangol hat, but unfortunately, the Guinness Book of records just wasn't interested.

DMV

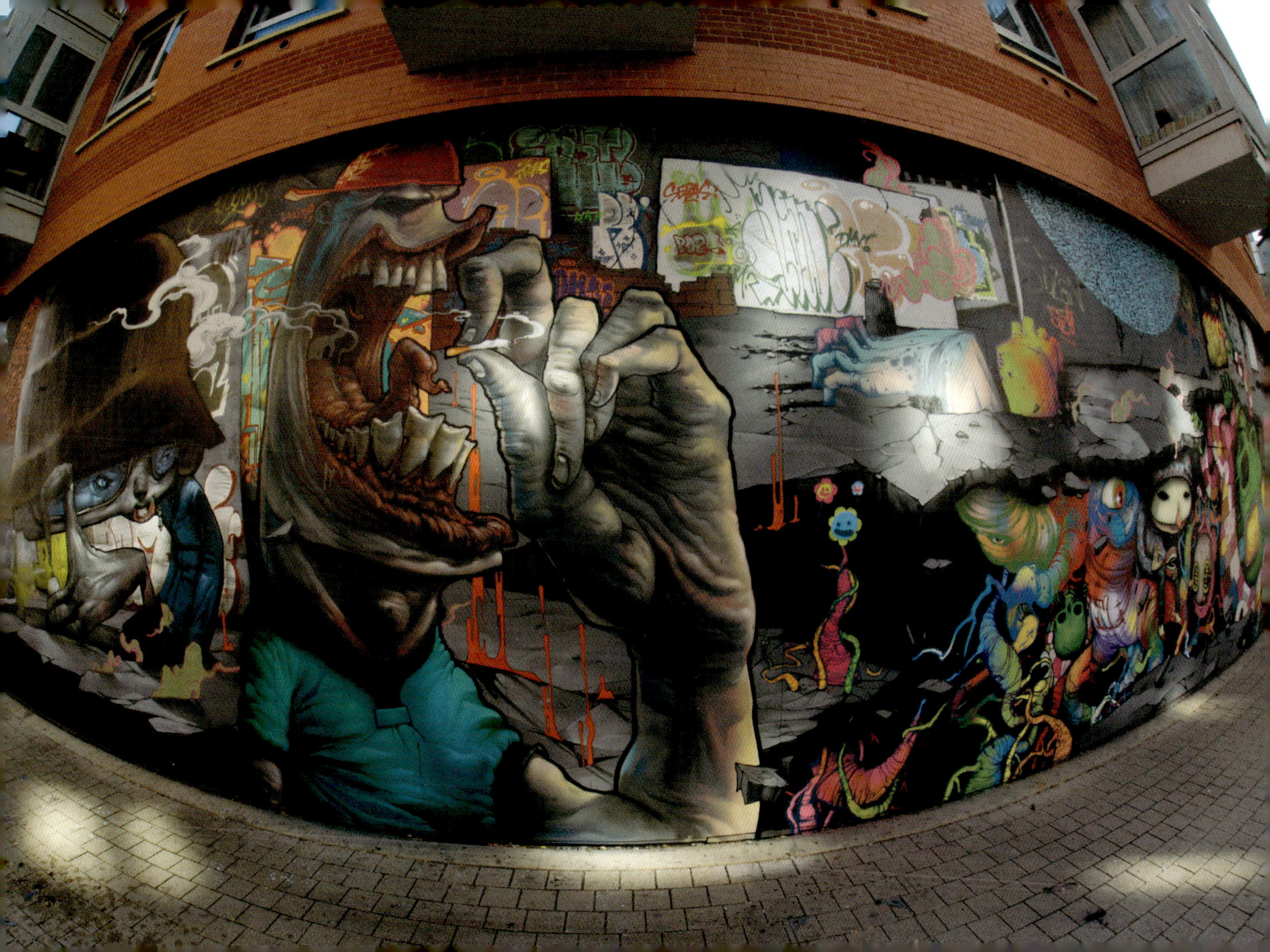

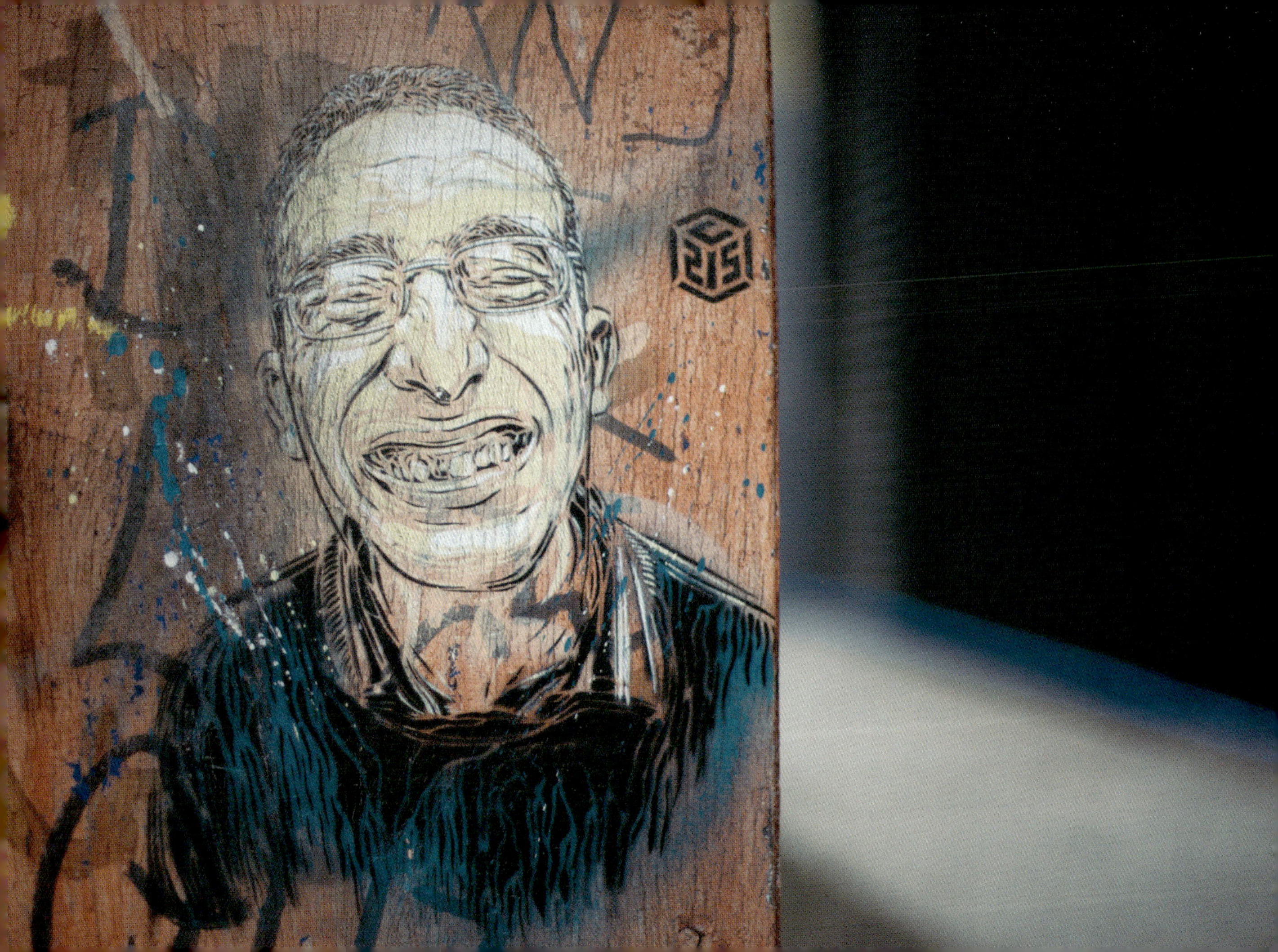

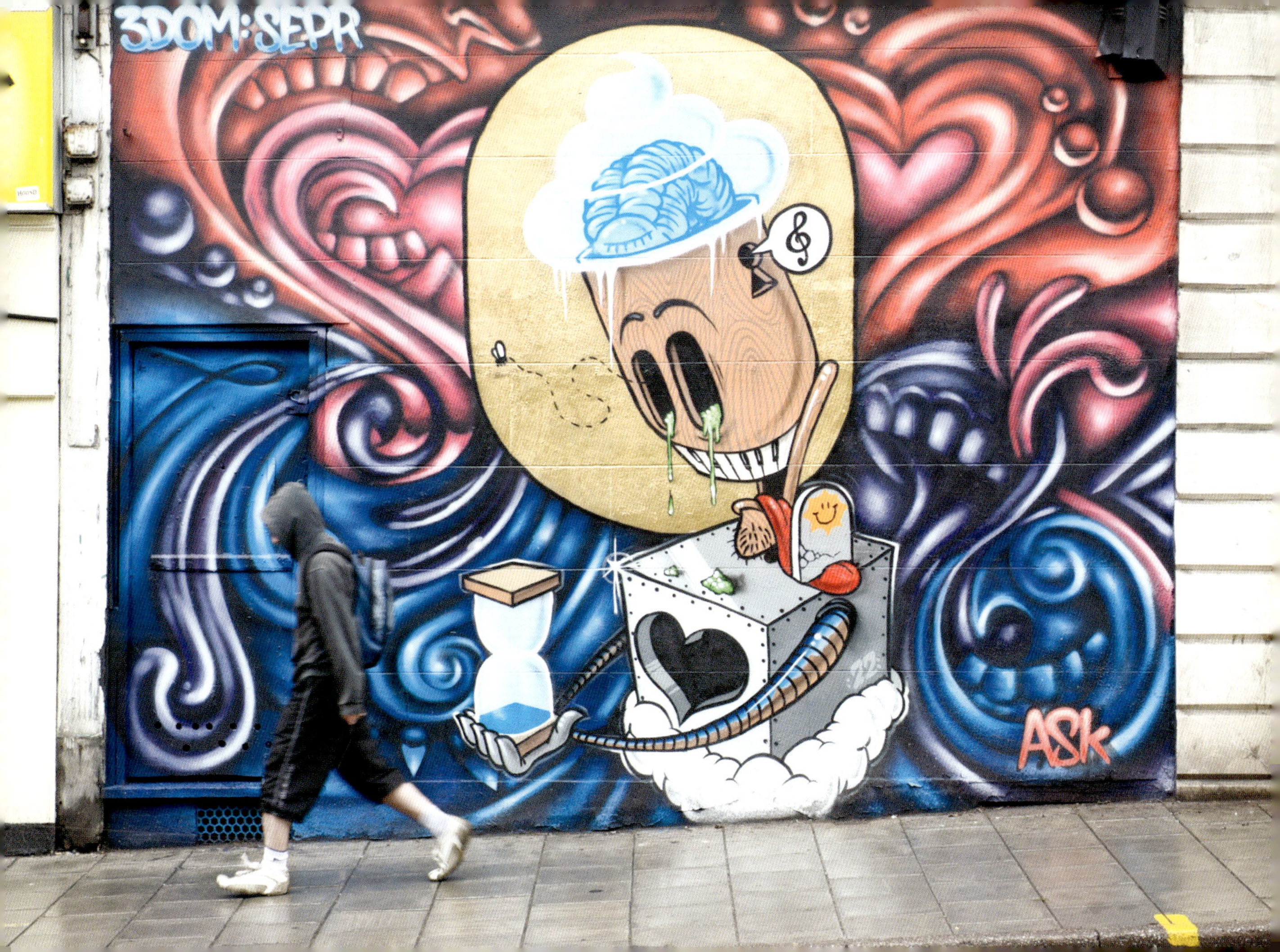
3DOM:SEPR
ASK

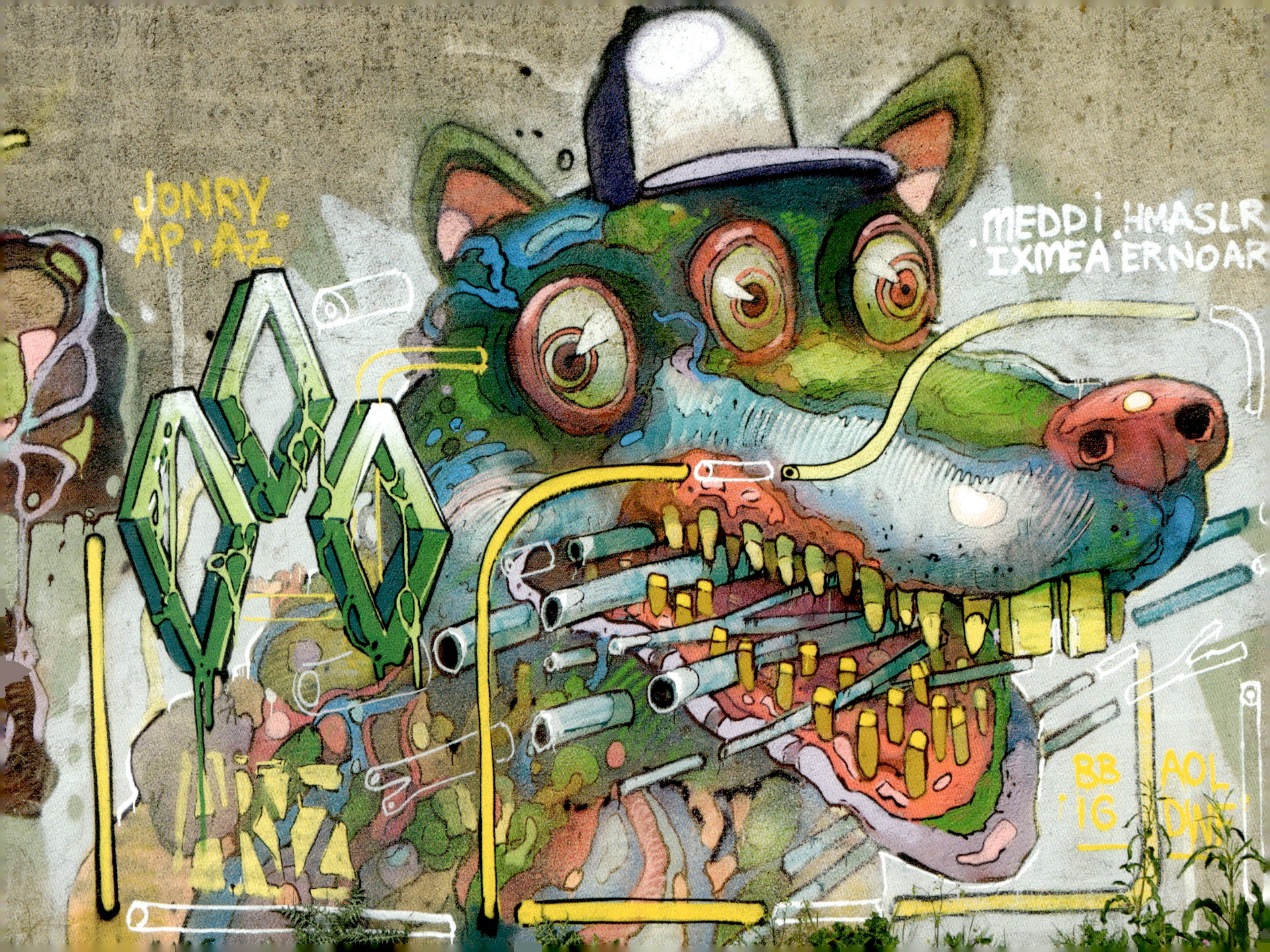
JONRY
AP AZ
MEDDi HMASLR
IXMEA ERNOAR
BB
IG
AOL

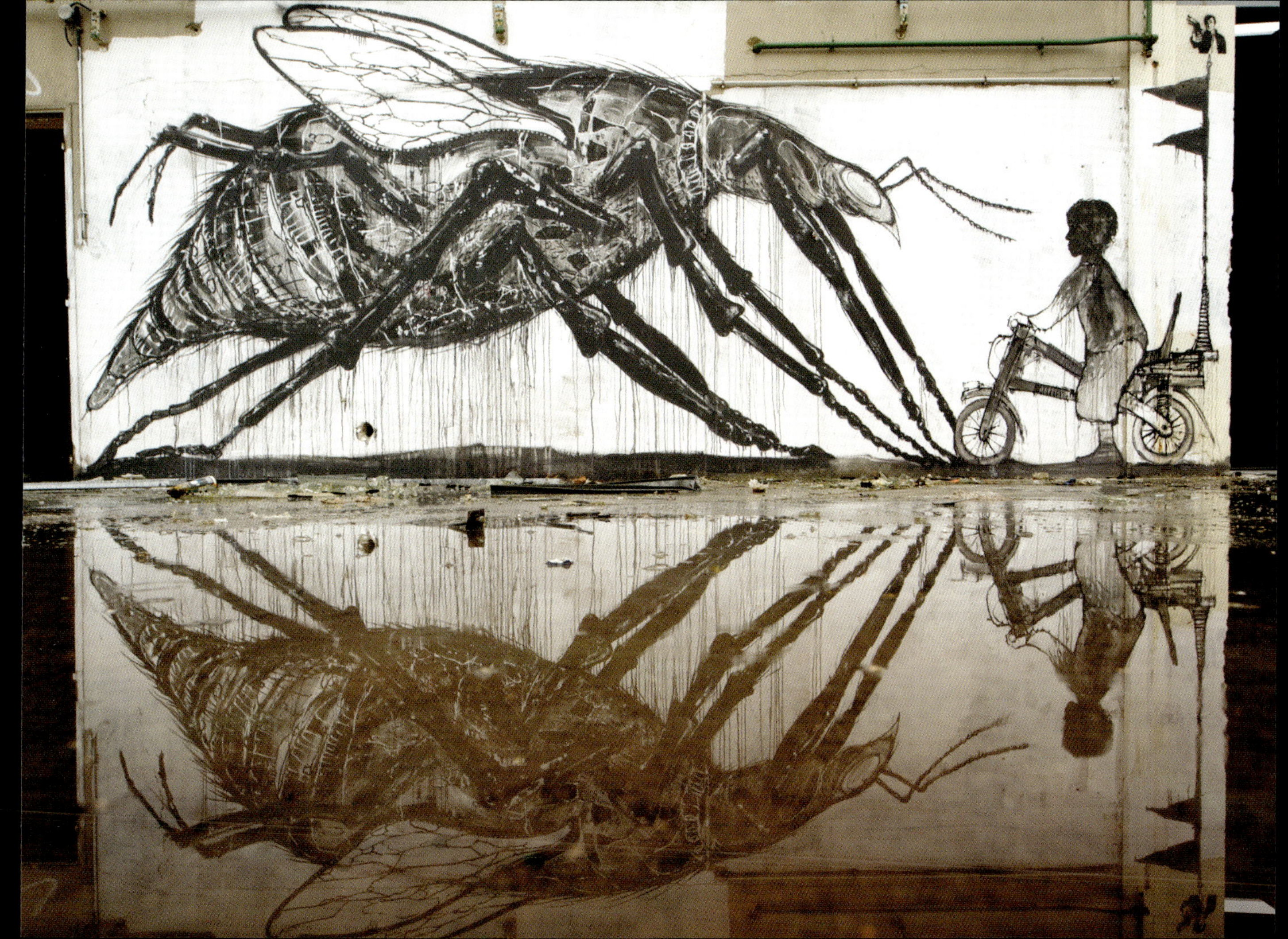

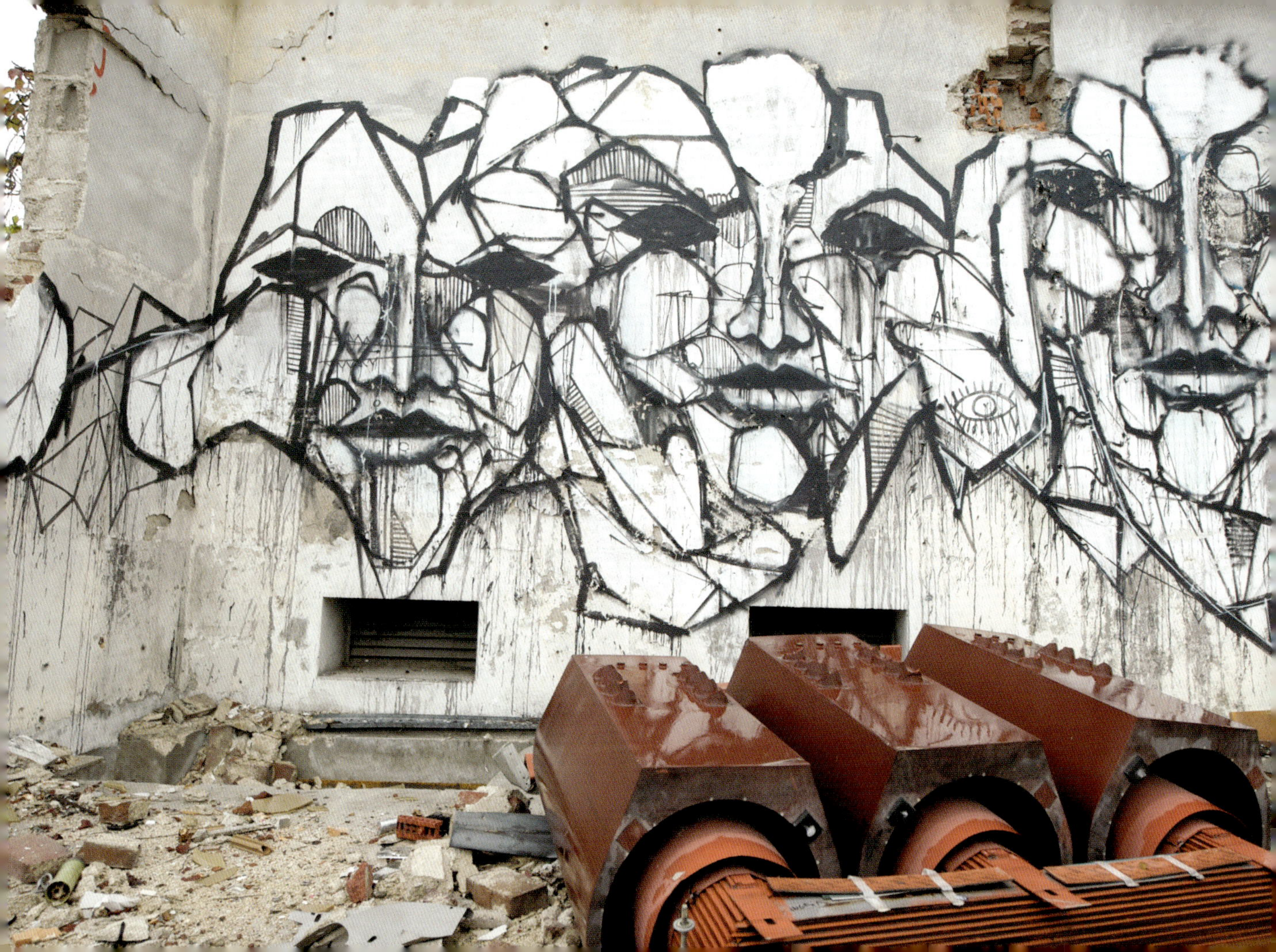

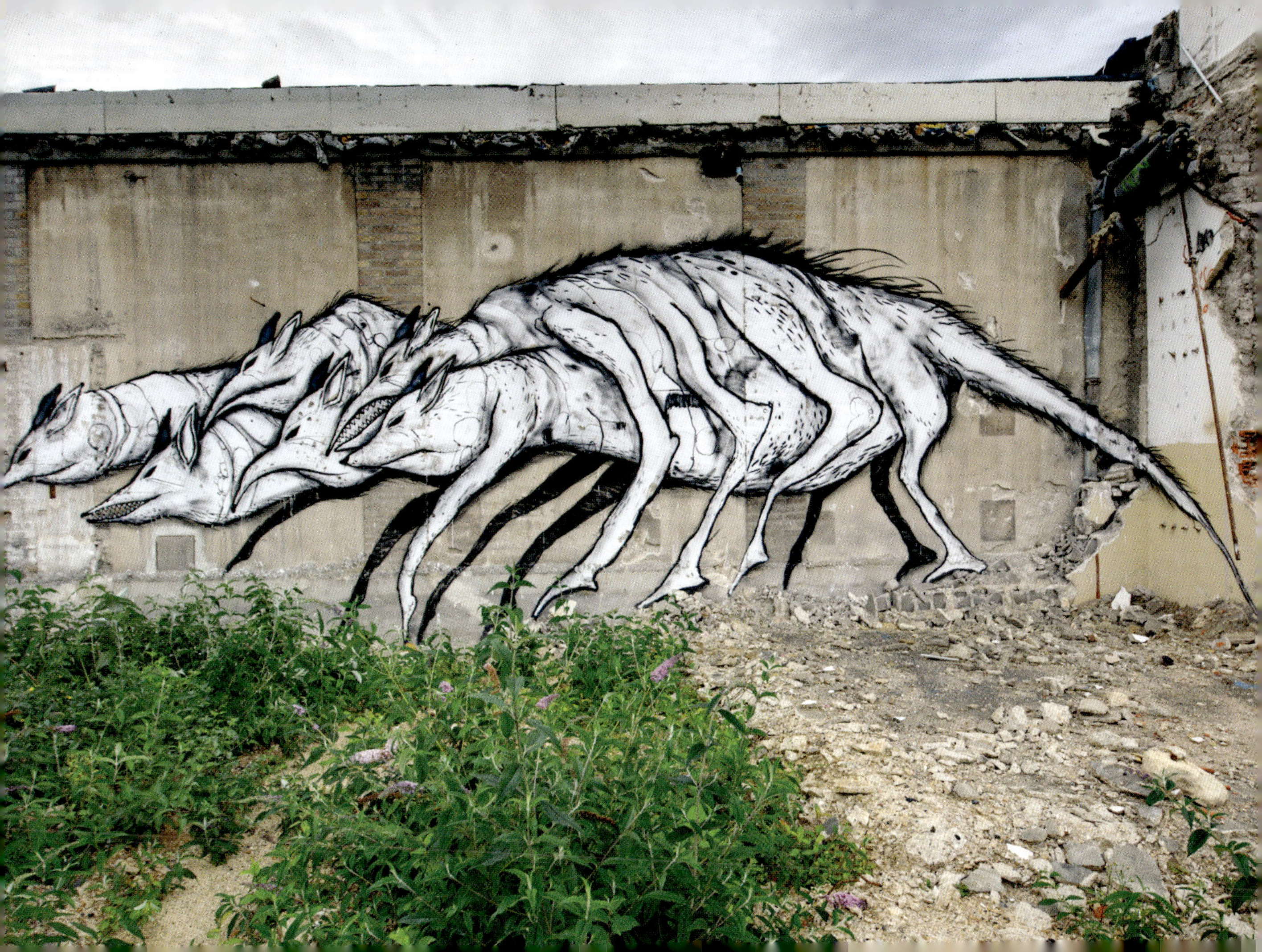

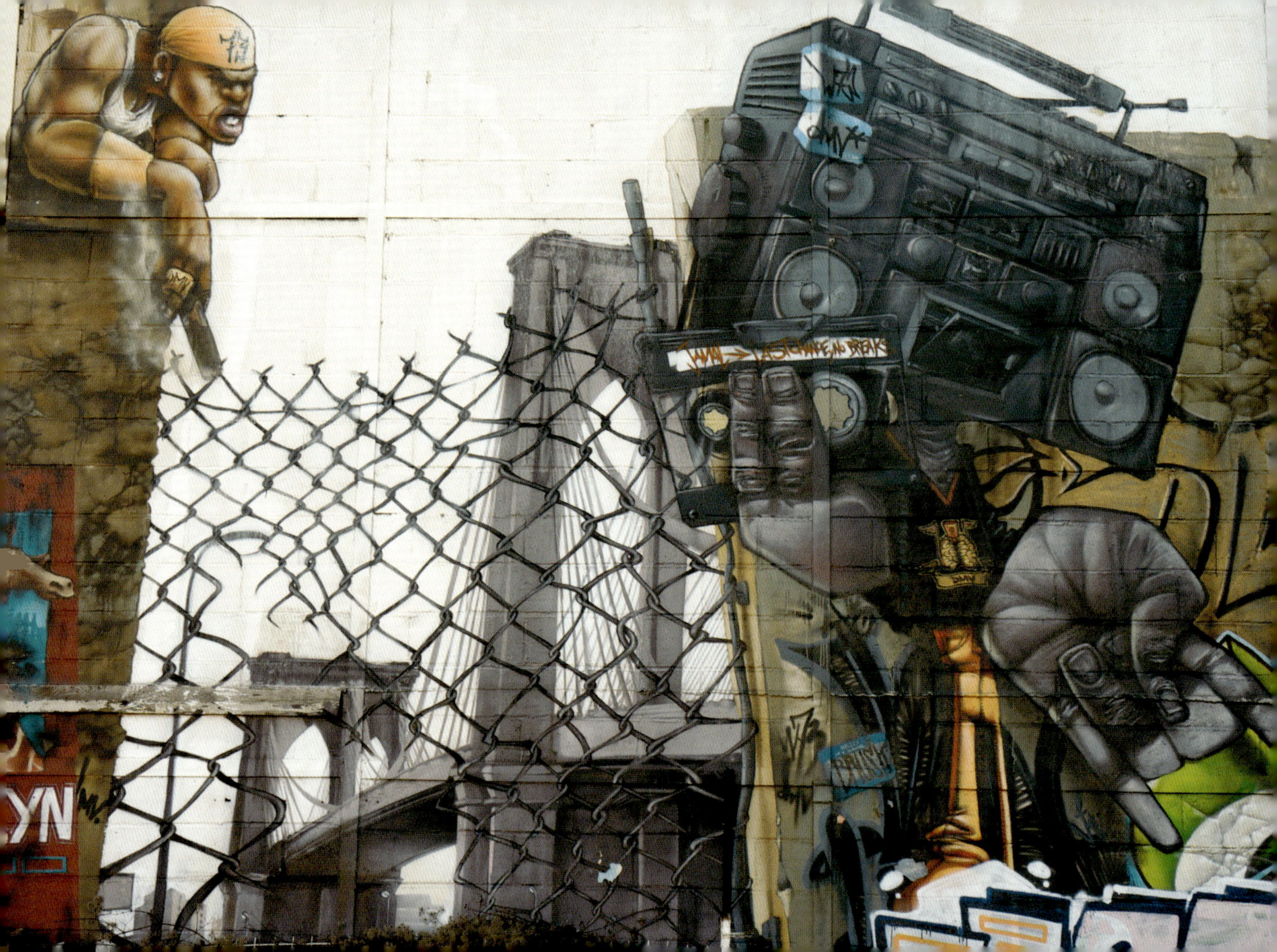

I started painting outside at 15, to impress my girlfriends.

At 20, I kept at it, hoping to impress my peers.

By 25, I was down to just trying to impress myself.

Now that I'm over 30, can my daughter really be impressed, with graphical nonsense, painted in the most desolate of places?

SOWAT (DMV)

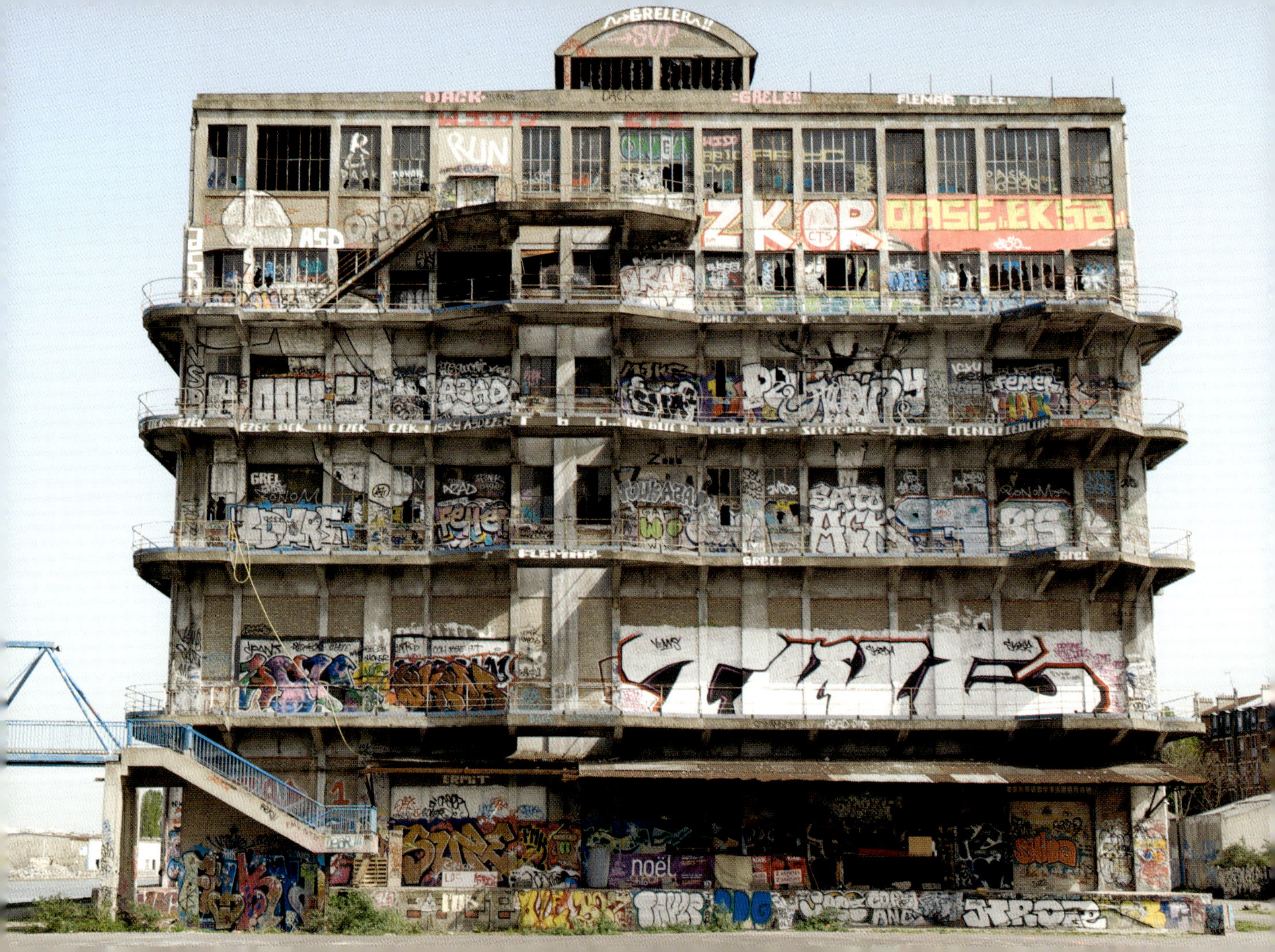
SVP
RUN
ASD
ZKOR
noël

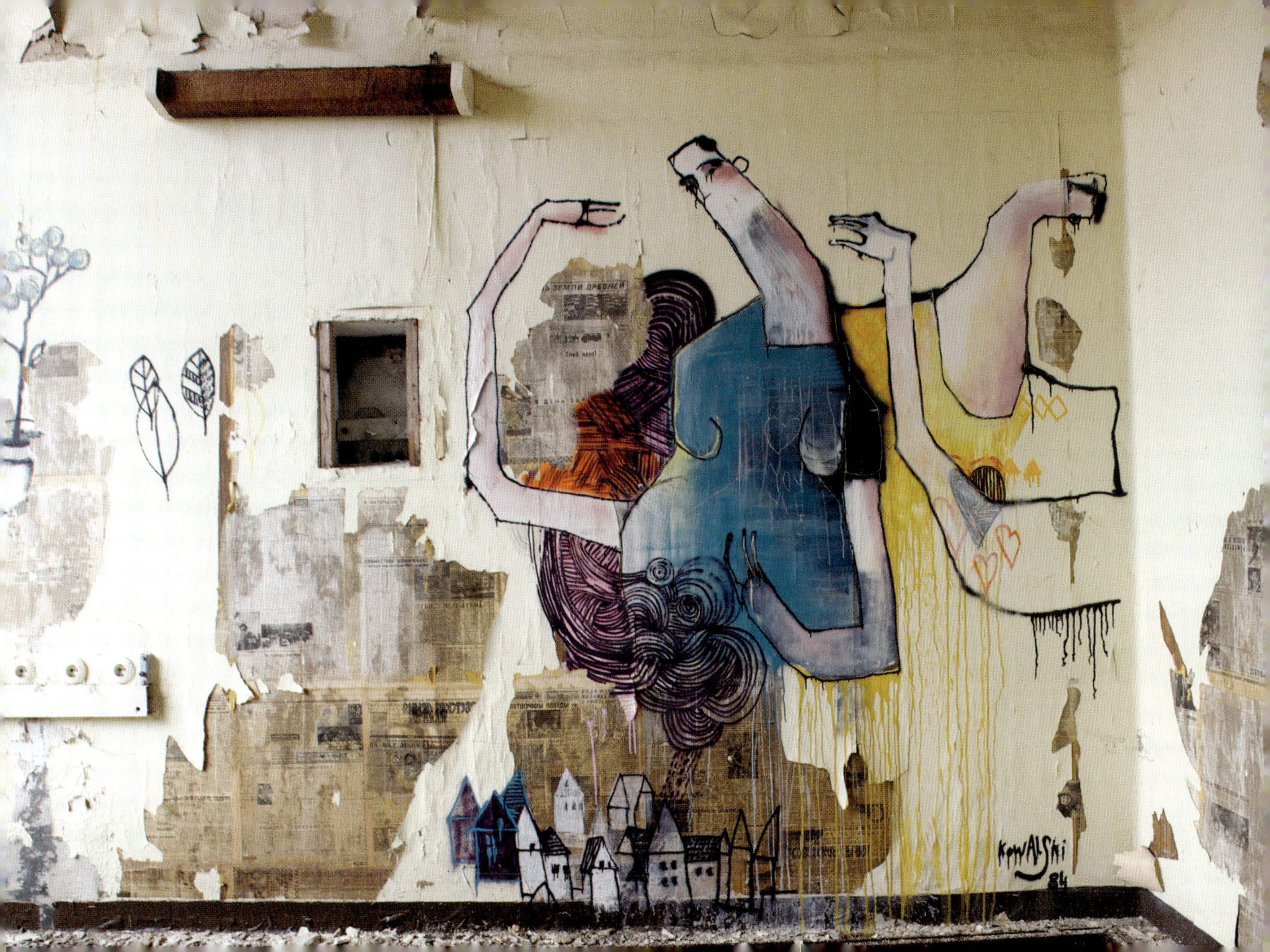
KOWALSKI
84

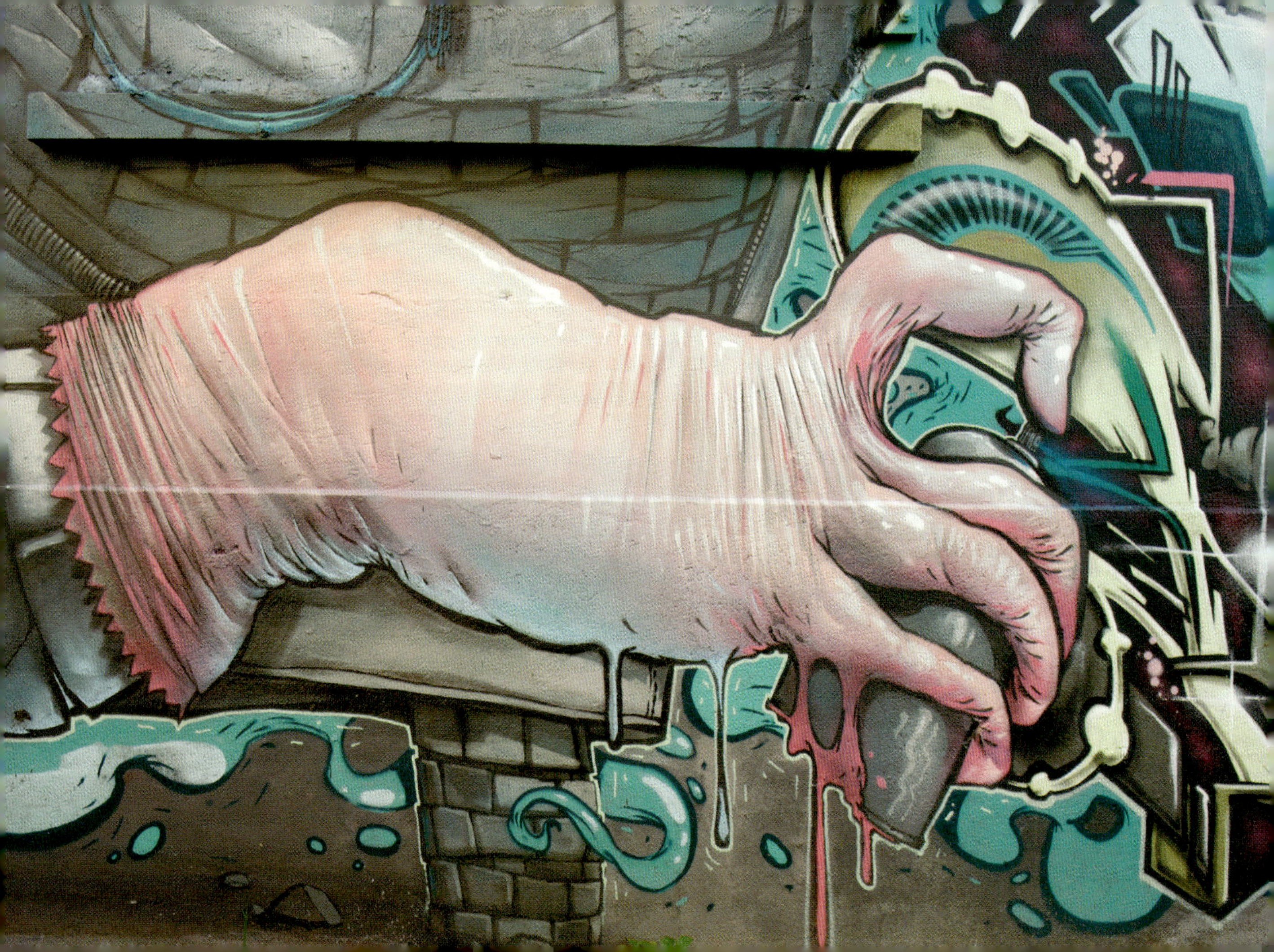

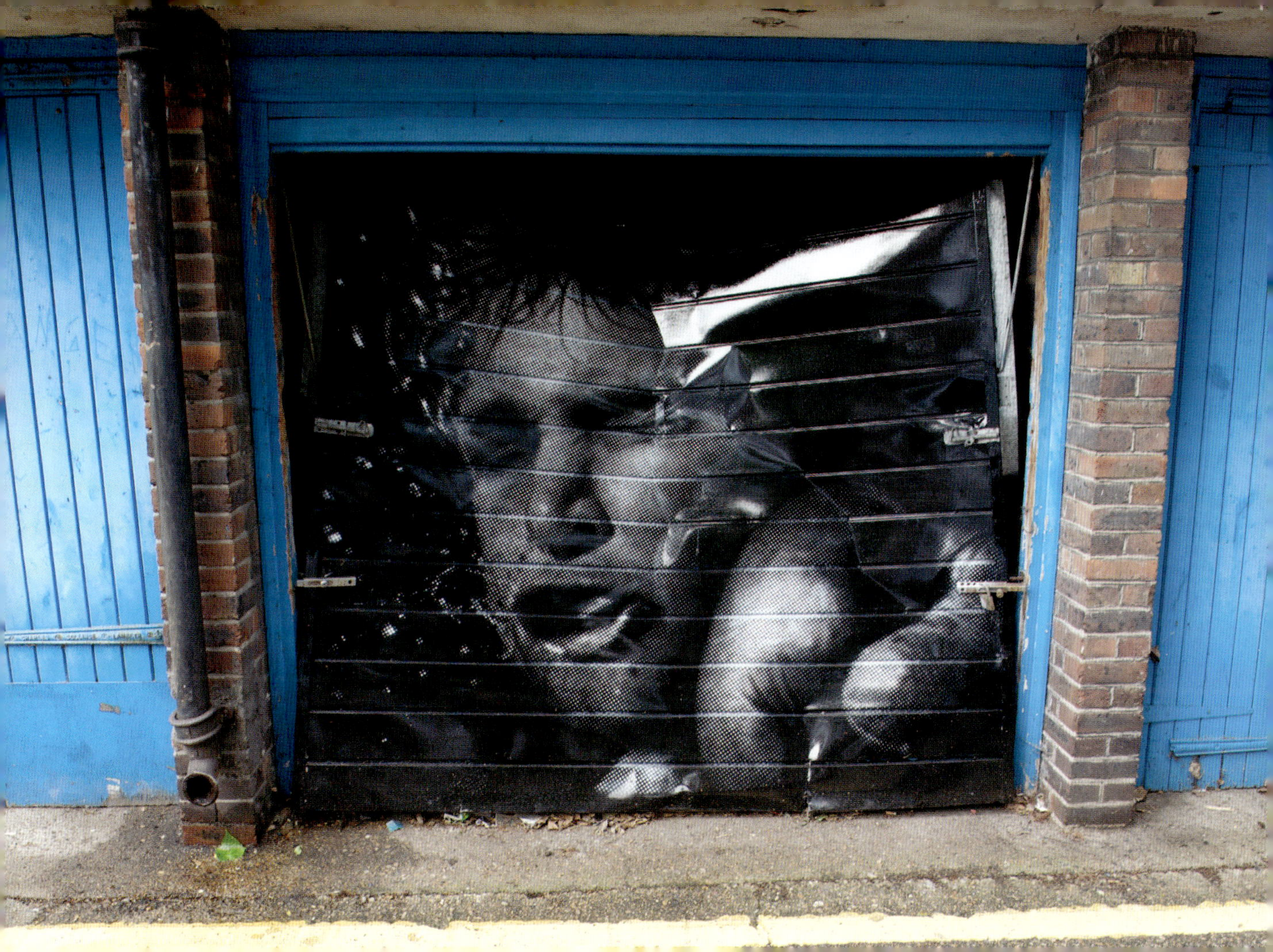

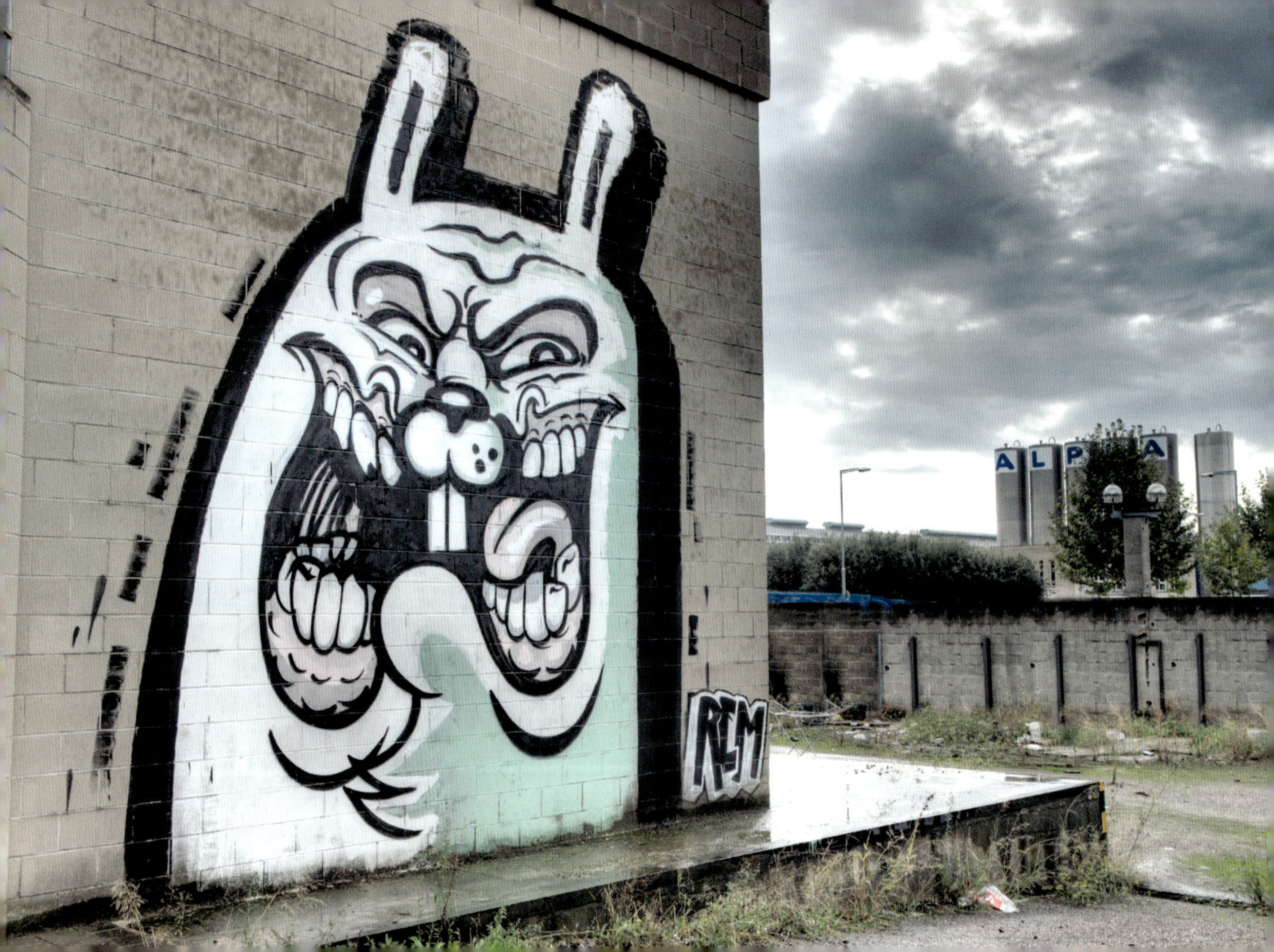

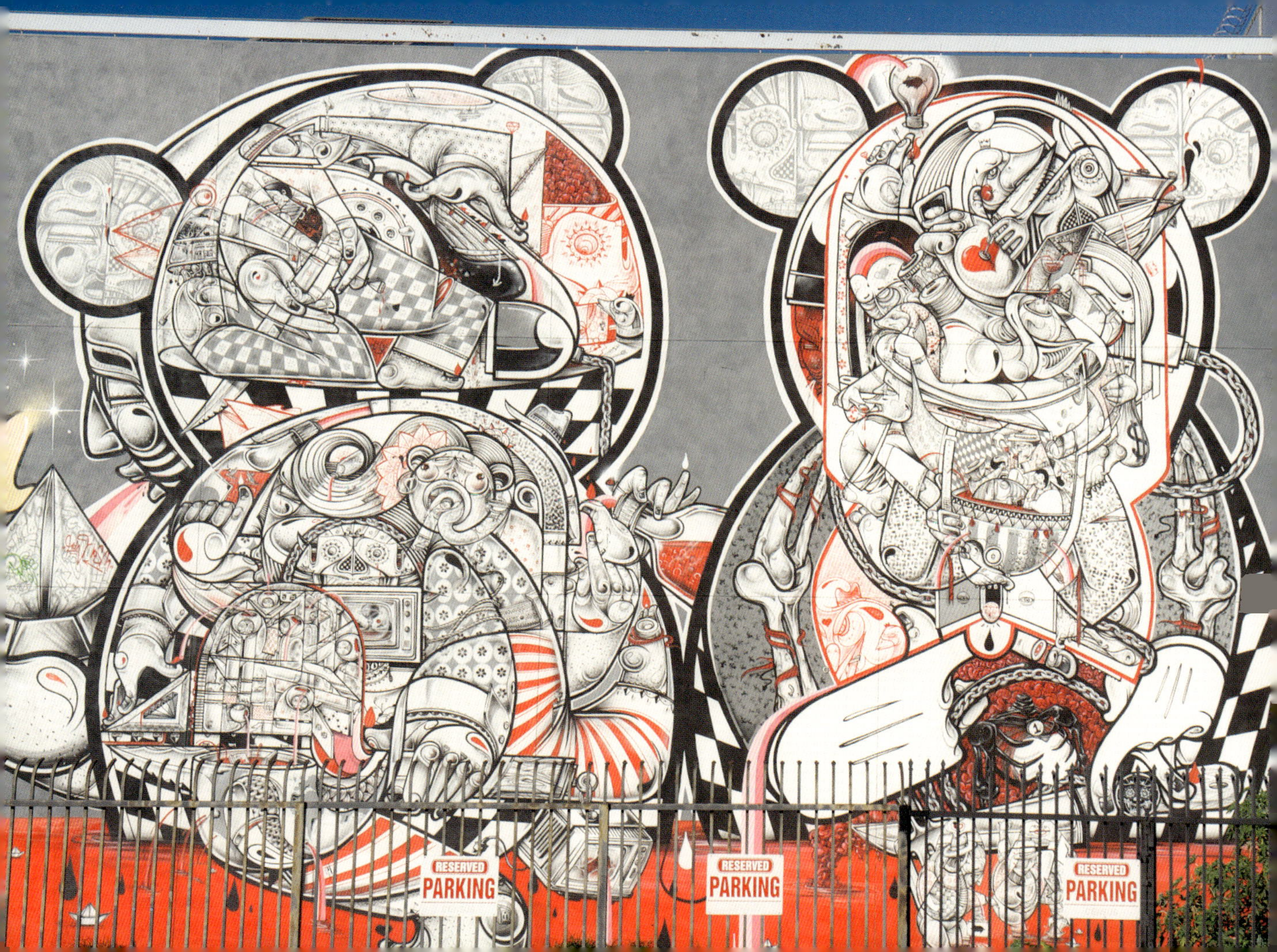
RESERVED
PARKING
RESERVED
PARKING
RESERVED
PARKING

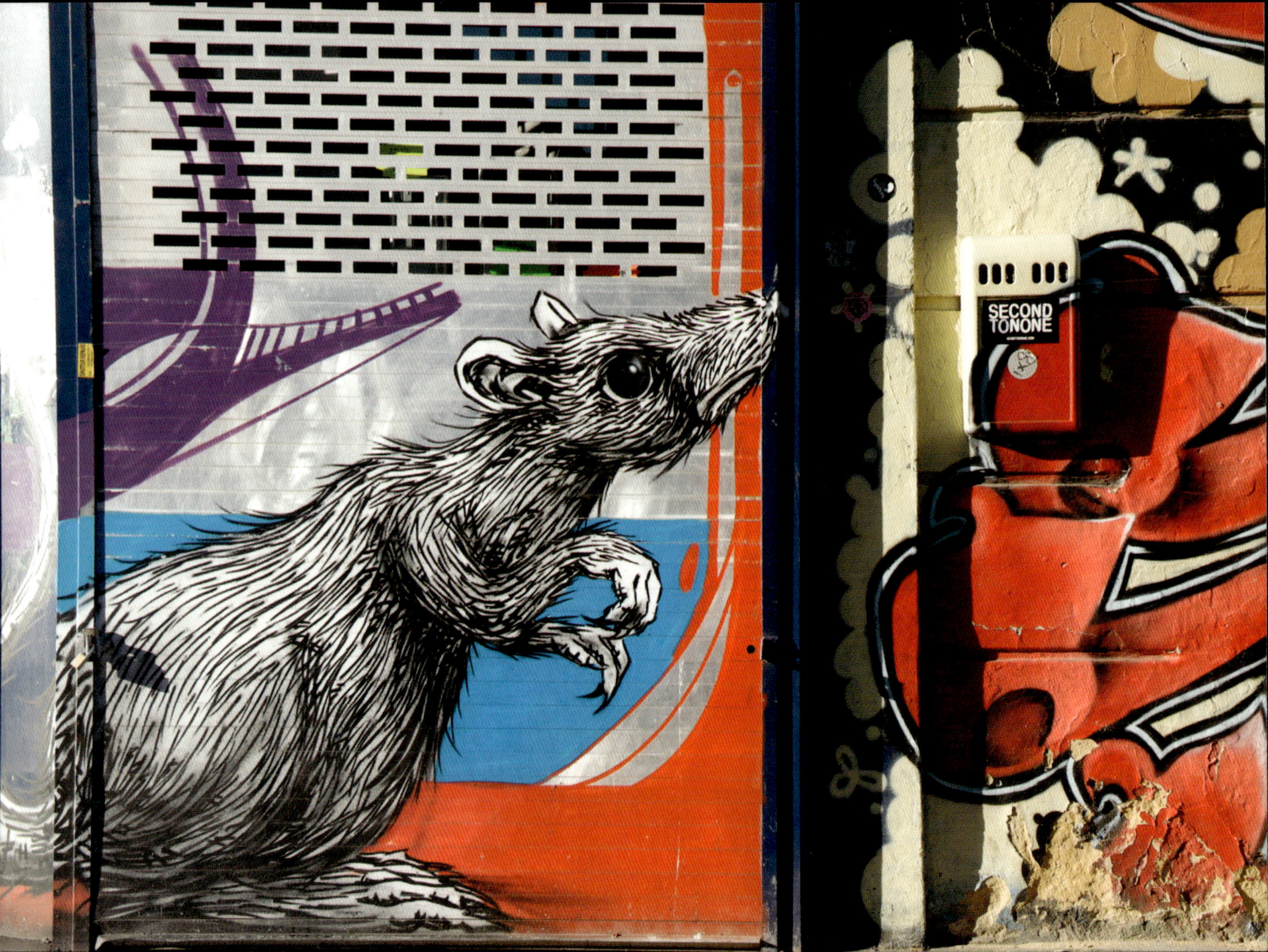
SECOND
TONONE

I like to paint in big cities because it's a totally different way to experience a city. You spend a couple of hours on a certain spot and get involved in that specific corner of a hood, you get to know the locals, the all day life of that particular micro space. For me it's a wonderful feeling to put up a big wall in London or New York, these cities I only knew as kid from graffiti, music and movies. It always give me an amazing vibe.

ROA

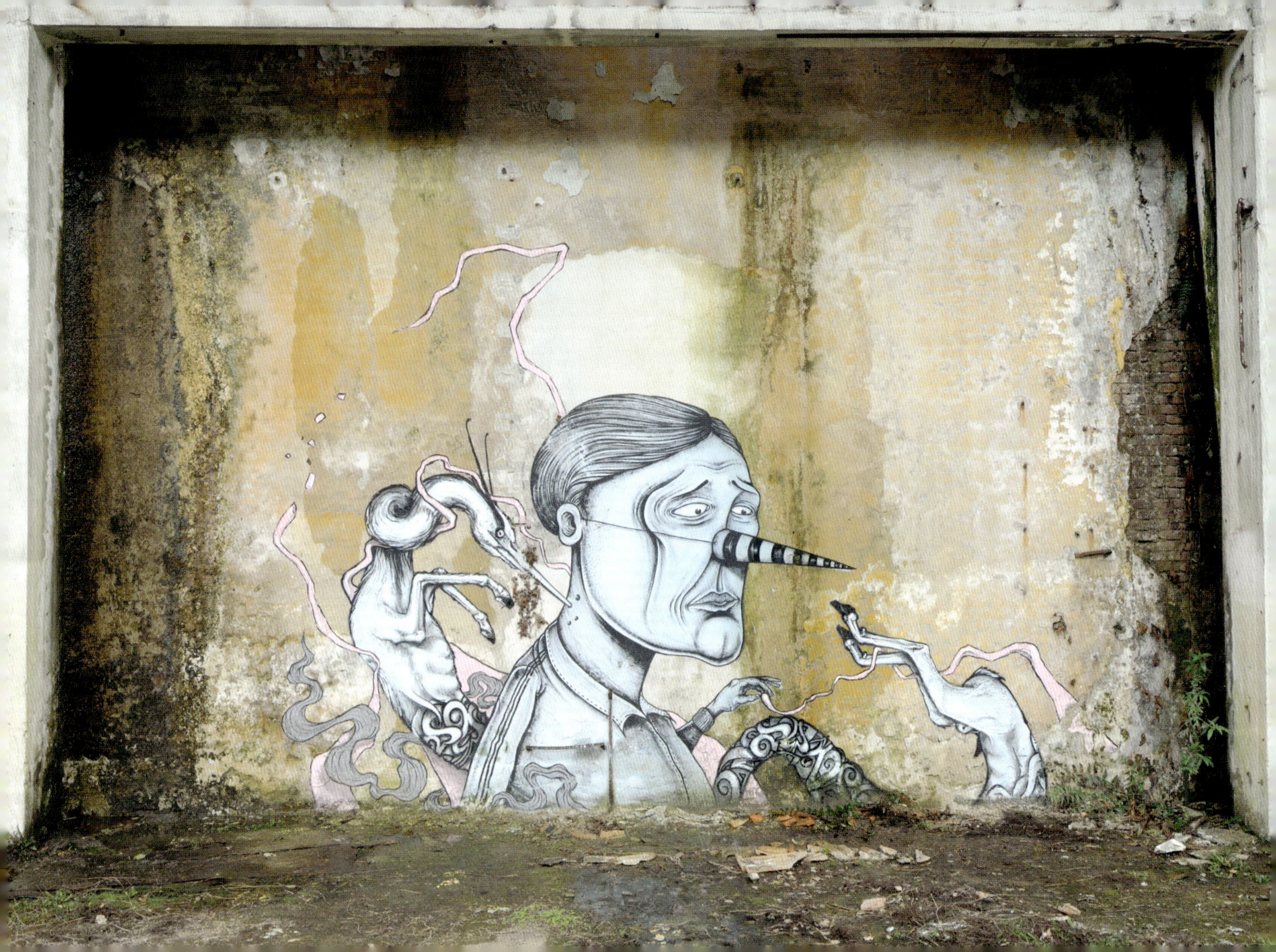

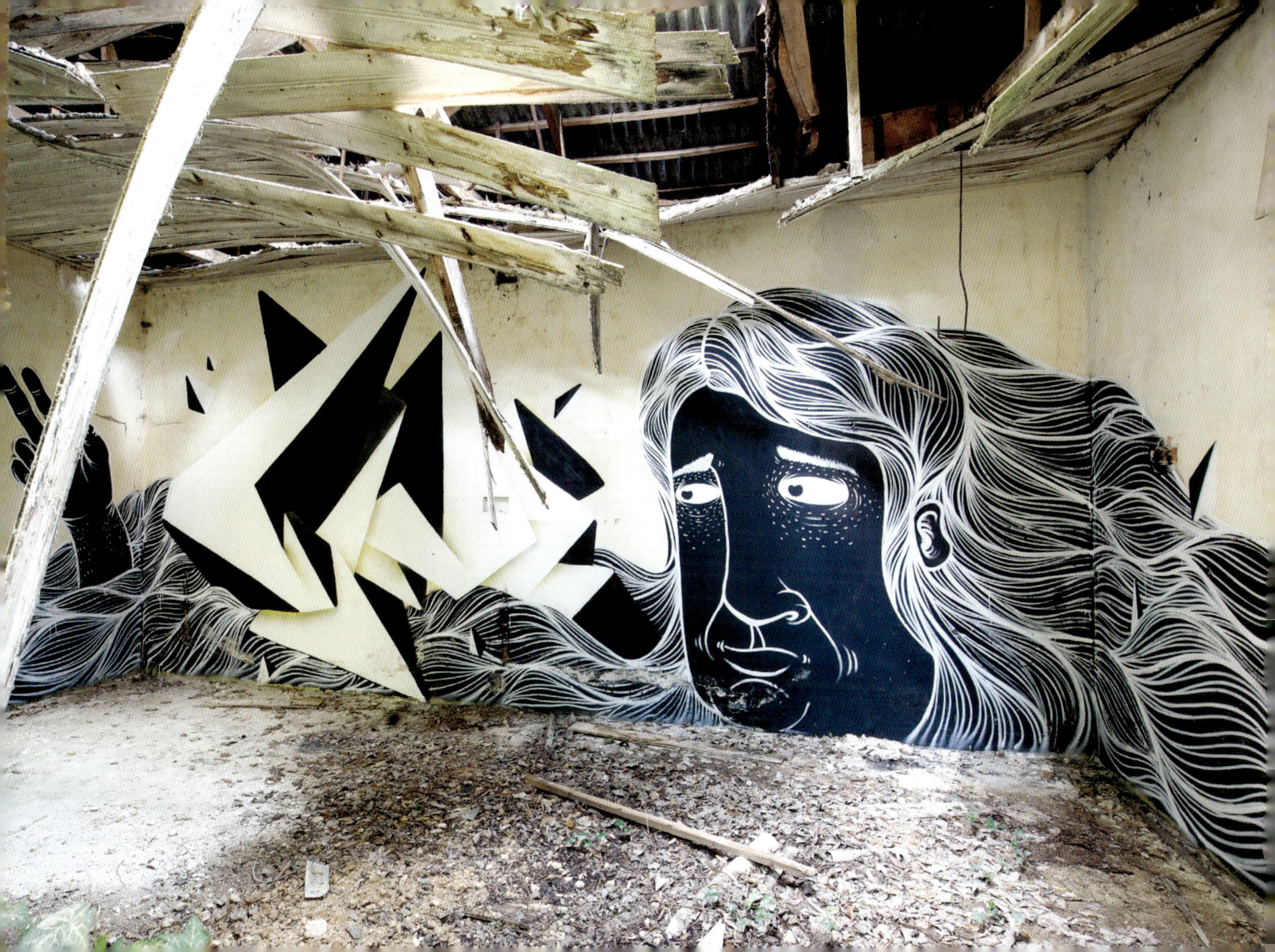

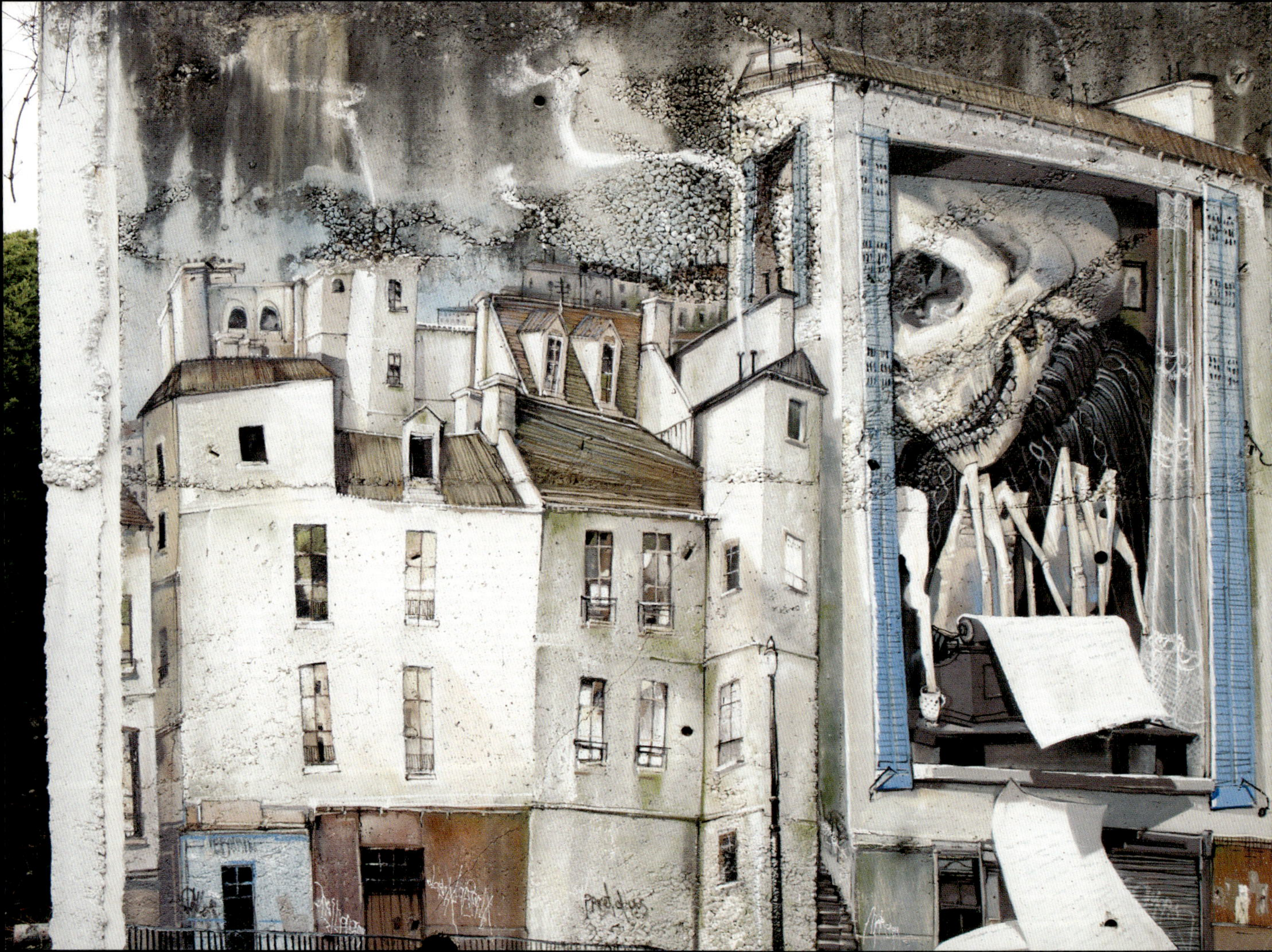

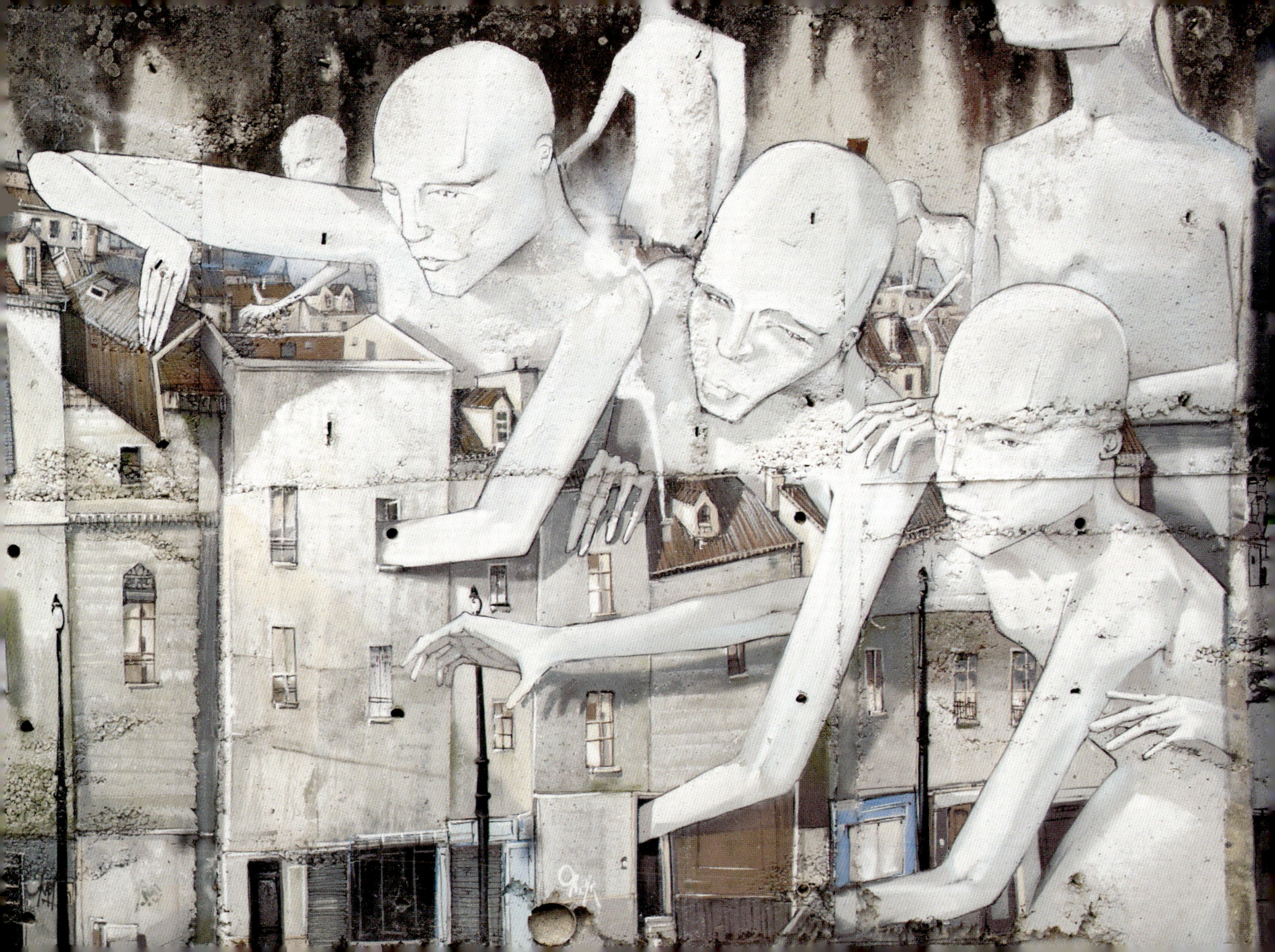

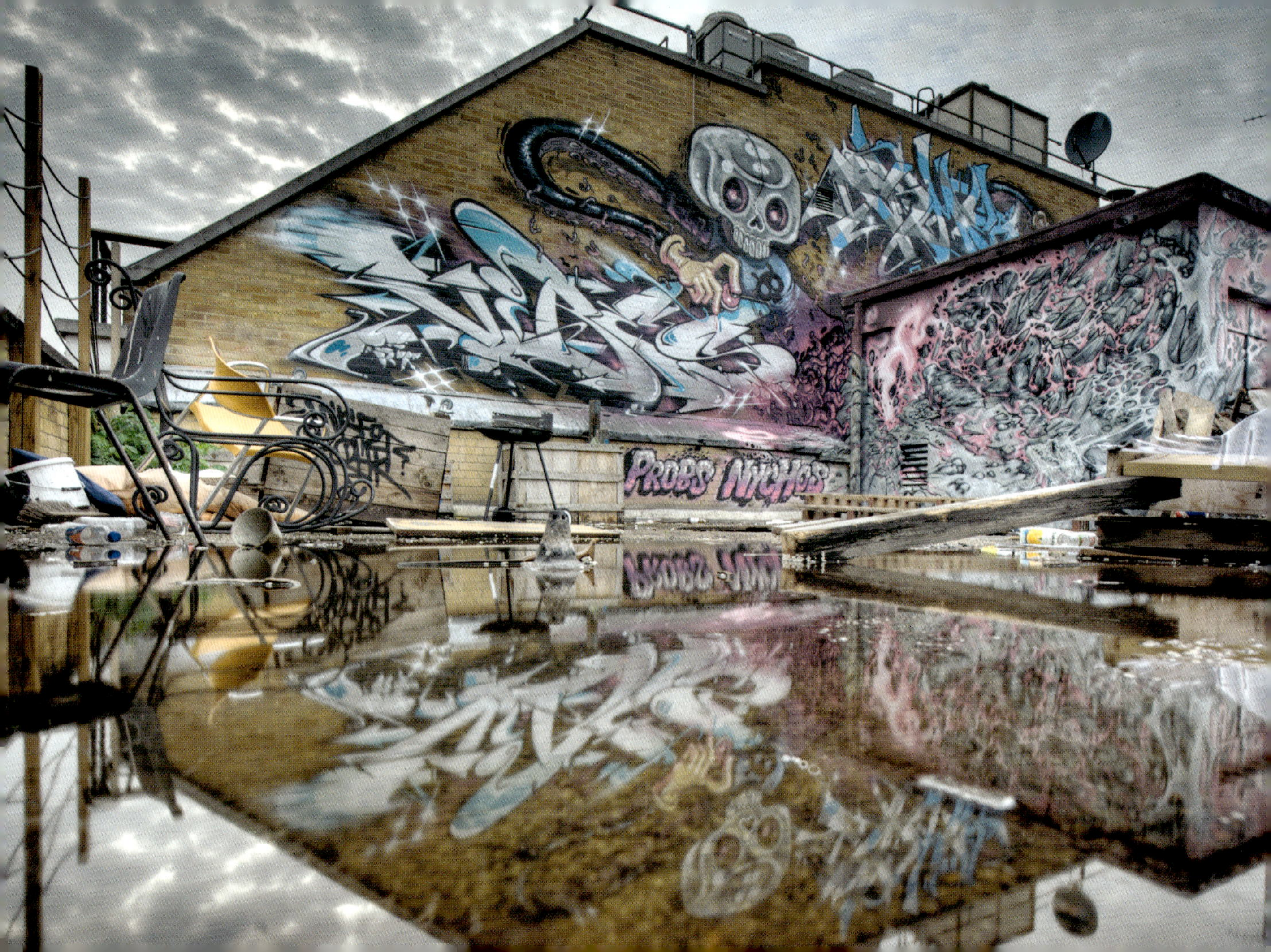
PROBS NYCHOS

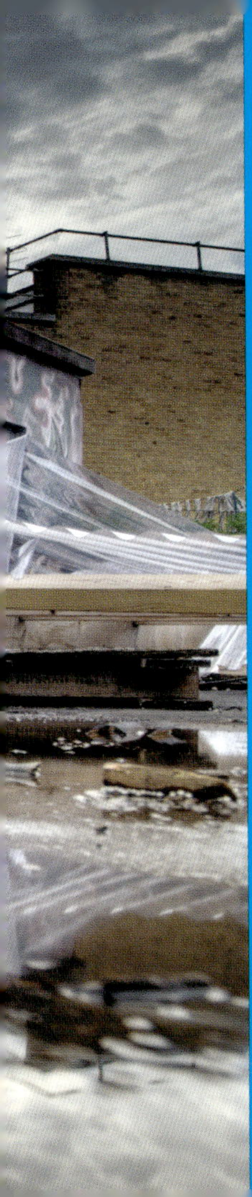

ECHOES OF '77

Like pollen blown across the world by an epic gust of wind, the explosion of youth culture in NYC 1977 fertilised the minds of a global generation of rebel kids. What was so magical about this moment in history that intoxicated a generation? The system broke down. The schools failed, the parents were working too hard to look after their kids or else on drugs, and the kids were left to their own devices with a rotten and collapsing city as a playground. They filled the vacuum with their own self-devised cultures. Hip Hop and Punk were at their apogees. And through Africa Bambaataa's block parties all the tribes came together at last. What provincial kid could resist this potent vision when it all hit the mass media in the early 1980's? Graff culture today is still an echo of 1977.

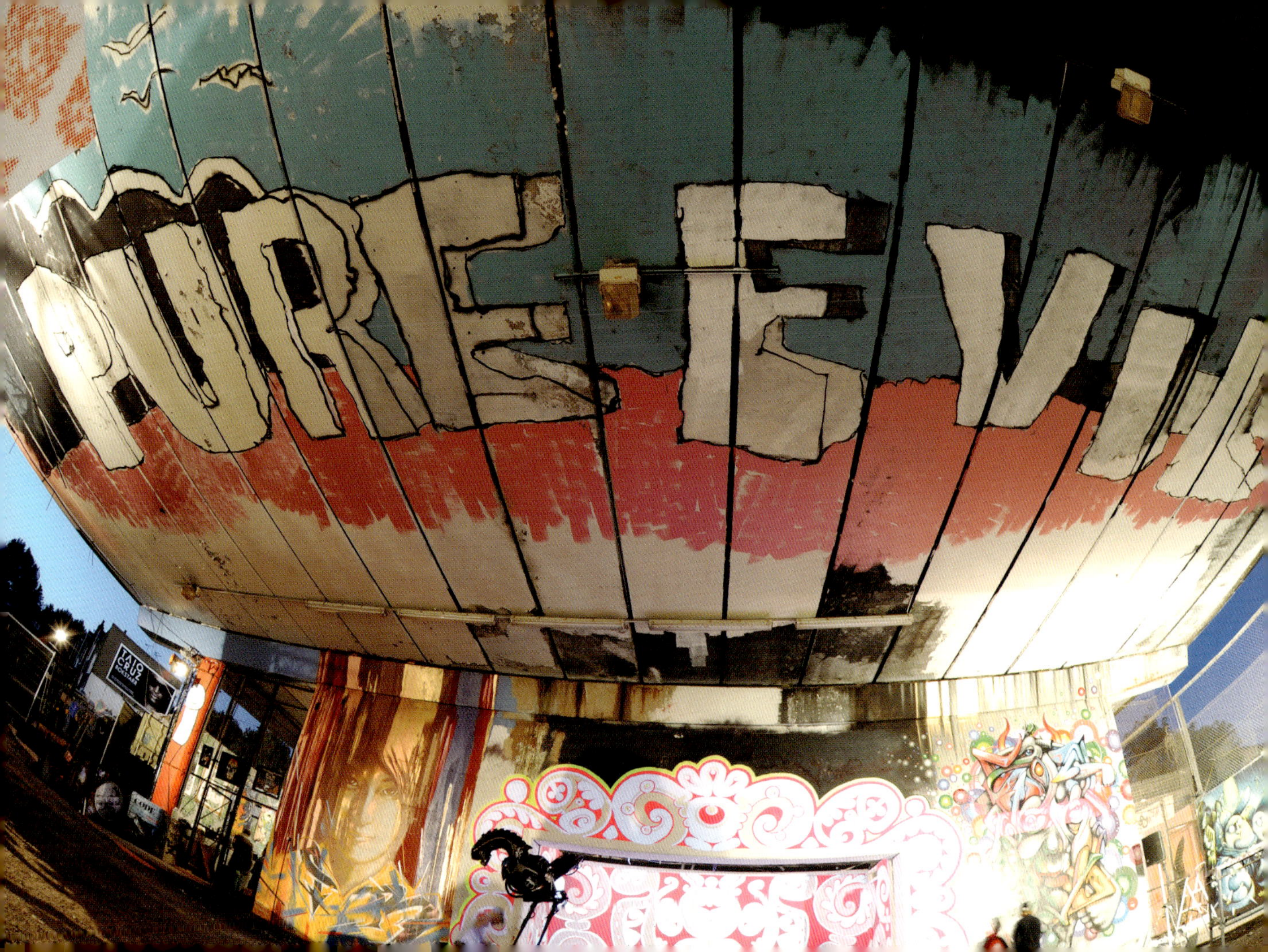
PURE
TAIO CRUZ

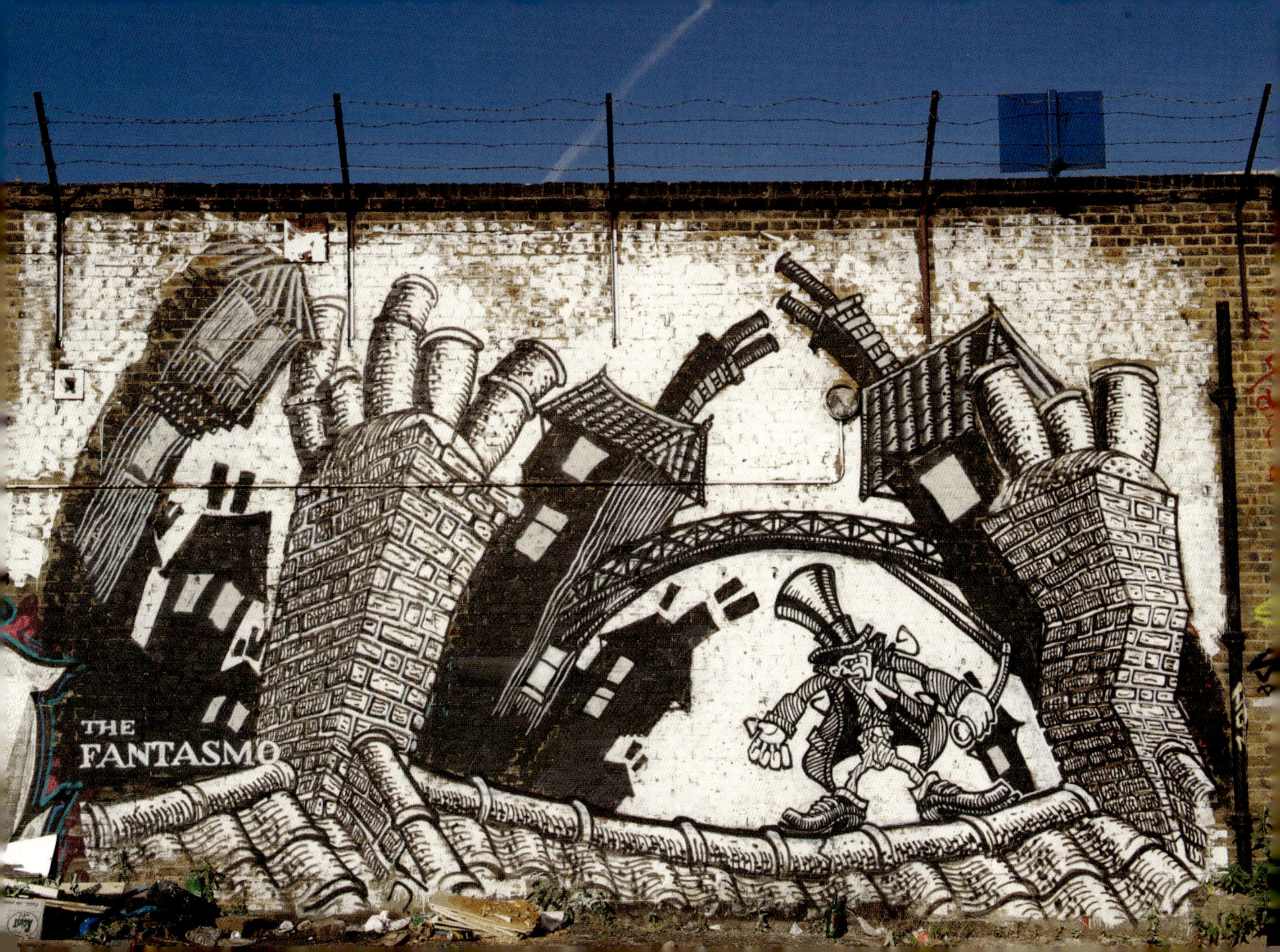
THE
FANTASMO

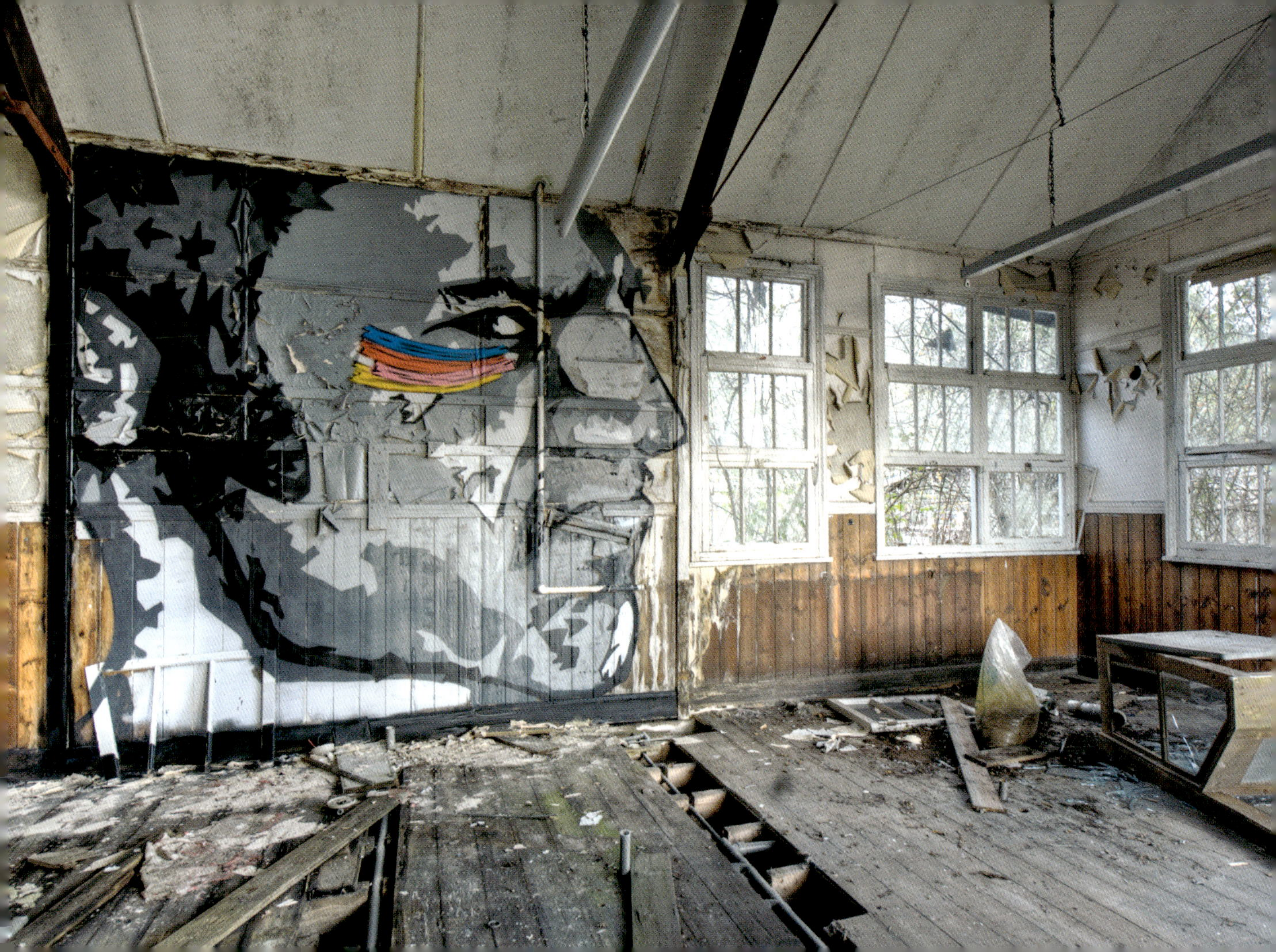

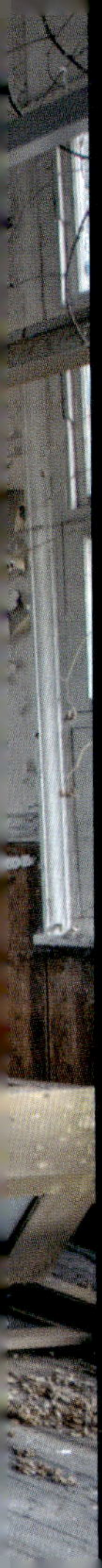

When I was a child I was always forbidden to paint on walls. Now painting on walls is both an expression of my freedom and a thrilling way to share my art for free.

THE MOUARF

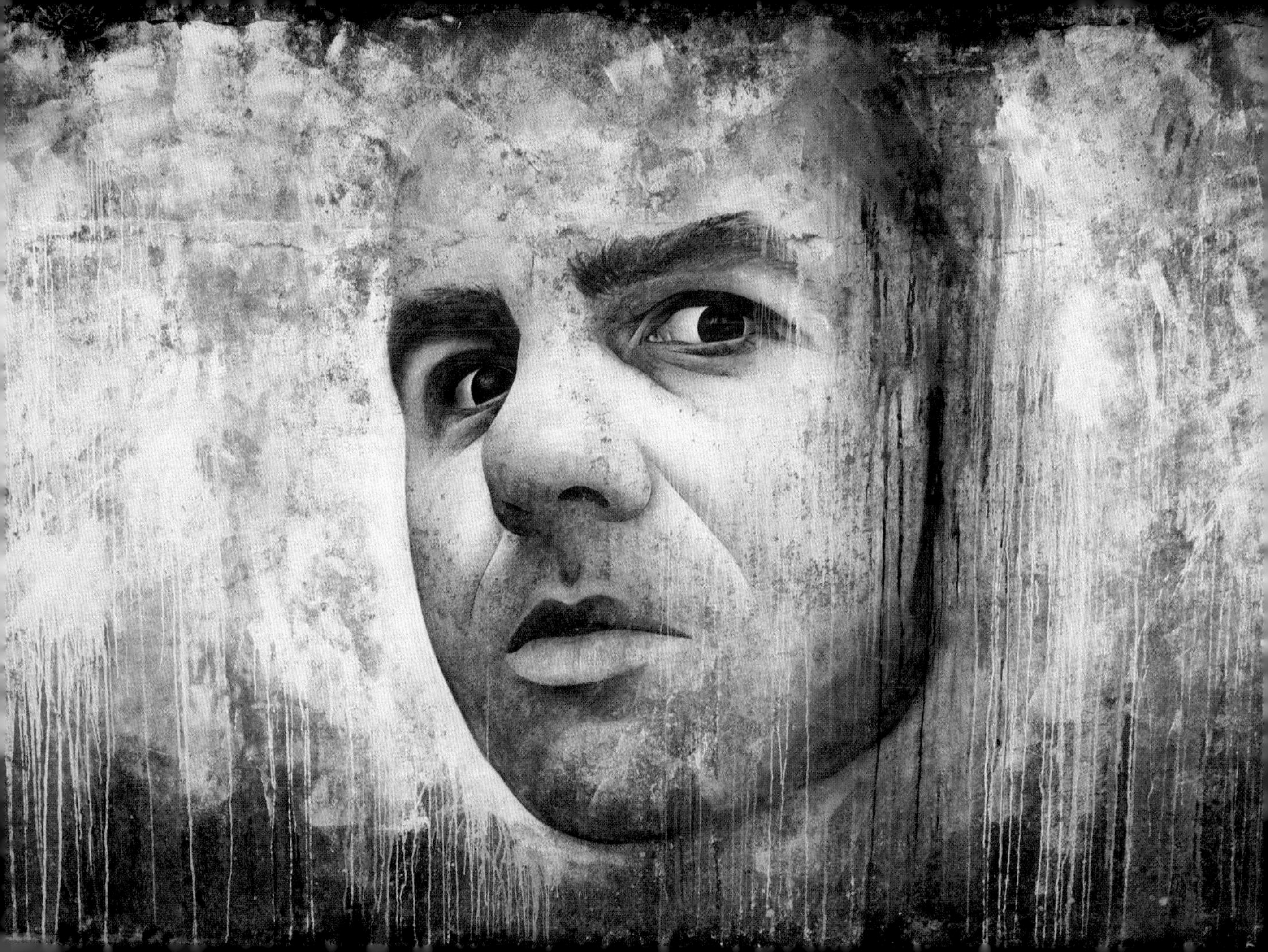

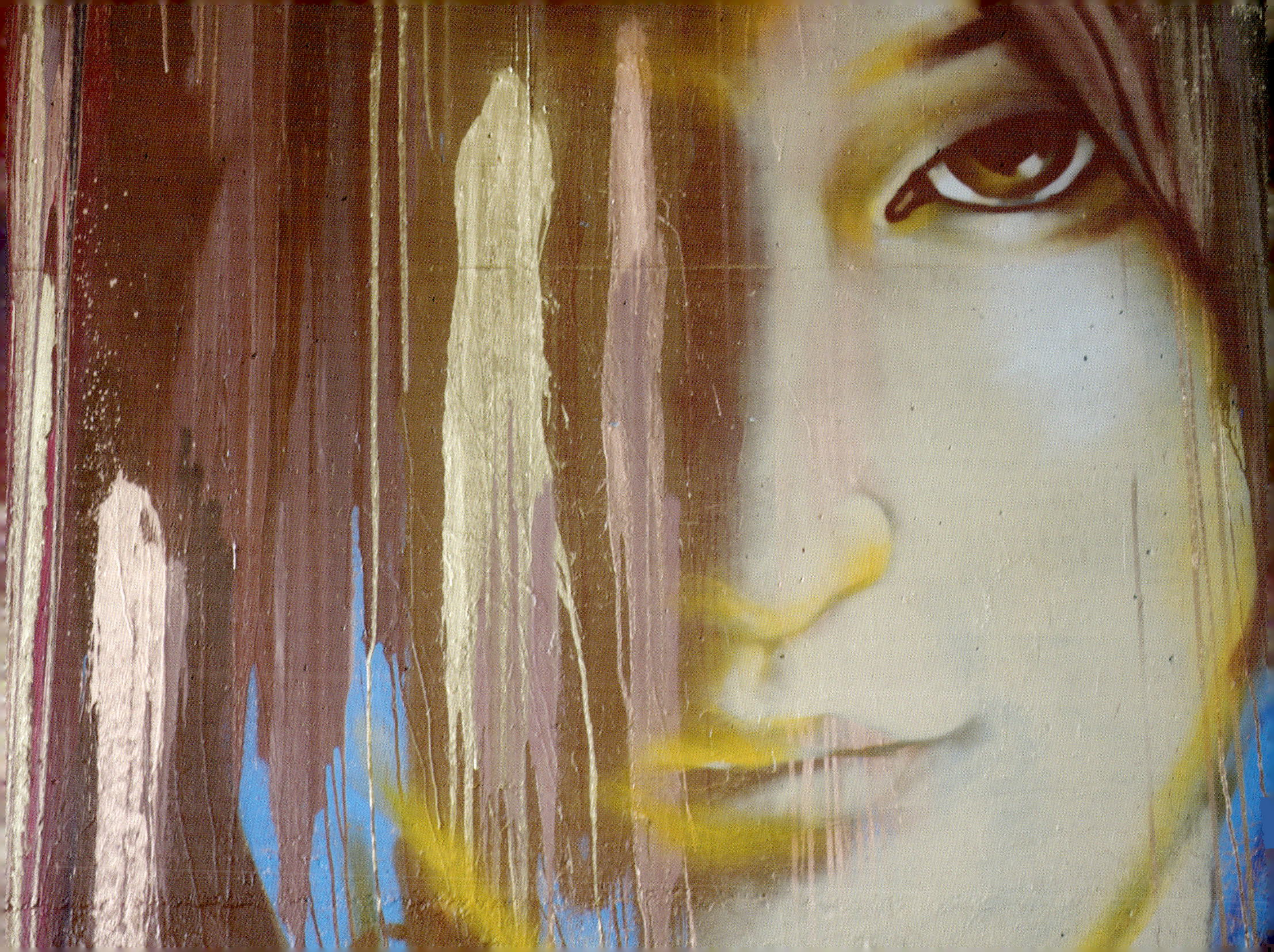

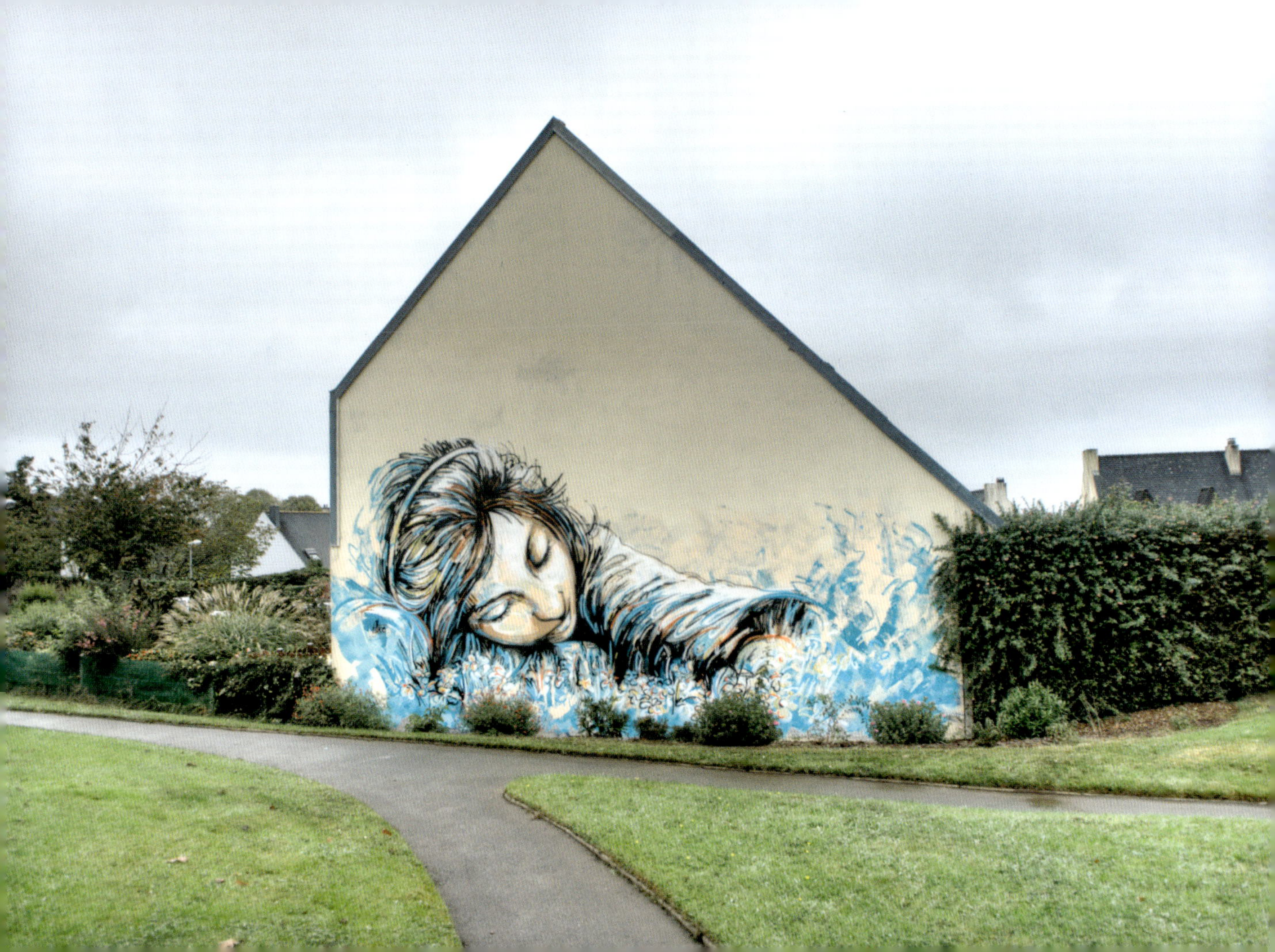

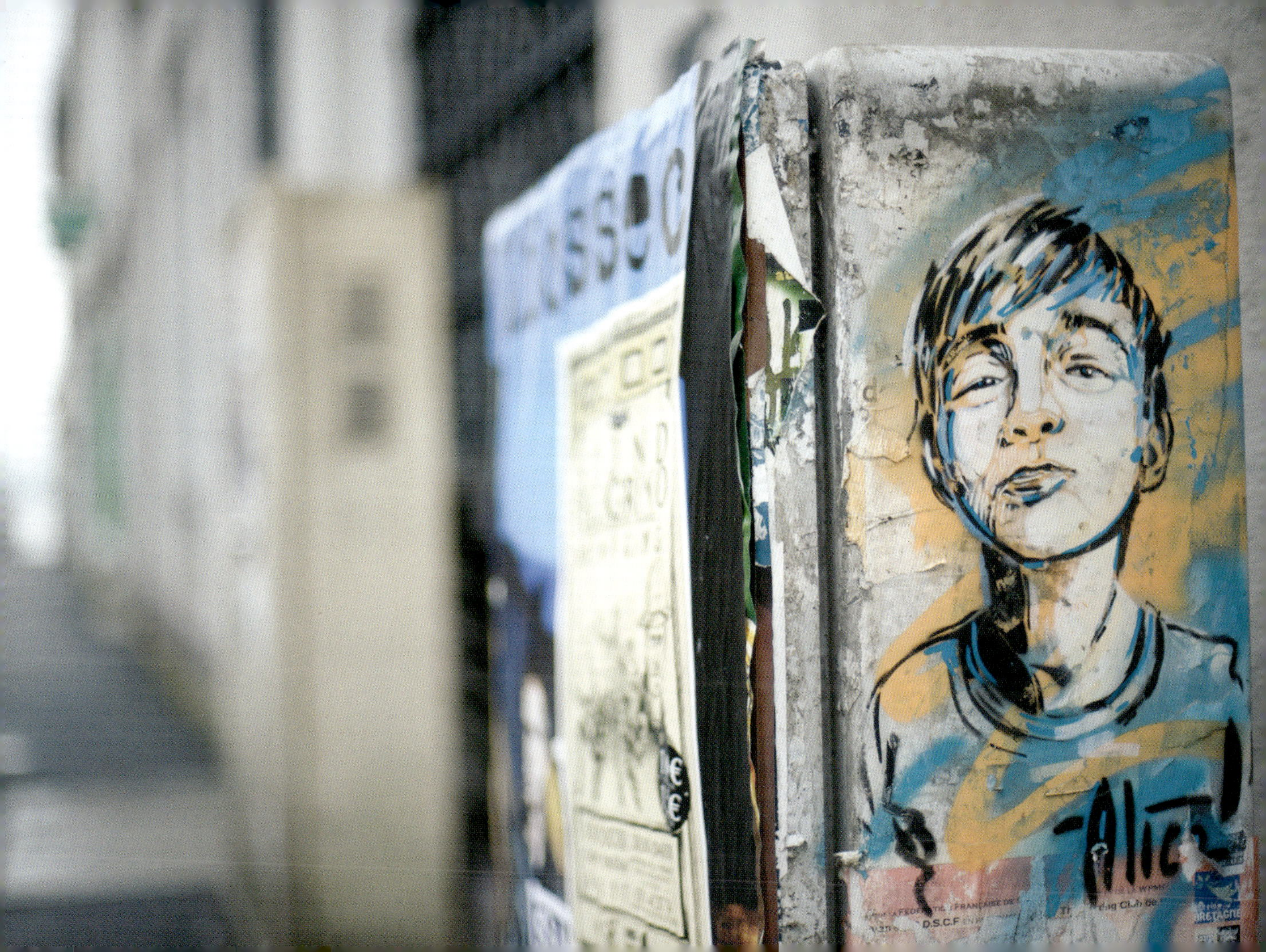
Alice

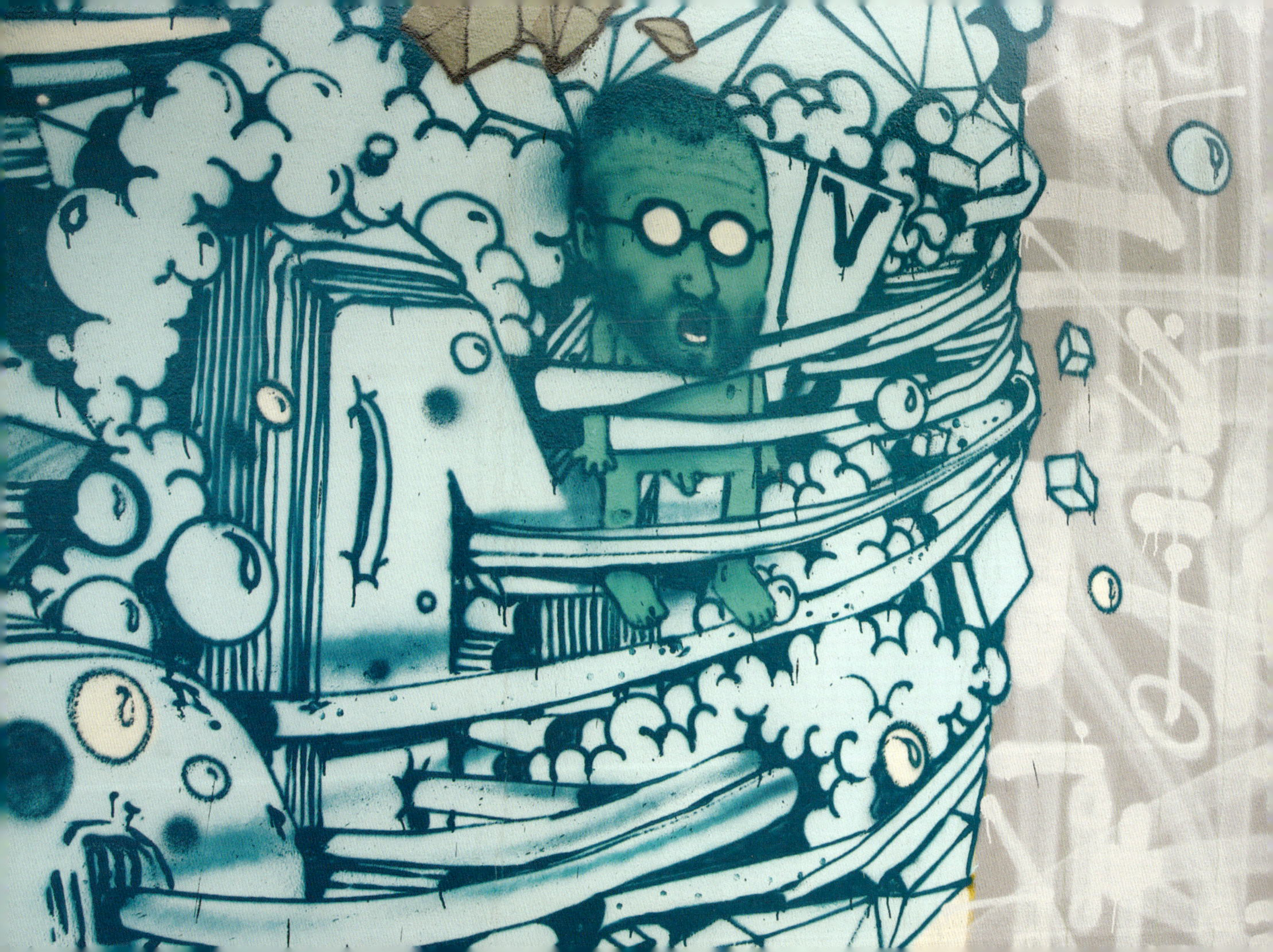
V

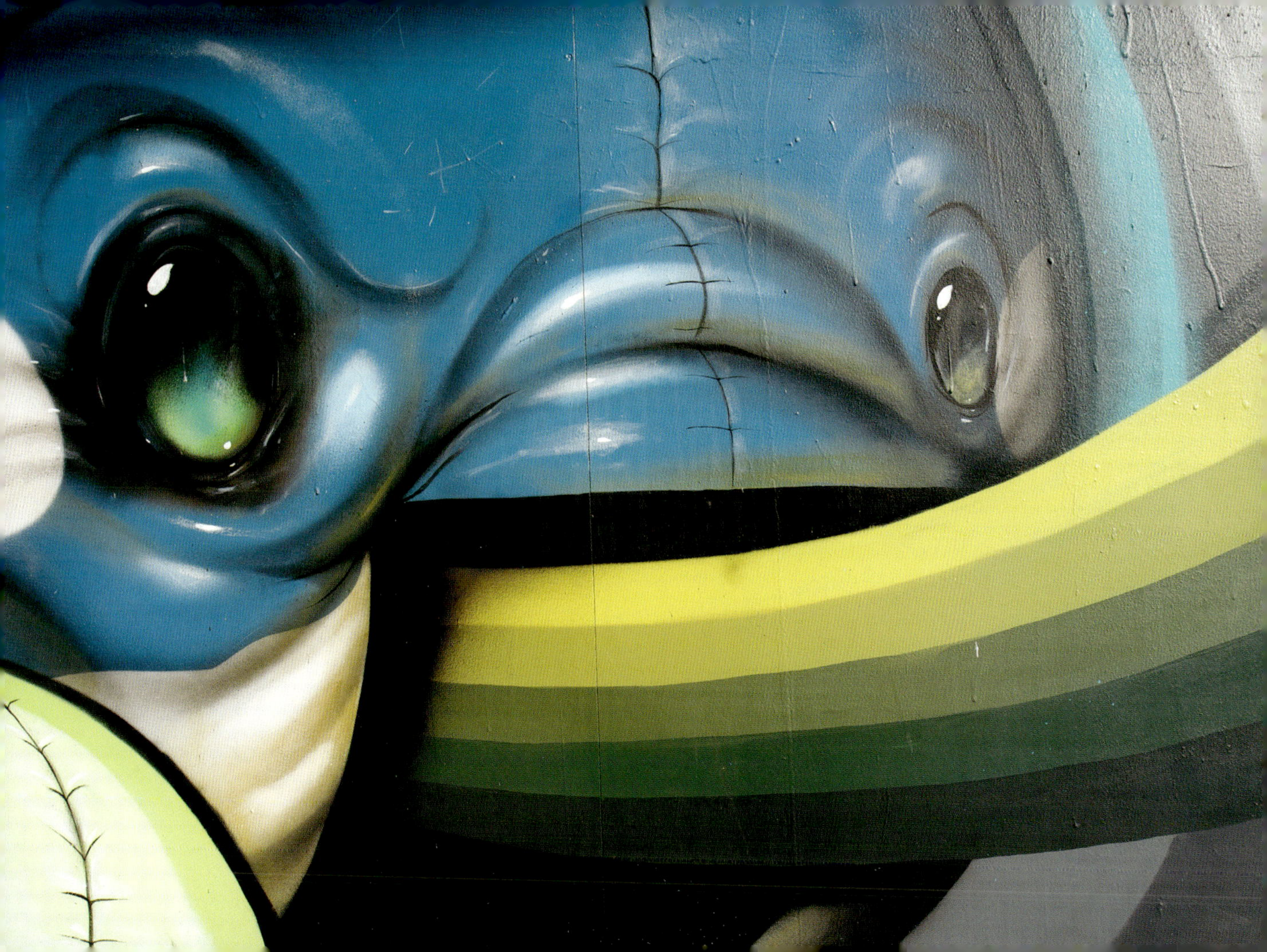

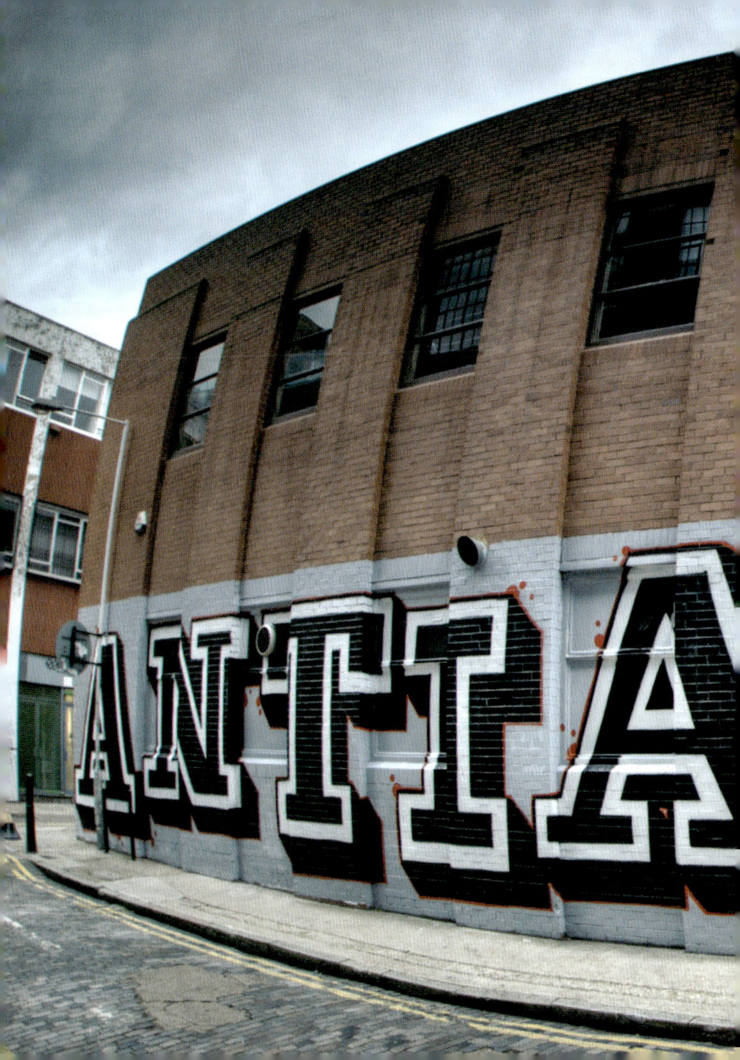
ANTIA

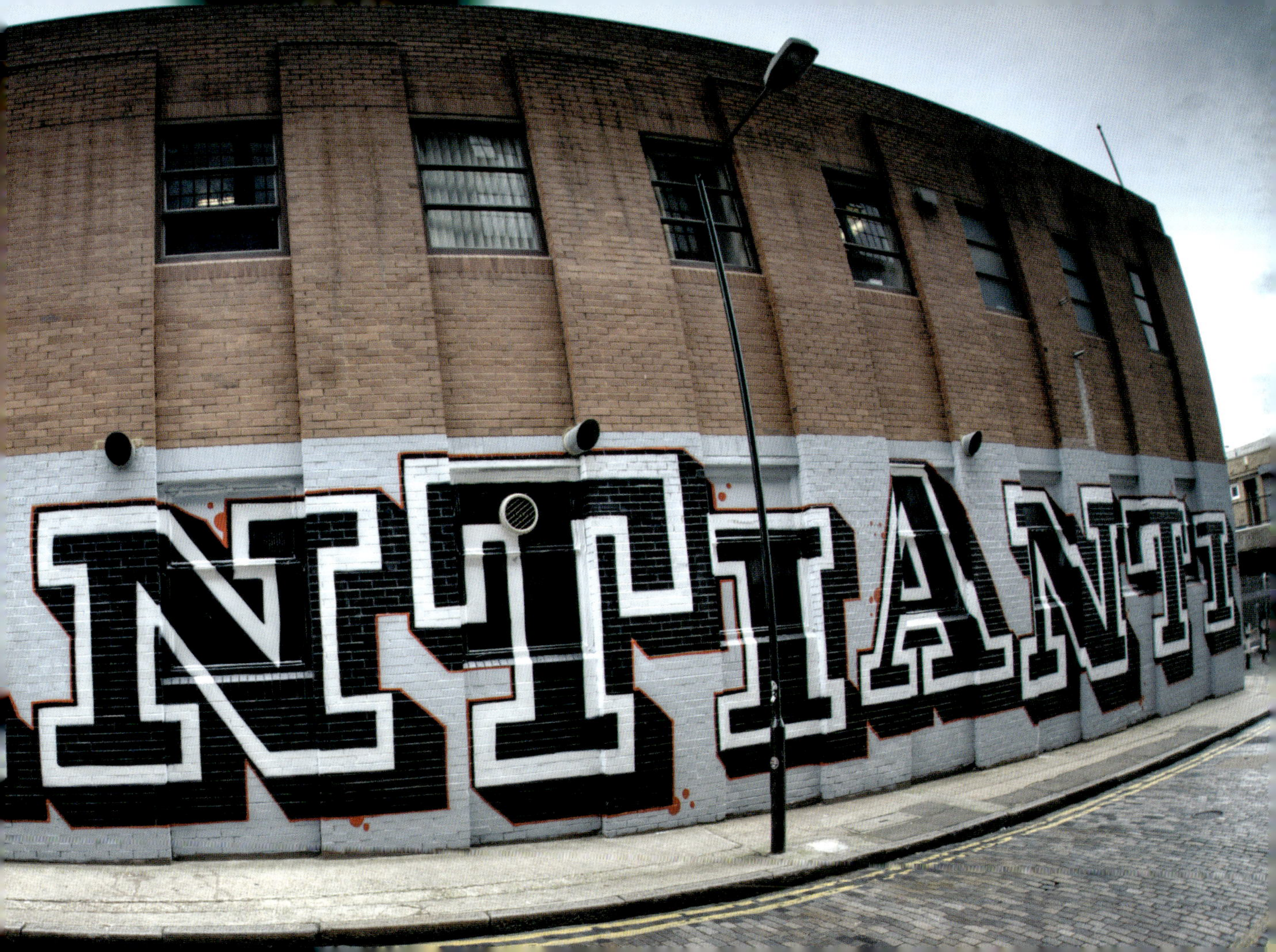
NITIANTI

I paint in the streets because you're free to choose your own space and there are no boundaries like there are when painting a canvas.

It's addictive and can be appreciated by many, you can go as big or as small as you feel and there's always a new surface waiting just around the corner.

FAUNAGRAPHIC

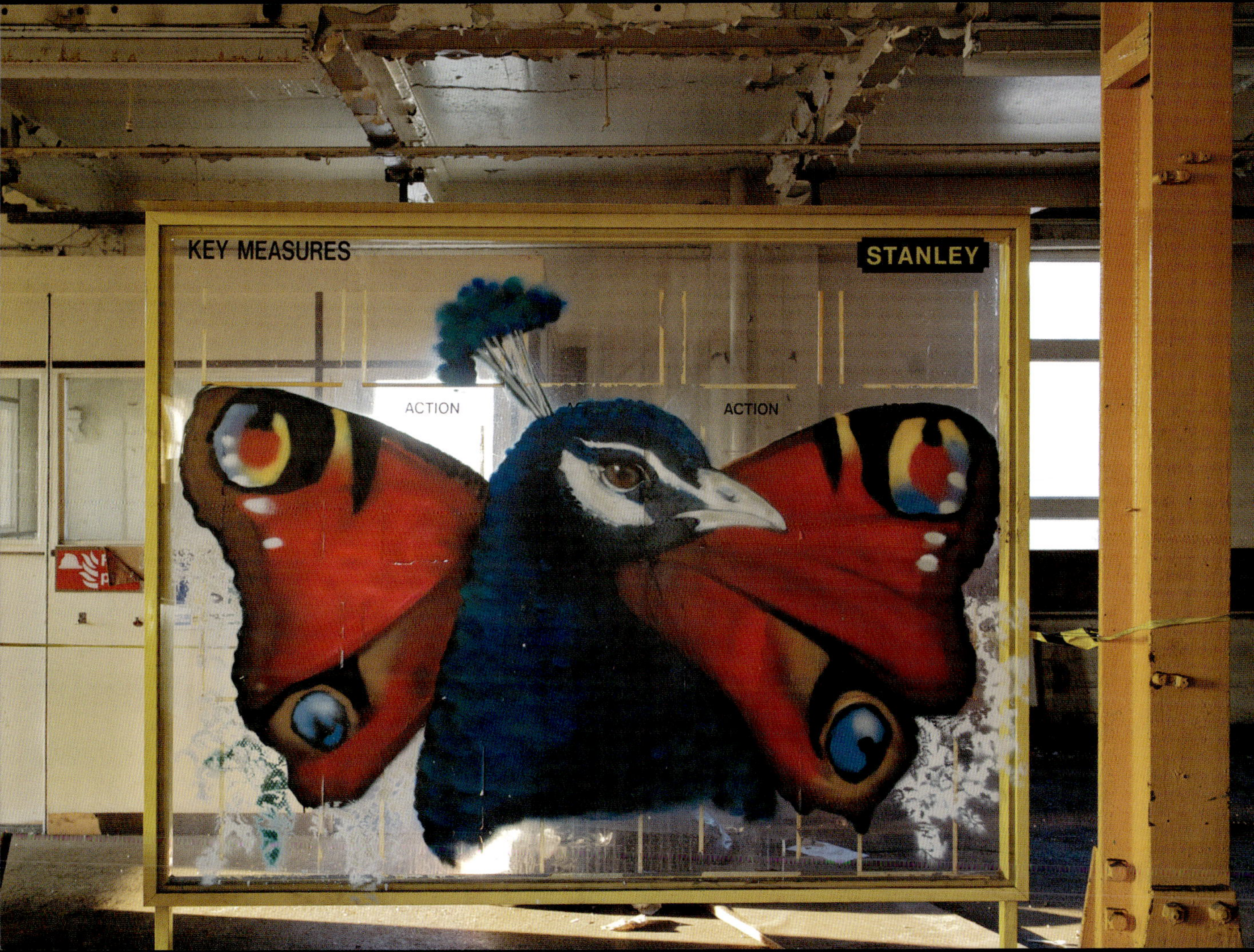
KEY MEASURES
STANLEY
ACTION
ACTION

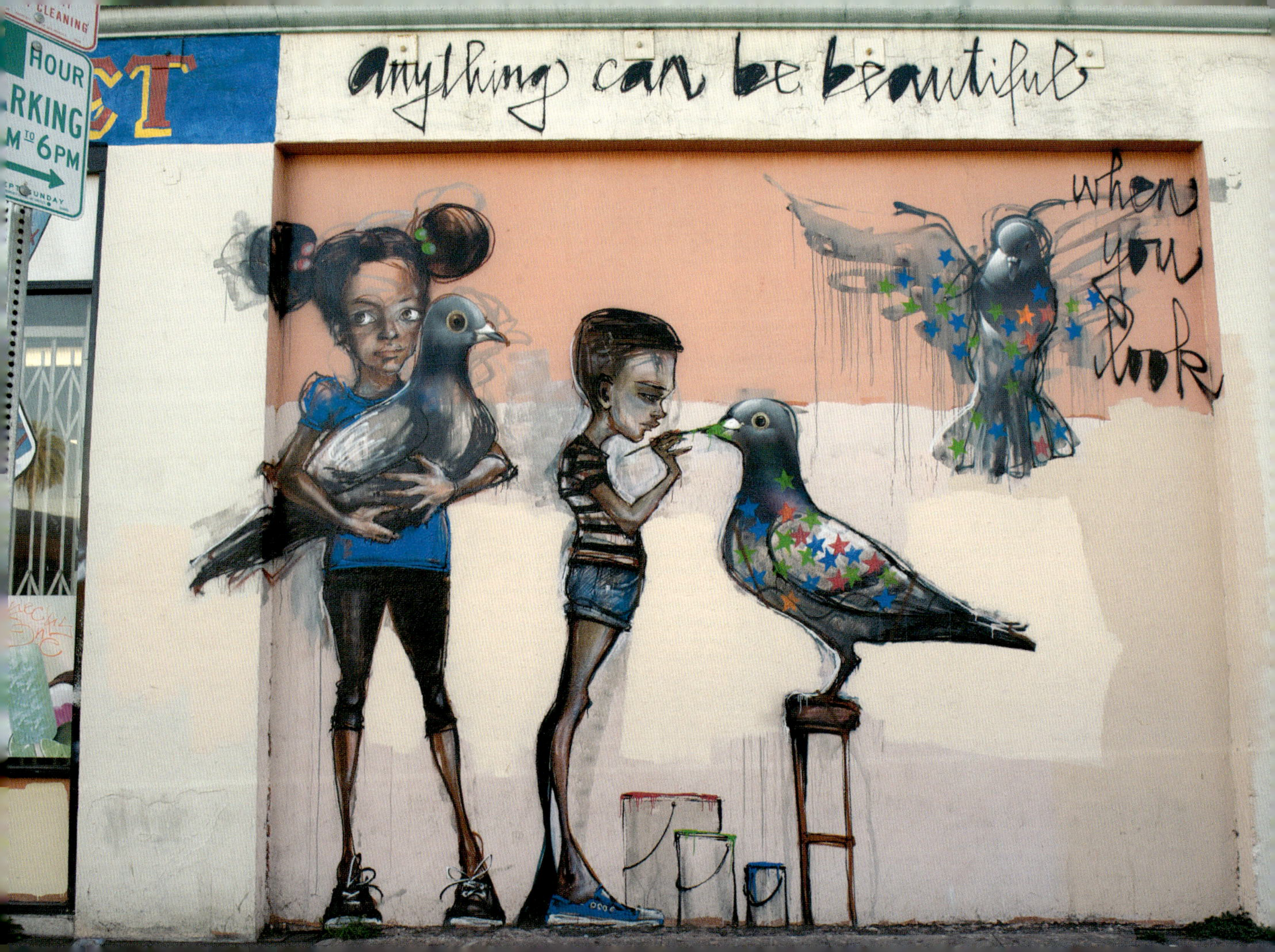
anything can be beautiful
when you look
HOUR
RKING
M TO 6PM
CLEANING

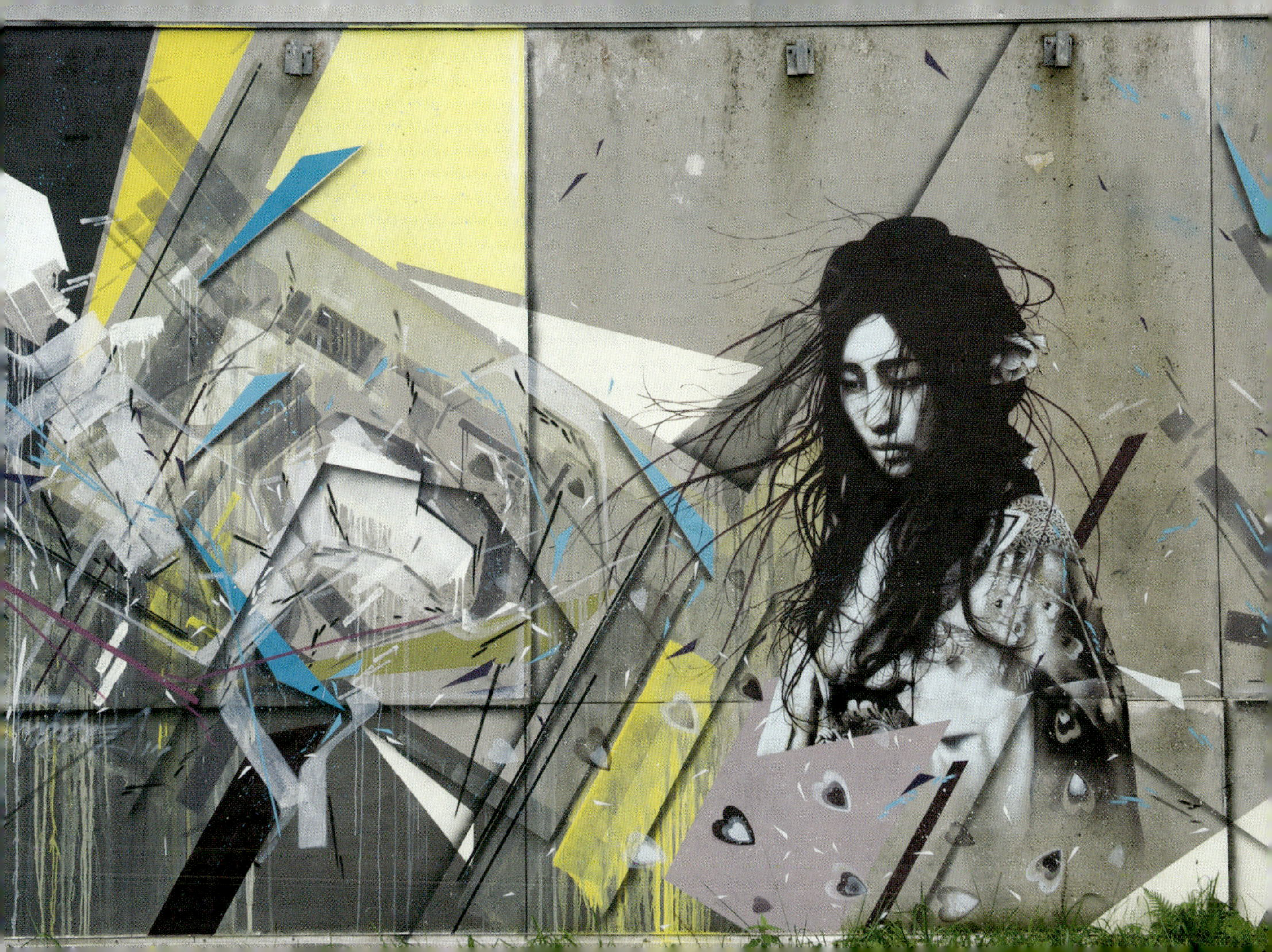

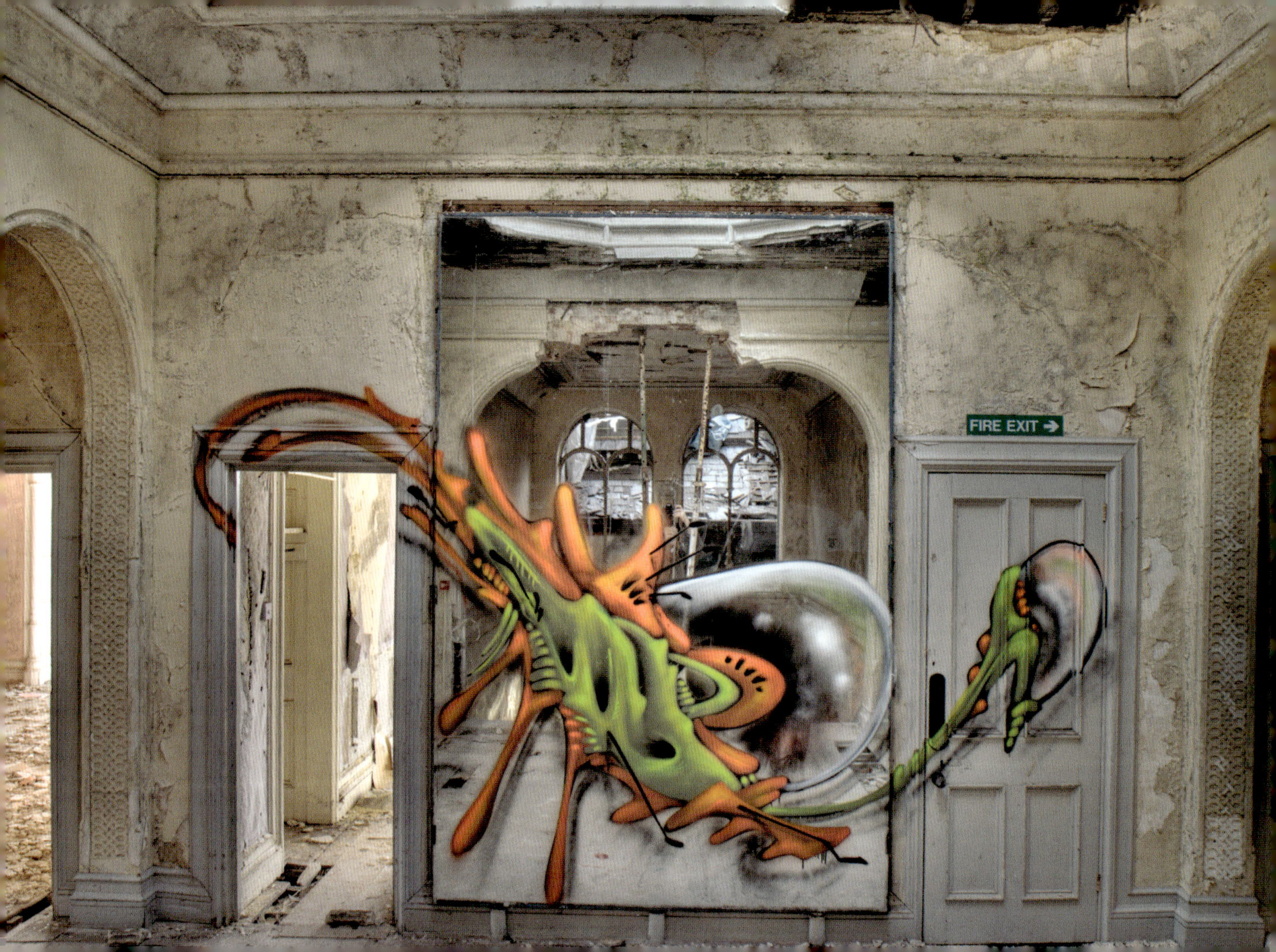
FIRE EXIT

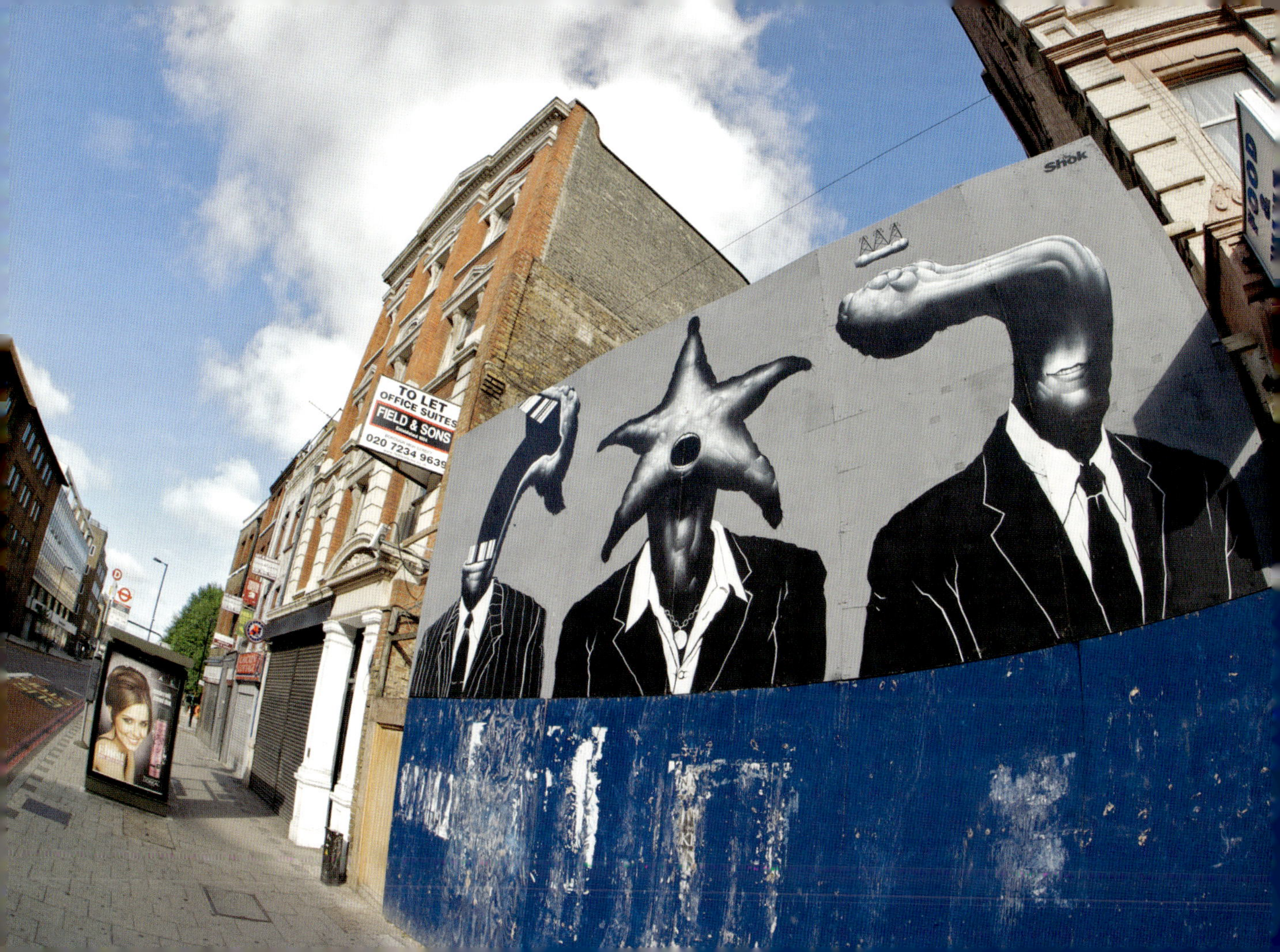
TO LET
OFFICE SUITES
FIELD & SONS
020 7234 9639
Shok

THE EUROPEAN DREAM

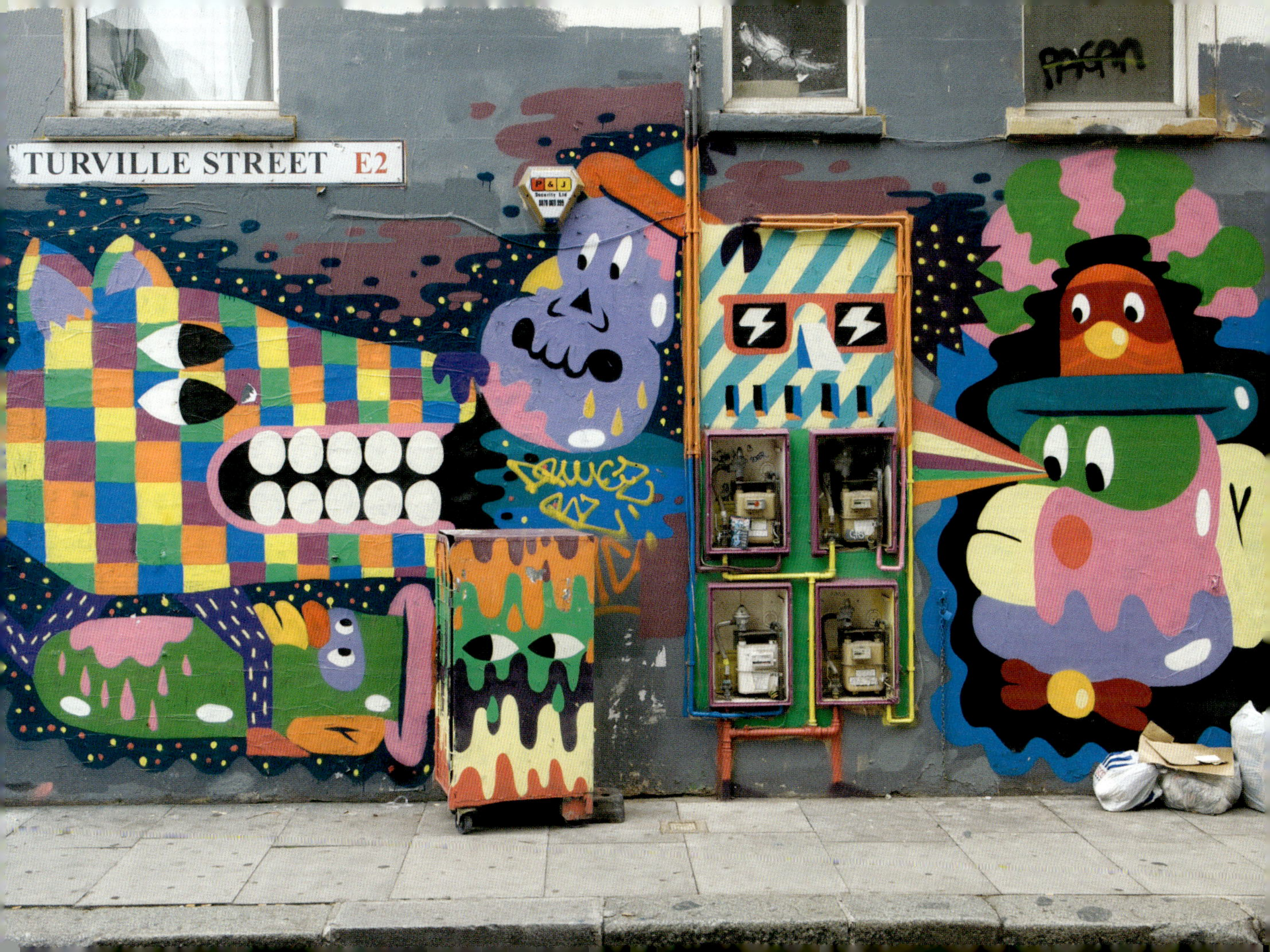
TURVILLE STREET E2

BERLIN
GRAFFITI CITY

The Allied powers split Berlin in half after the second world war. The Allies gave the East to the communists, a prize for Russia. In the 1970's the great wall that ran through the city divided it in half. On the East side Stazi patrols shot anyone who tried to approach the wall. On the West side nobody gave a damn. The desolate area gave a home to immigrants, draft dodgers and bohemians. This melting pot of the poor and the rebellious created its own graffiti culture in parallel to developments in New York. They covered the West side of the wall in writing and images. And when the city was reunited, the bohemians moved East and began to cover the other side of the wall too. Now many call Berlin the graffiti capital of Europe.

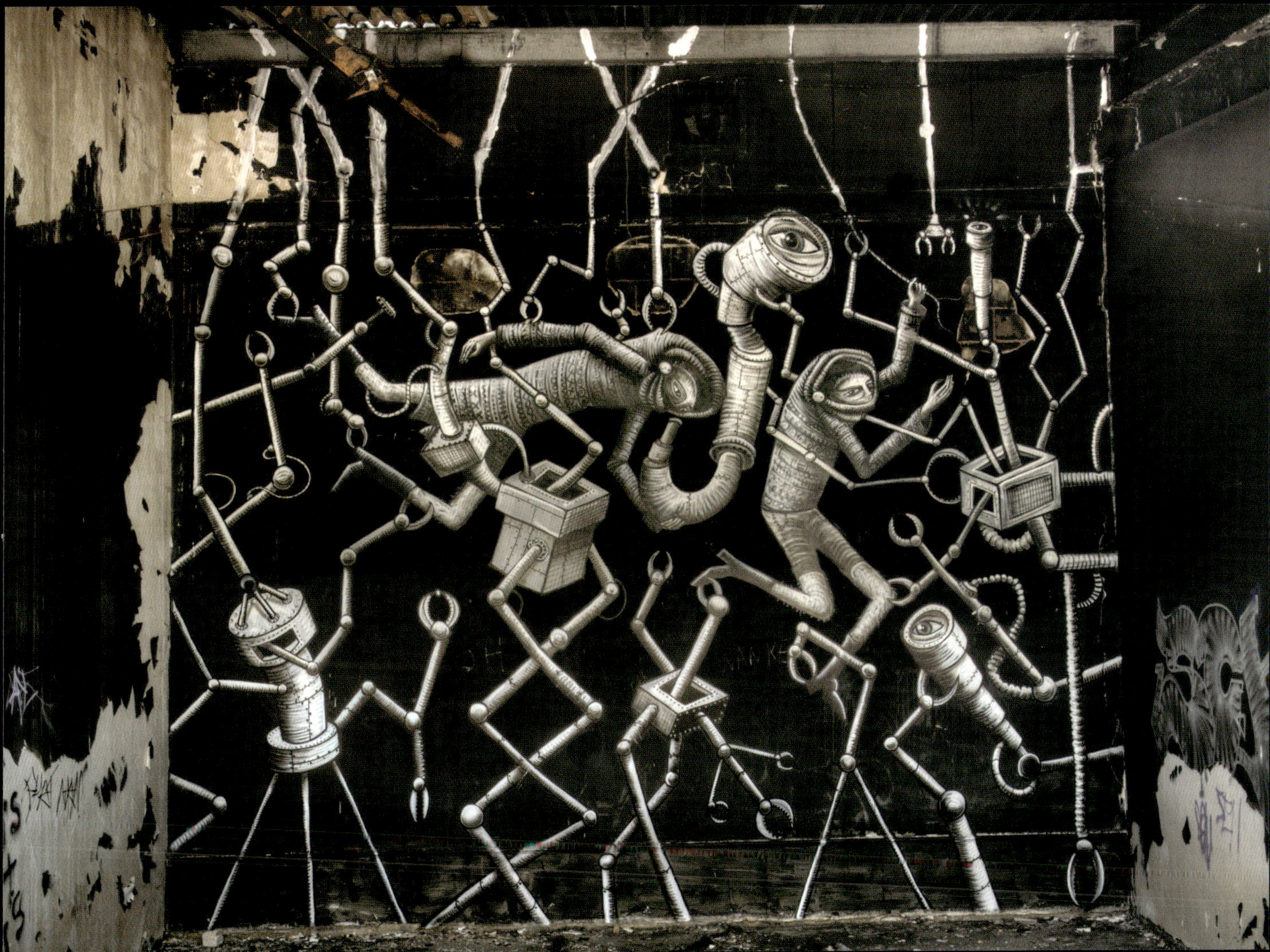

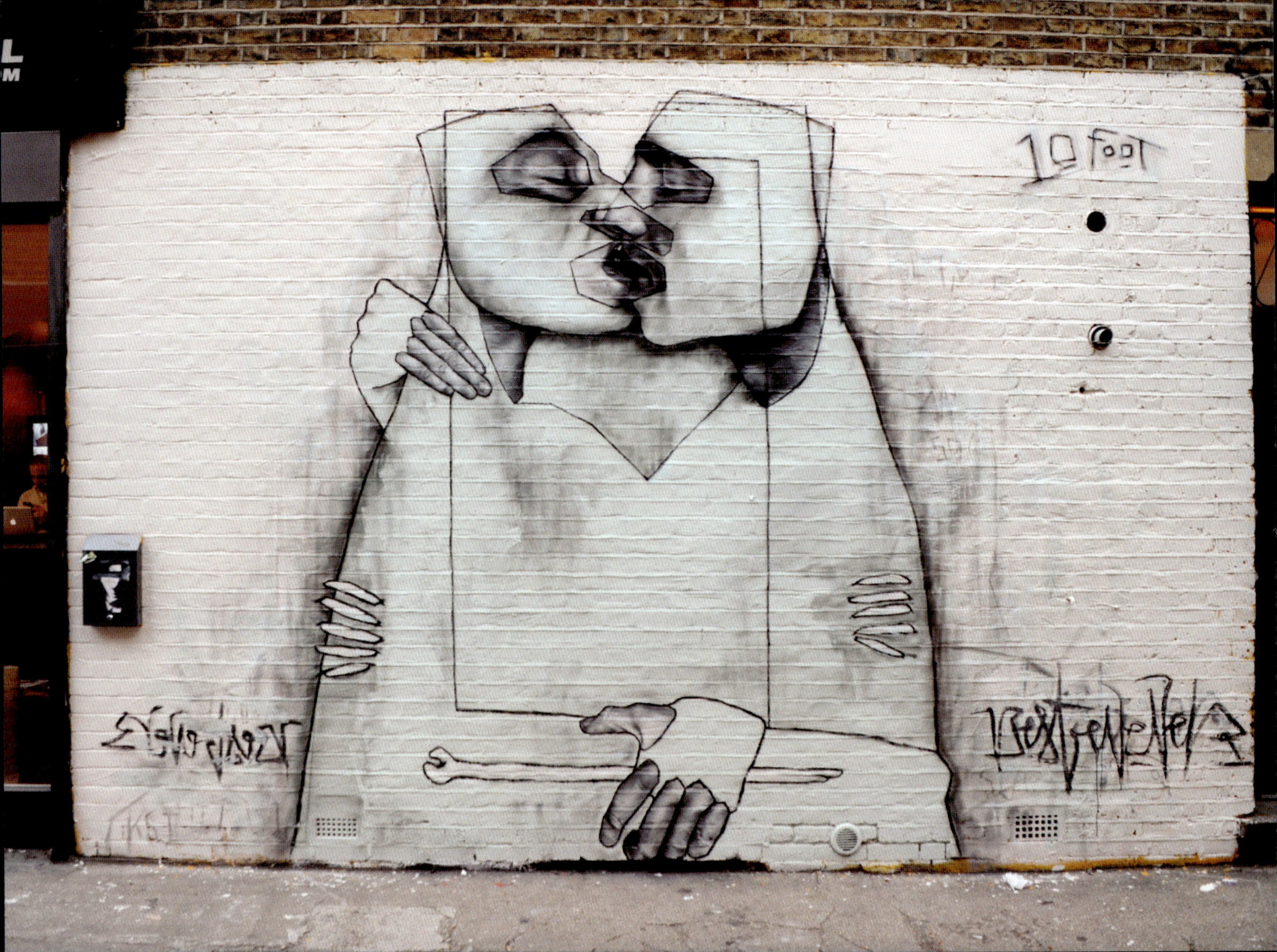
10 foot

PARIS GRAFFITI CITY

As early as 1981 Paris played canvas to the Stencil artwork of Blek Le Rat. New York inspired him but he changed the style to something new. Whereas writers like Bando brought pure NYC style Graff to the city with his silver and black throw ups. Le Rat felt the city needed something better suited to its look and feel, so he pioneered stencils and wheat pastes, techniques that would later flood the scene with the rise of so called 'street art'. Blek painted swarms of rats all over Paris. Generations of writers have risen and fallen since then. The culture lives on just as the inequality. As long as the kids in the suburbs are angry and excluded, they will bomb the city.

LONDON GRAFFITI CITY

In the early 1980's King Robbo and his contemporaries brought the NYC style graff to London. The legendary Mode 2 immersed himself in the Covent Garden Hip Hop scene in 1984 and his characters brought him huge respect. He made the front cover of an influential book 'Spray Can Art' in 1987, demonstrating that the new focus of writing was international. These days London is a tough city to bomb. There are more surveillance cameras in London than any other city in Europe. Writers have had to evolve more and more complex ways to work without getting caught. London was the mecca that drew Banksy from the provinces to make his international fame and the Bristol boy continues to work the city. East London is a major attraction for the international street art set.

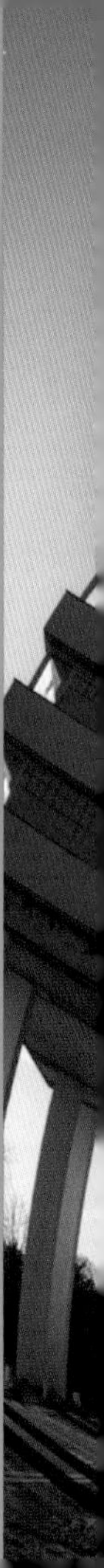

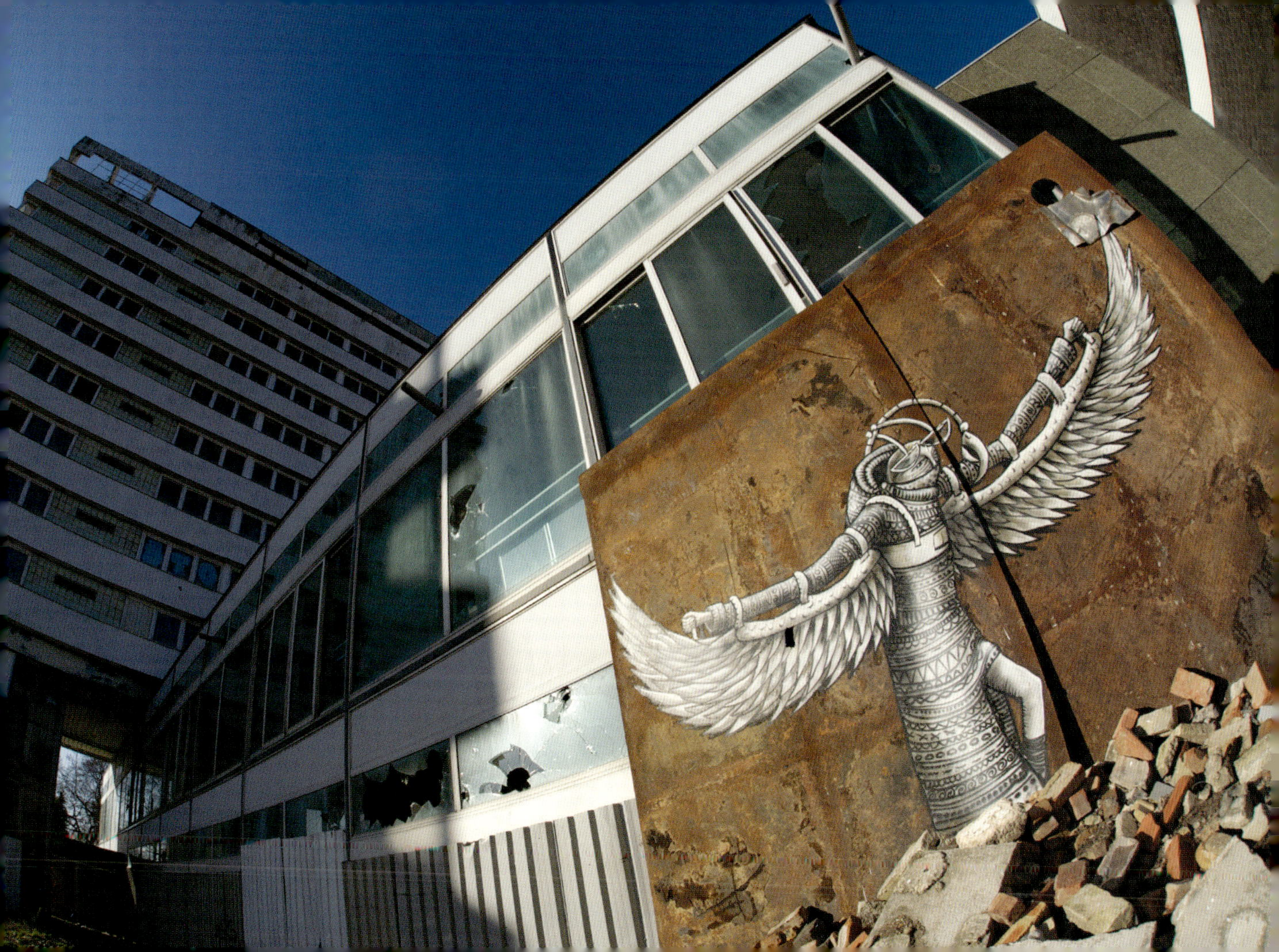

BARCELONA GRAFFITI CITY

When Hip Hop came to Europe, Barcelona was only six years free of a military dictatorship. The city had been unleashed after decades of oppression and the young people were expressing themselves without fear for the first time in their lives. The new government was young and the city was liberal. Writers were free to work with almost no interference from the authorities. Huge sections of the city became semi legal or at least tacitly ignored graffiti spaces. This combined with the Spanish sunshine led to a generation of writers developing flamboyant masterpieces, able to spend whole days at the wall. Only recently has the city begun to tighten up control with urban regeneration picking up pace. The city council and the city police are driving BCN graffiti culture back underground. Even so, the home of Montana paints still offers more legal spots than many far bigger cities in Europe. If you visit the city the one thing you'll see everywhere is a grinning fish. Pez is certainly the cities most visible writer.

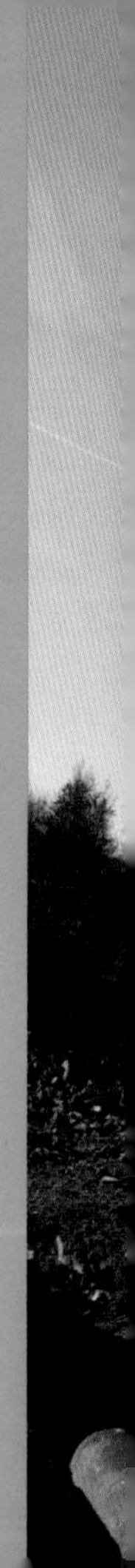

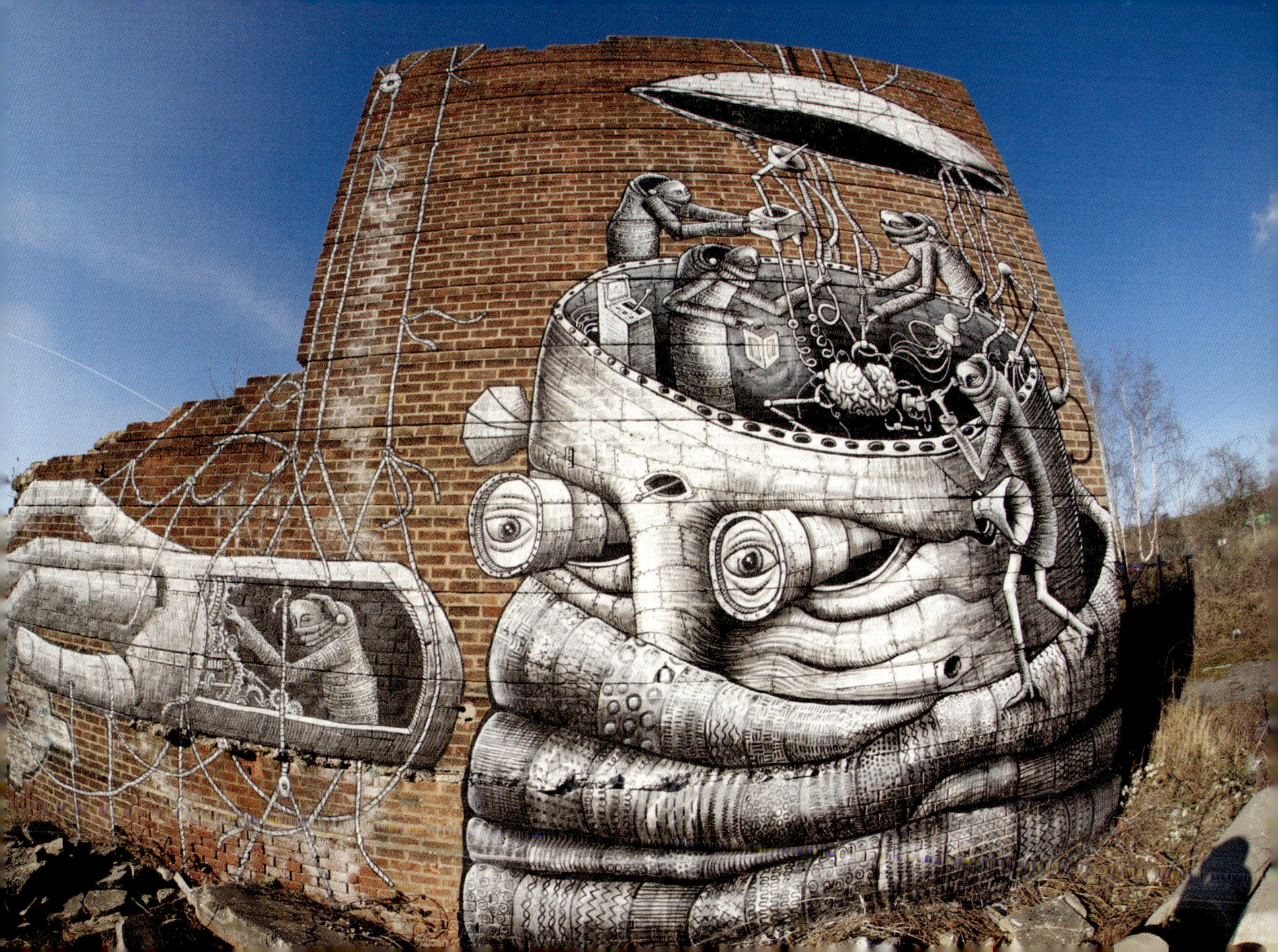

AMSTERDAM GRAFFITI CITY

Amsterdam always was a rebel city and in the 1970's the city had a hardcore punk scene. Dutch punks were already writing their names on walls before the US style came over. The king of the punks was Dr. Rat who painted his cipher in Gothic letters. Writers competed to bomb the city throughout the 1980's although they still had time to share a joint, the 'walking joint' character was a communal symbol used by lots of different writers. Shoe was one of the original international guys who went to meet other first generation legends like Bando from Paris and Mode 2 from London and represented the Hip Hop style in Holland. And Delta really pushed the envelope in 3D lettering, influencing many writers after him.

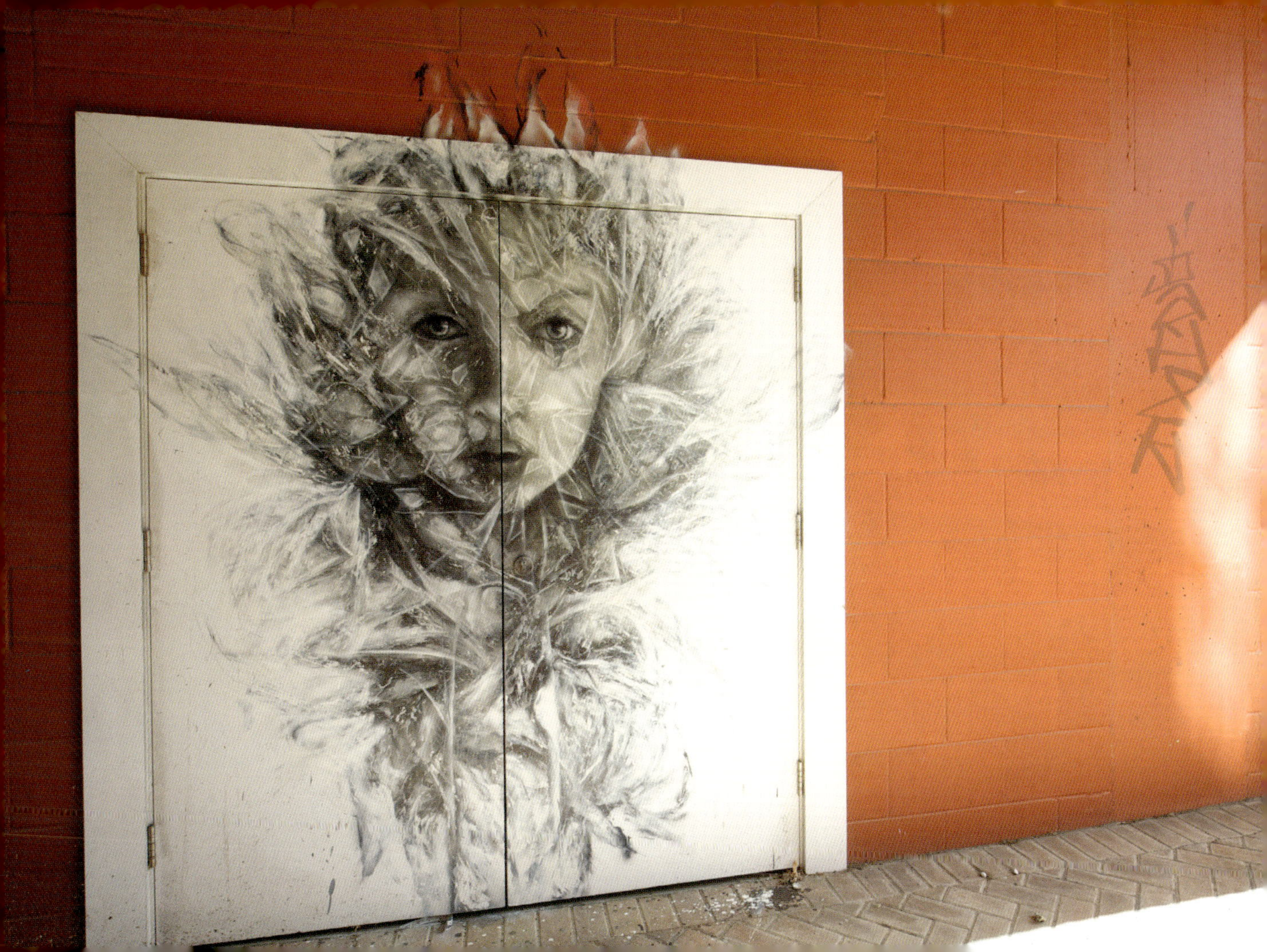

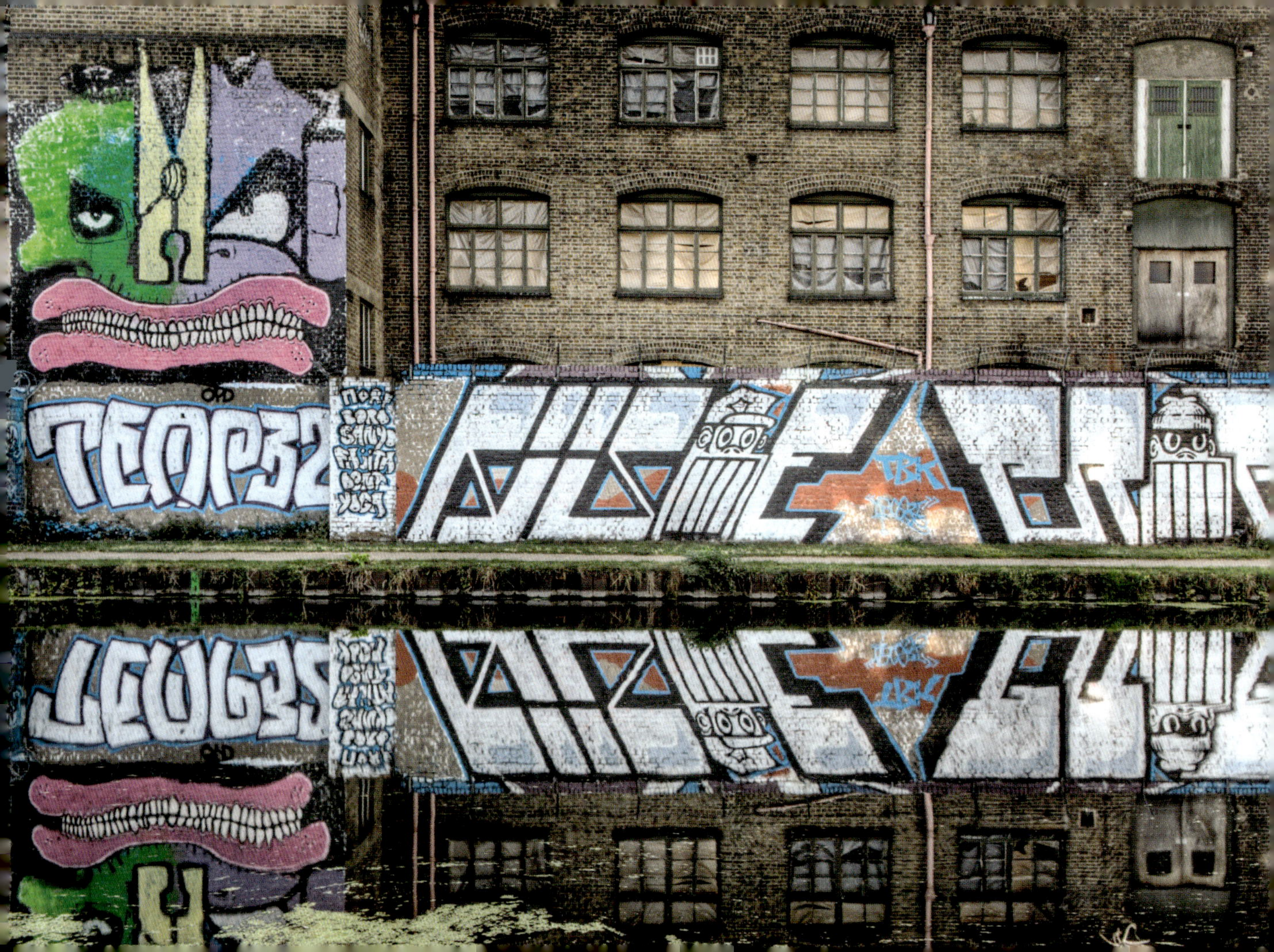

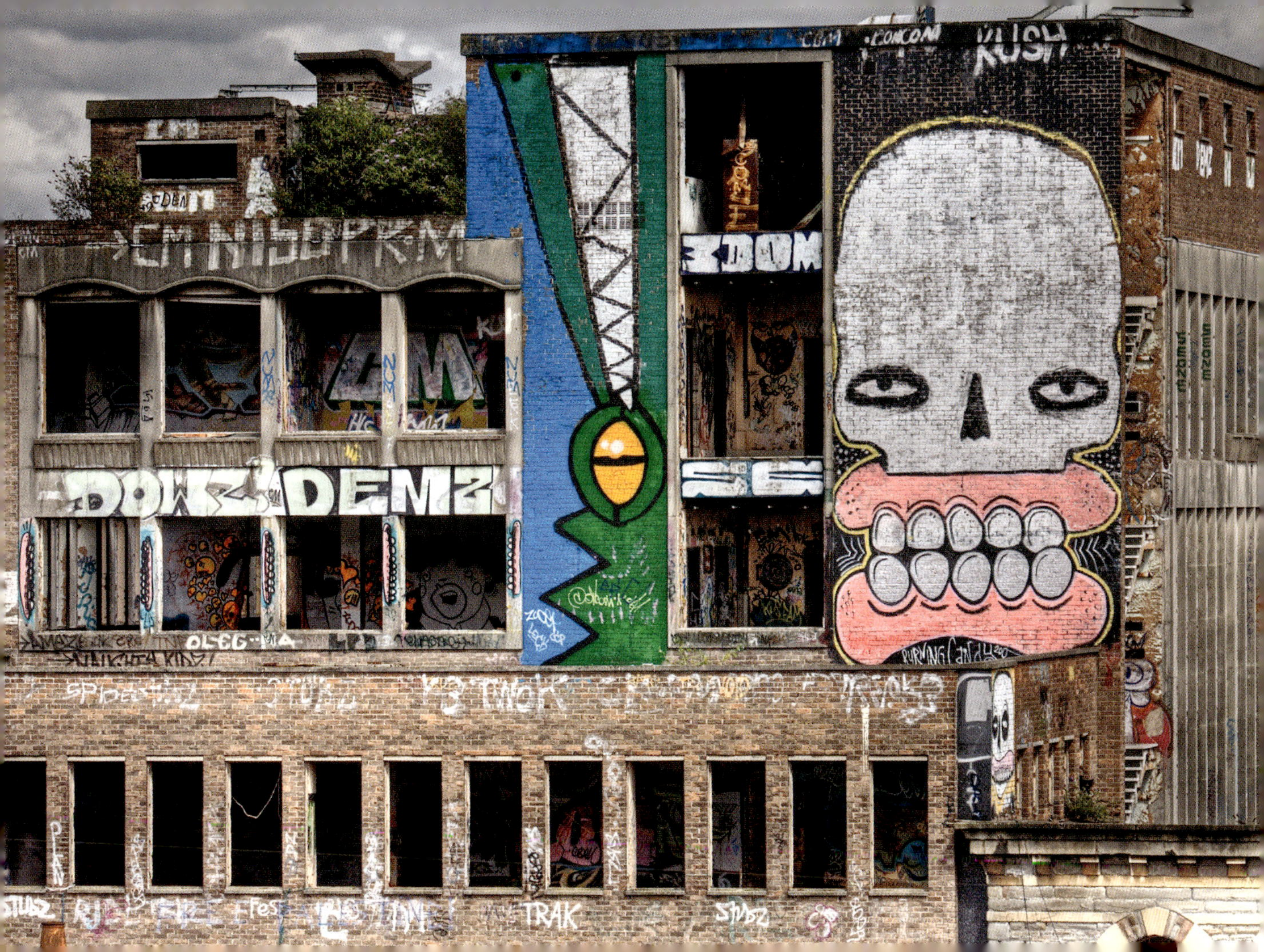
KUSH
DEMZ
TRAK

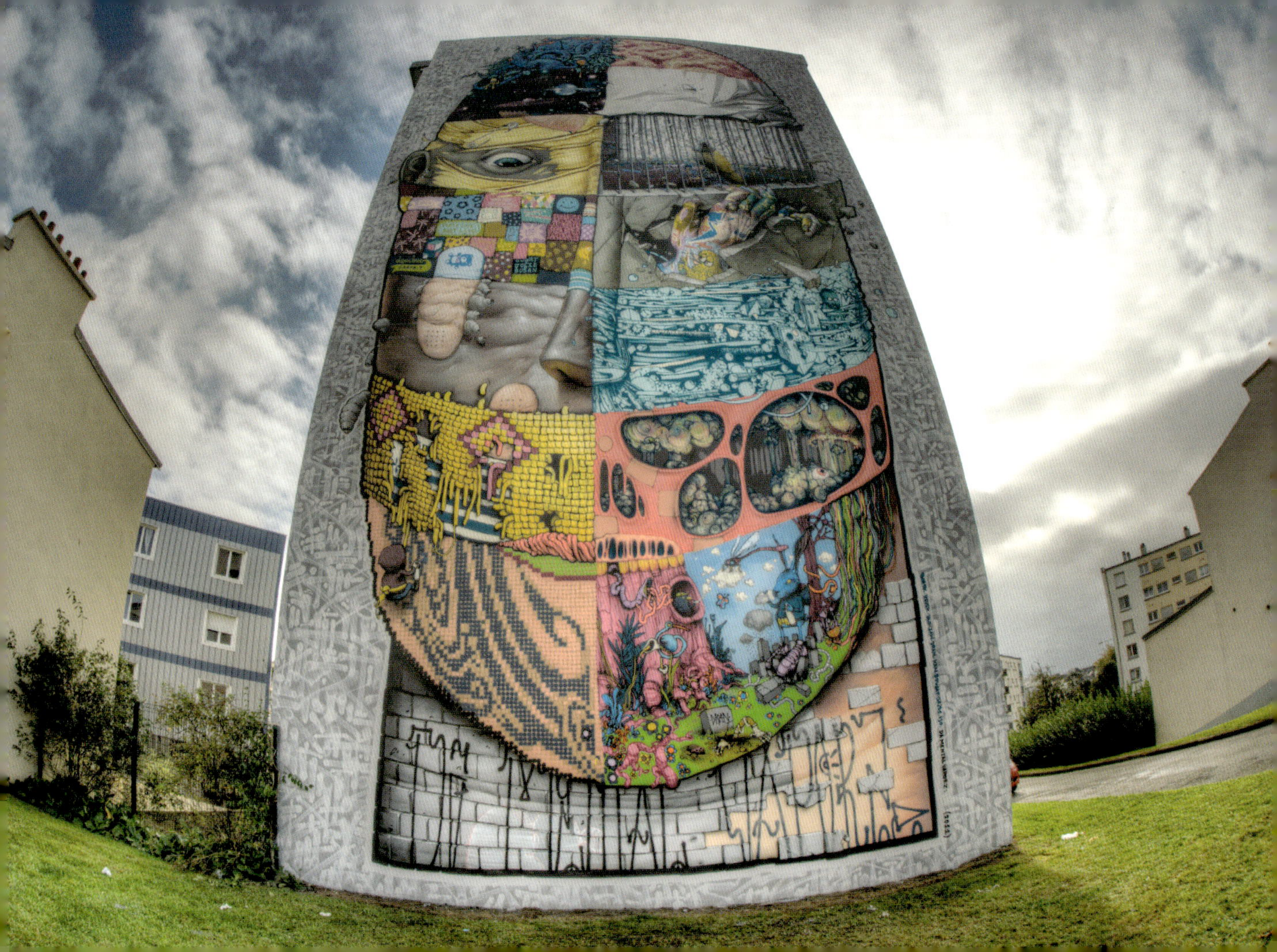

For me it's a total act of freedom to paint in the streets. There is no censorship, people are free to accept the message or not, I invite them to discuss it.

KAN (DMV)

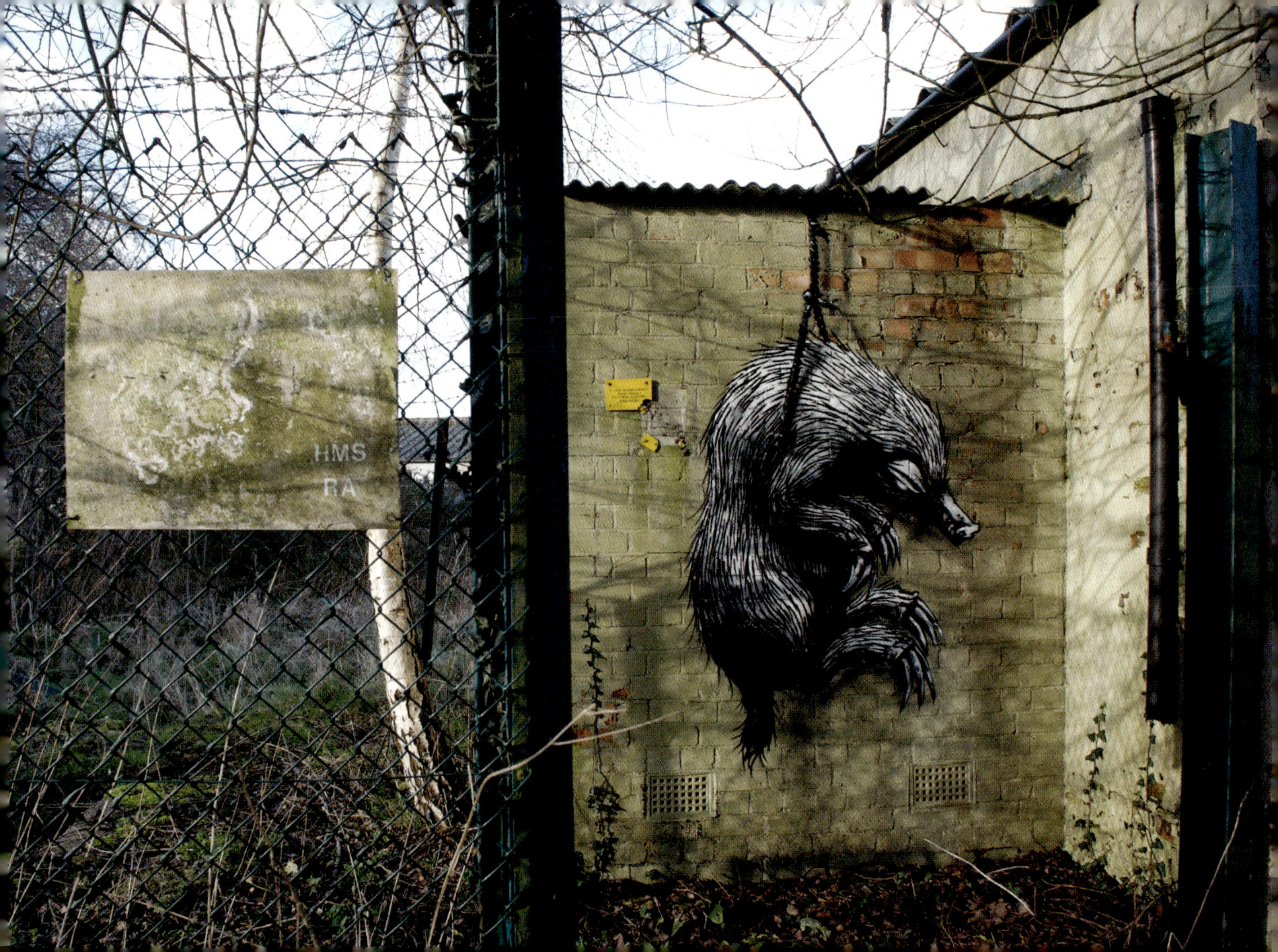
HMS
RA

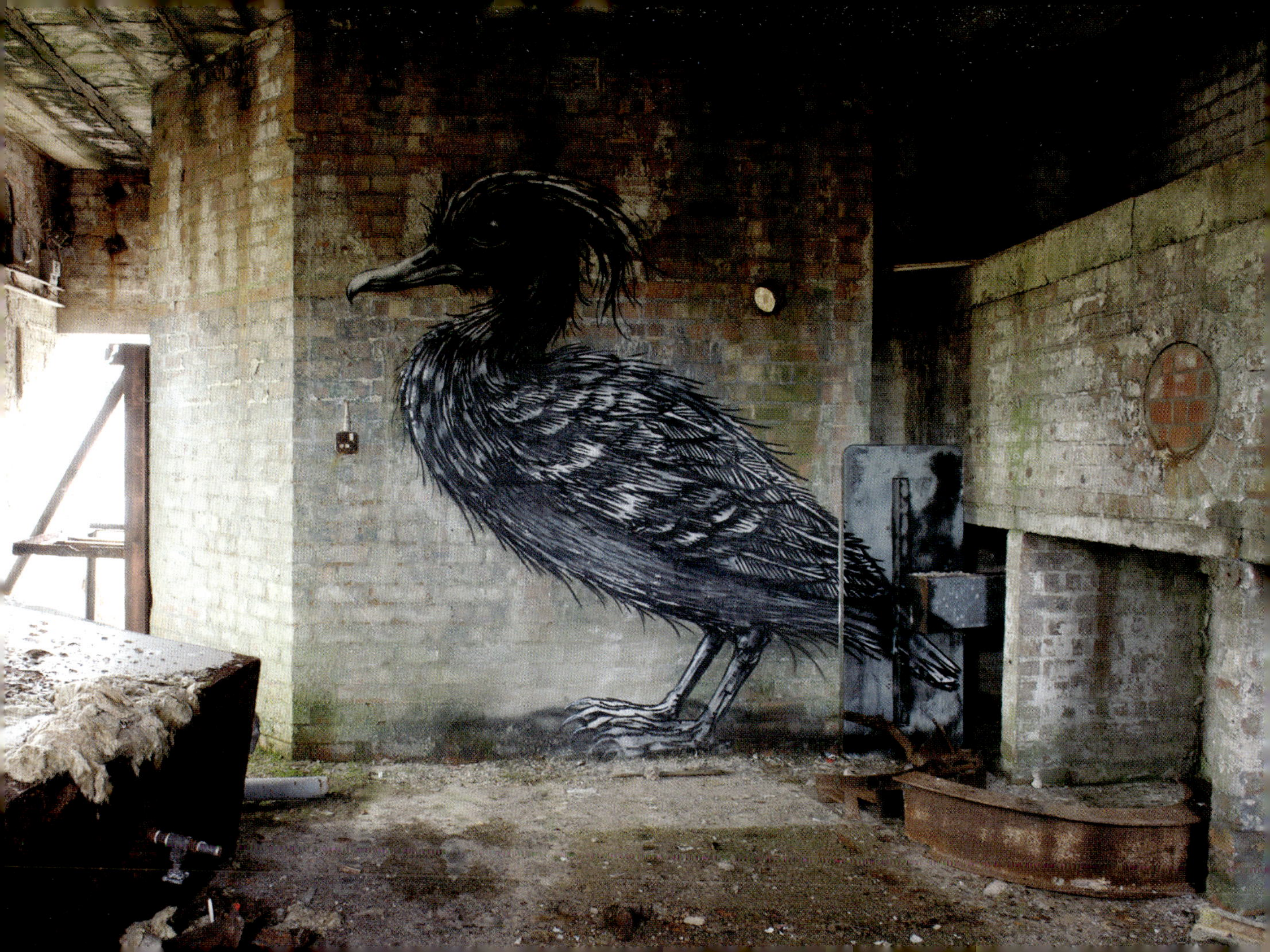

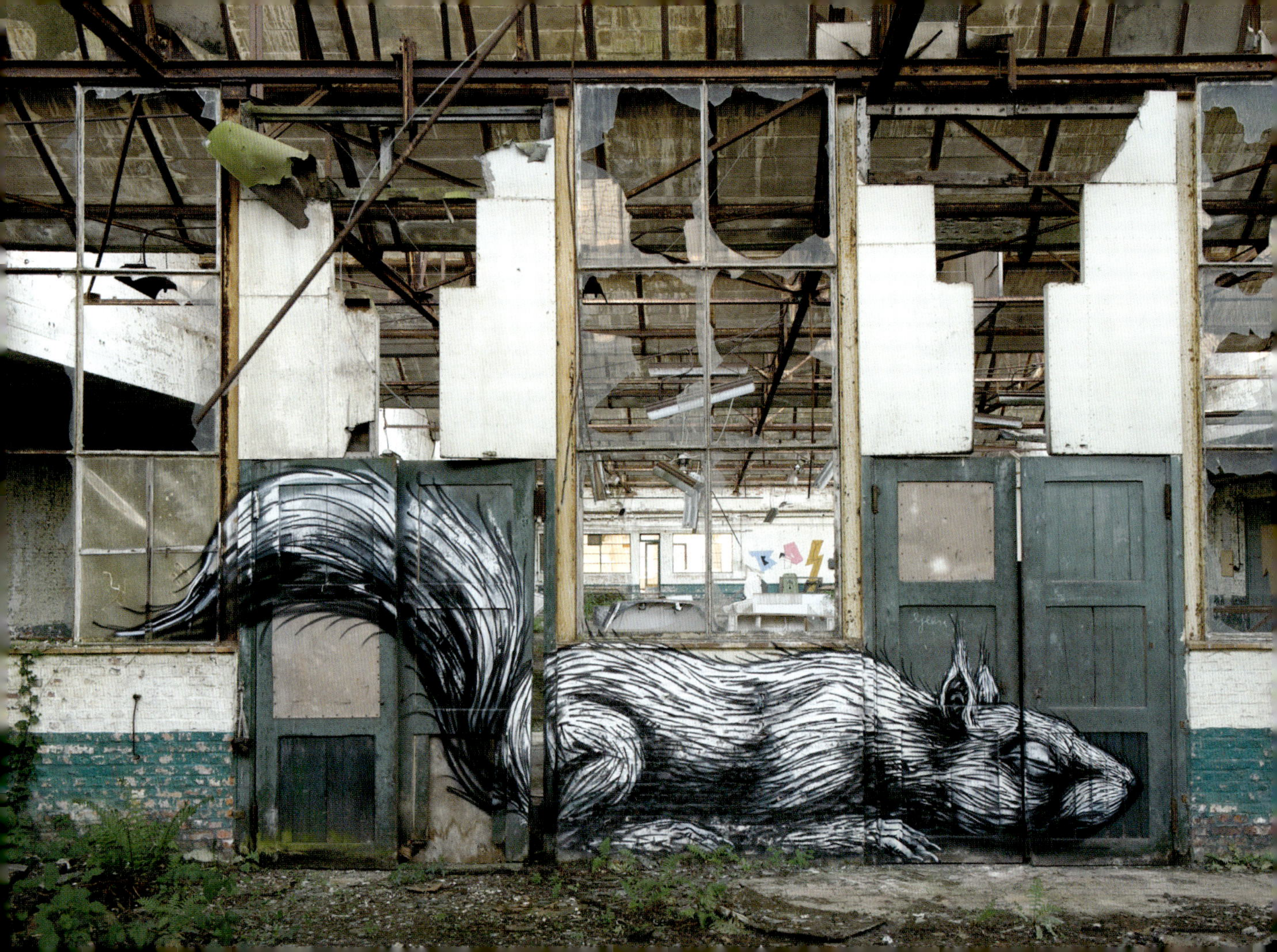

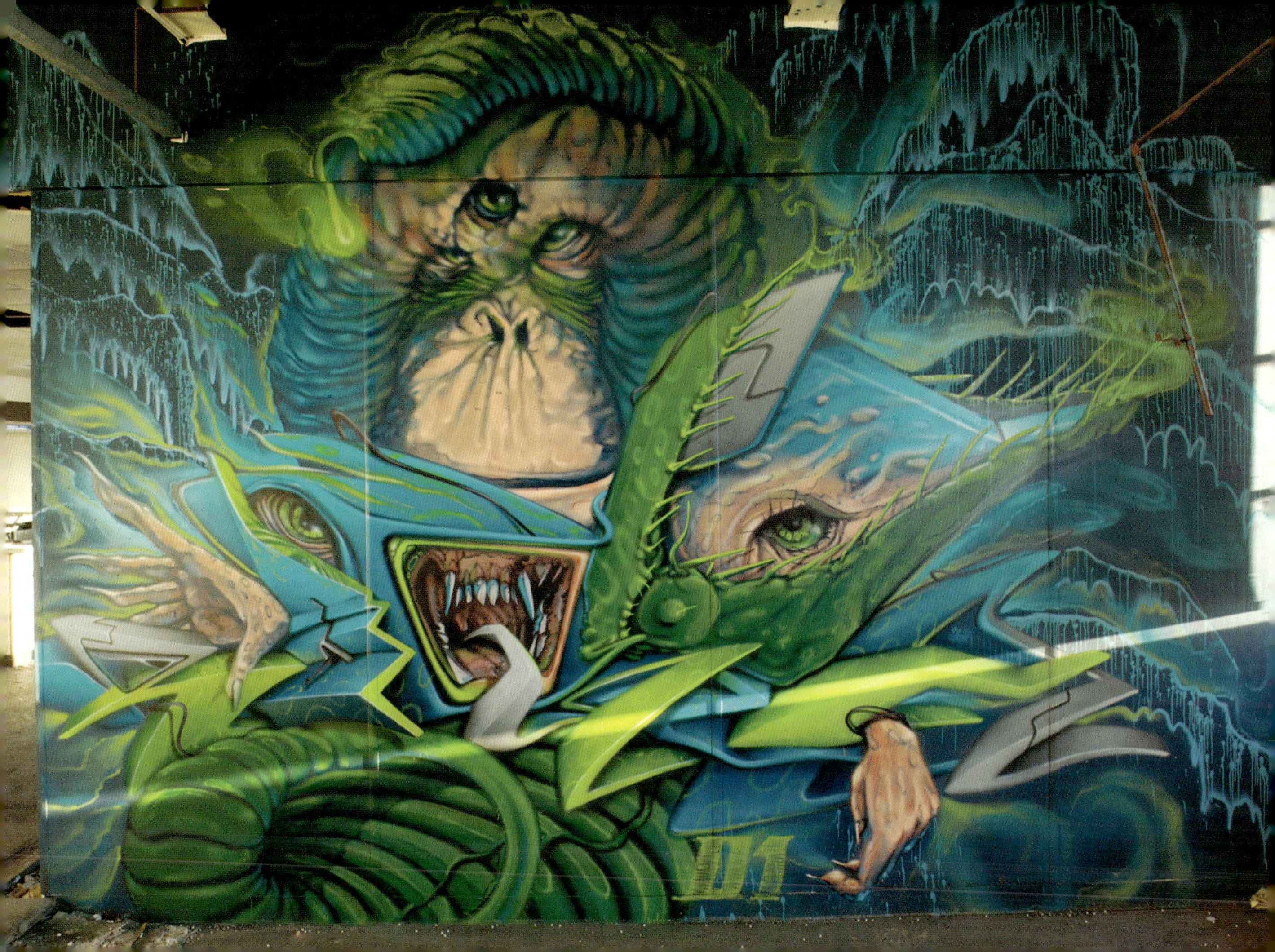

LURID EVOLUTION

In graffiti the goal was fame right from the start. 'Getting up' was everything. This was the new game in town and that was the difference between Graffiti culture as we know it now and the political graffiti or territorial gang graffiti that preceded it. When TAKI 183 and other contemporaries became famous, the game was born. The one prize - to be king. The one strategy - numbers. The more bombing you do, the more famous you get.

Like in evolution, male birds compete for attention from females to get laid with ever more stylish displays of dance moves or plumage or song. Hip Hop was a pure reflection of this.

The tagging style became a victim of its own success. When the trains were saturated in tags how could you get up? How could you get famous?

Necessity is the mother of invention.

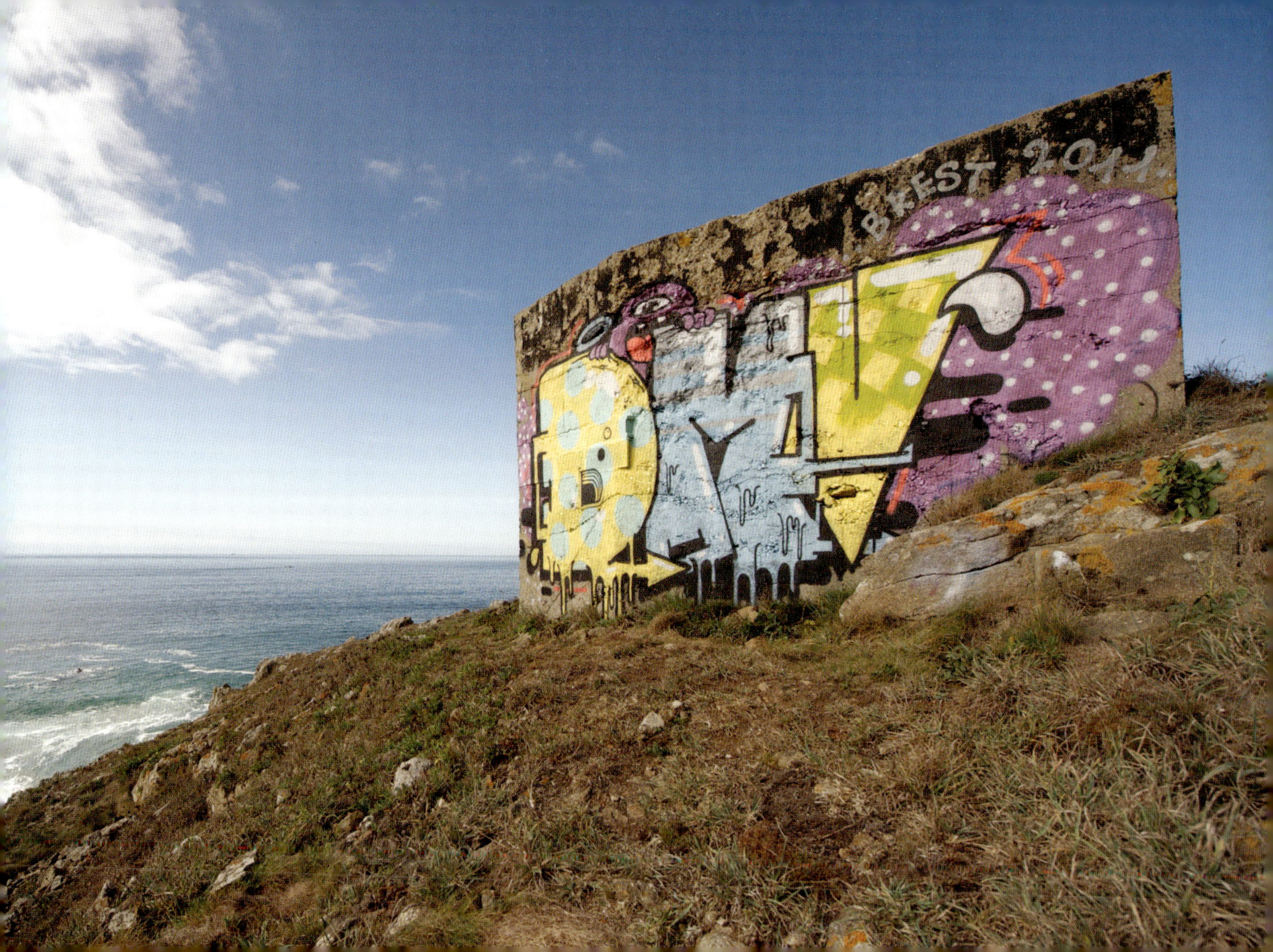
BREST 2011.

Size became the new weapon. Writers competed to put bigger tags up. These moved to the outsides of the trains for more space and exposure. They evolved into 'throw ups', block letters came into play, writers throwing up a quick outline. The outline didn't have enough impact on its own so they naturally filled it in, 'designs' were born, filling in the letters with stripes, dots or other patterns. People began to use symbols. A crown for a self-proclaimed king. Then the style wars began.

Writers competed for firsts, the first 'top to bottom' covering the whole side of the train changed the game. Writers competed to invent new styles of lettering. Broadway style, block letters, bubble letters and leaning letters came in. Three-dimensional lettering became dominant.

Writers would rip each other's developments off and push them further, raising the game with every piece. The addition of design elements grew with arrows, curls, connections and twists along with punctuation marks all growing into one another to finally result in 'wild style' the now familiar form of graff where only the initiated can read the word because it is so heavily stylised.

In addition to these developments some writers began to frame their work in landscapes and surround them with characters. These murals became known as 'pieces' (short for masterpiece) and often were collaborations of crews working together.

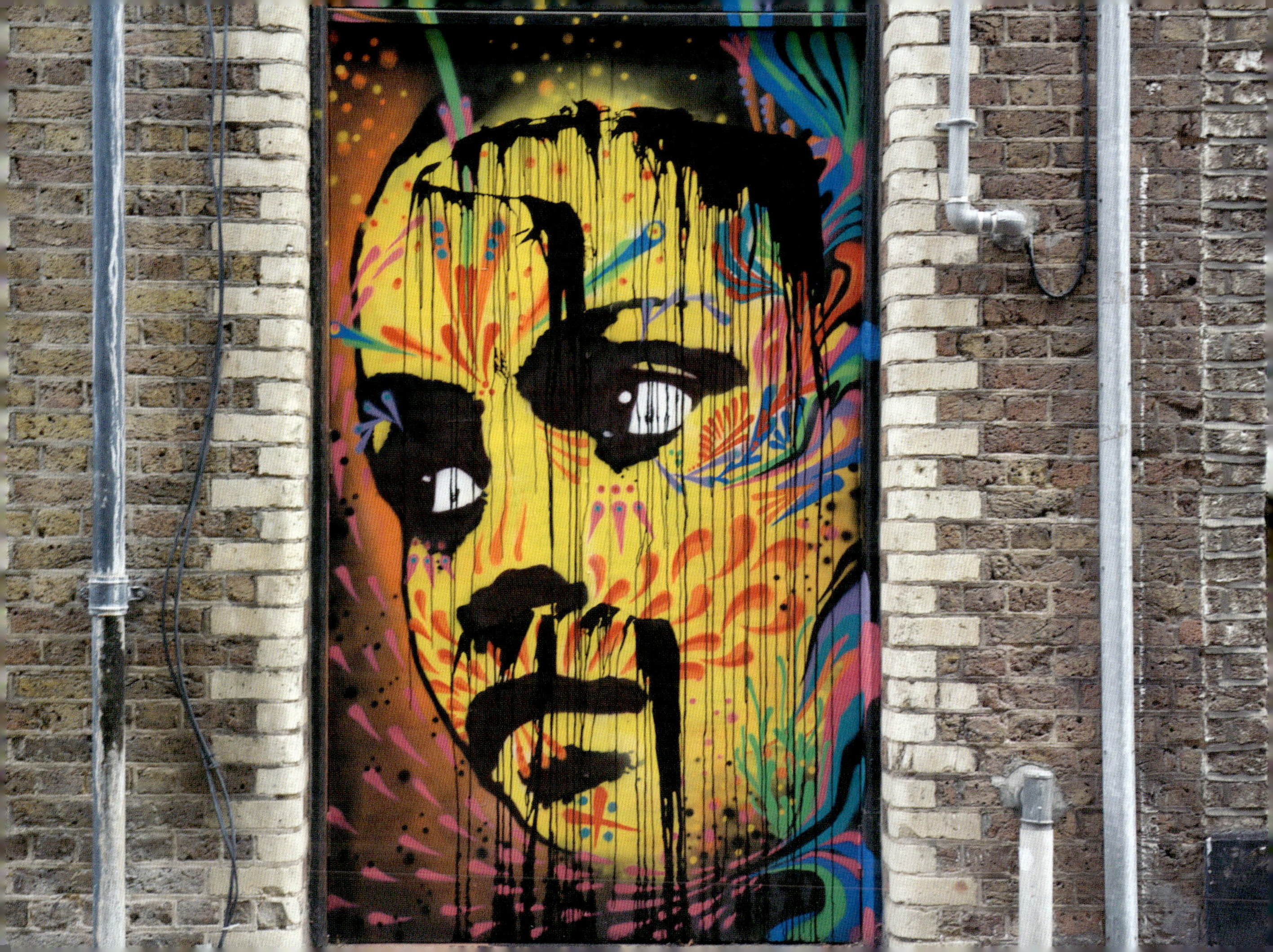

Graffiti finally came up against environmental pressures in the form of an aggressive and well-funded campaign by the Metropolitan Transit Authority in the early 1980's. The number of train yards that could be hit dwindled and competition between crews to control these yards became violent. Under these conditions only the strongest crews survived.

Finally, Graffiti left the subway and spread out into the city. Just like in evolution, the species diversified to survive.

Today it's a worldwide phenomenon. However, in first world countries, as the technology of state surveillance reaches higher and higher levels of sophistication, it gets harder for illegal graffiti to survive. These days a full-scale piece in Europe or the US is usually only done with permission. Is this the twilight of the art form?

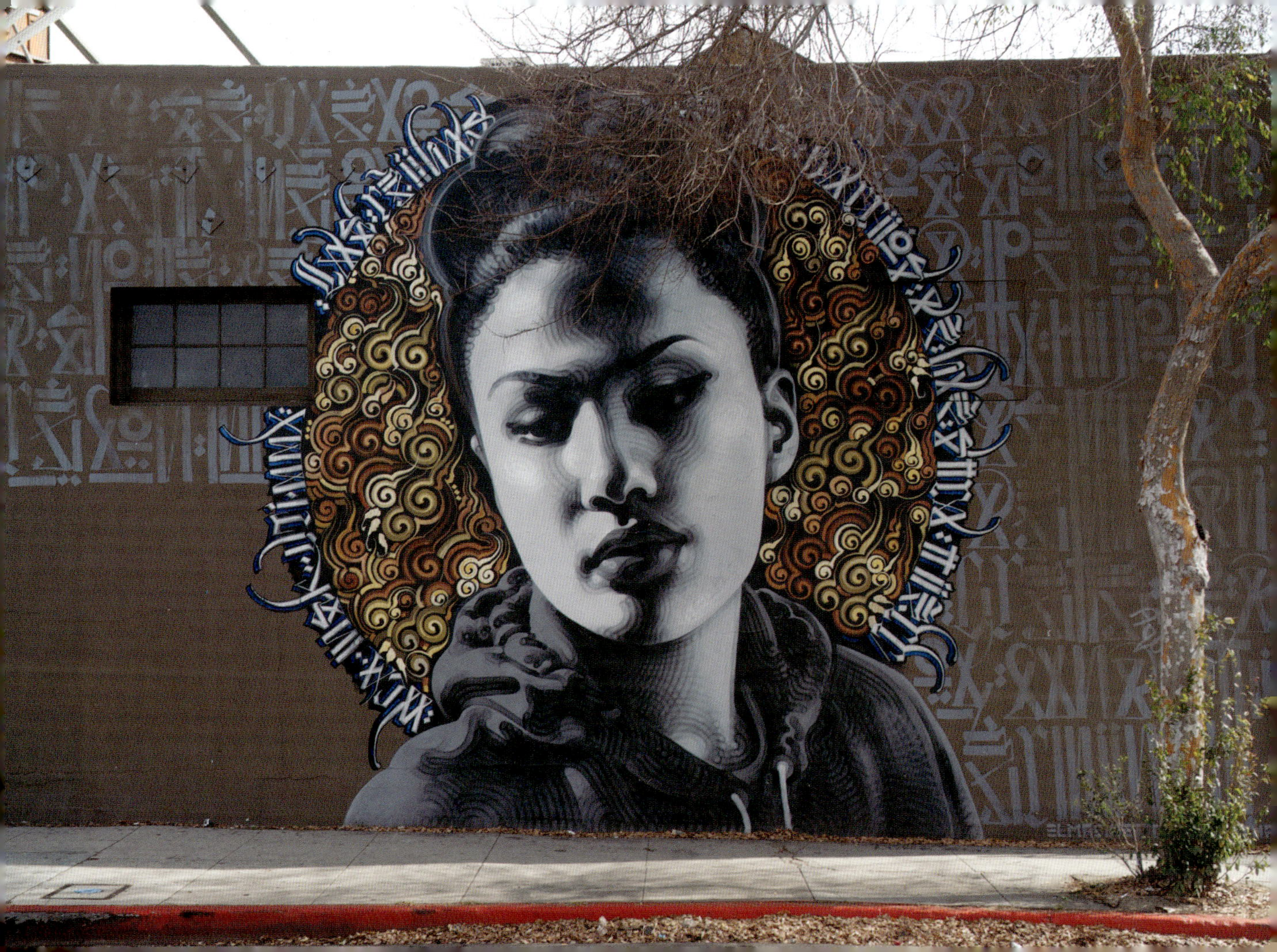

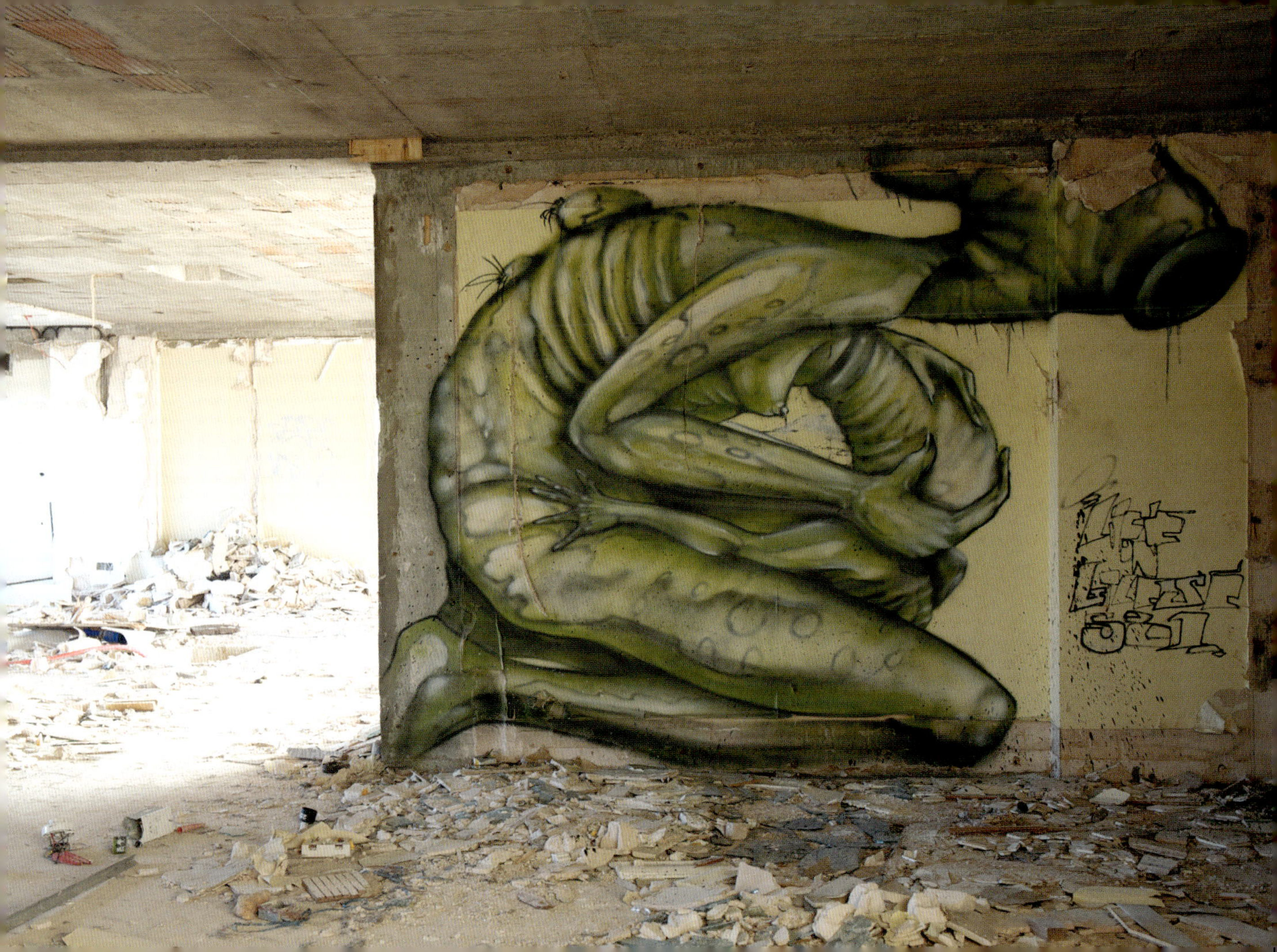

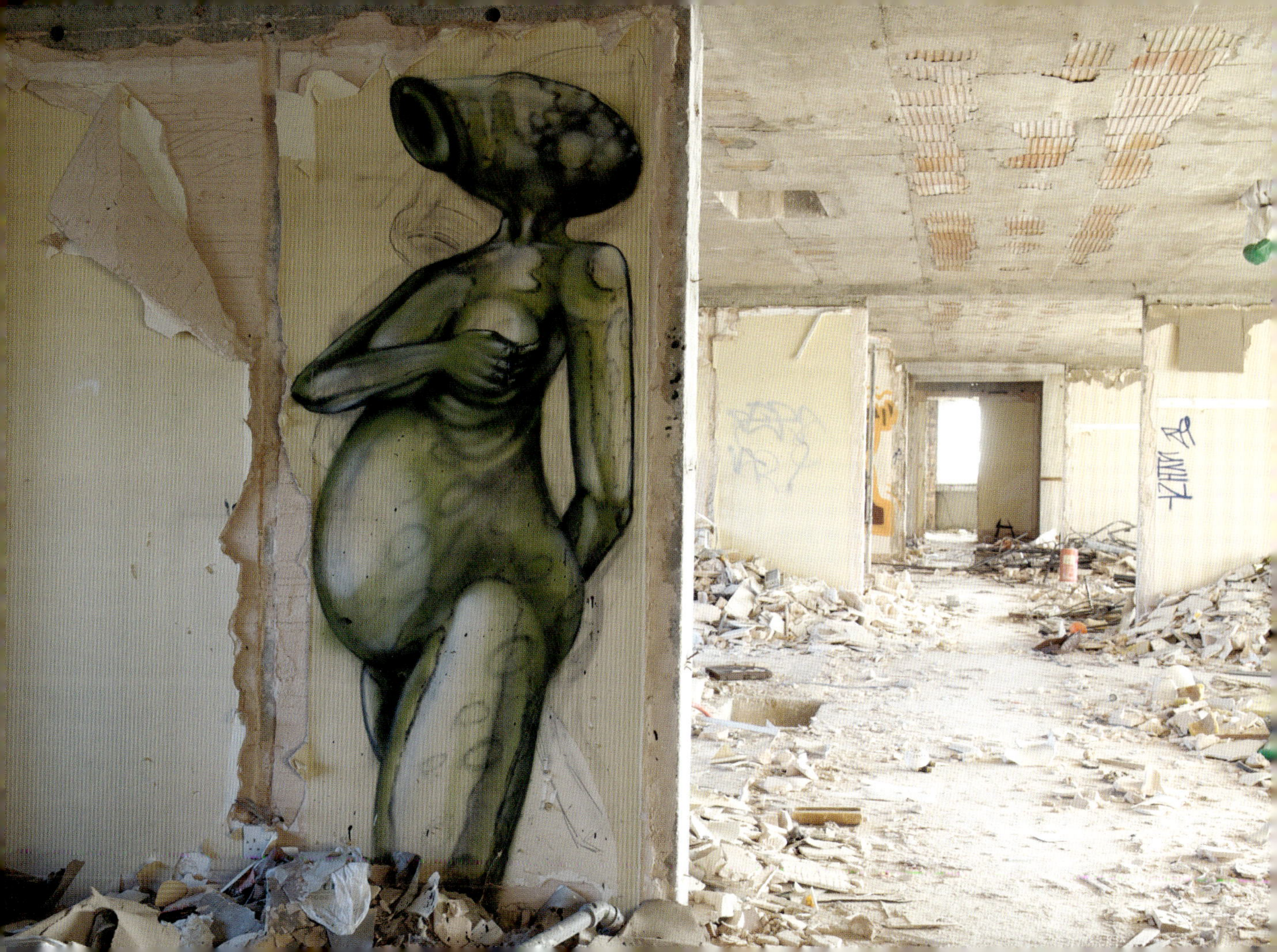

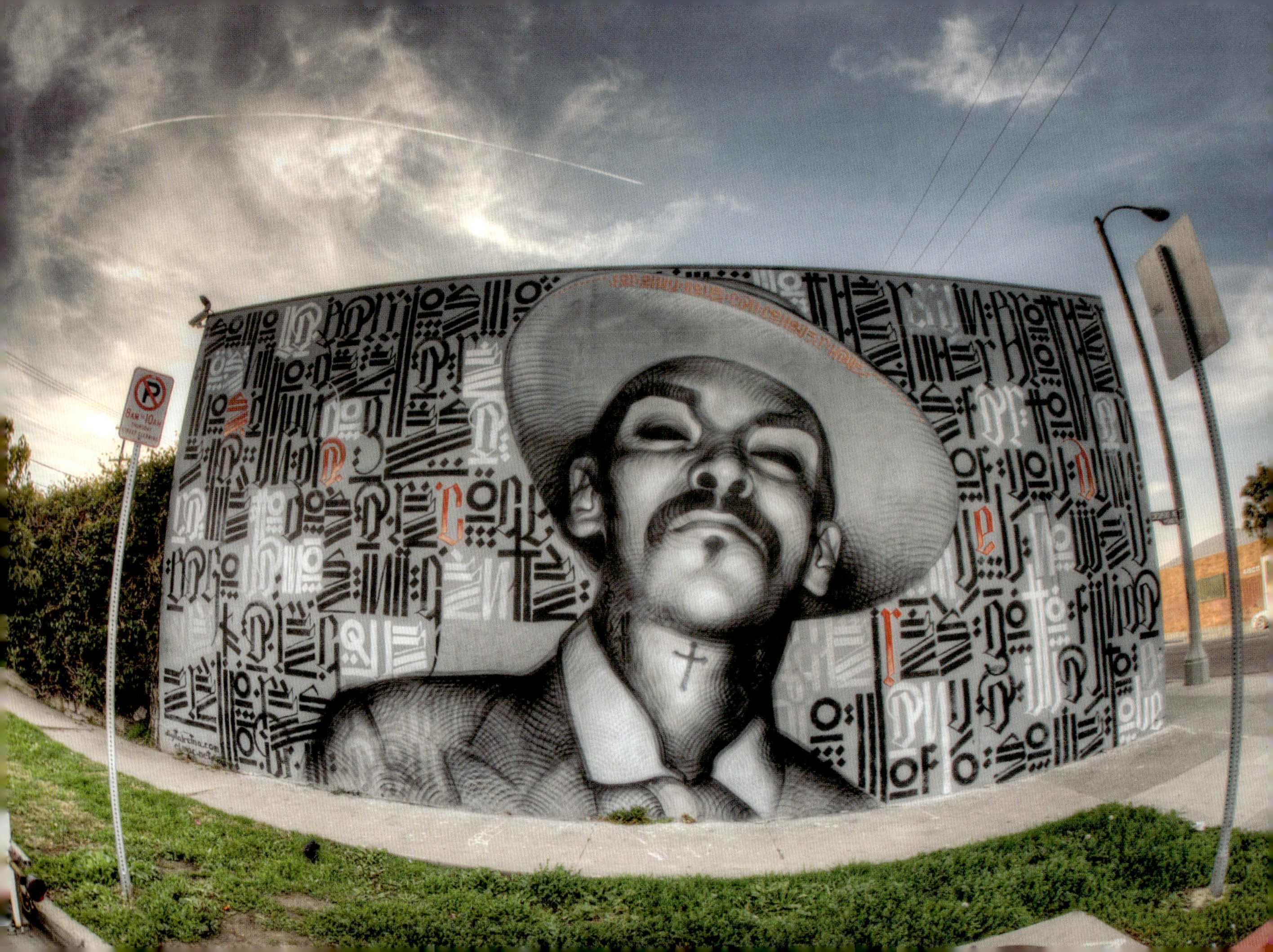

GROUND ZERO

Imagine a time when alpha males ruled the world, bare chests displaying their wealth in gold medallions and beach tans, designer suits and frequent flyer miles, disco, cocaine, sex before HIV, studio 54, Bianca Jagger riding a white horse on the dancefloor. Whores on Broadway, Son of Sam, Bronx Burning. This was American life in the 1970's. The hippy dream long sold off for scrap, excess was the watchword and those who could, pretended to be rich and those who were rich shoved it right in your face at every possible goddamn opportunity.

The city was laced up in tangled networks of power, organised crime at a peak, street gangs, corruption and the sparkling, glittering lights of the spectacle, the newborn forms of mass media, lifestyle advertising and trash pop culture, the era when the very idea of 'fifteen minutes of fame' was born - and then there is you.

You. Stuck on a street corner in hand me down clothes in a no hope barrio in a fuck you city.

Those excluded from the gangbang were forced to watch from the sidelines, punk kids written off by society, working desperate jobs if at all.

Gangs of no hopers, riding the city with nothing but pocket change or delivering packages on foot or just killing time. Days spent riding the subway armed with nothing more than a permanent marker pen. Writing their names. Ride/write, ride/write, they just couldn't stop. They were addicted. Before long, the whole of New York city knew their names. They had found a way to be famous. This is where it all started.

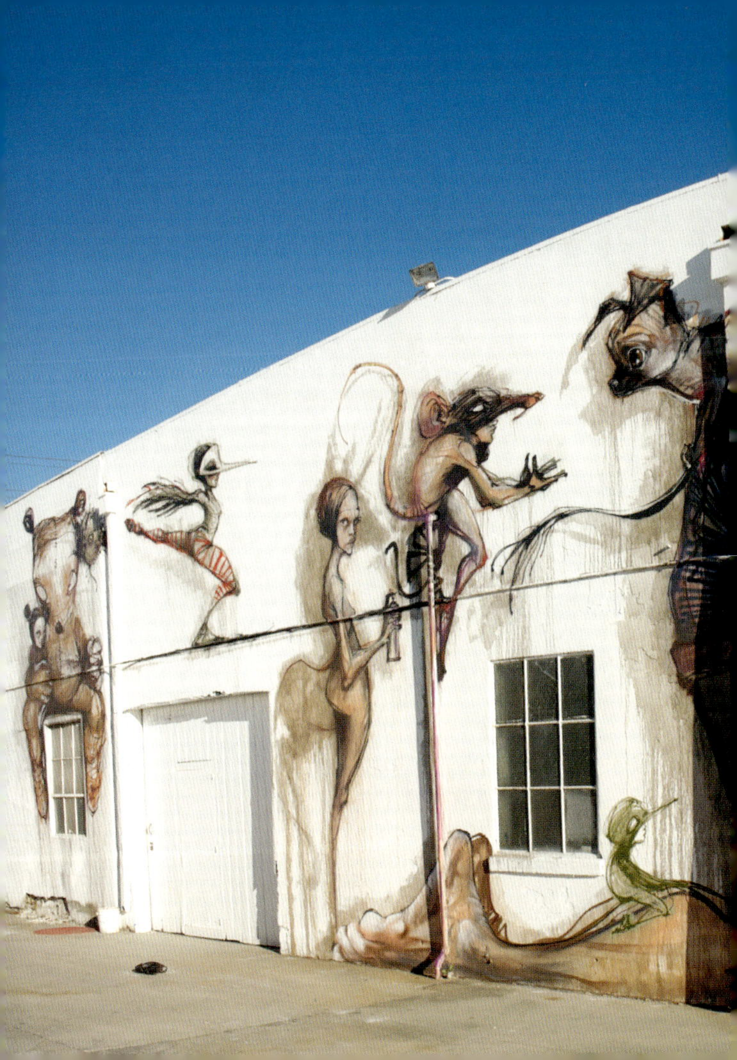

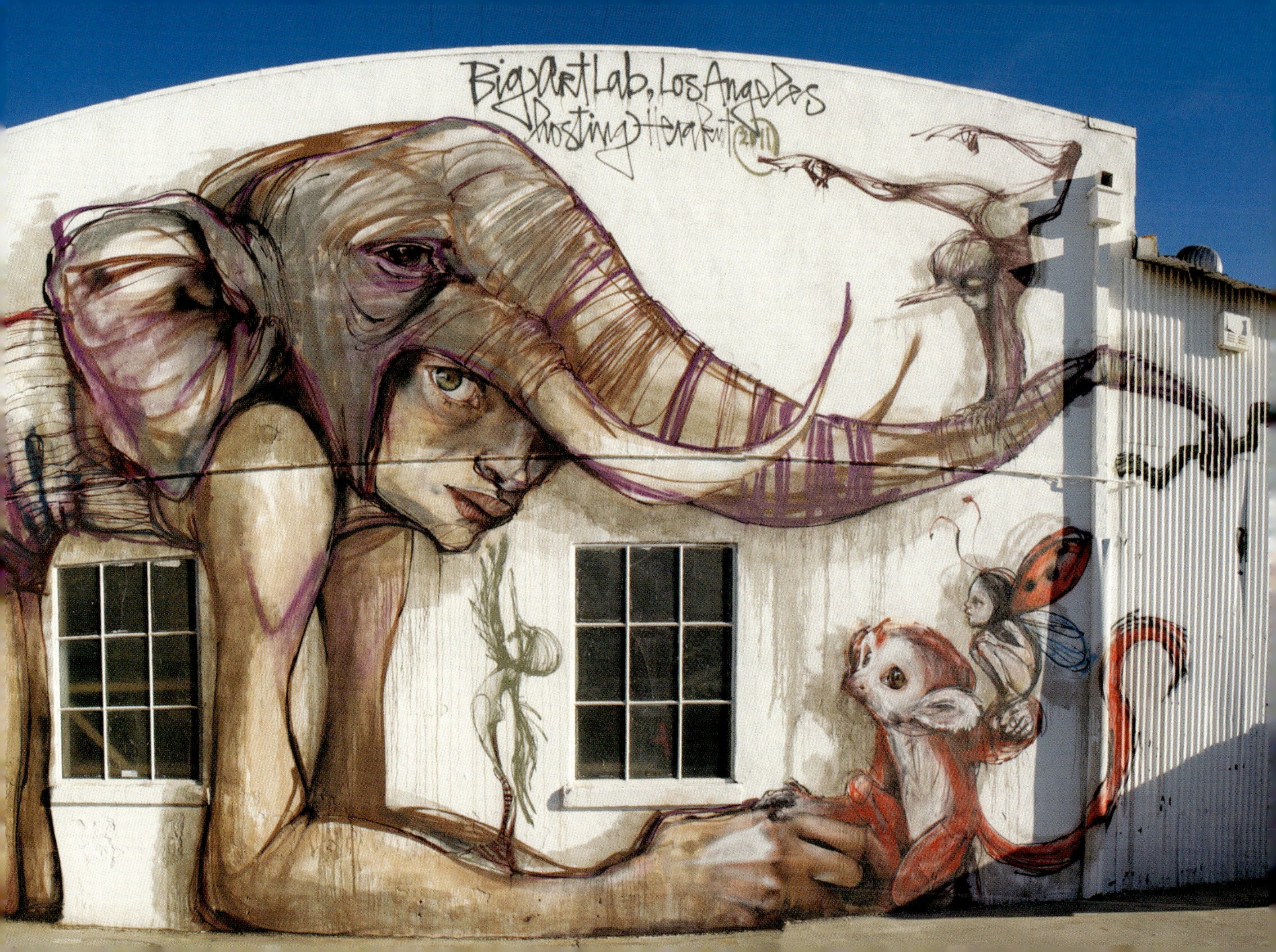
BigArtLab, LosAngeles
hosting HeraKut 2011

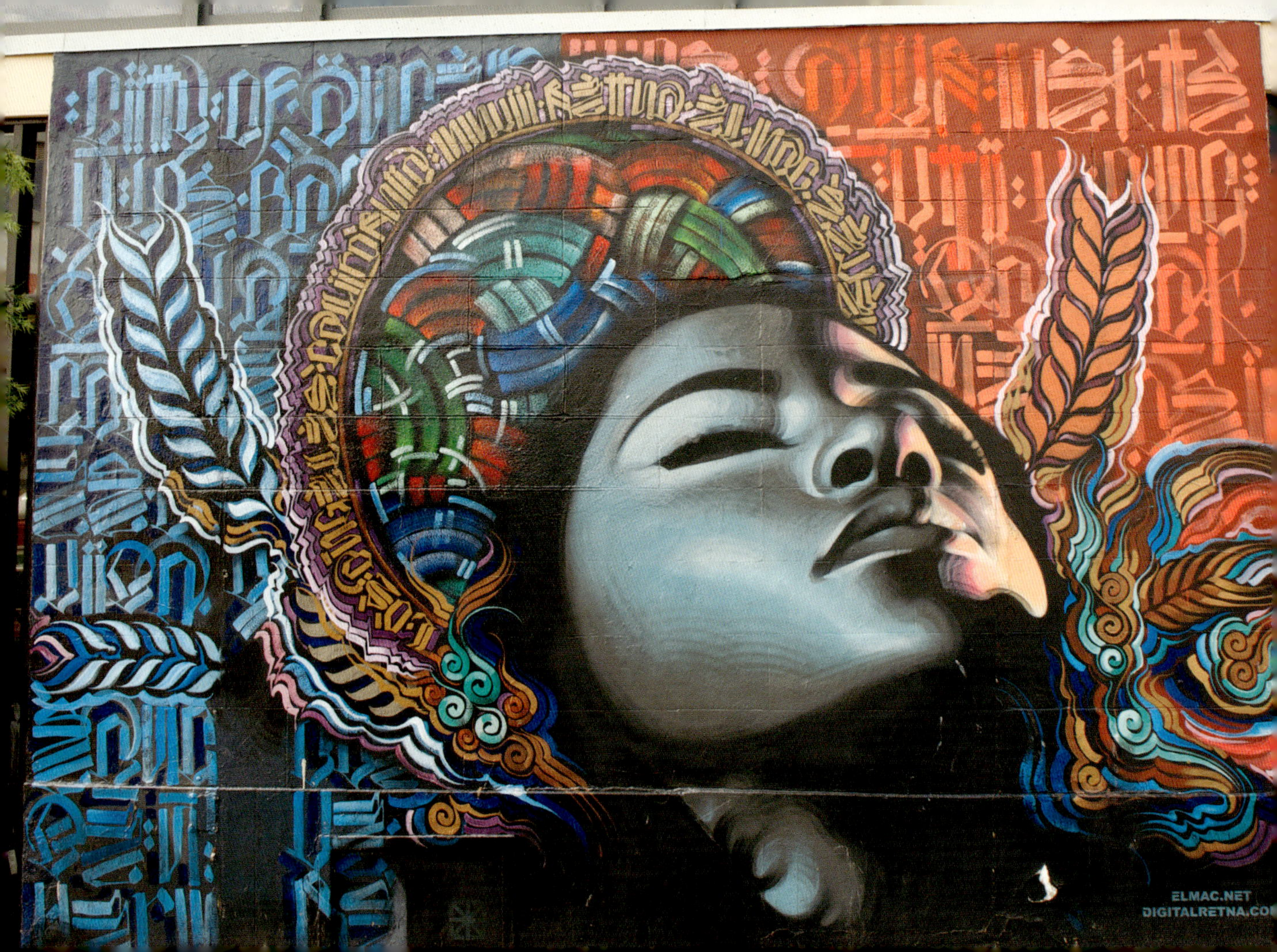
ELMAC.NET
DIGITALRETNA.CO

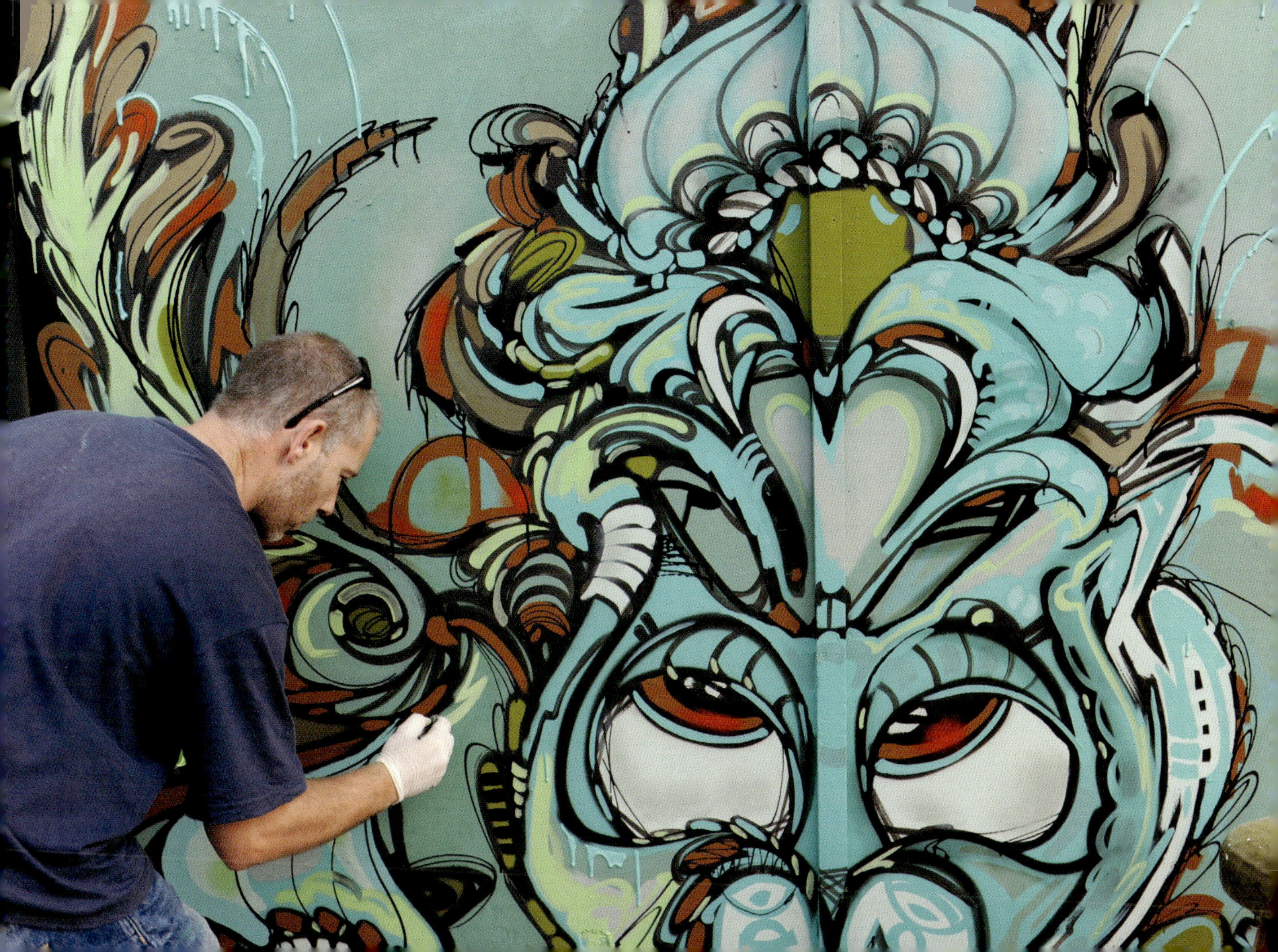

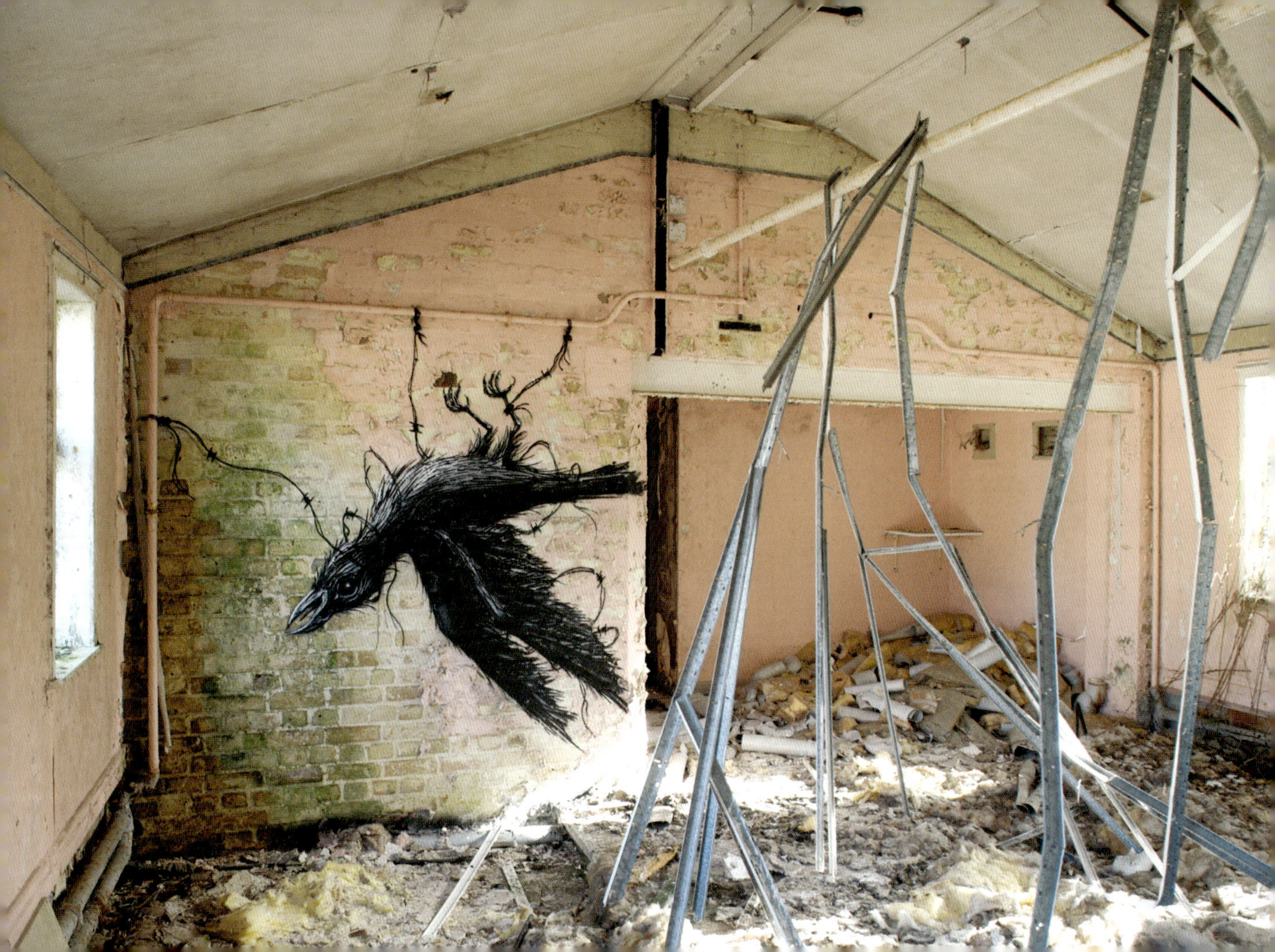

It doesn't matter for me if every painting is either elaborate or well considered, it's all about the action, the expression, the creation, . . . call it what you like.

ROA

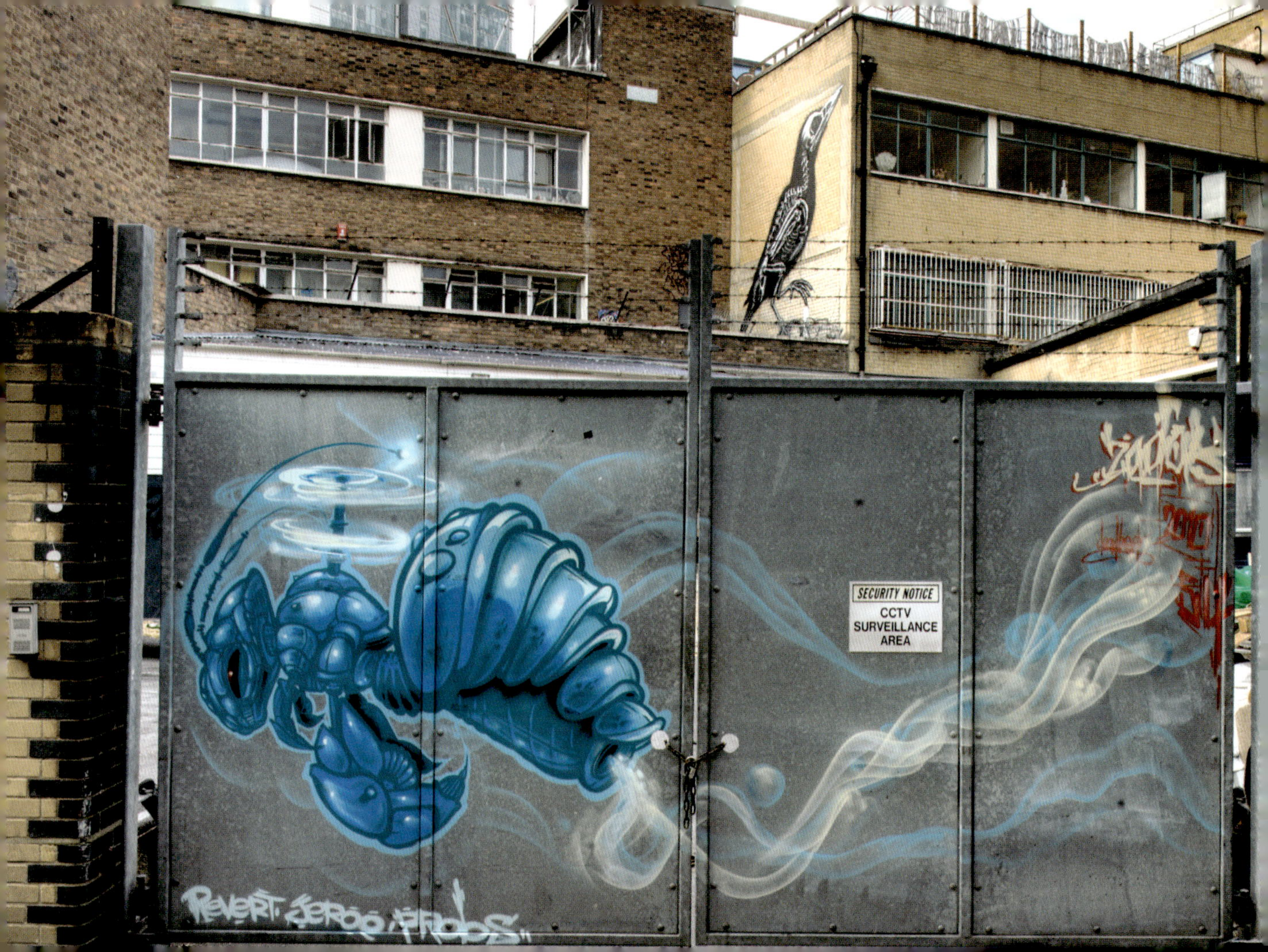
SECURITY NOTICE
CCTV
SURVEILLANCE
AREA

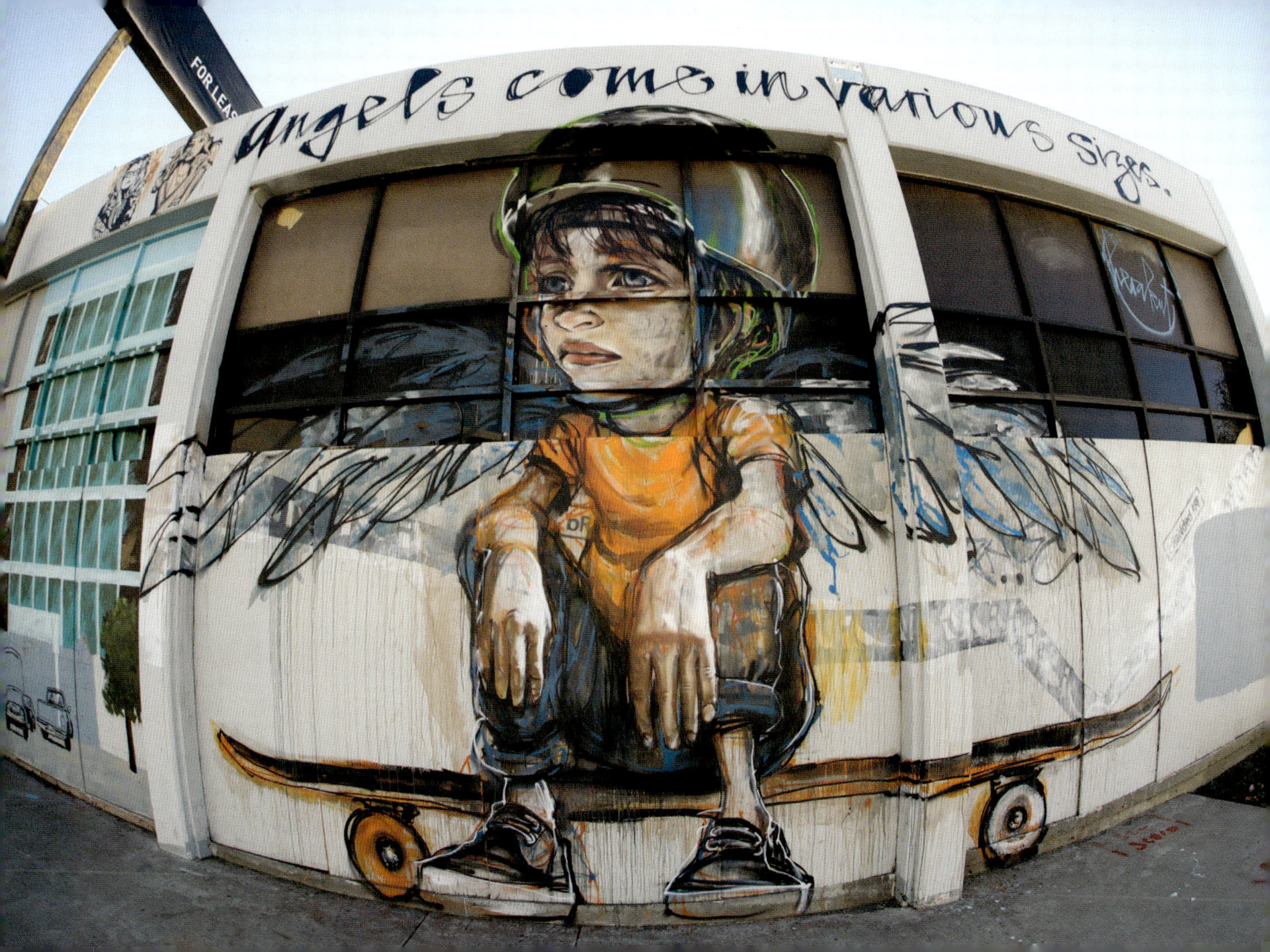

angels come in various sizes.
FOR LEAS

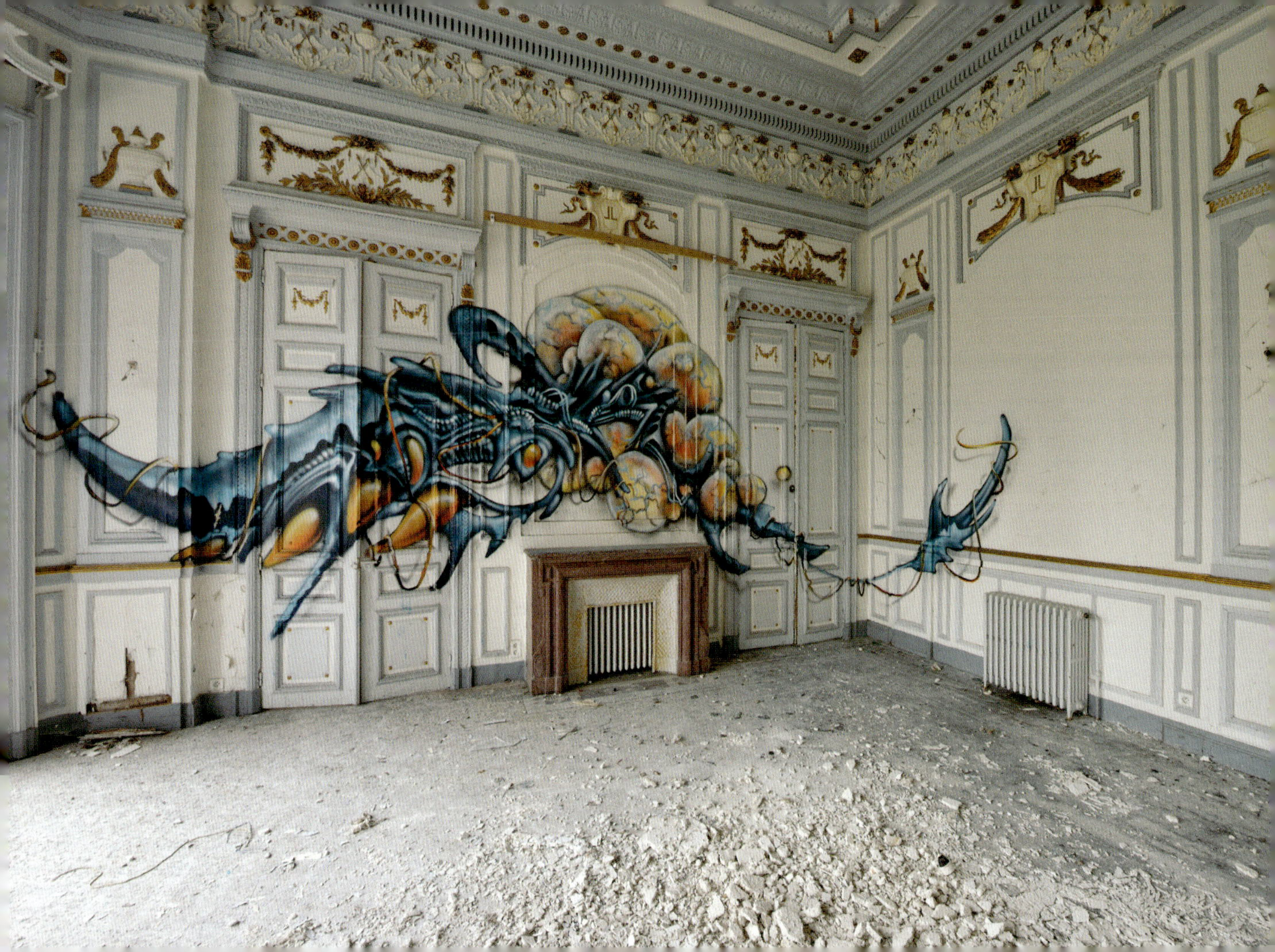

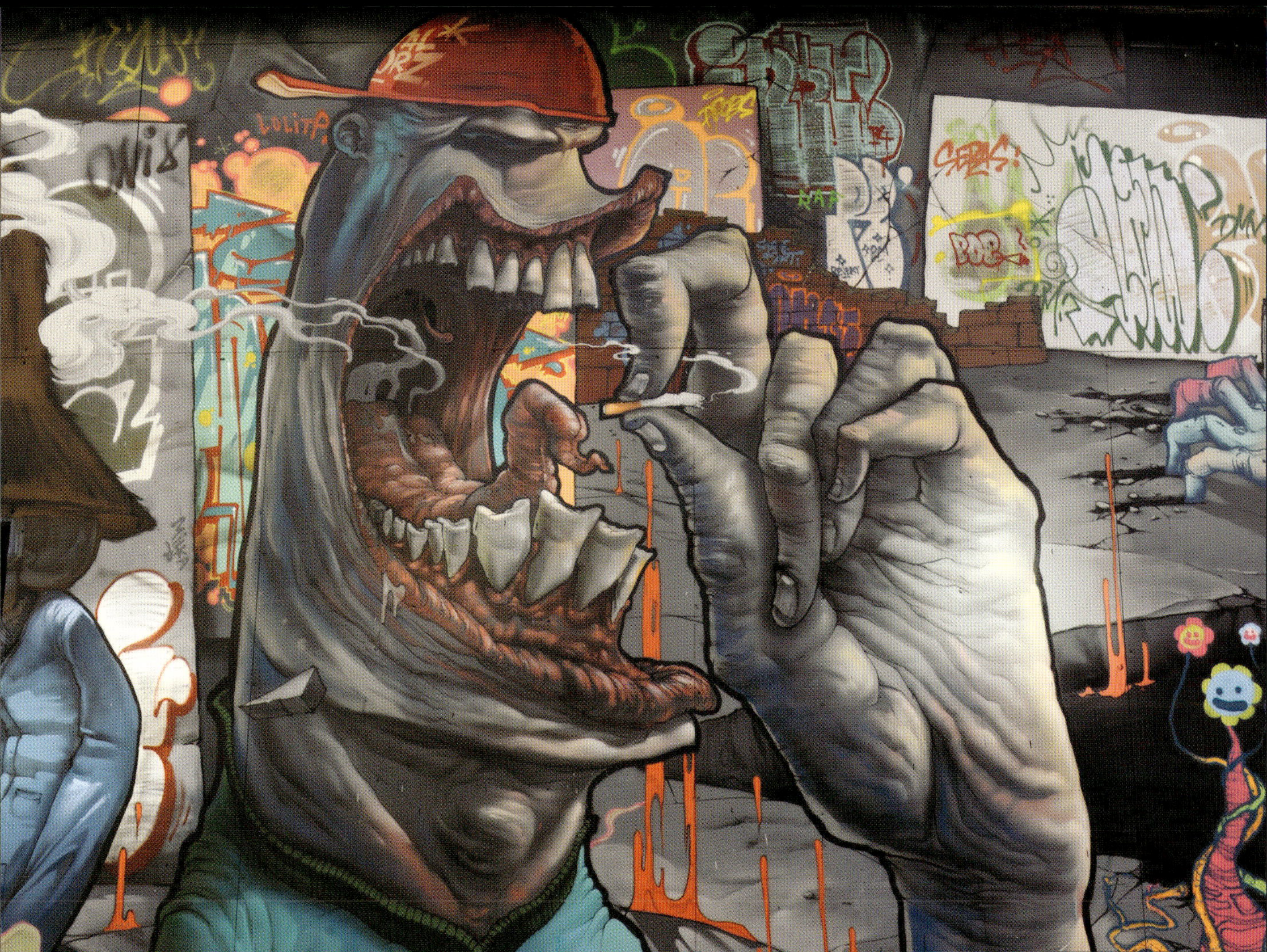

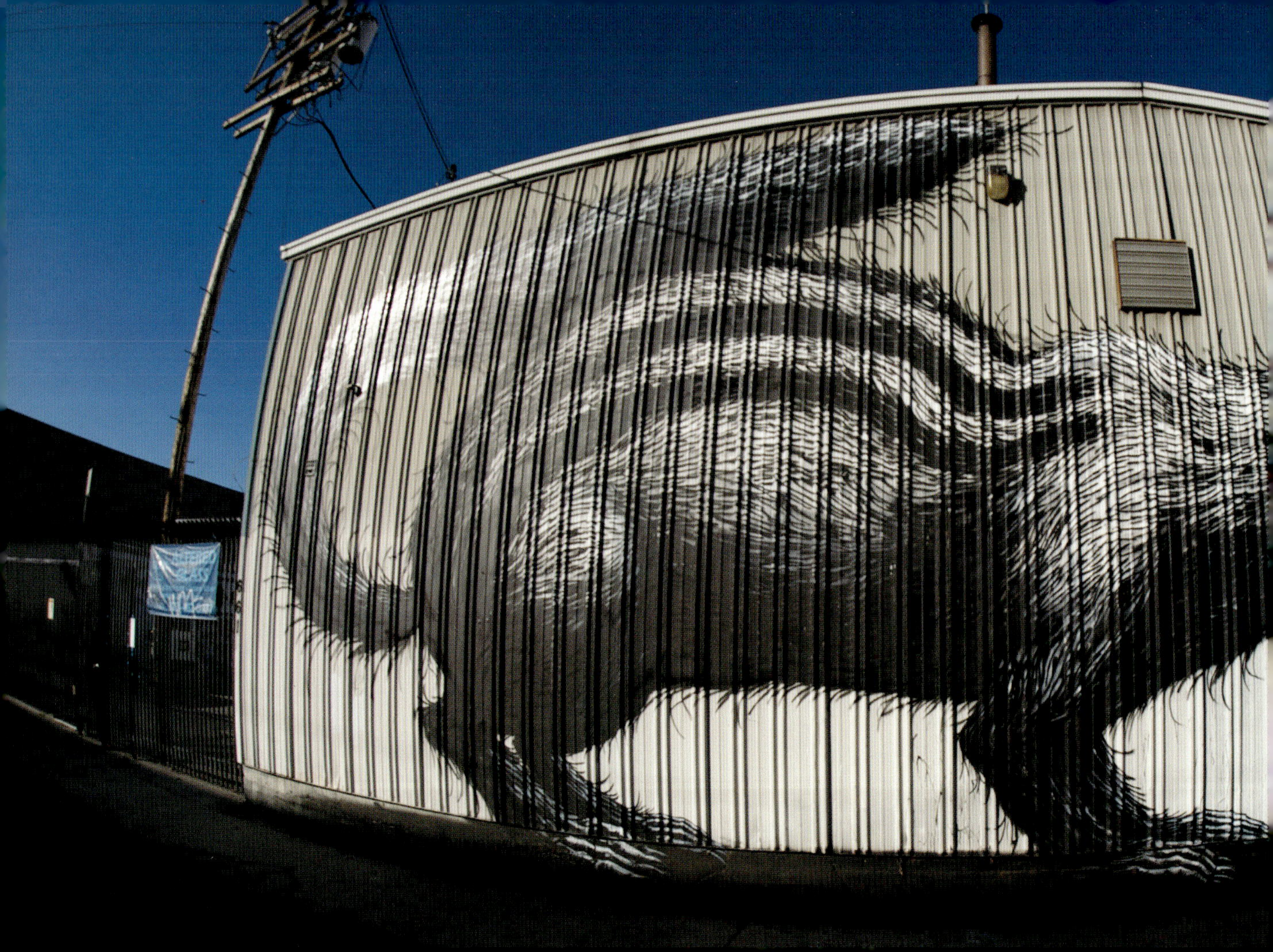

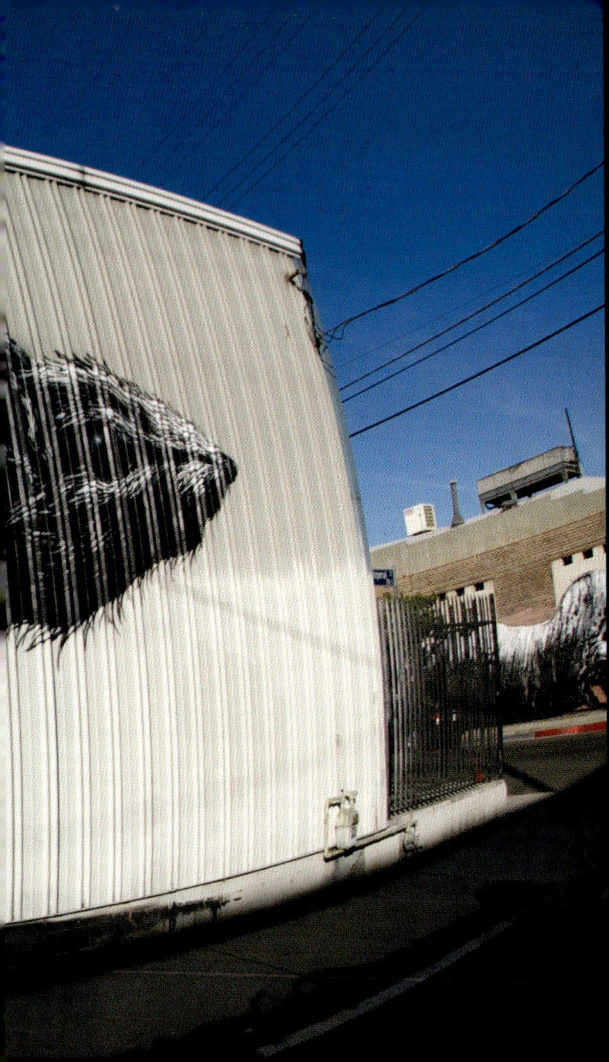

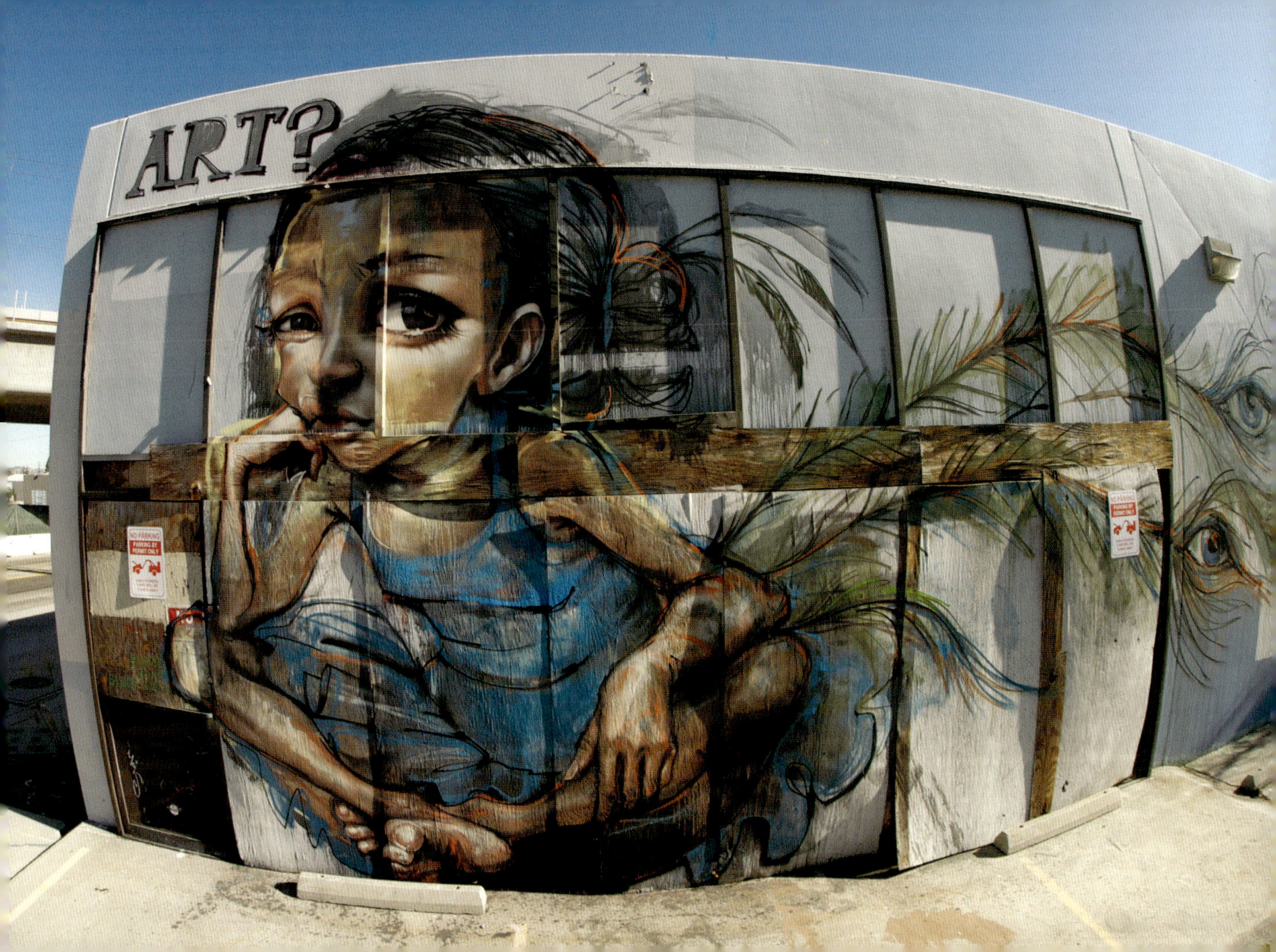
ART?

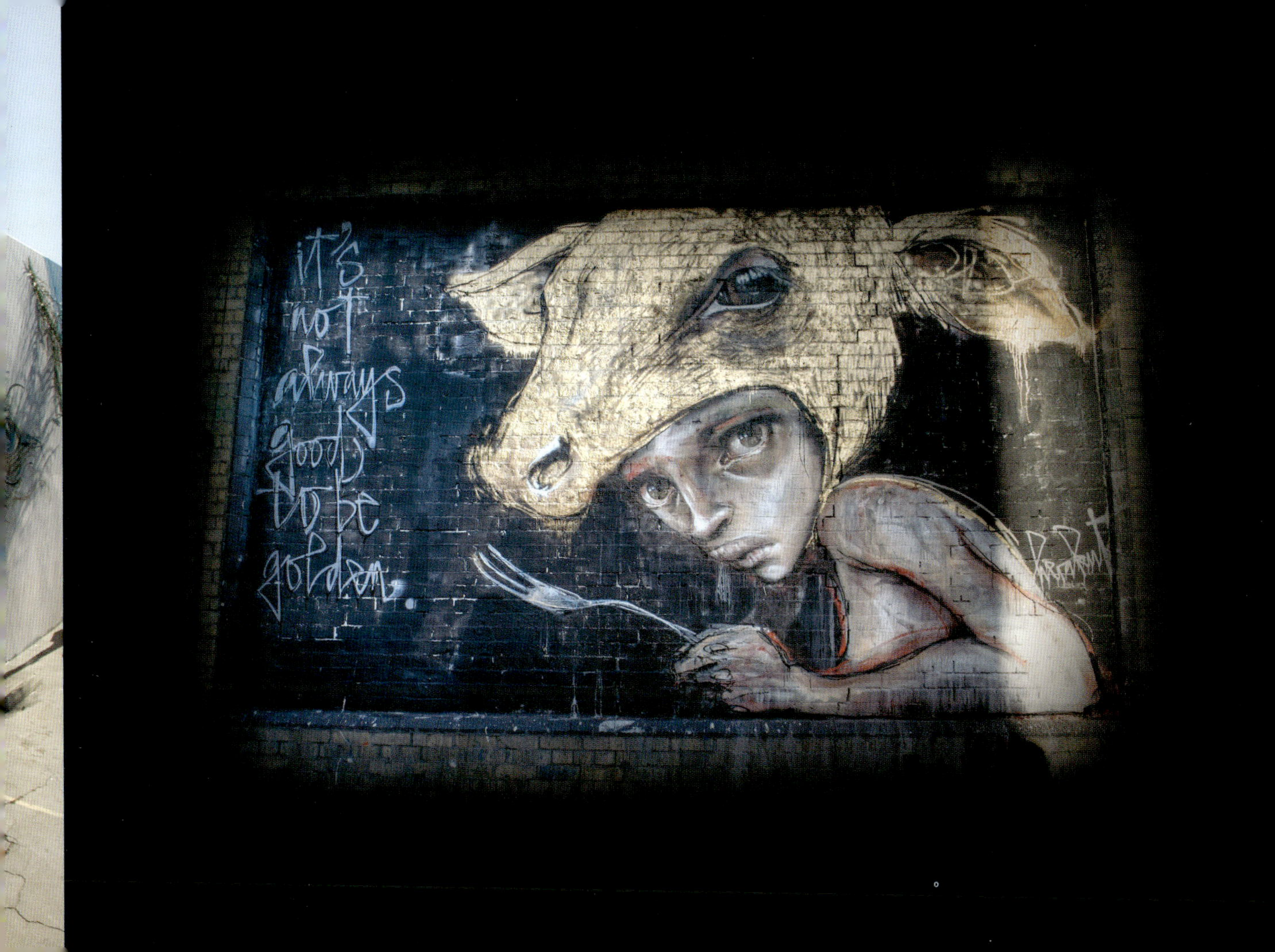
it's not always good to be golden.

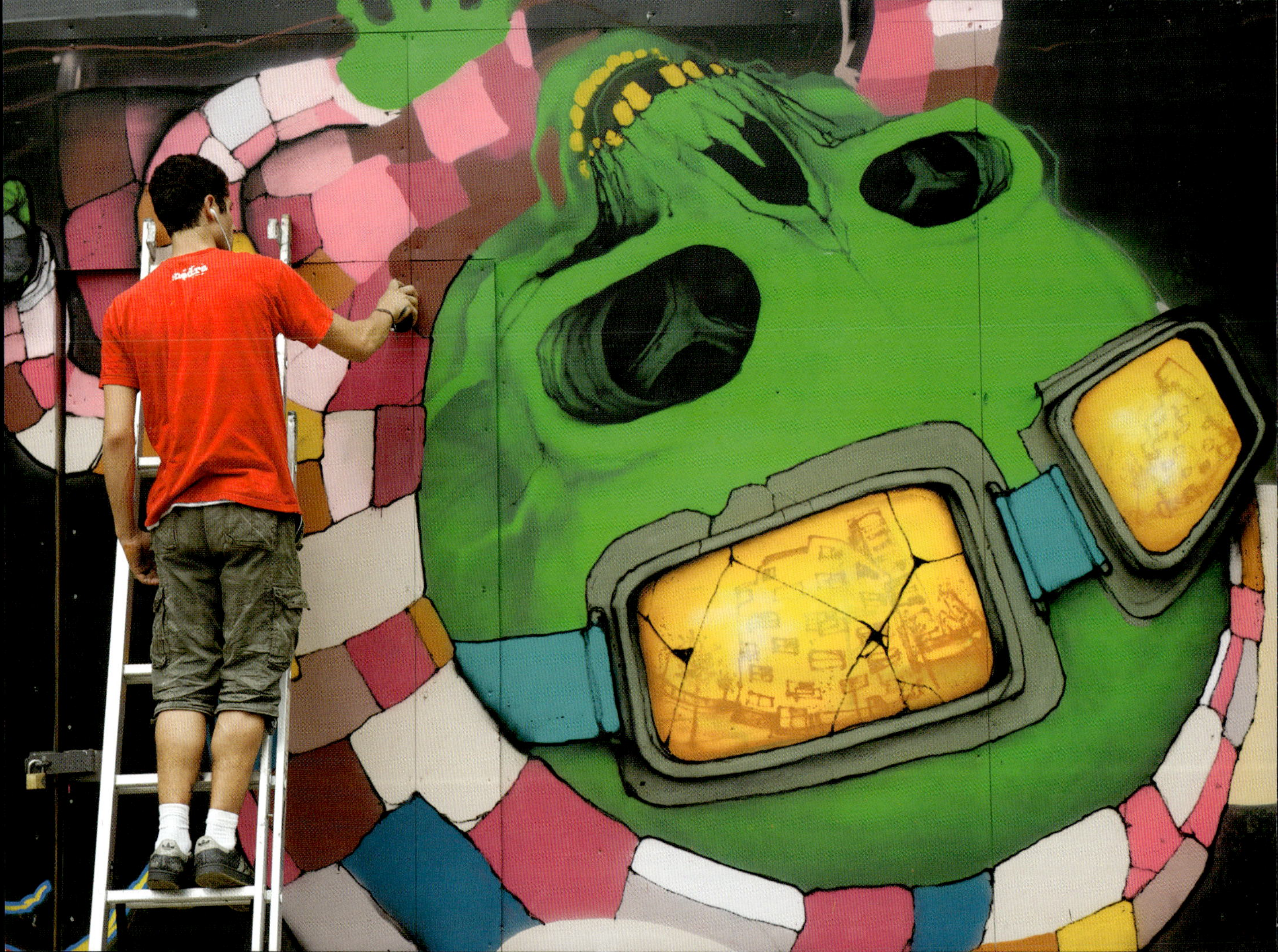

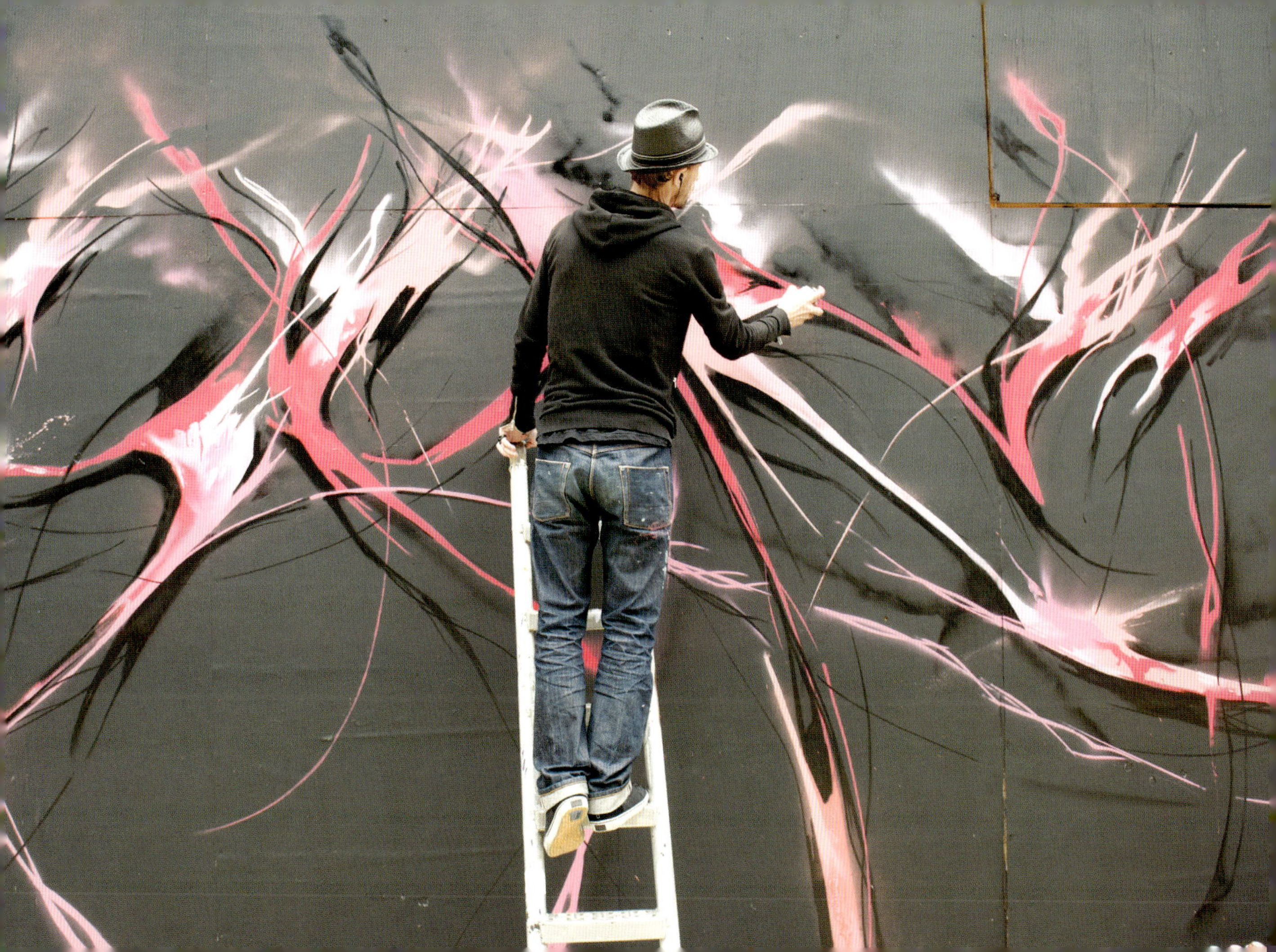

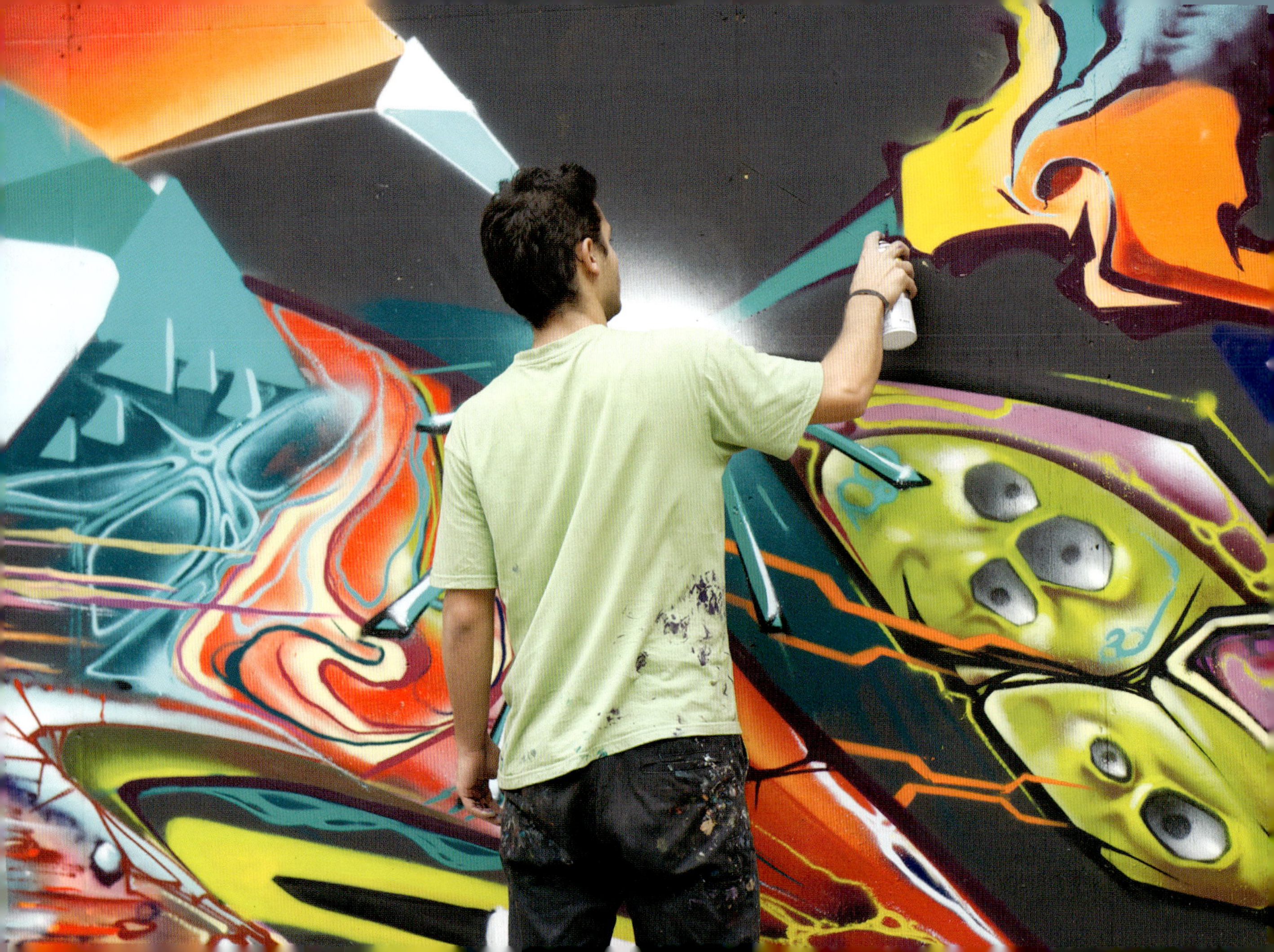

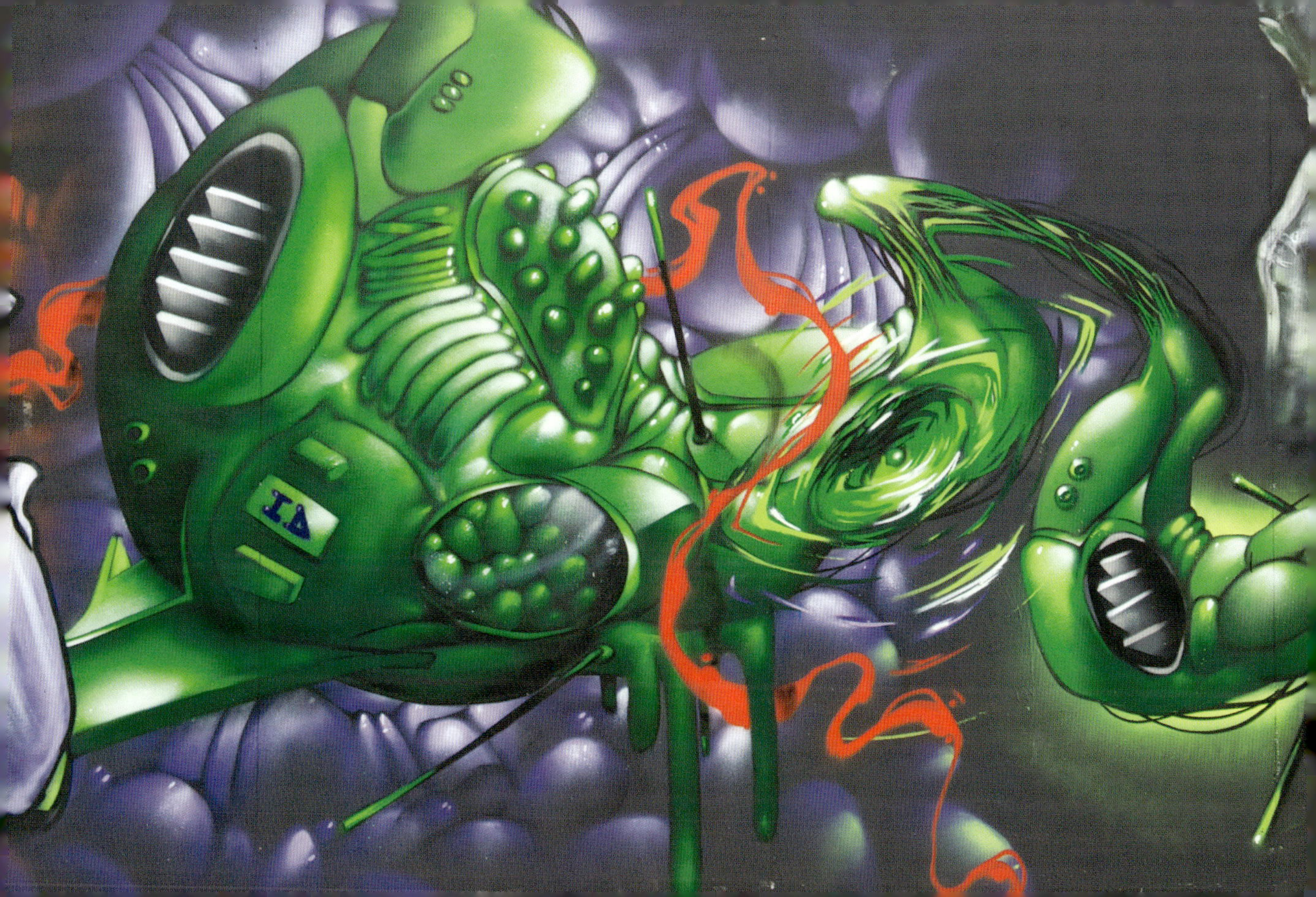

I started painting on the streets thinking it could really change the world but one thing is for sure . . . it has completely changed my life.

C215

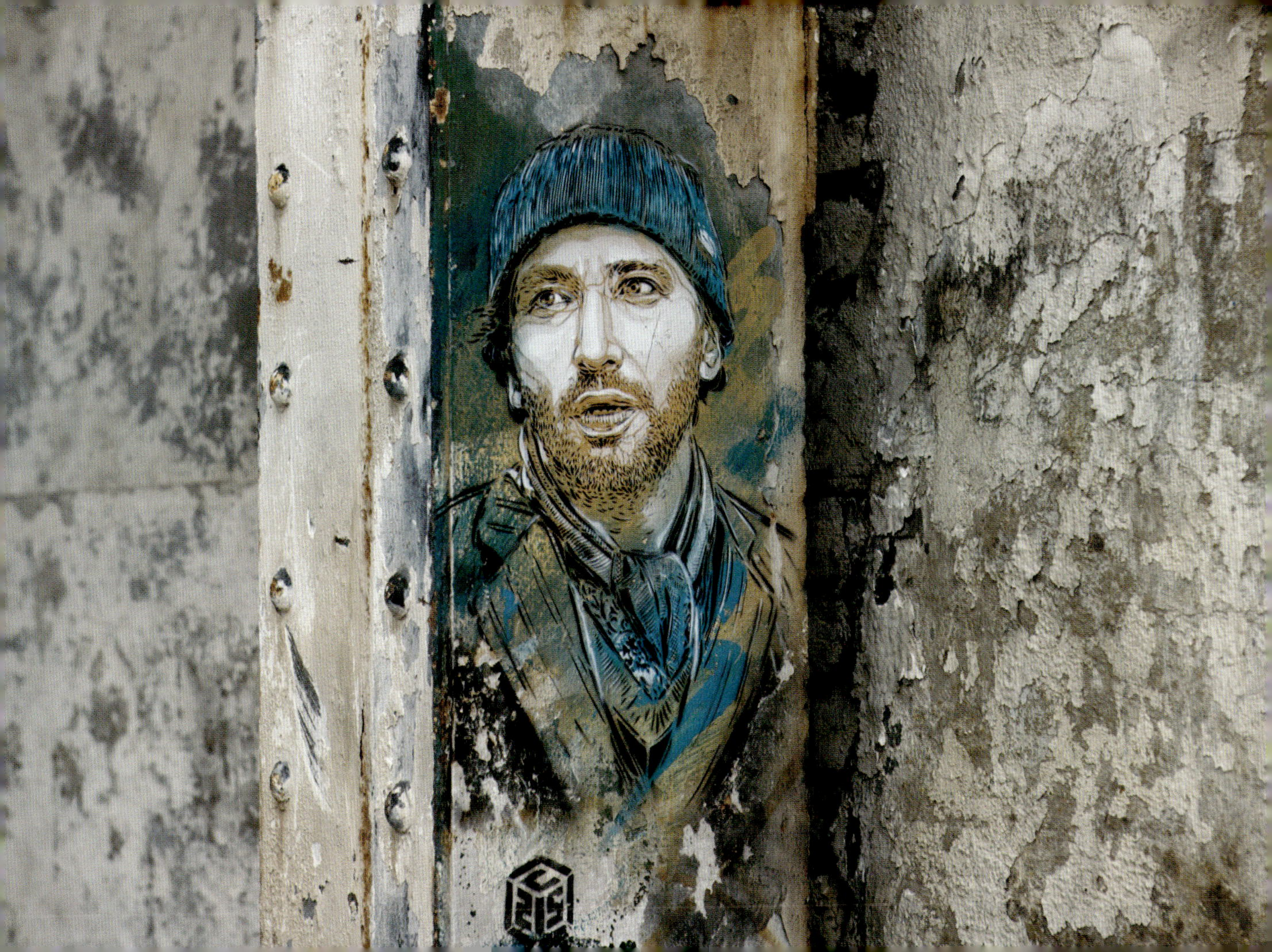

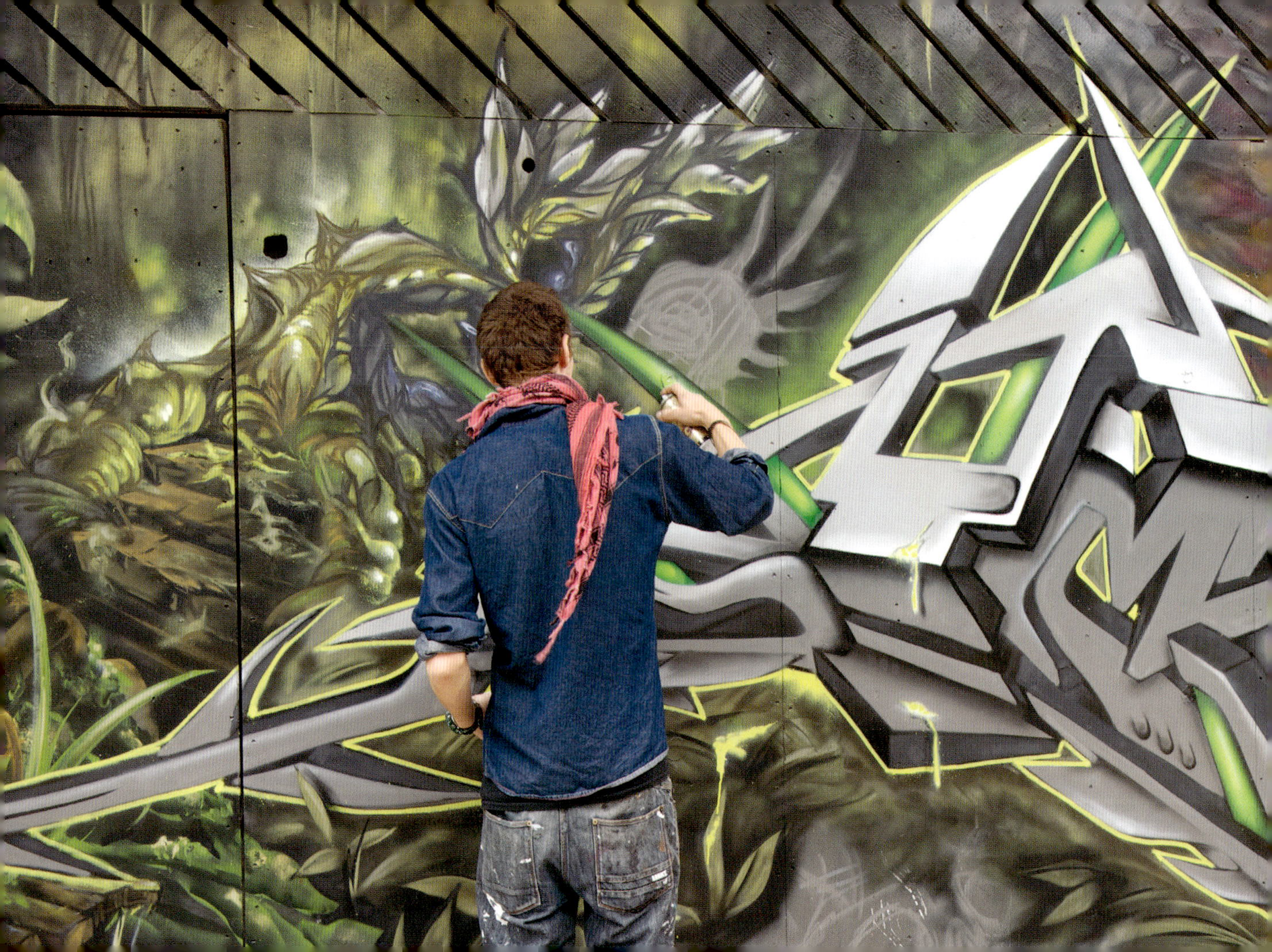

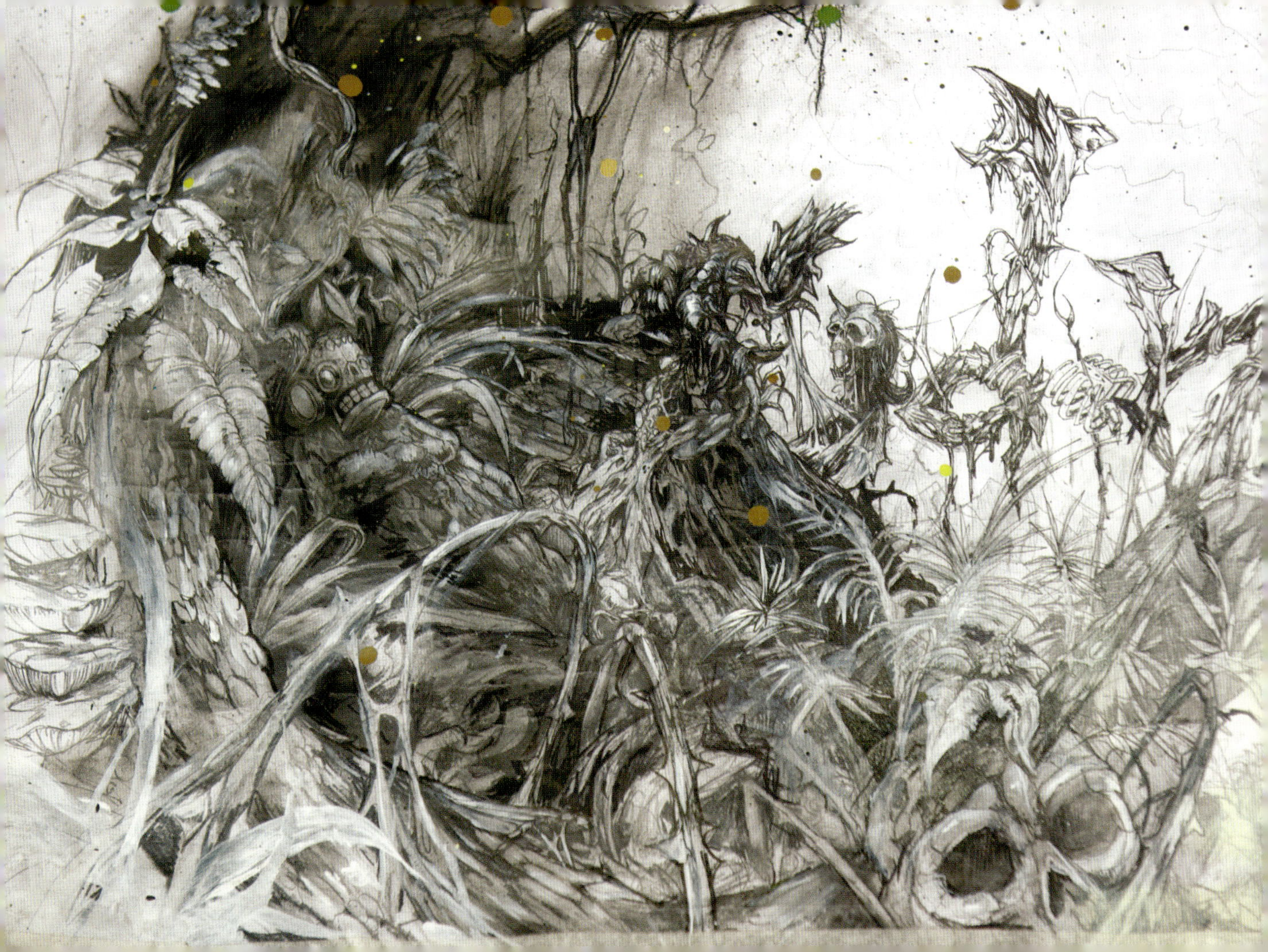

FAMILY STRIFE

If Graffiti is the mother of Street Art then you could expect to hear an argument or two in their household, ending with street art shouting 'I hate you!' and running upstairs like a herd of elephants to slam the bedroom door. Graffiti is a rough mother, the type to tell you to punch the bully in the mouth rather than grass on him. Street Art is the sensitive child, insistent on 'meaning' something and disillusioned with the unabashed pursuit of fame insisted upon by her mother. Graffiti wouldn't understand if Street Art wanted to go to University. *You think you're better than your old mum dontcha sweetheart?*

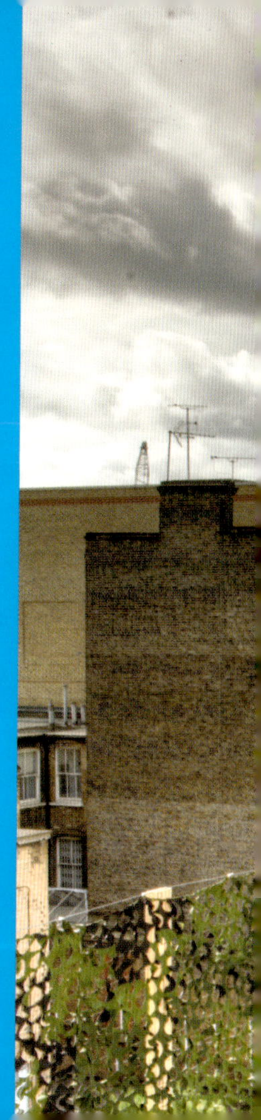

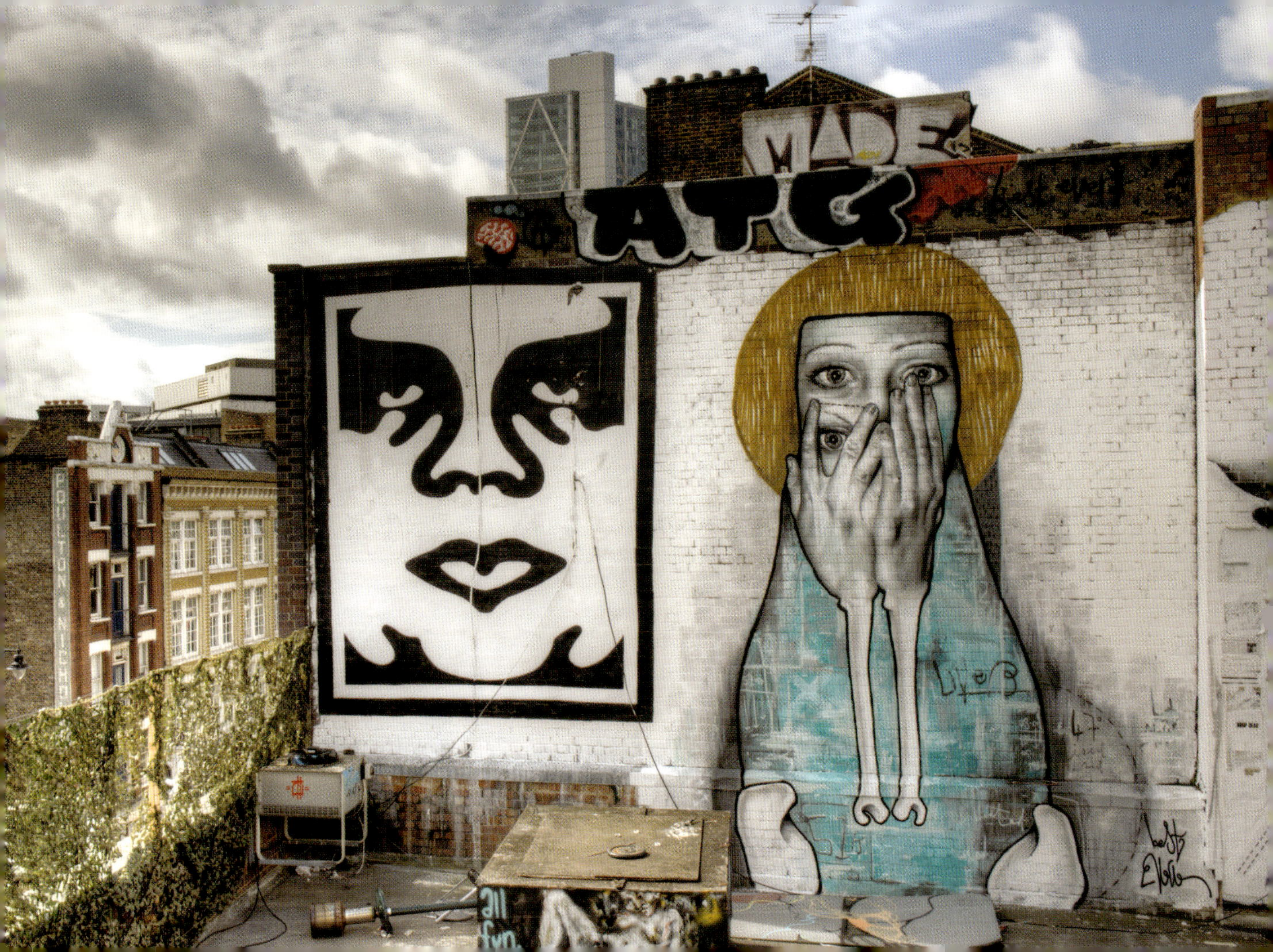
MADE

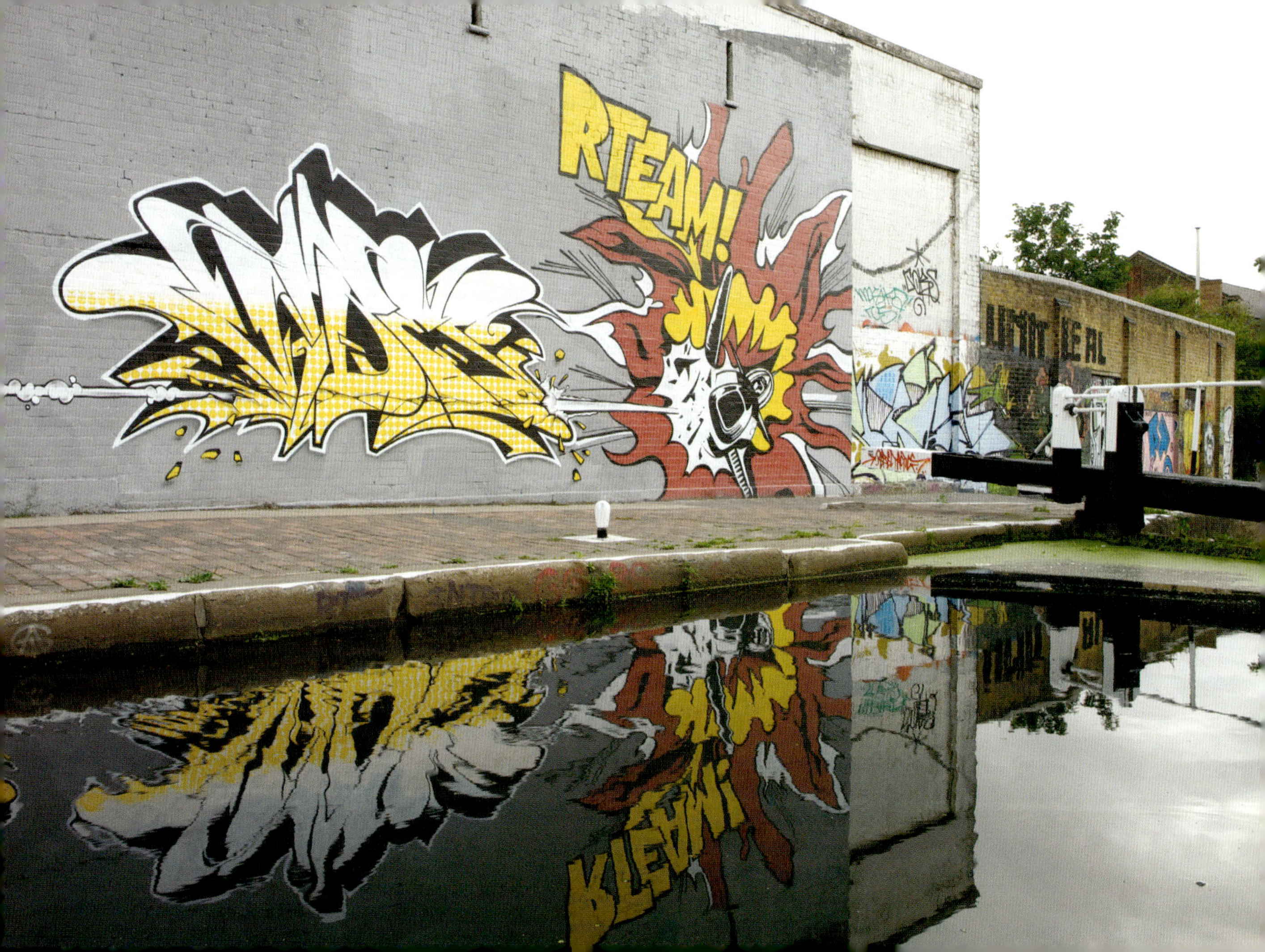
RTEAM!

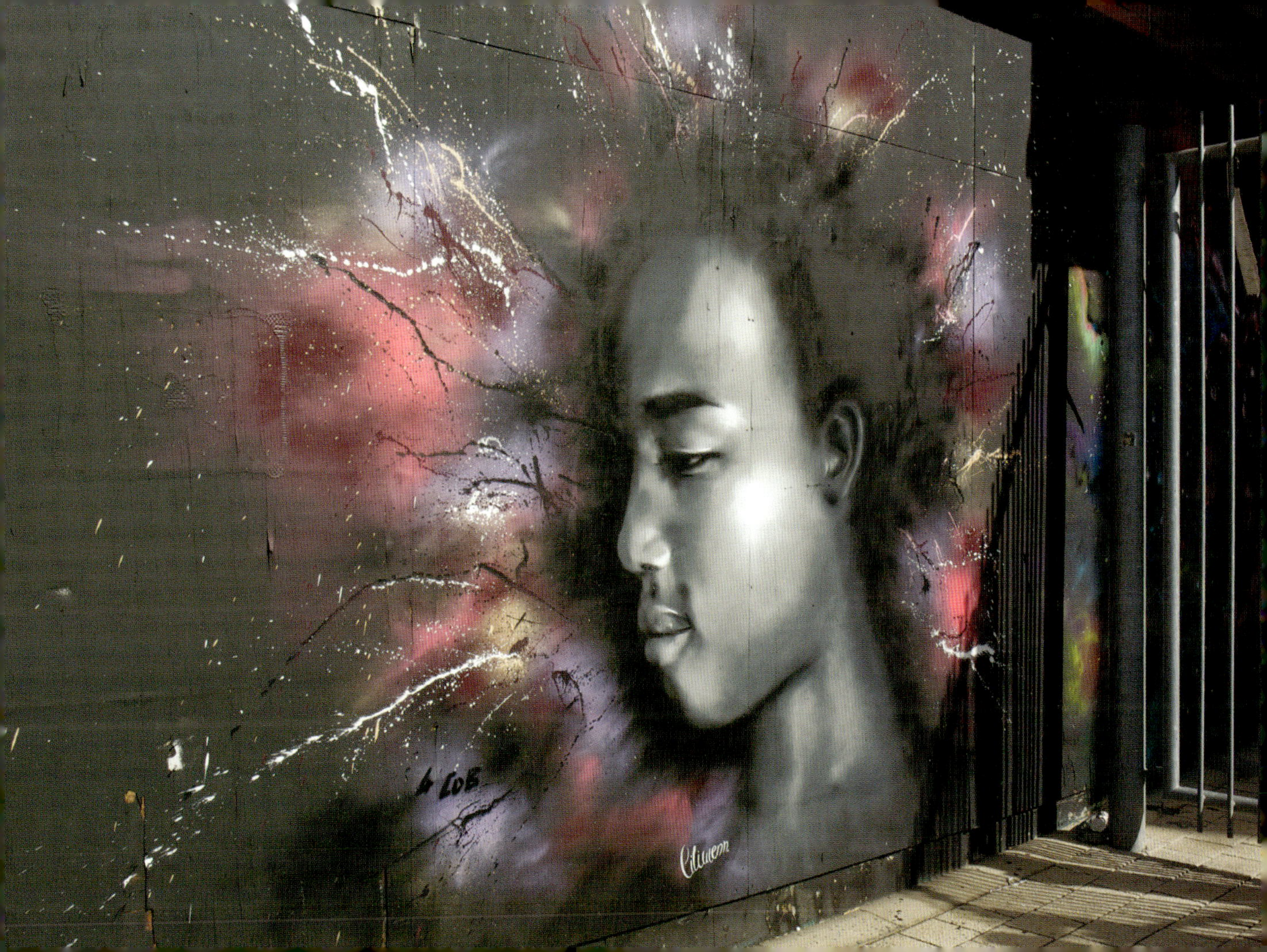

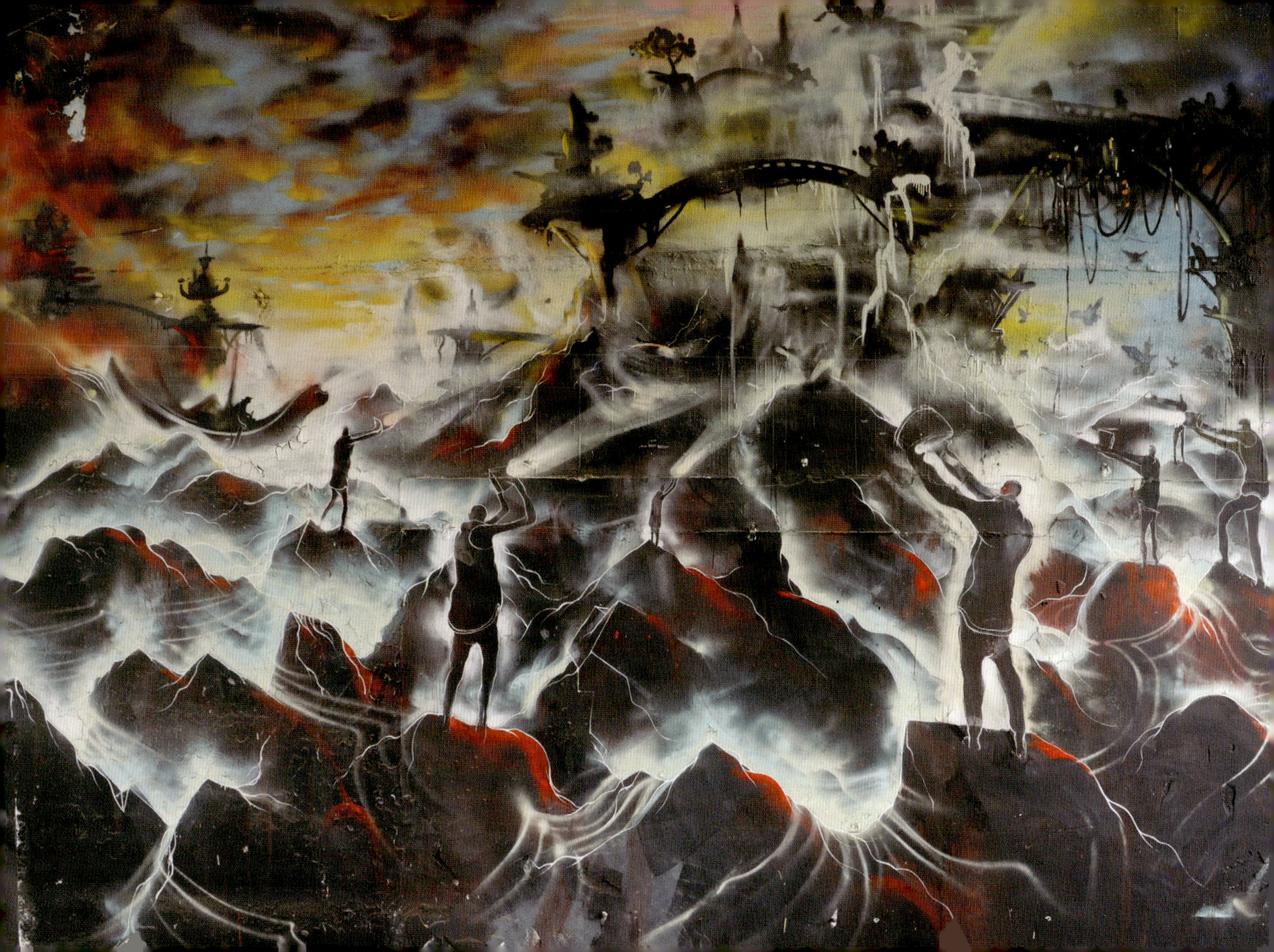

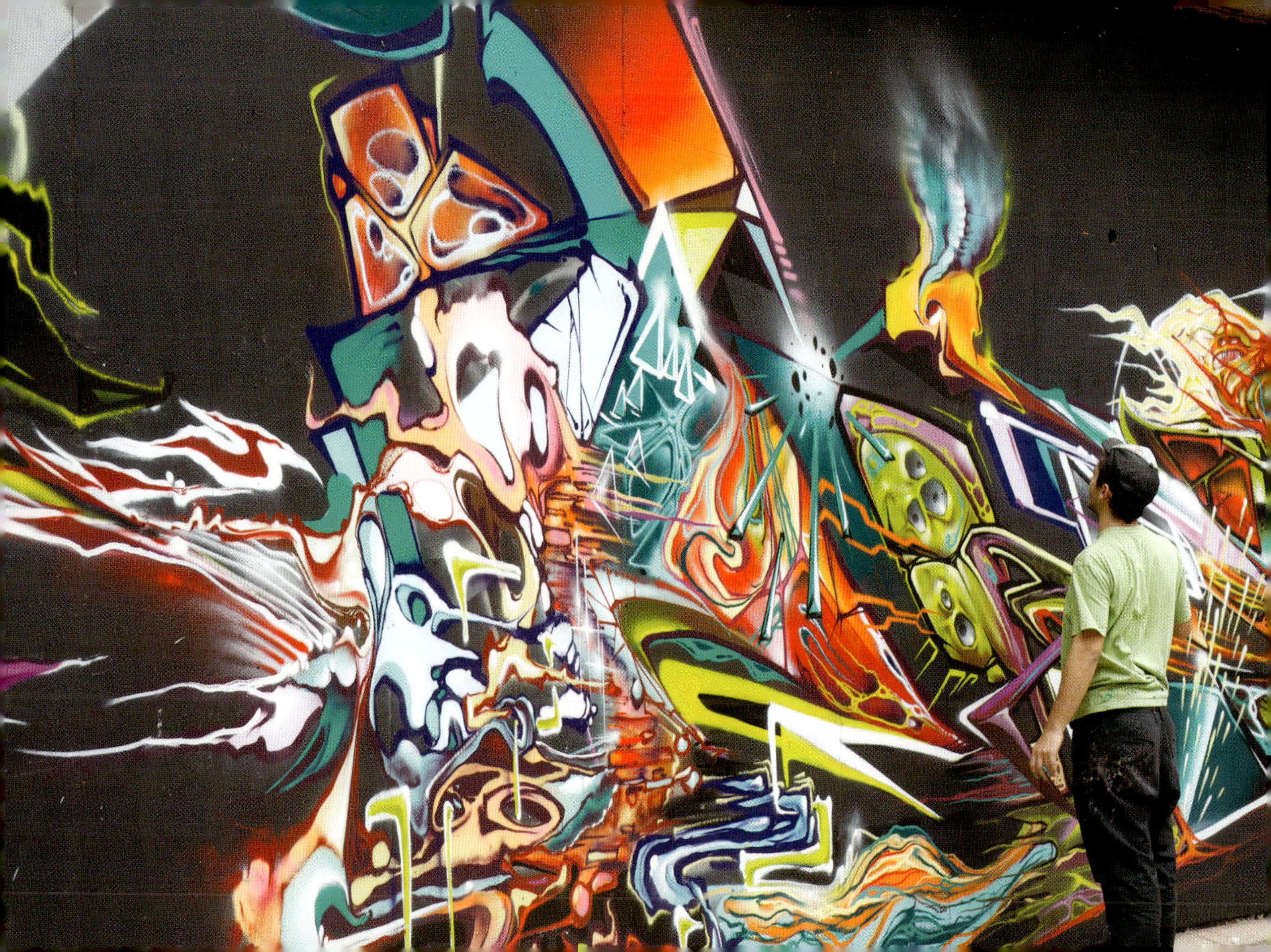

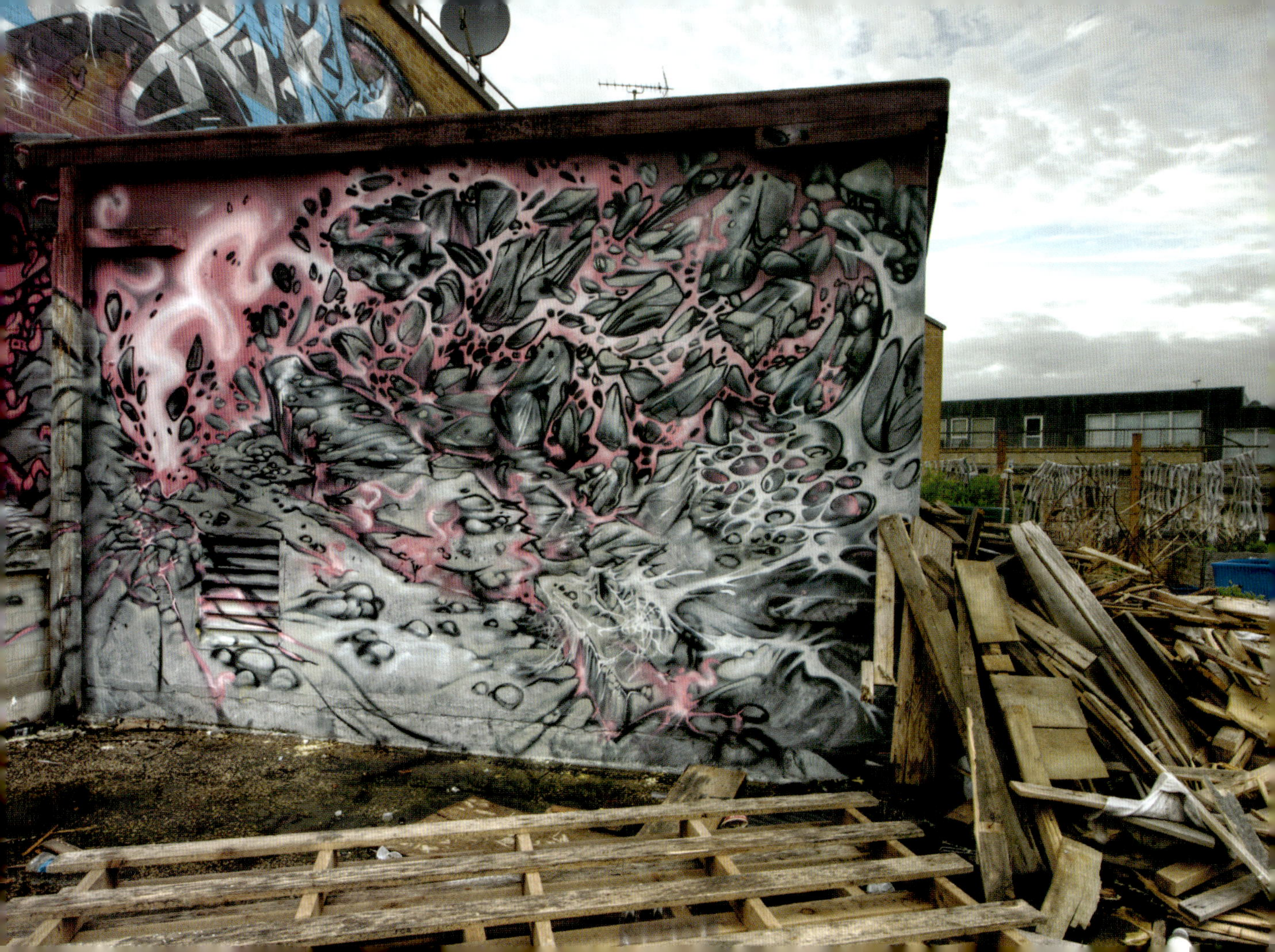

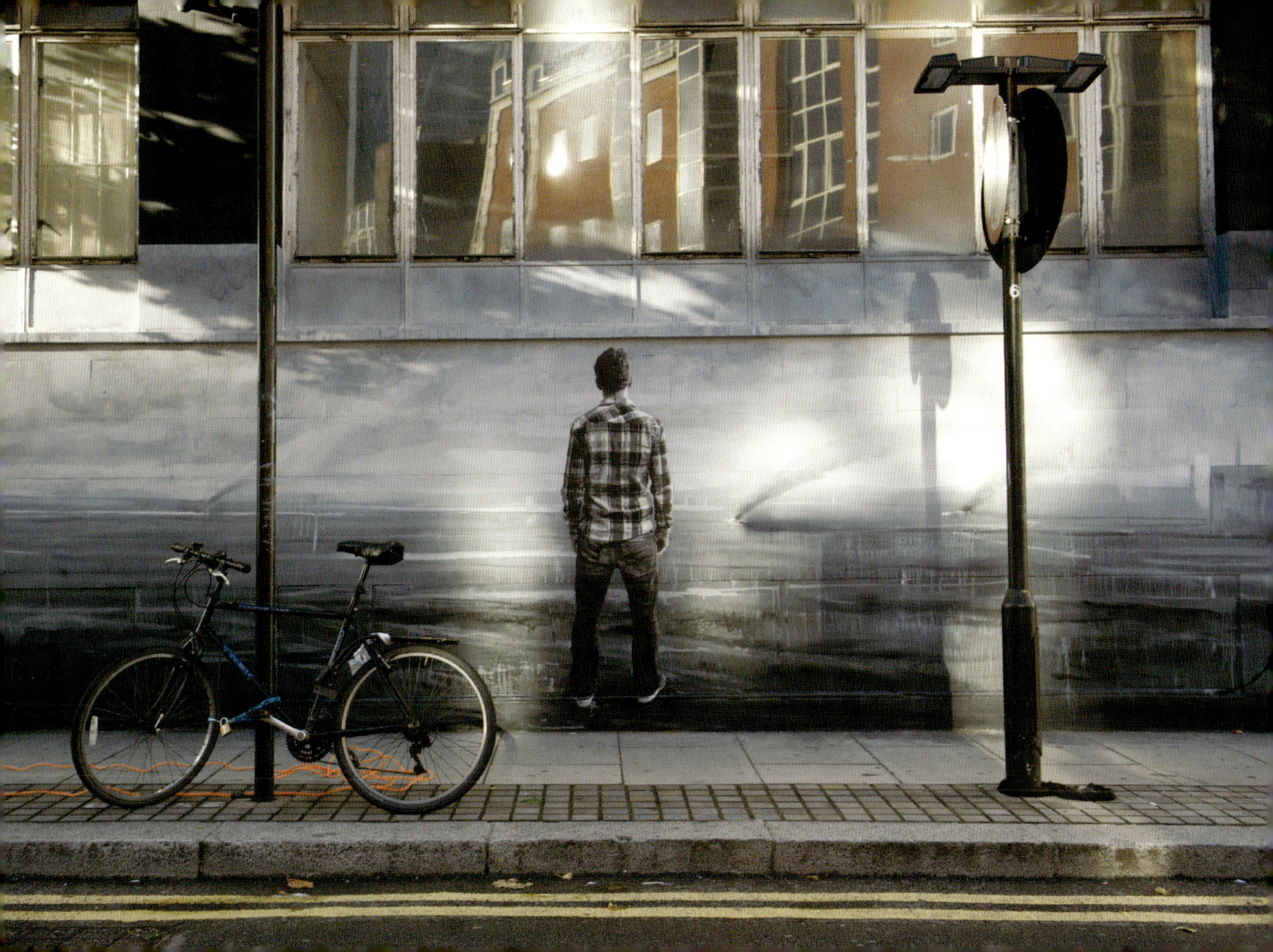

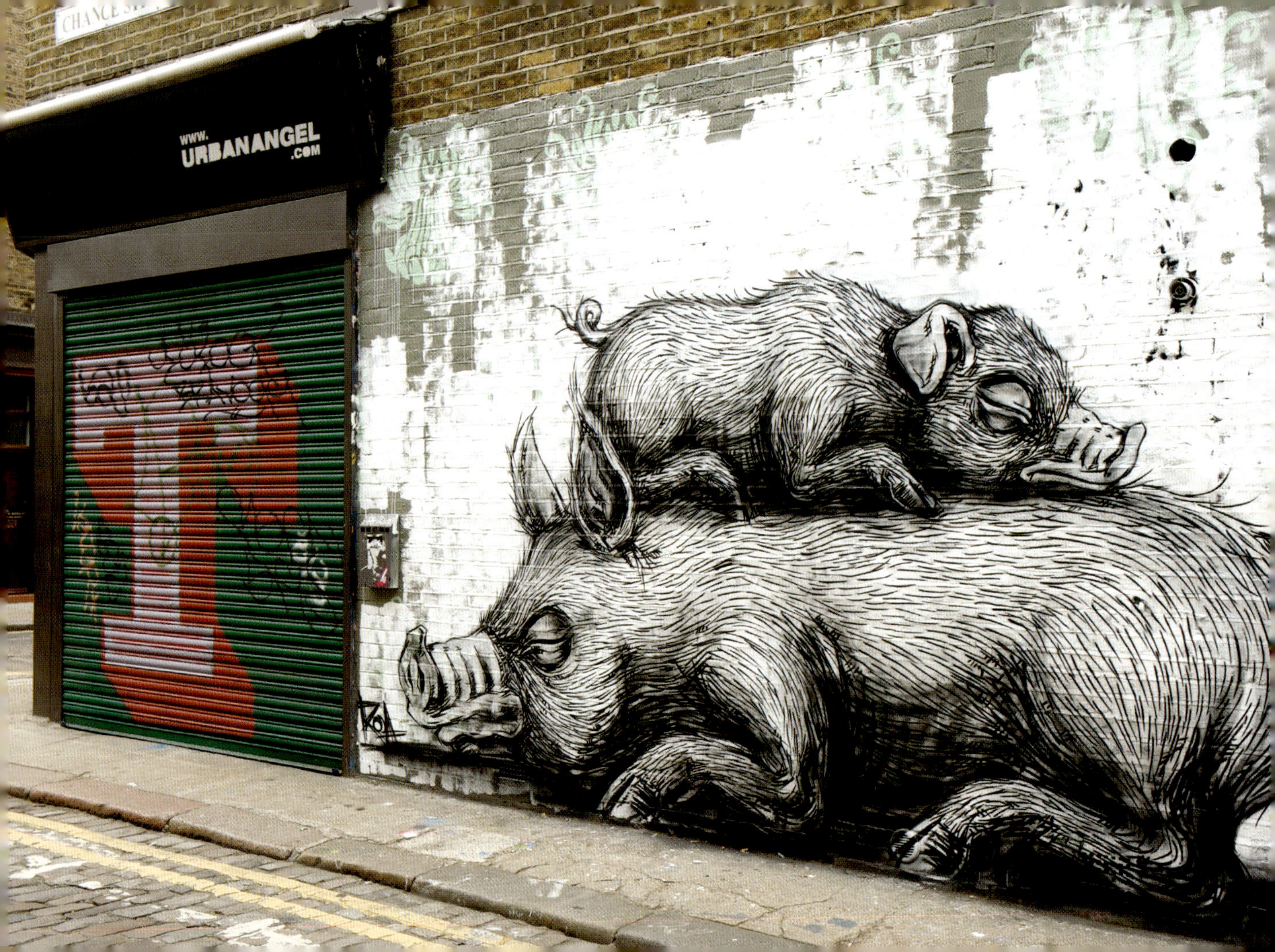
WWW.
URBANANGEL
.COM

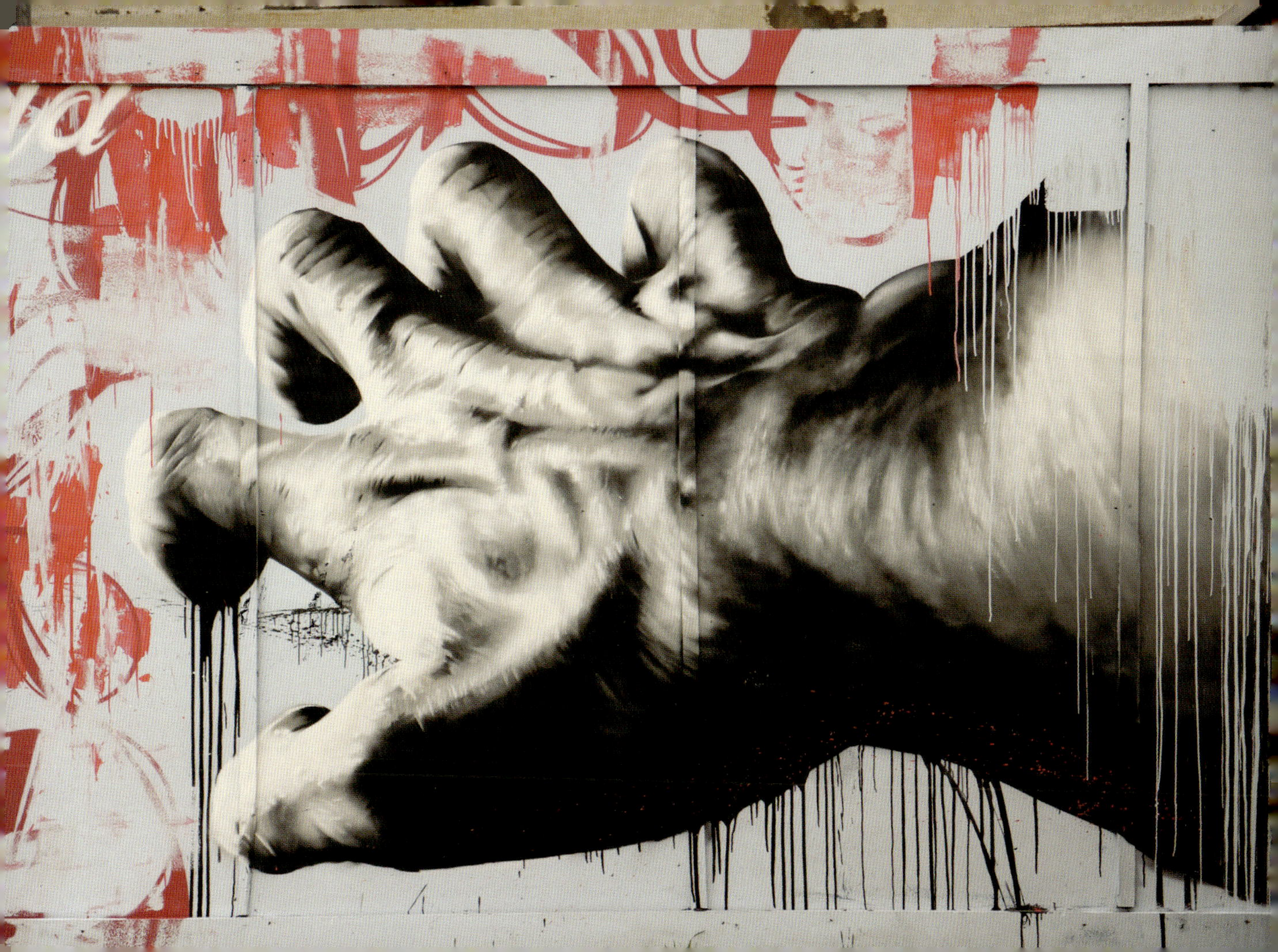

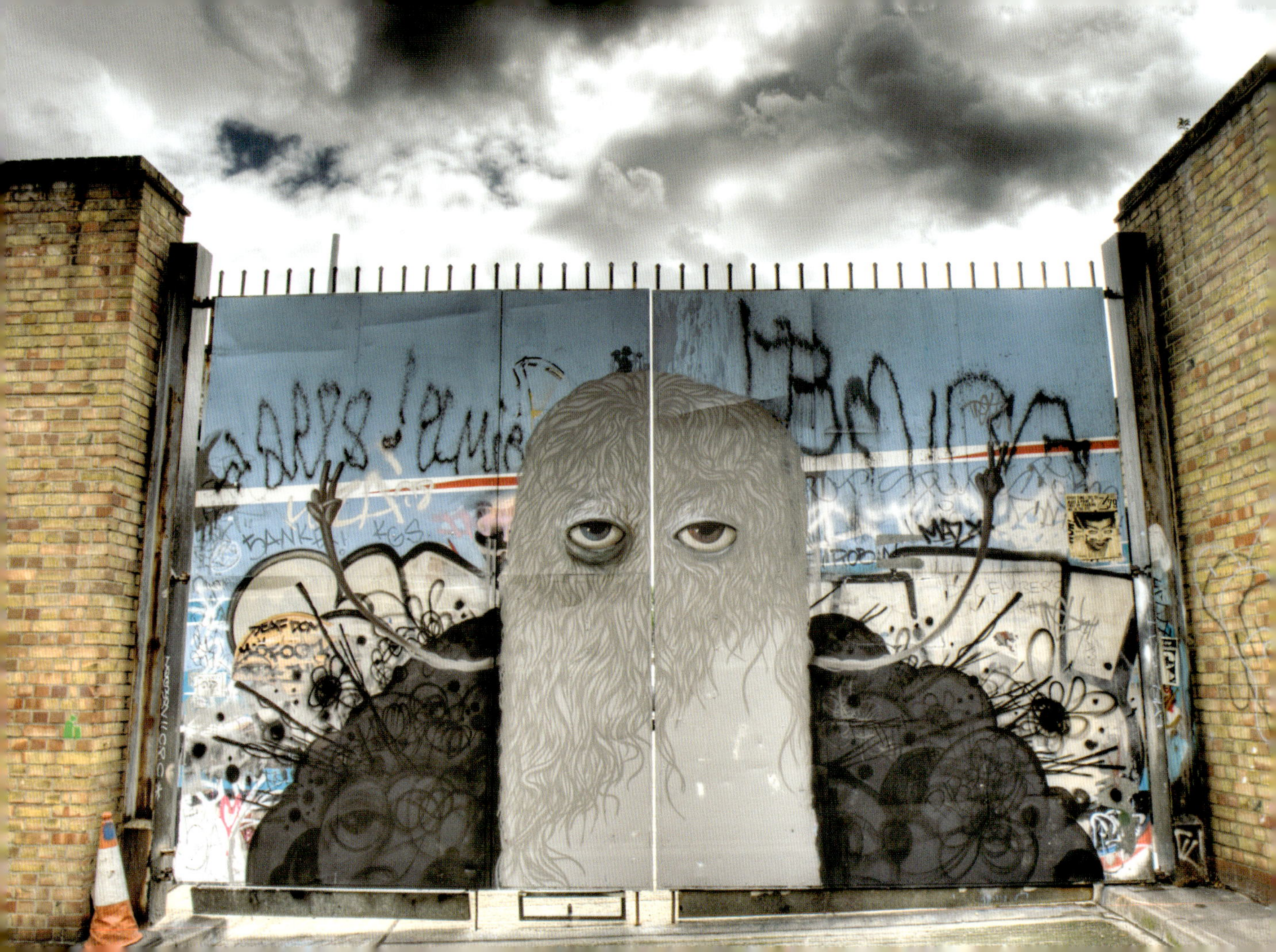

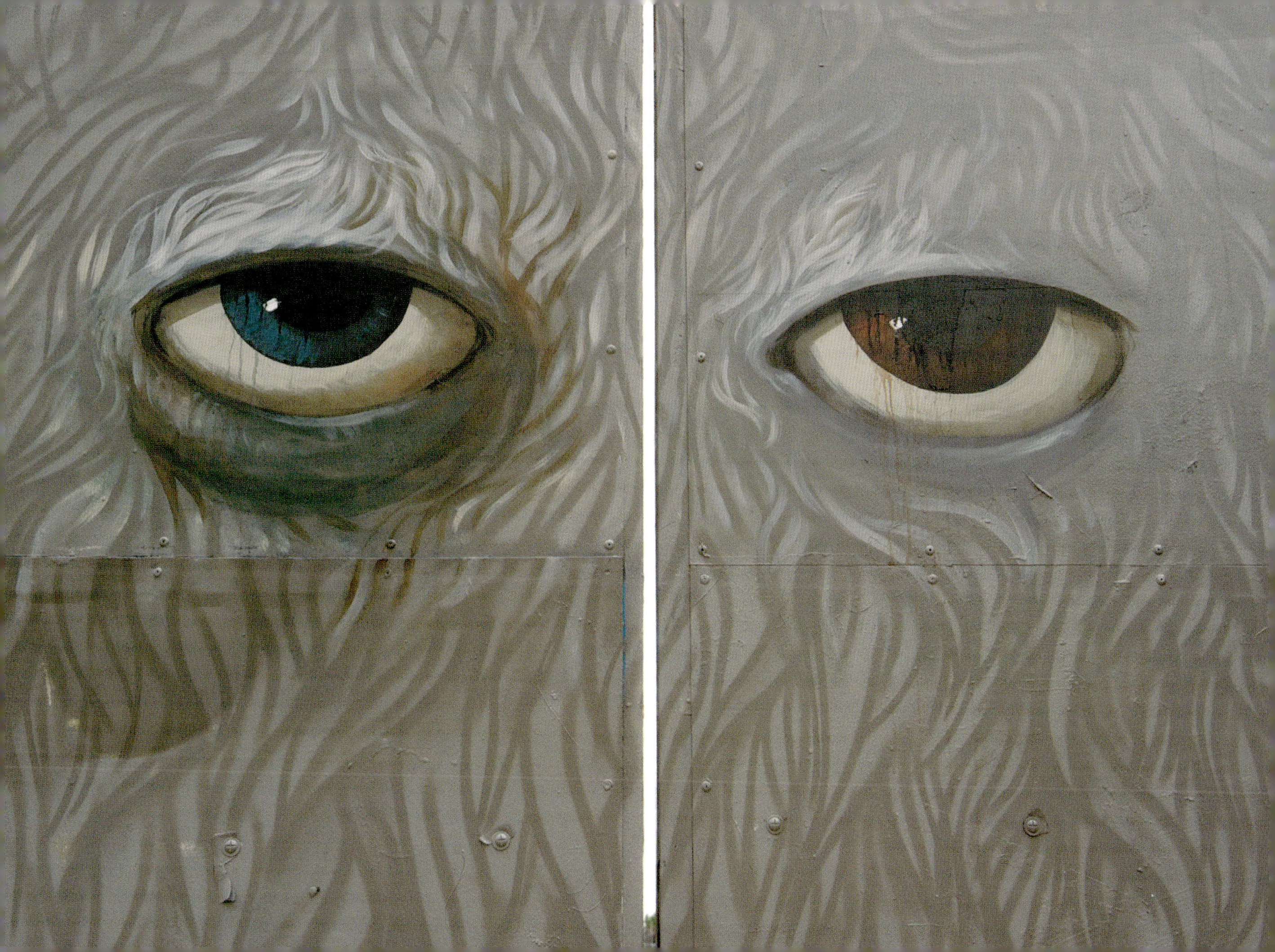

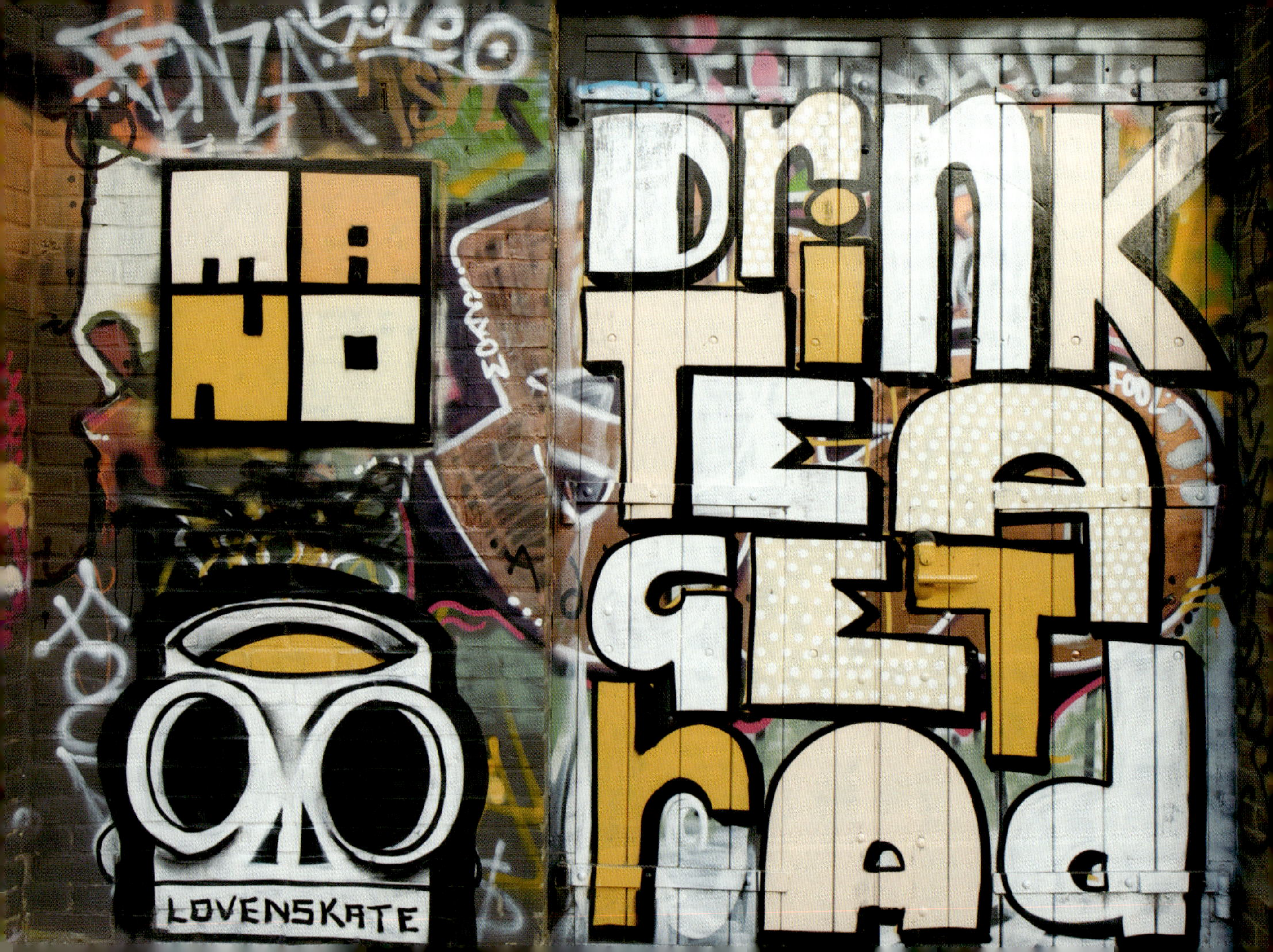
Drink Tea Get Rad
LOVENSKATE

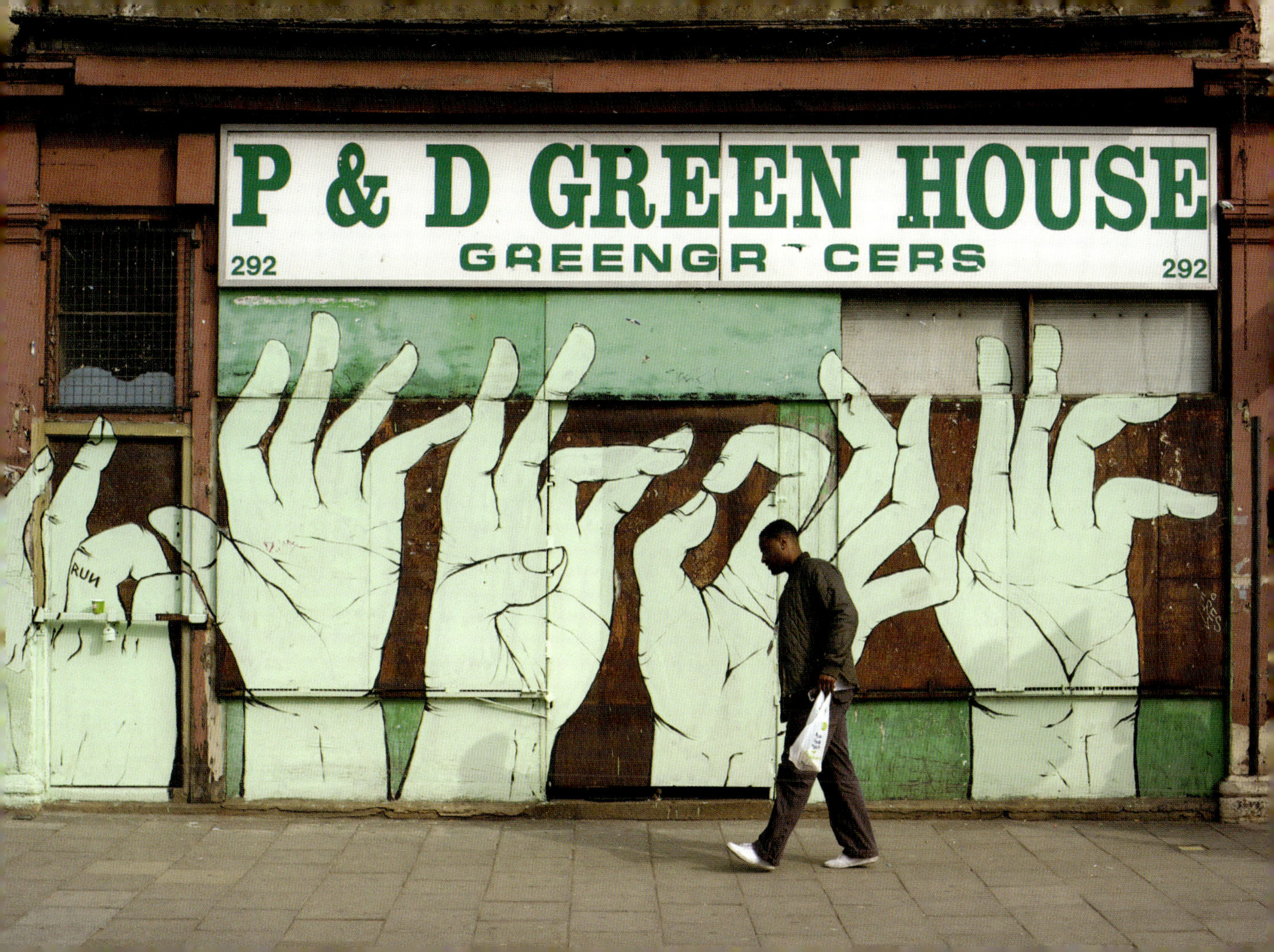
P & D GREEN HOUSE
GREENGR CERS
292
292
RUN

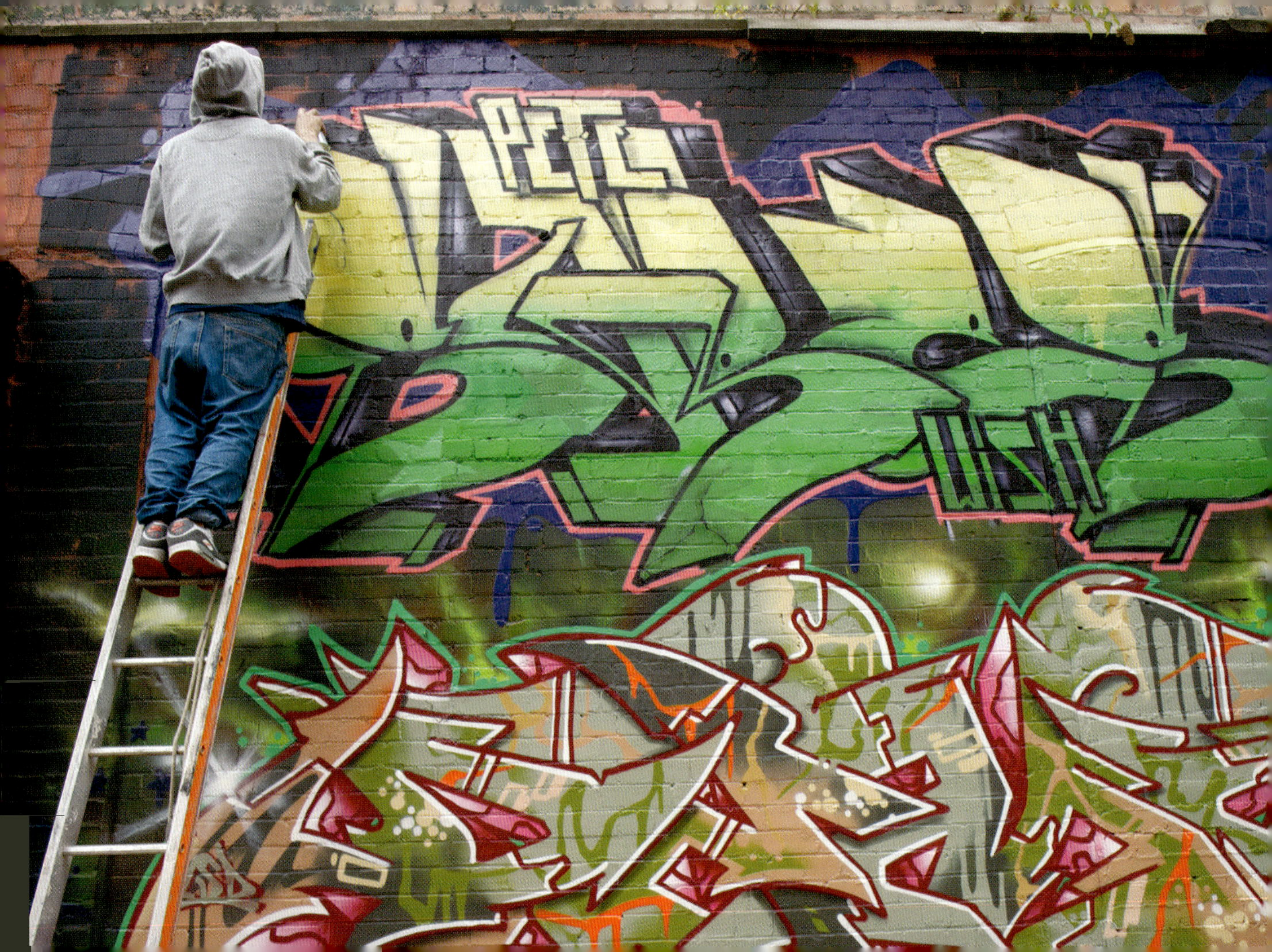

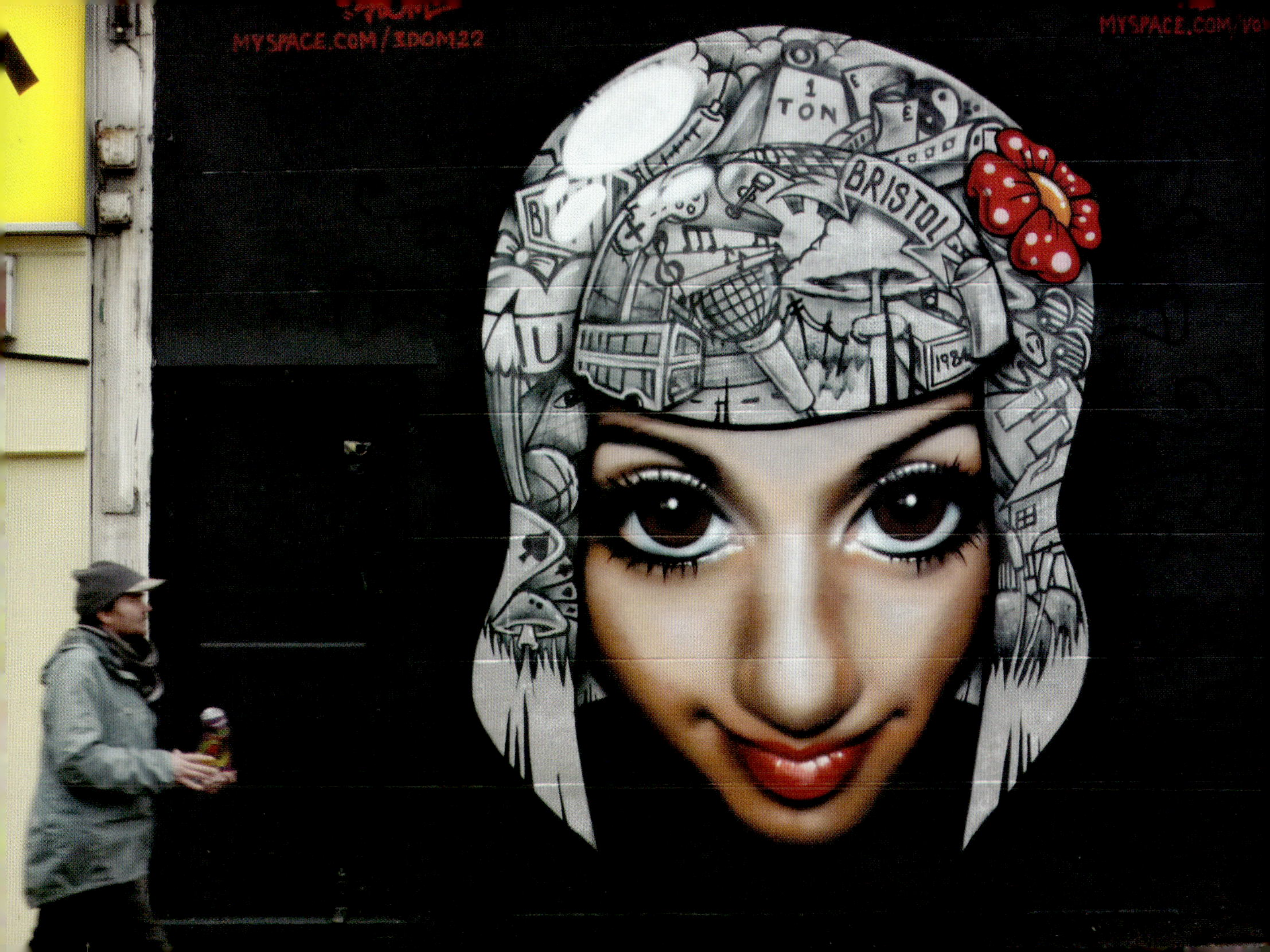
MYSPACE.COM/3DOM22
1 TON
BRISTOL

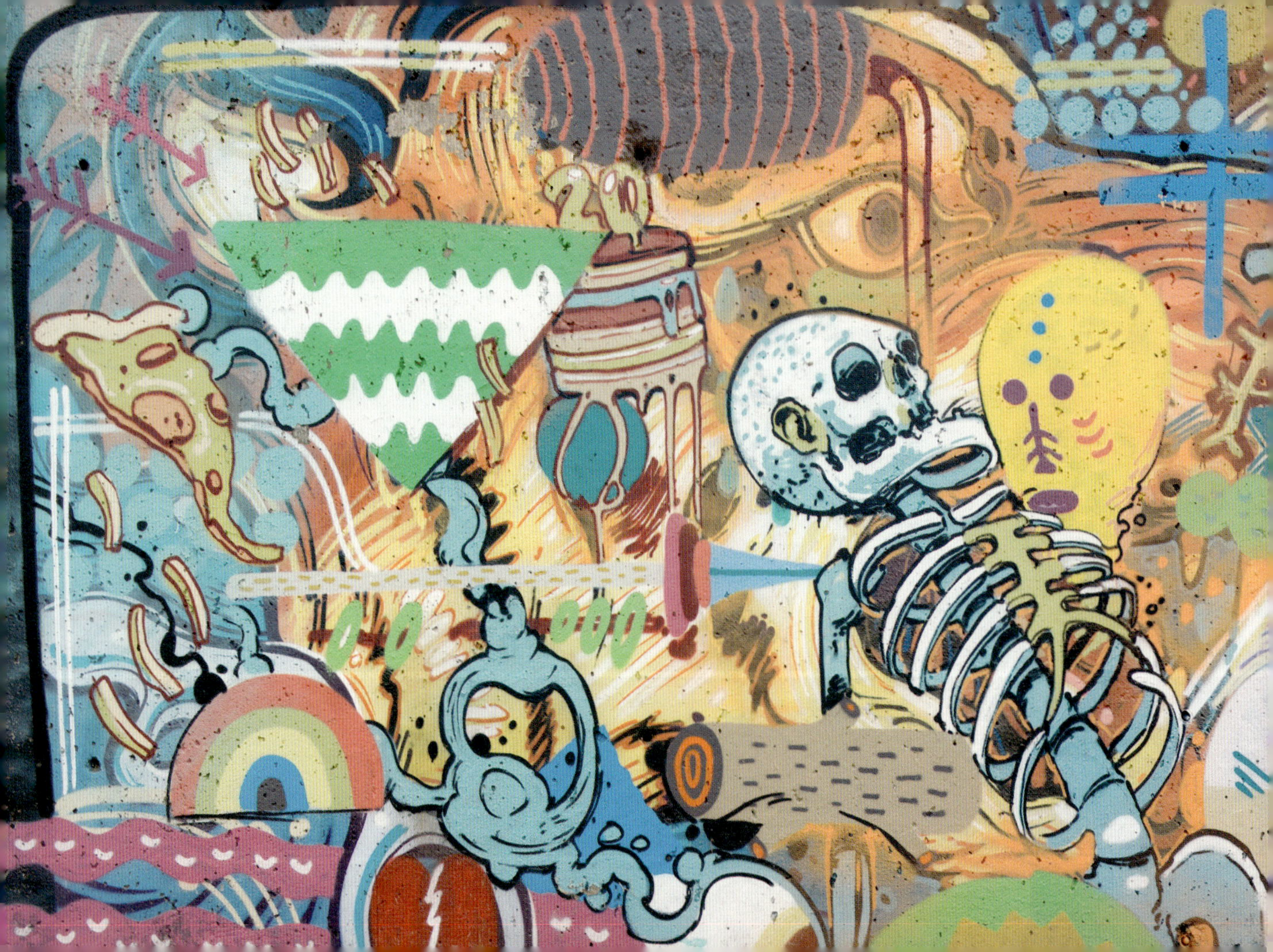

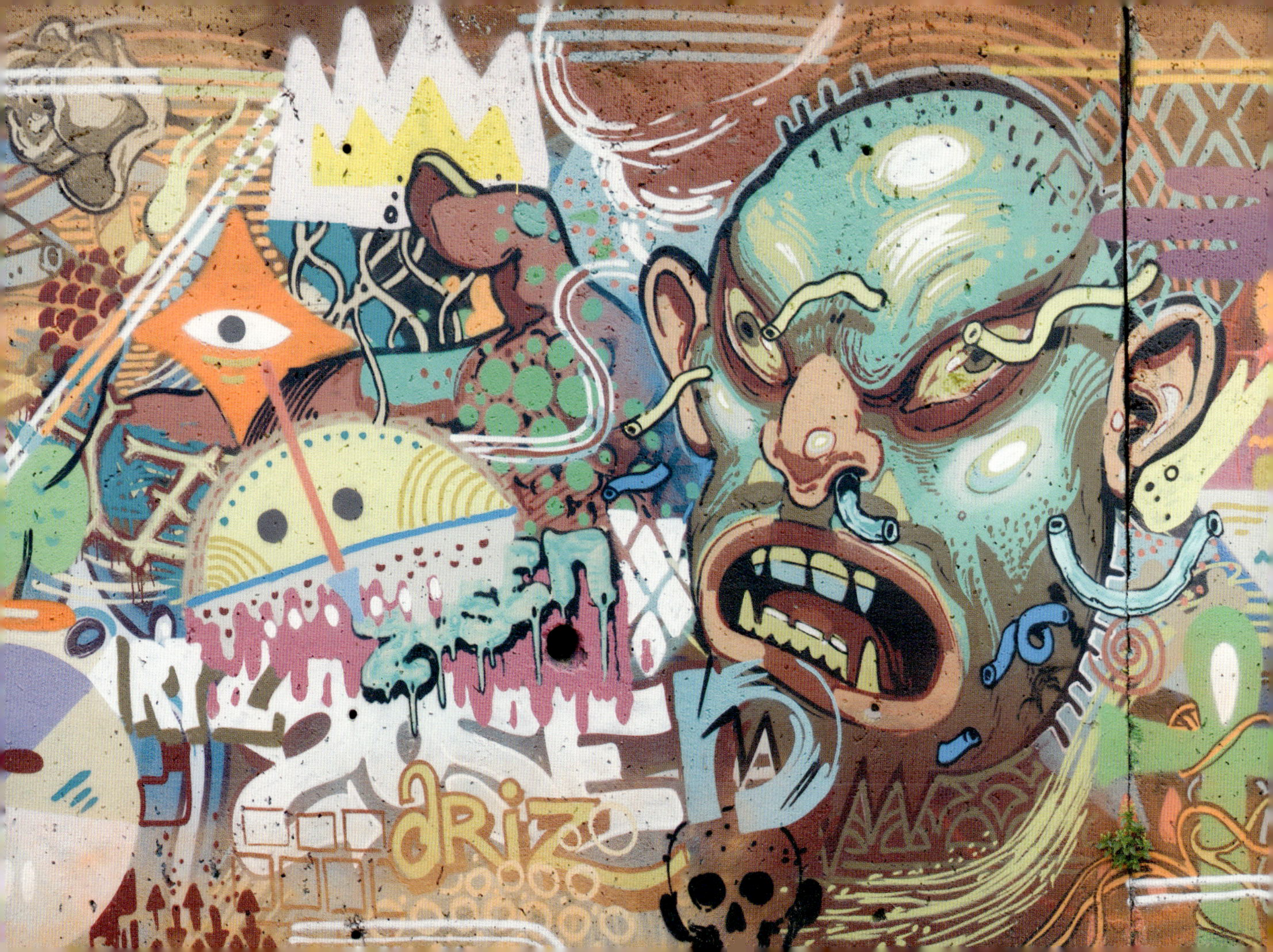
dRiZo

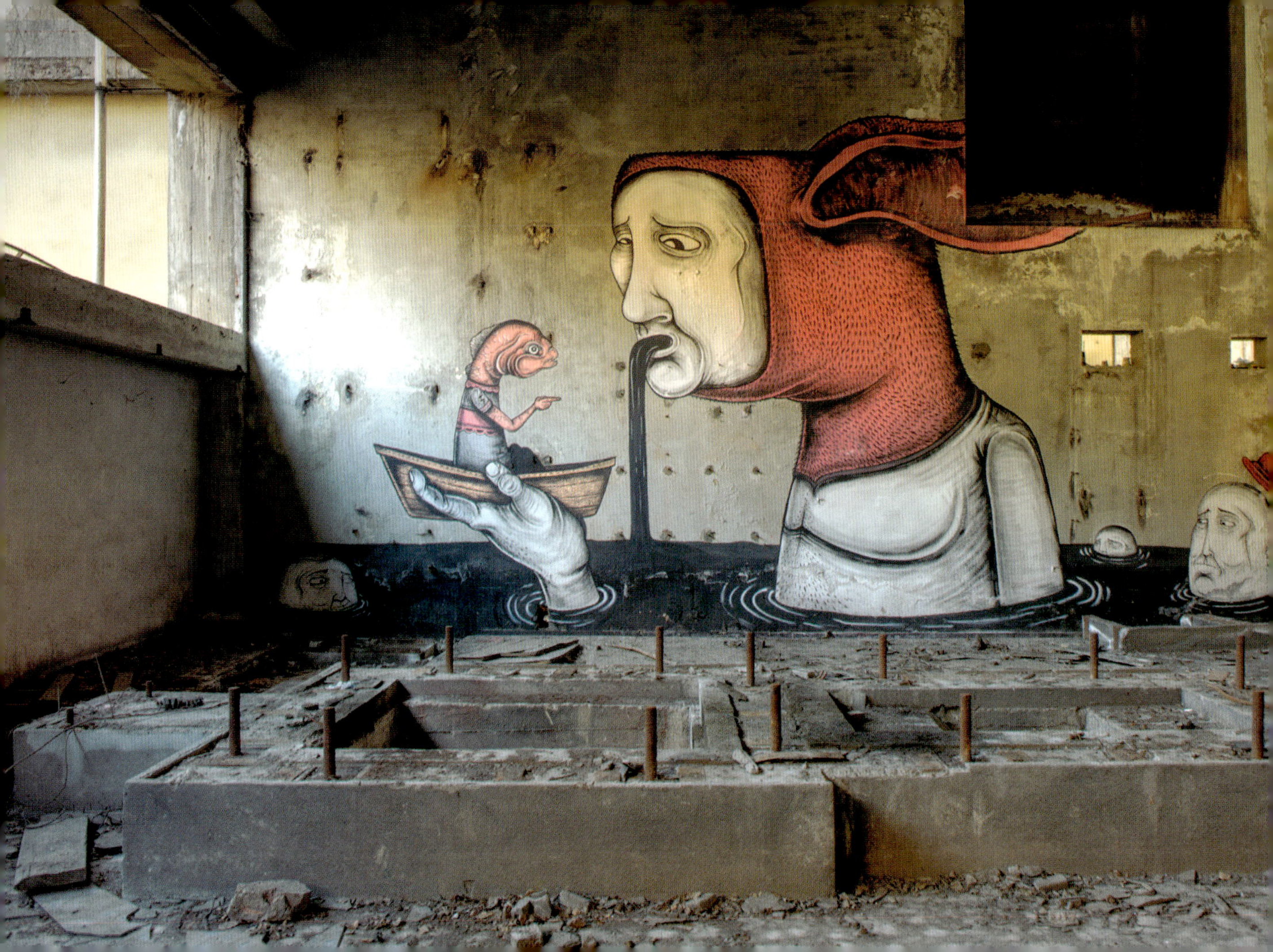

I've been doing street art mainly because I started out with graffiti. It is something that comes naturally to me. I do happen to do some art works for galleries and others, although I always go back to the street as if it were a sort of a love-hate relationship.

The street itself is indeed a gallery - for better or for worse - it gives everyone a chance to see and value one's work. Most of all though, you don't need to either send out invites to people or be on a guest list or be recommended to come enjoy street art!

SEA

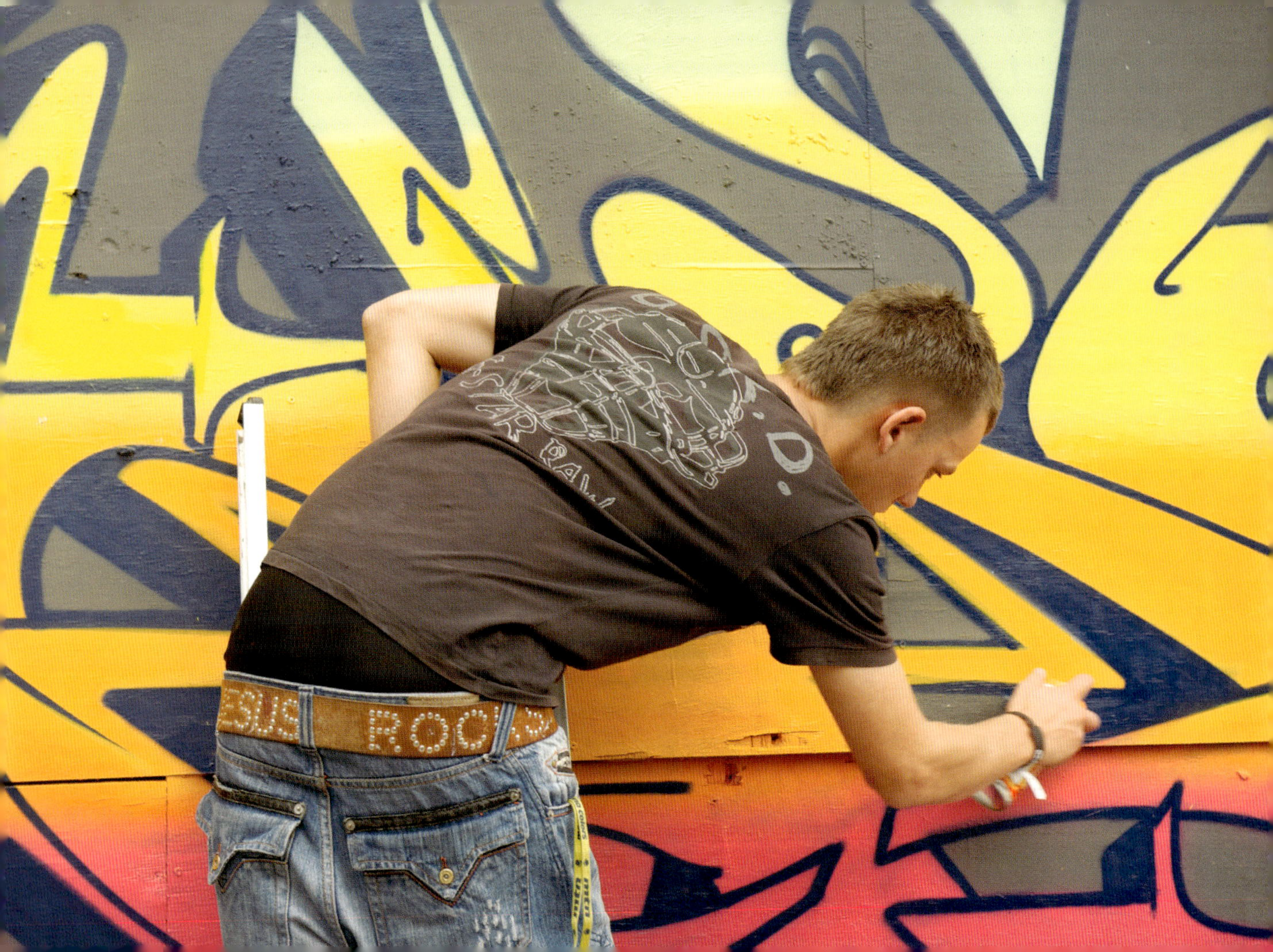
ESUS ROCK

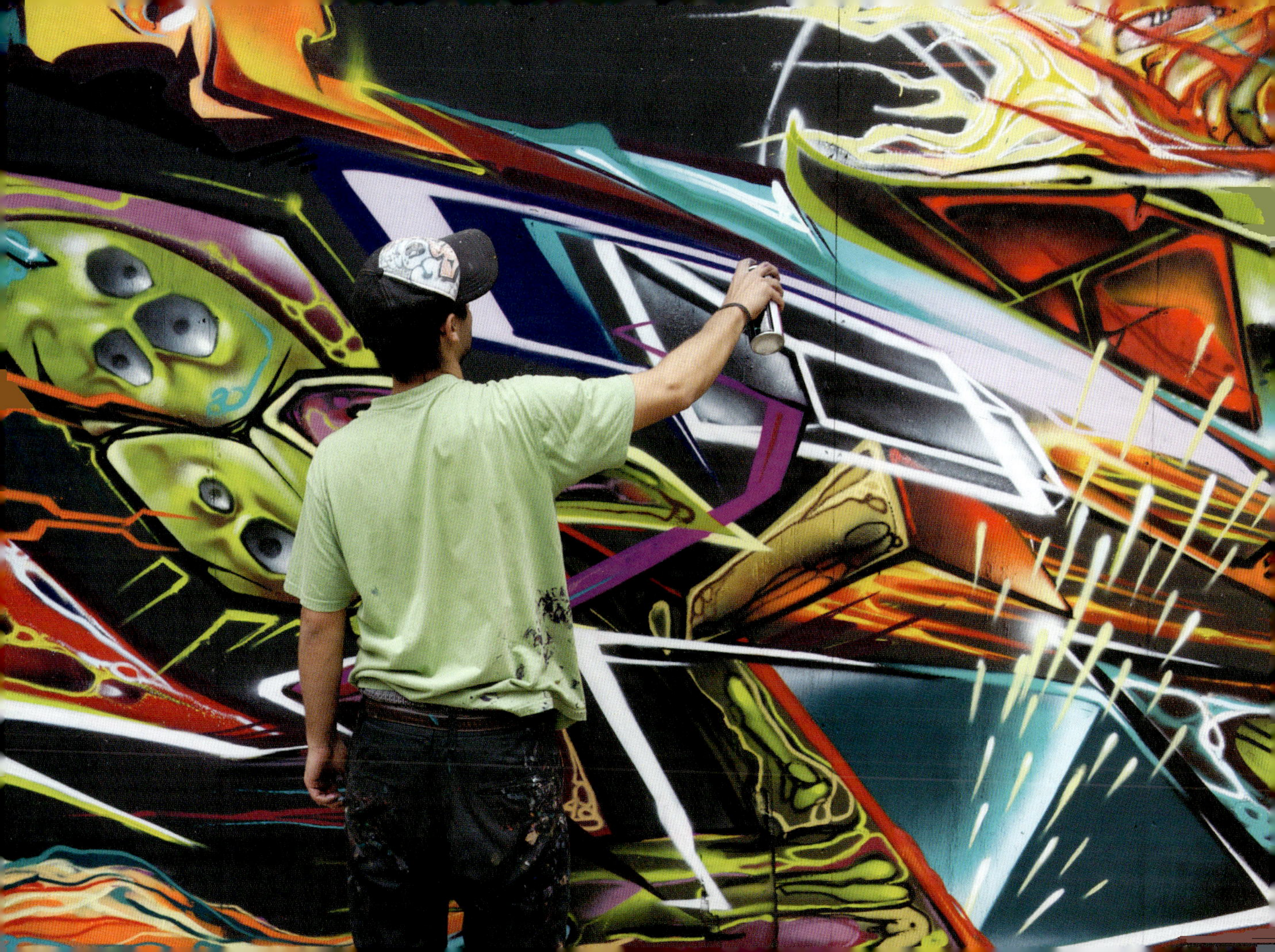

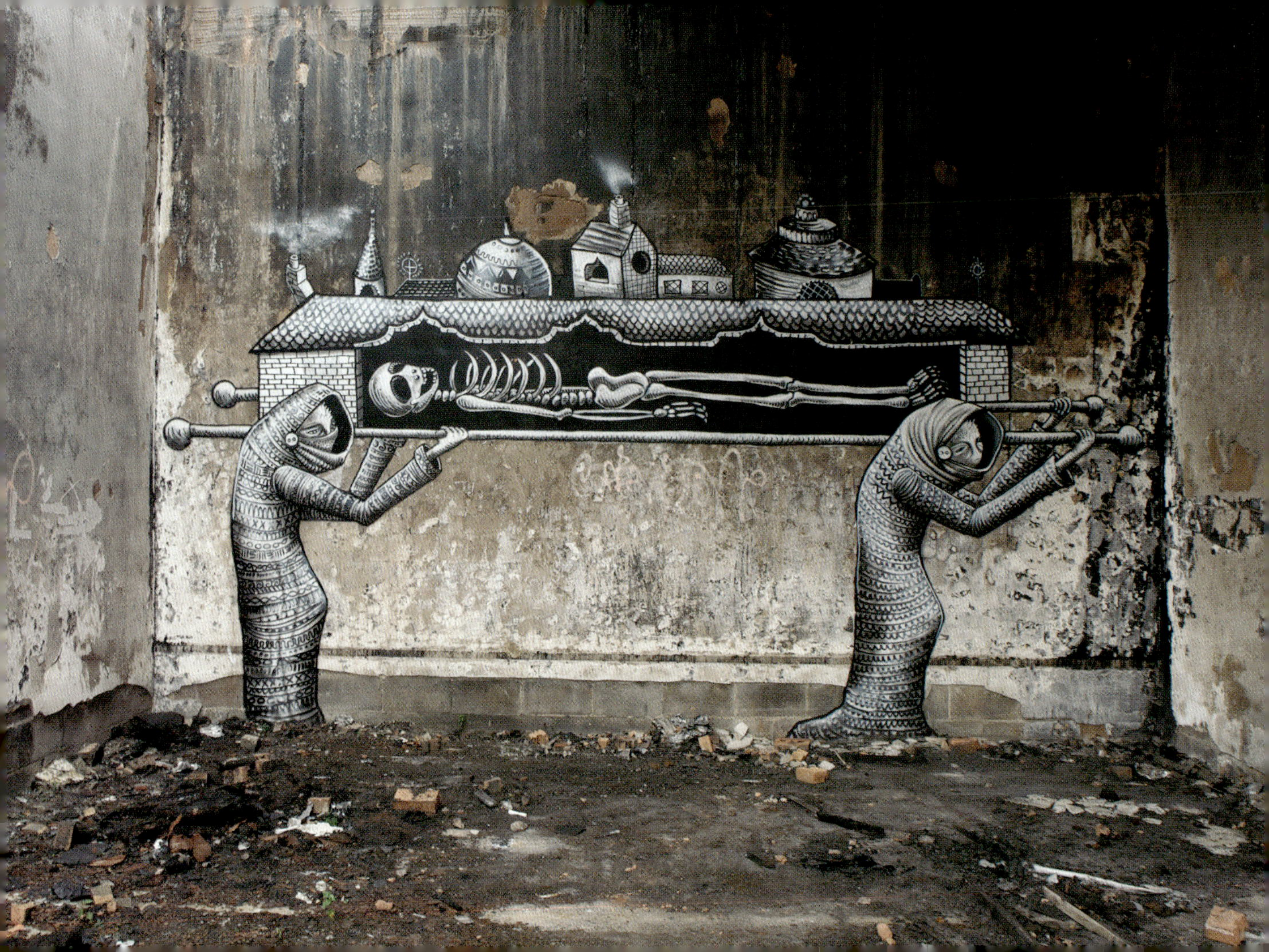

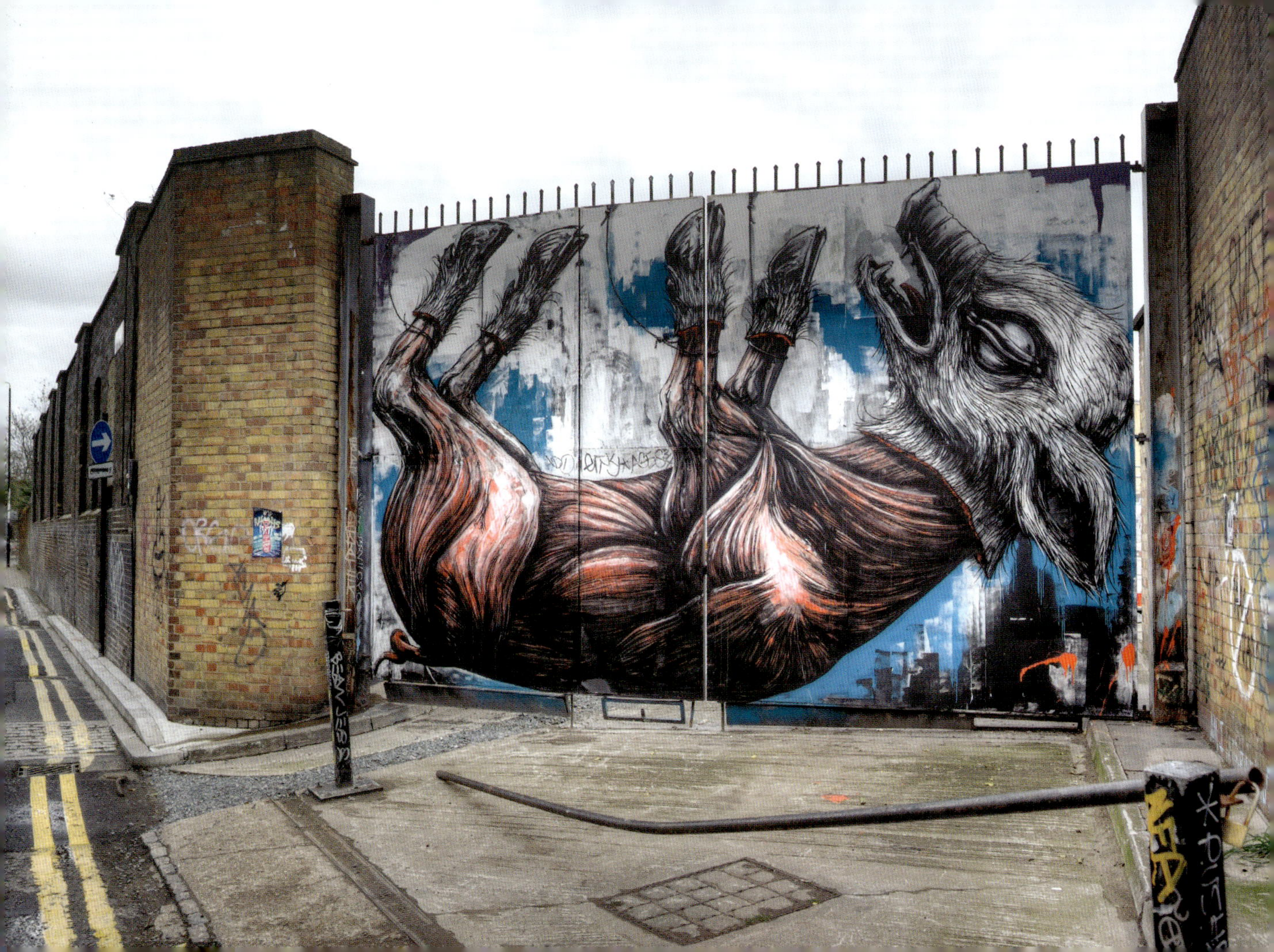

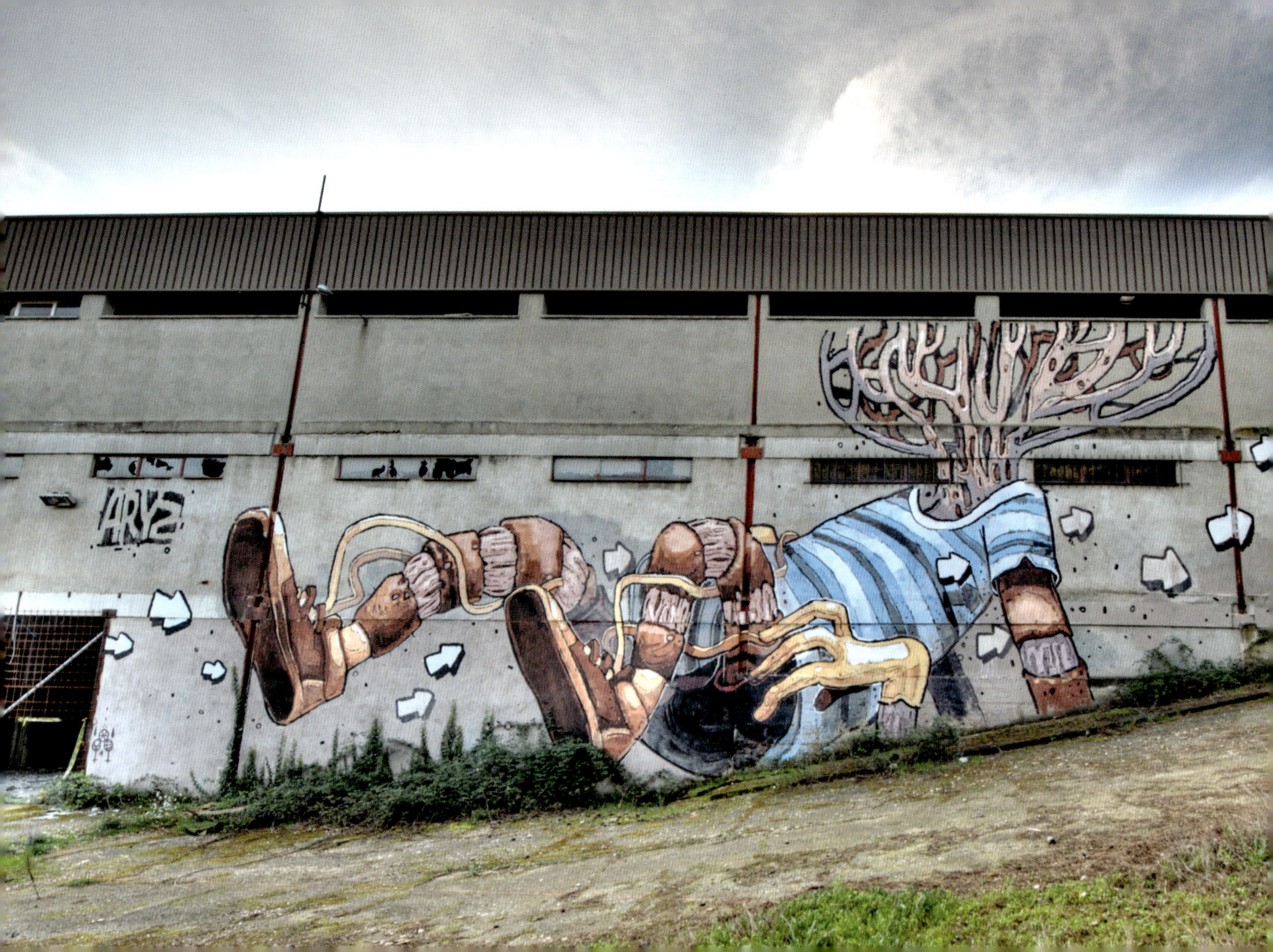
ARYZ

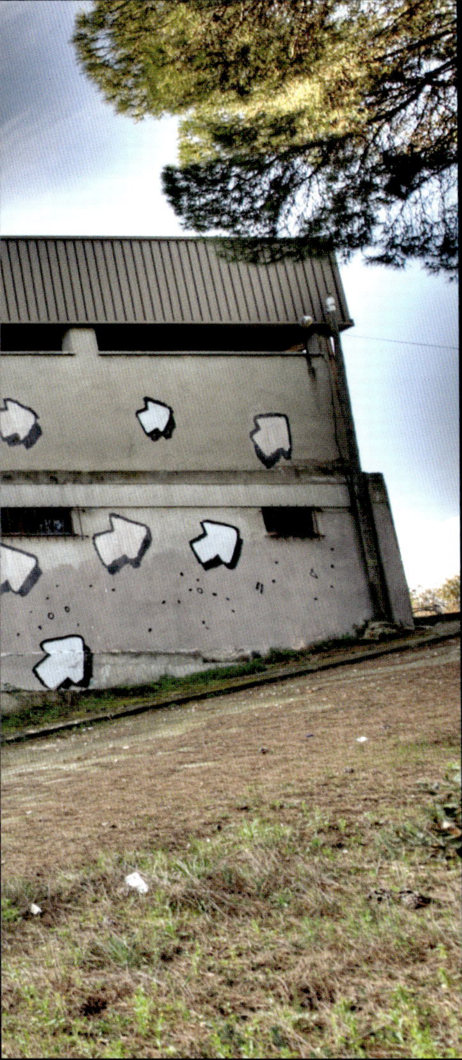

When you stop to think, it's both sad and poetic that these routine spaces, where people worked their whole lives, are now empty....giving us space where we can create

ARYZ

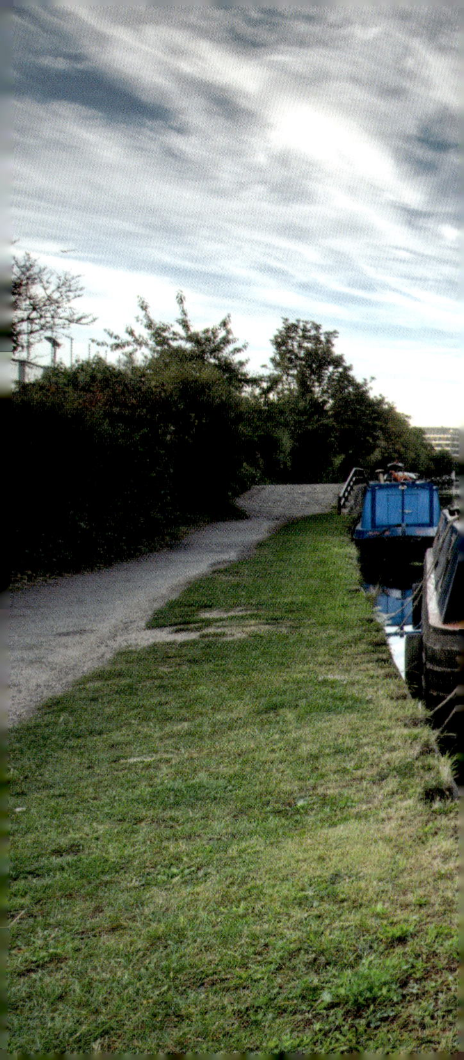

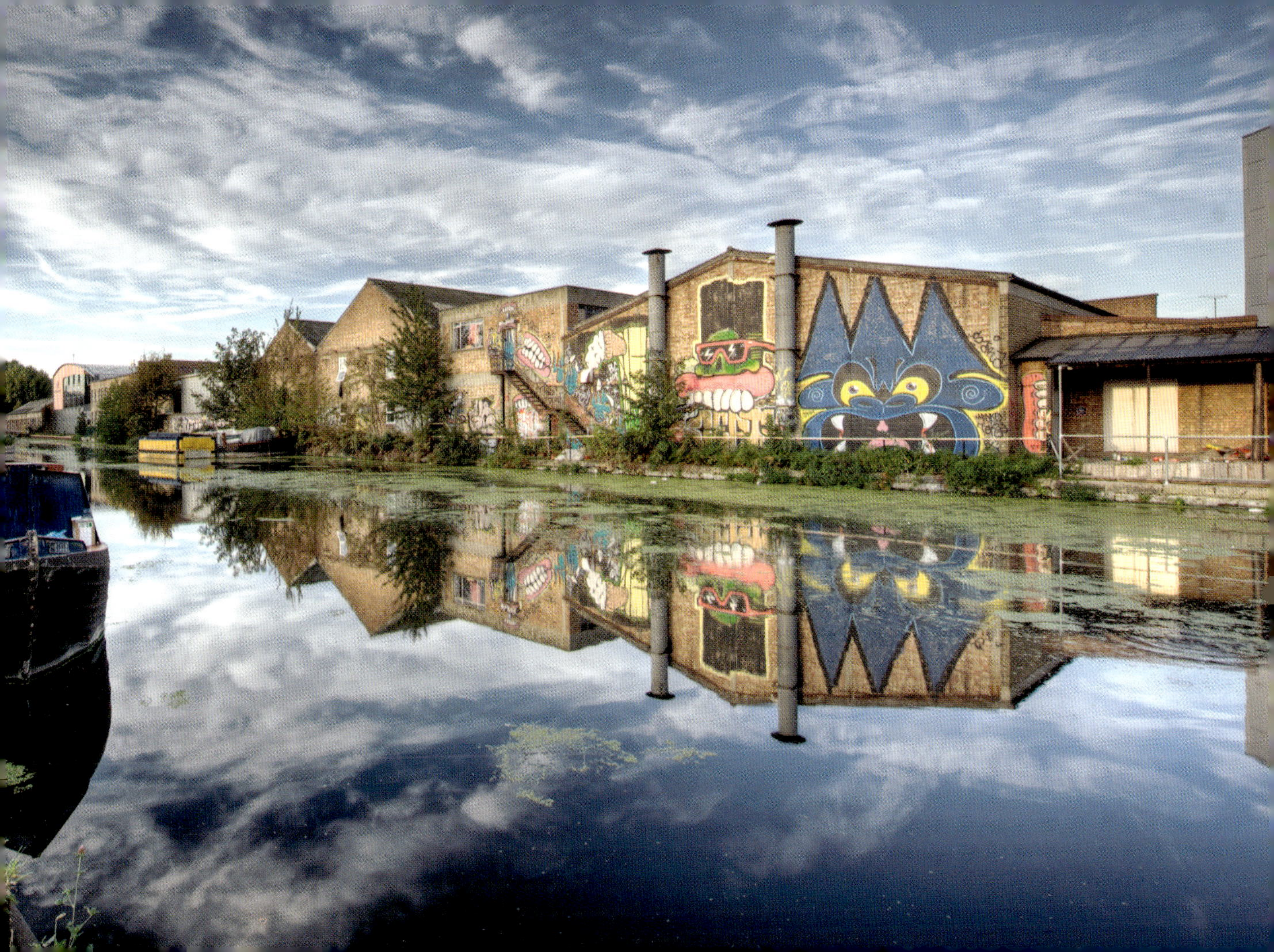

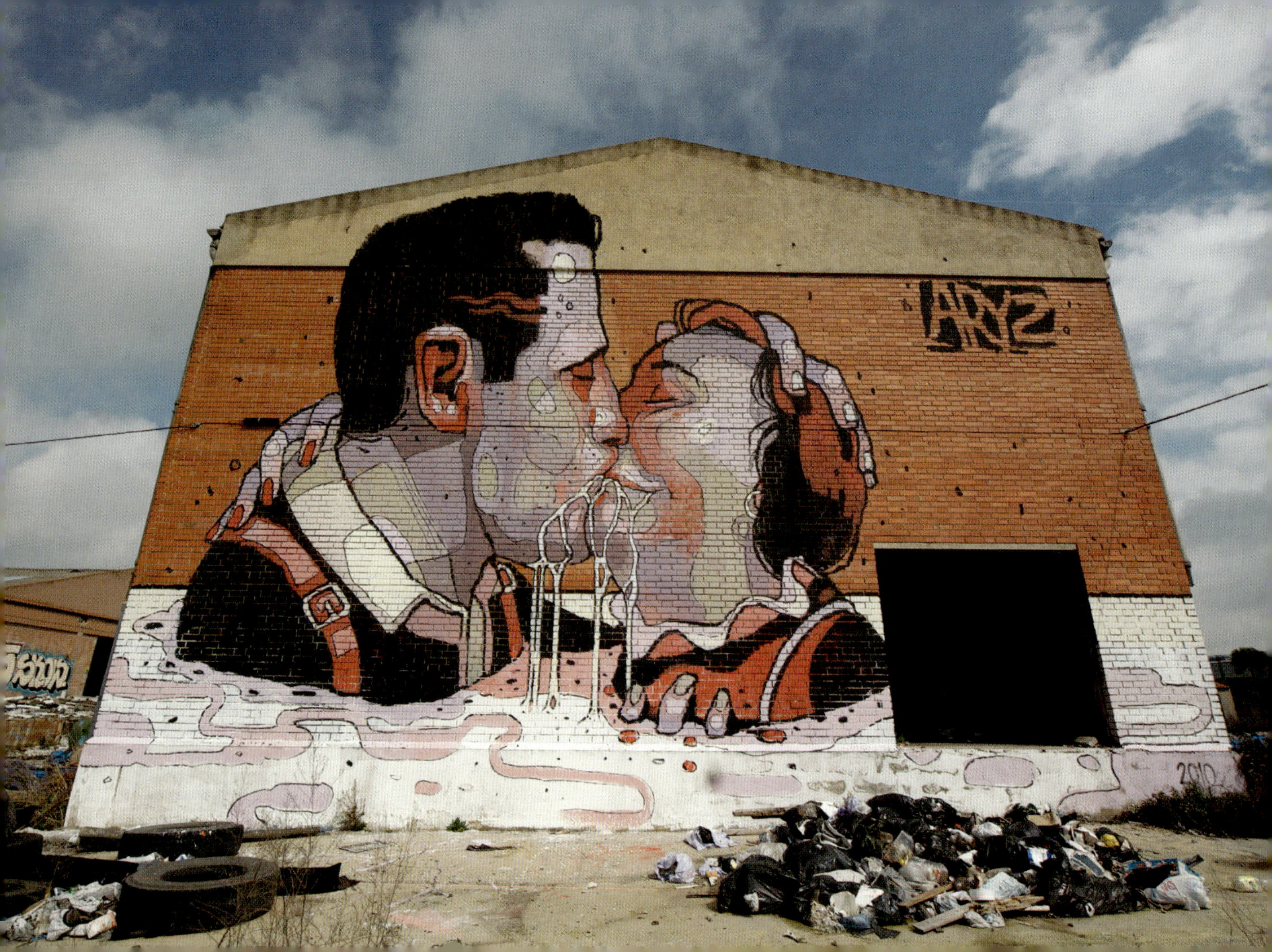
2010

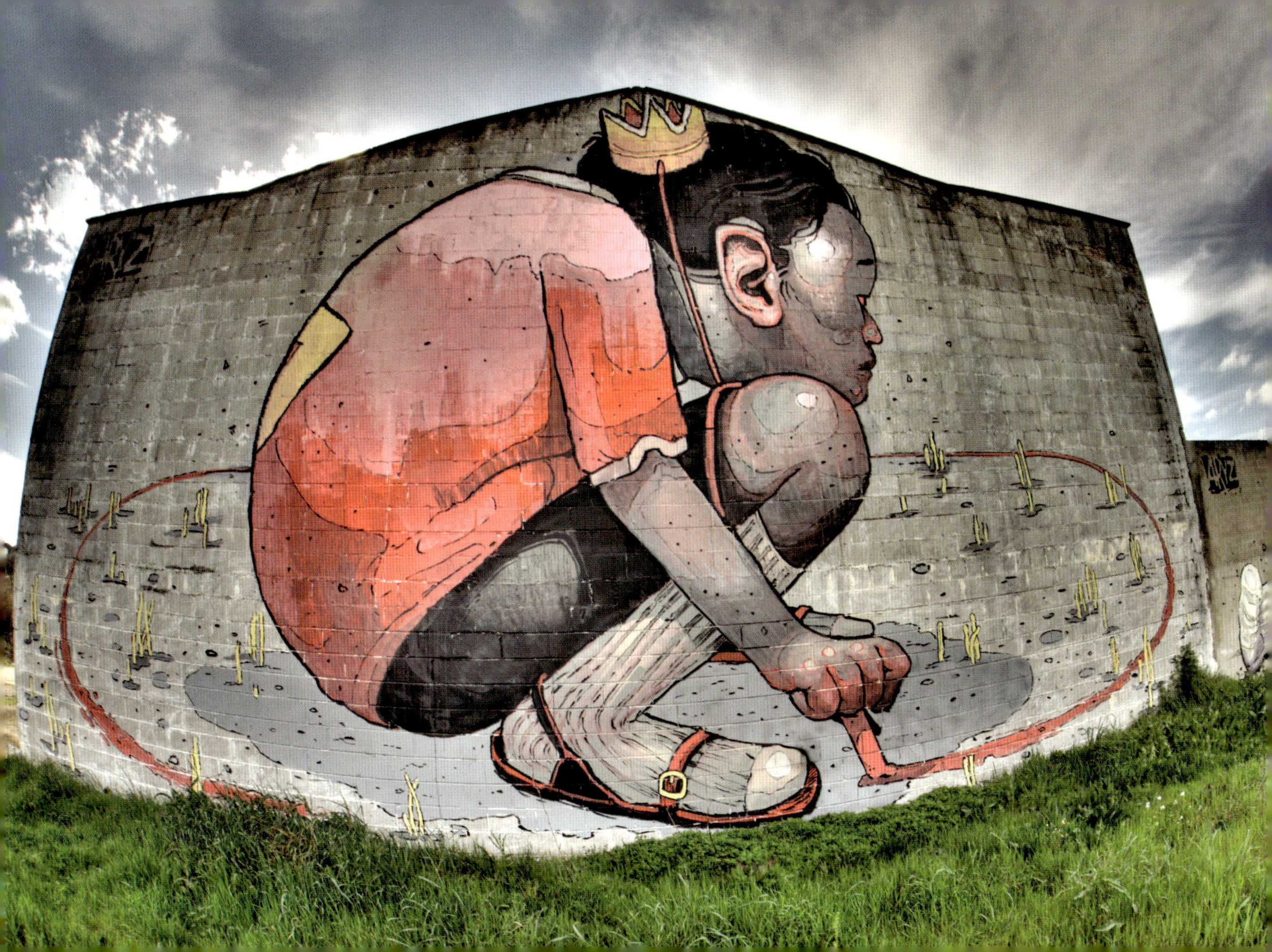

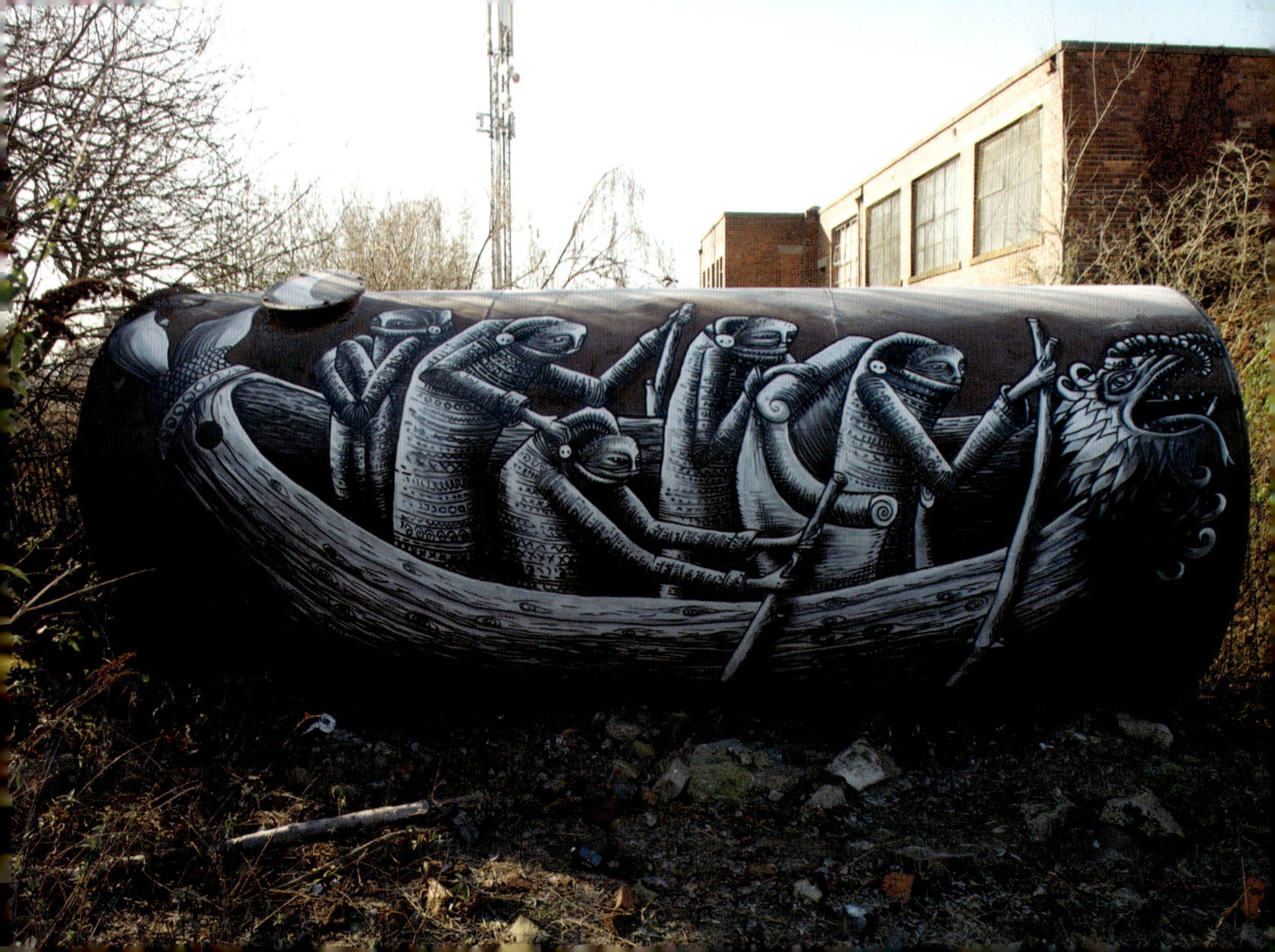

I don't want my painting to be important; I like it to remain ephemeral and unobtrusive.

PHLEGM

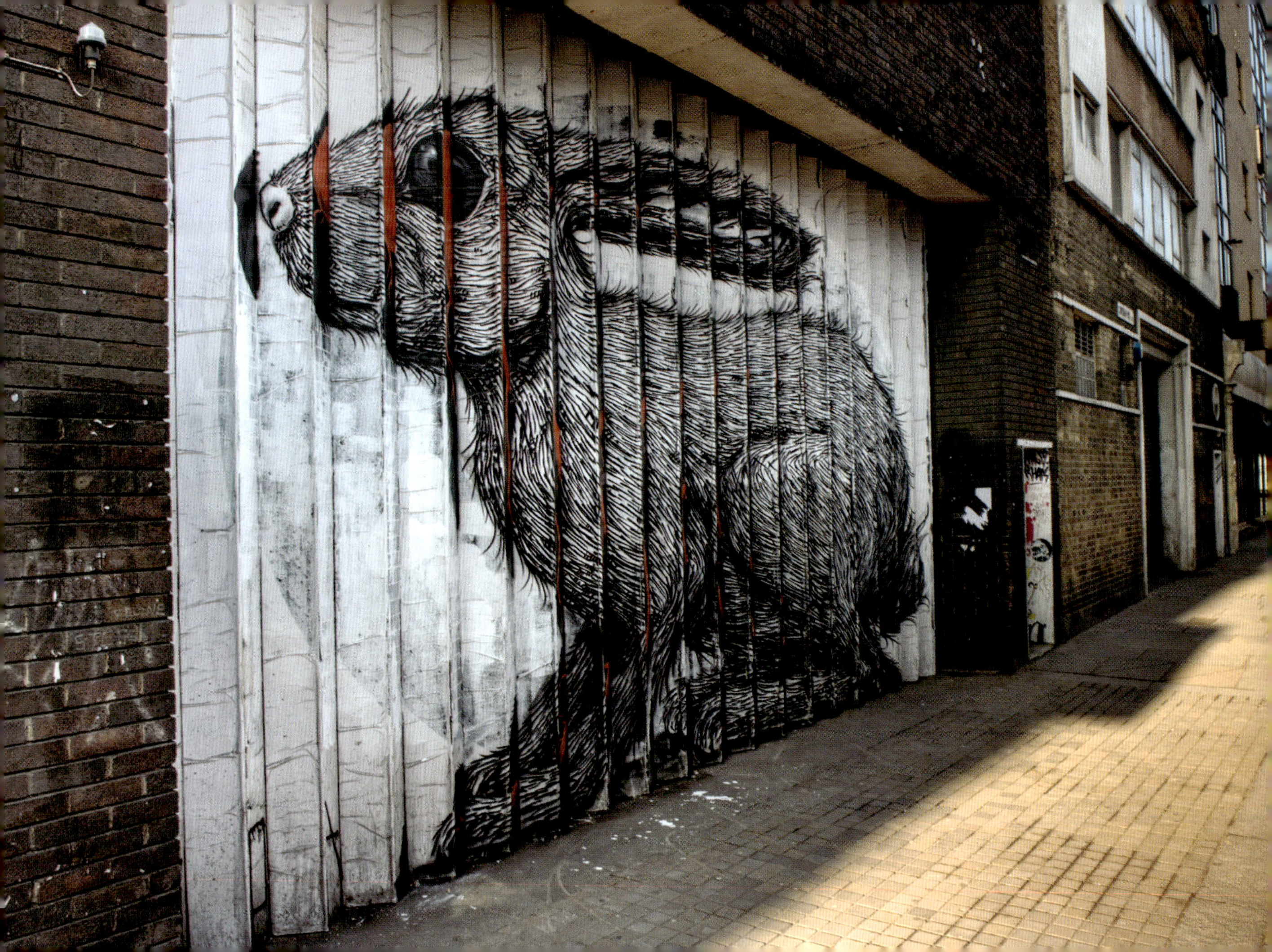

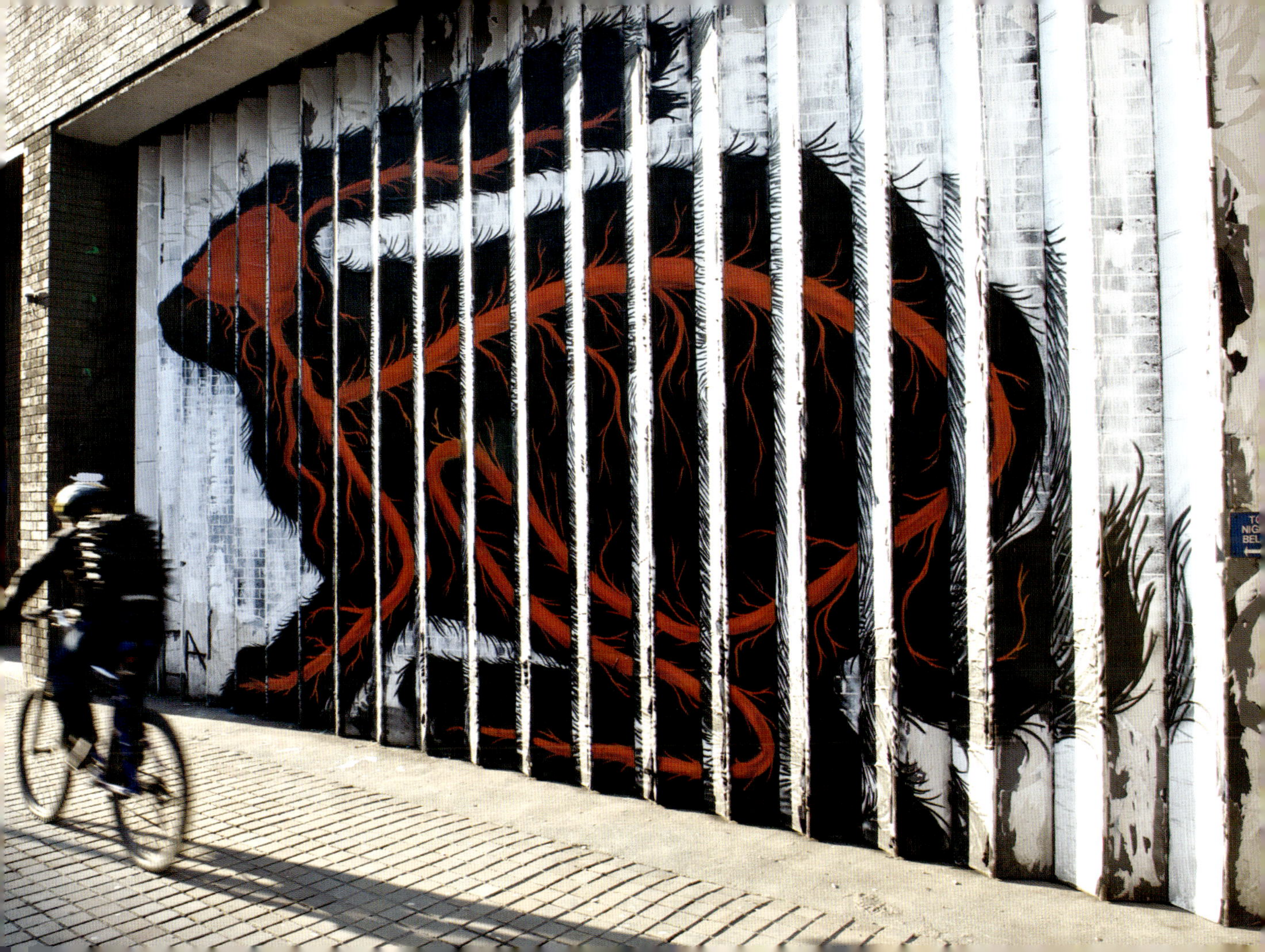

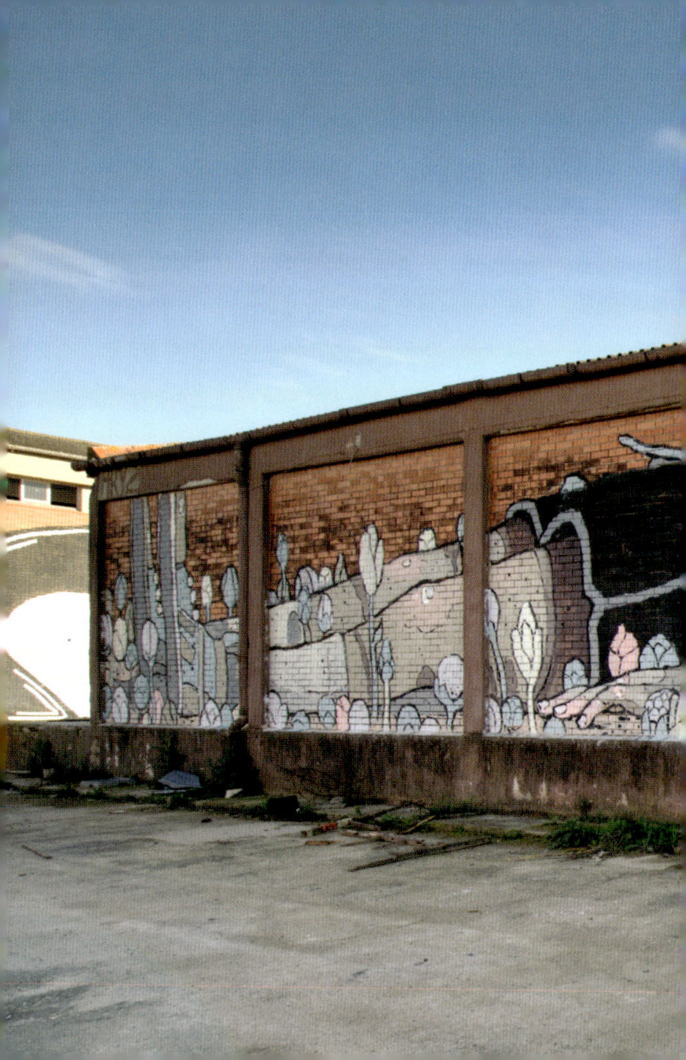

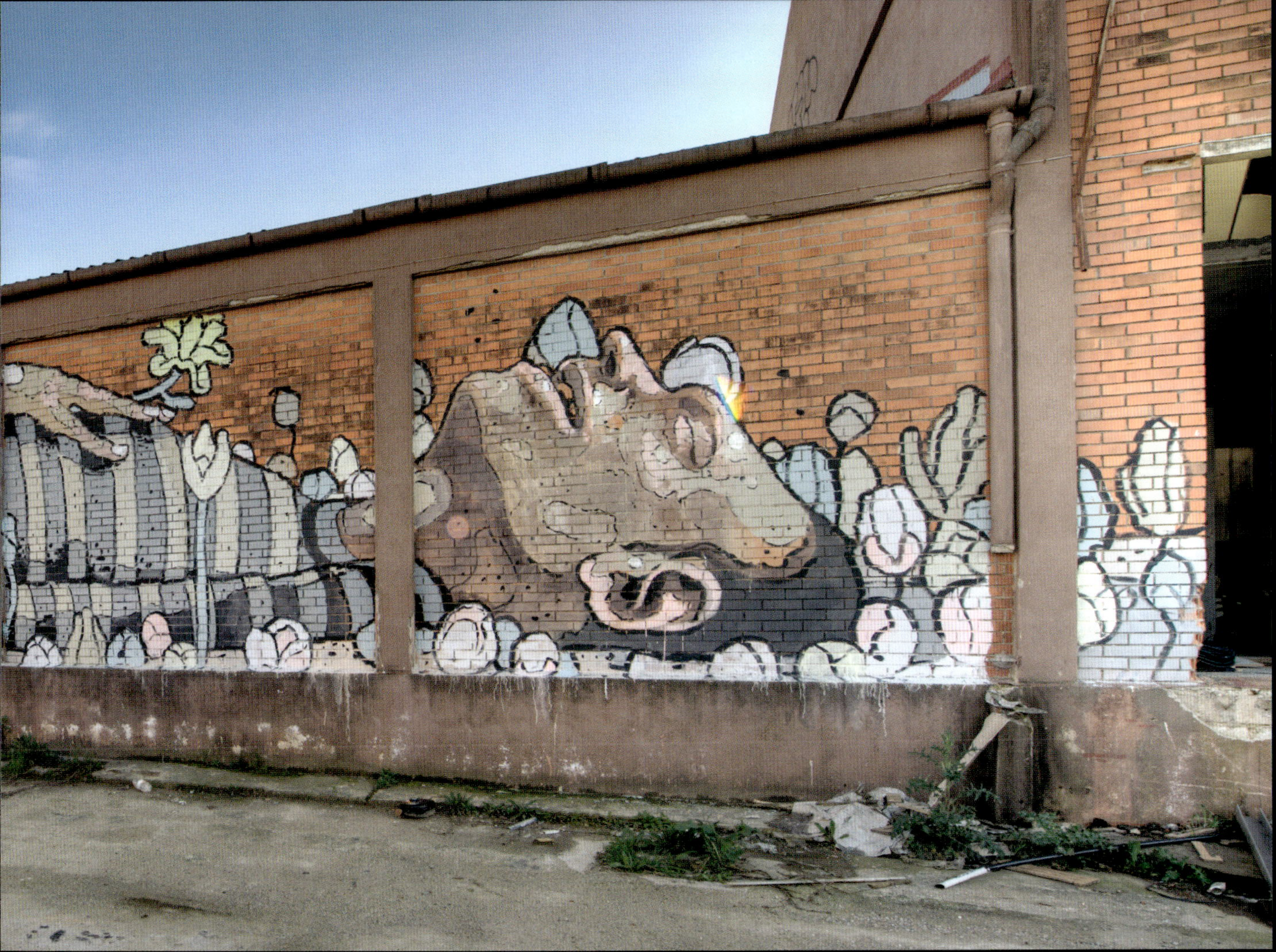

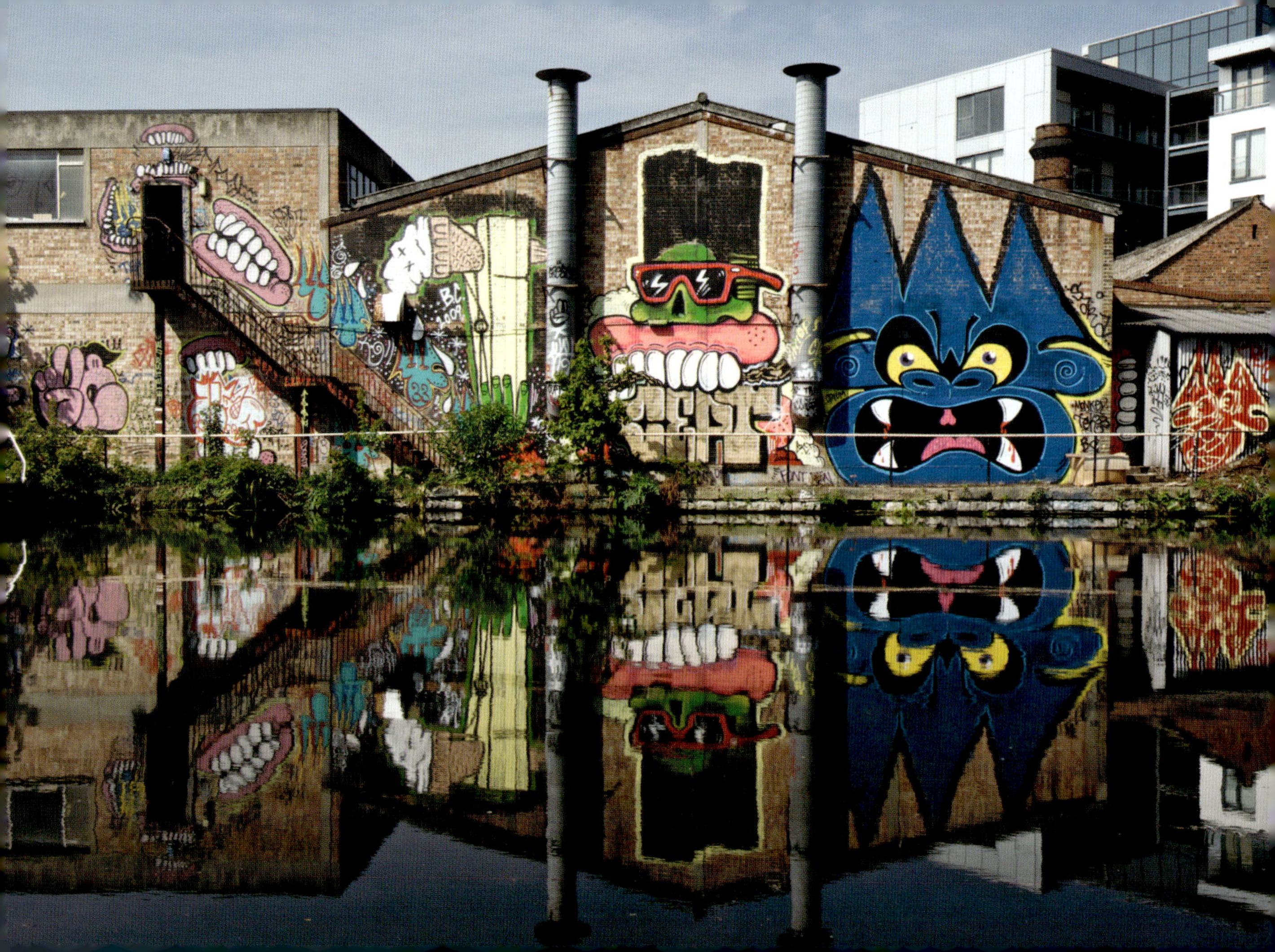
BC
2009

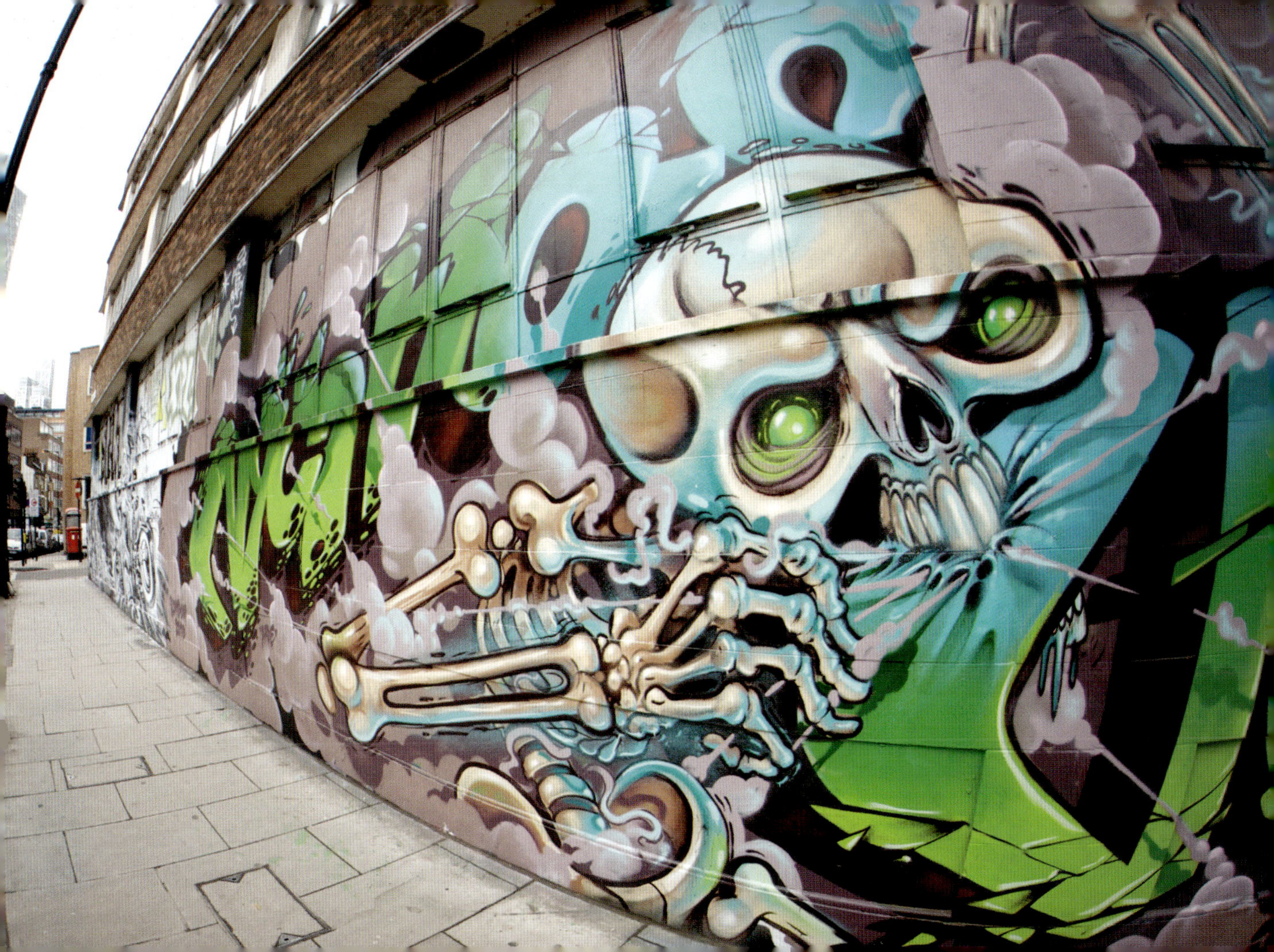

For me abandonment gives me a place where I can give life to my creations . . .

These spaces add value to my characters; it feels like they're able to integrate themselves within their surroundings.

SEA

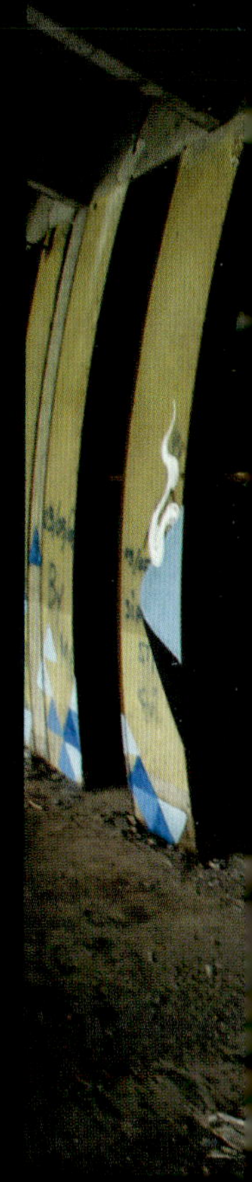

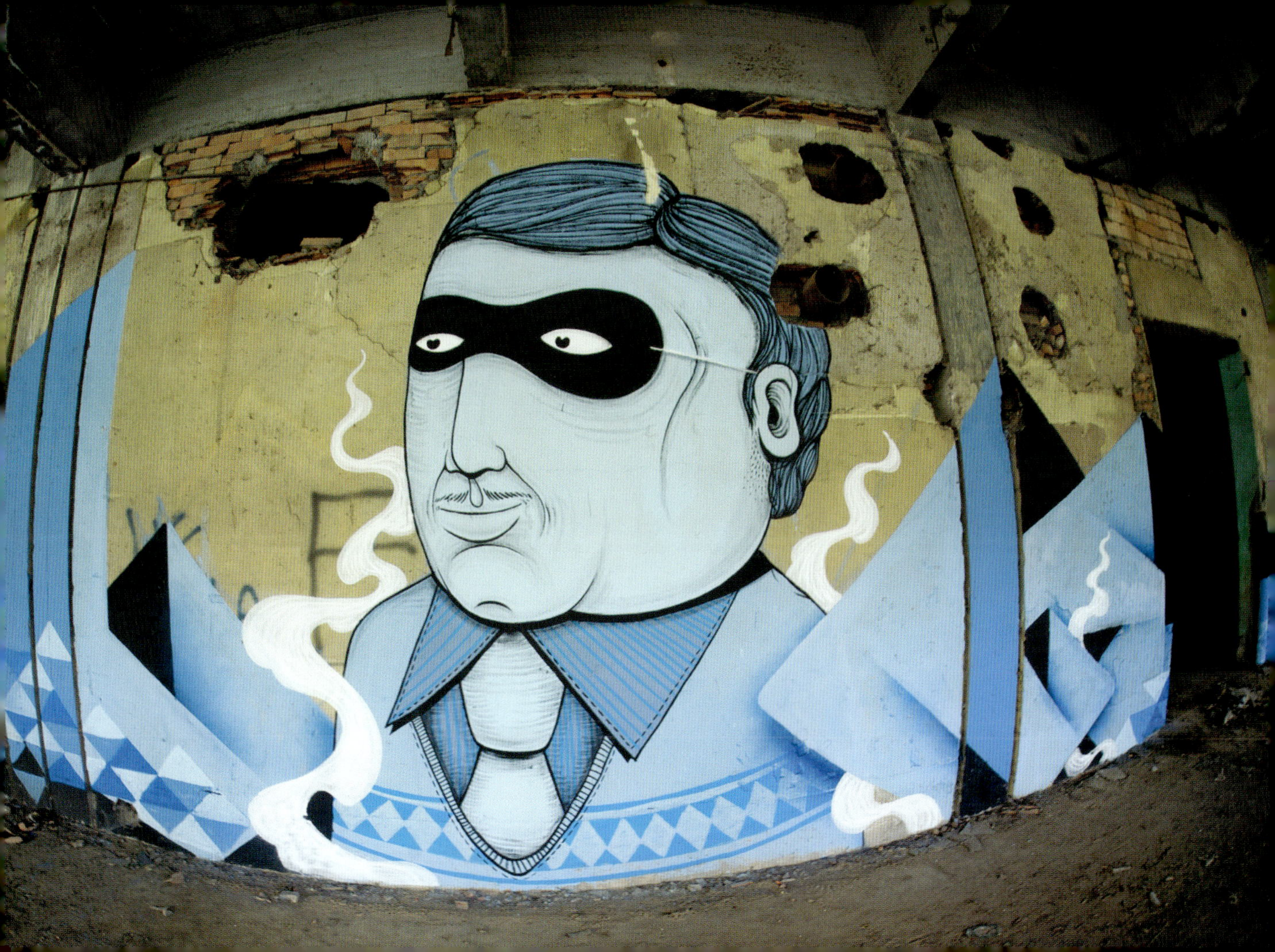

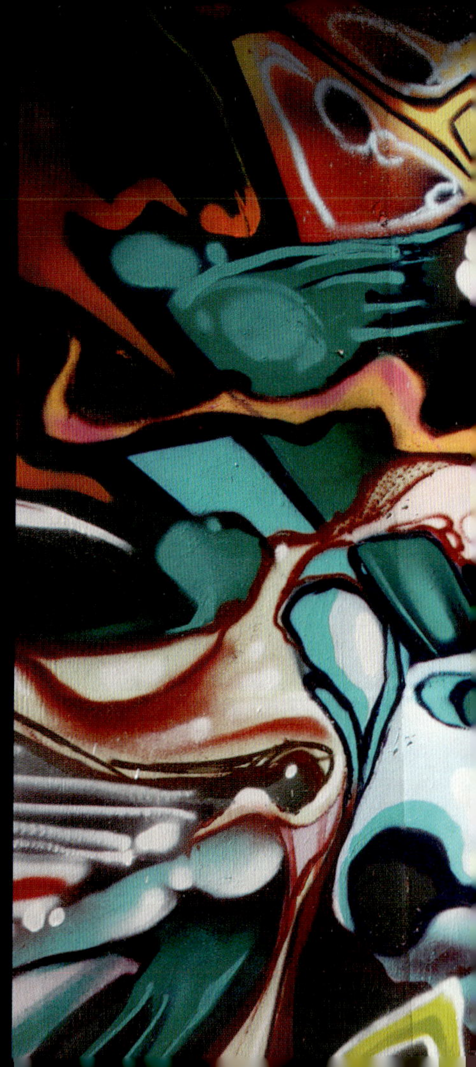

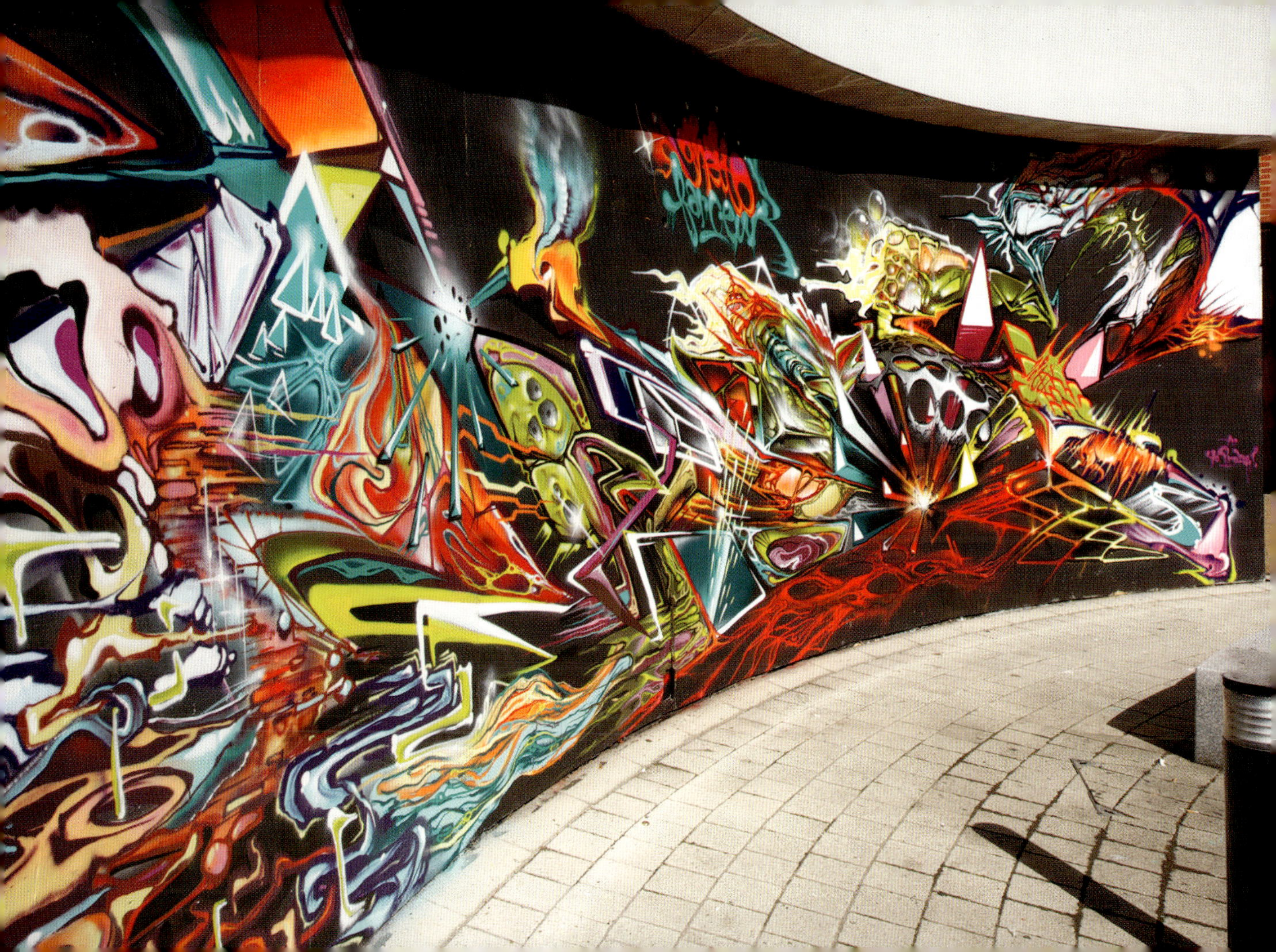

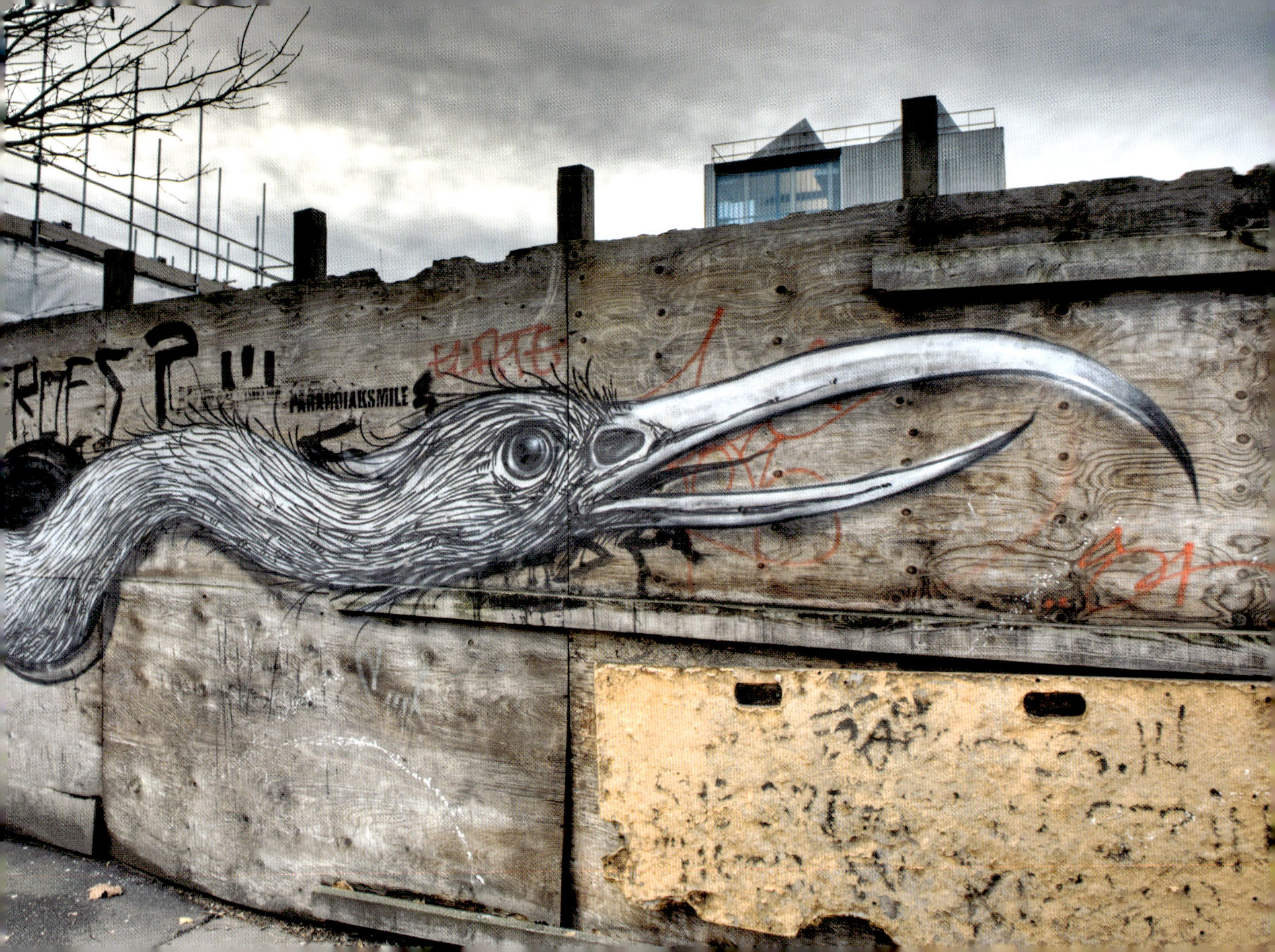
PARANOIAKSMILE

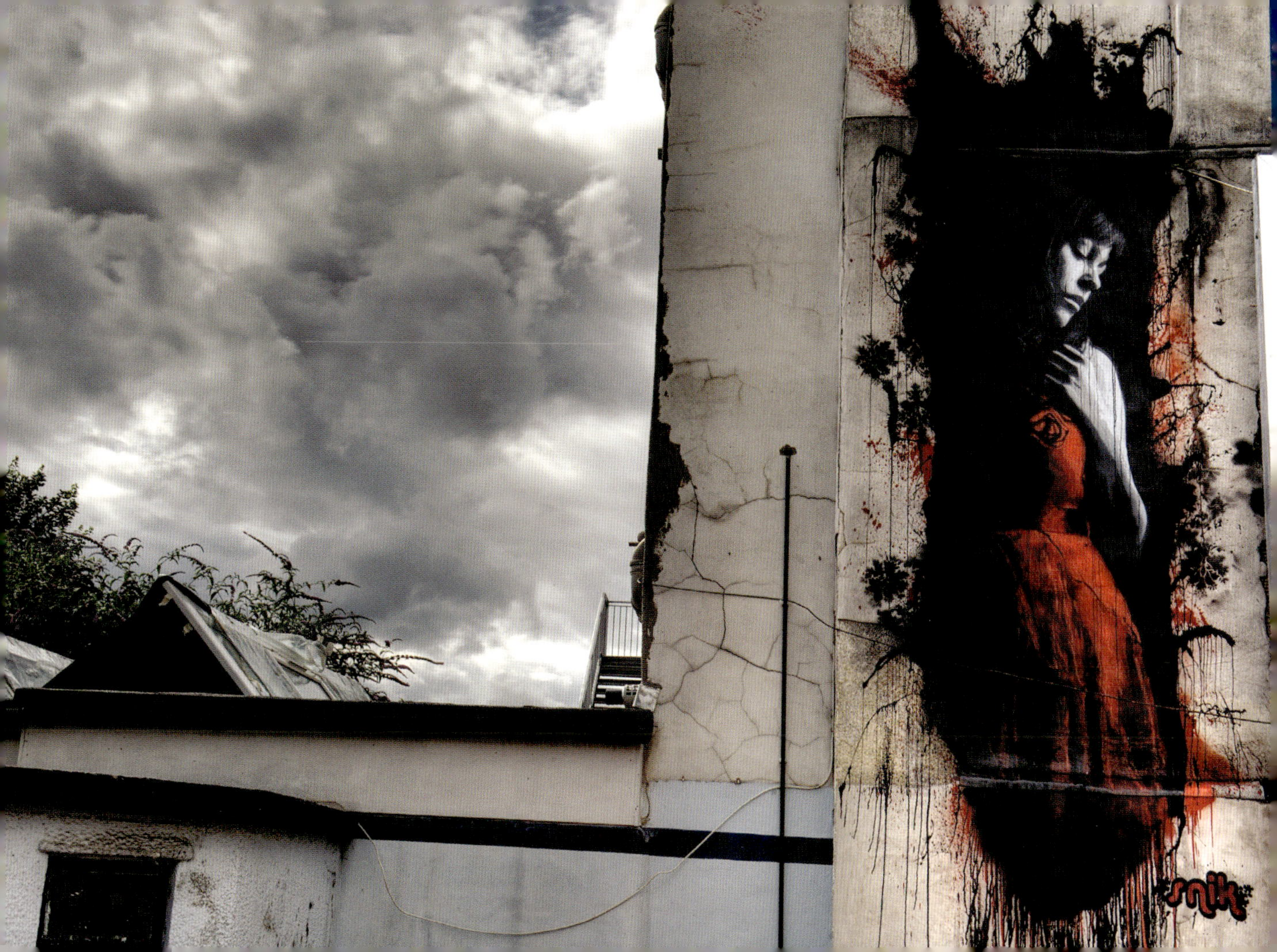
snik

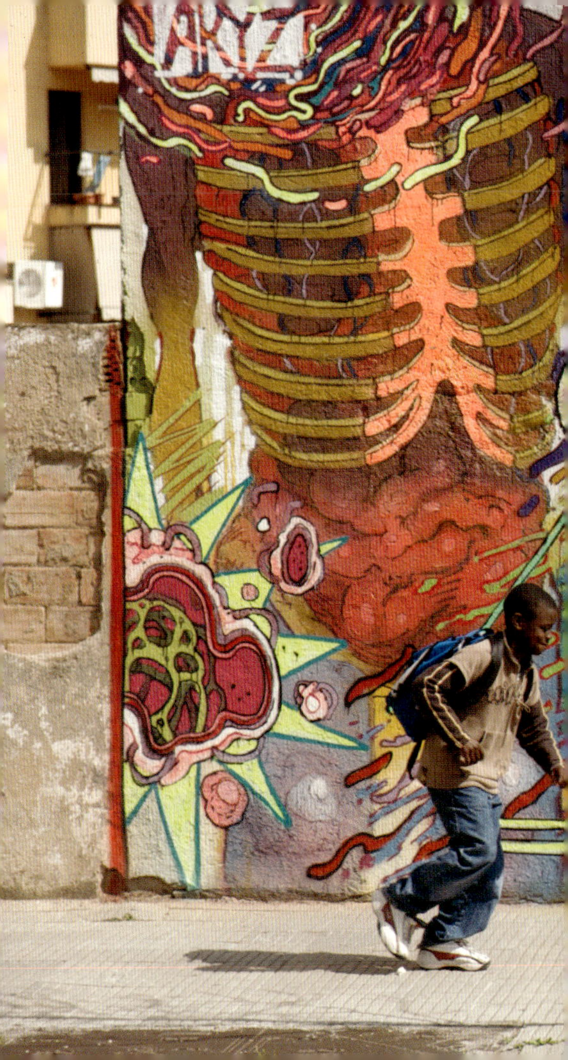

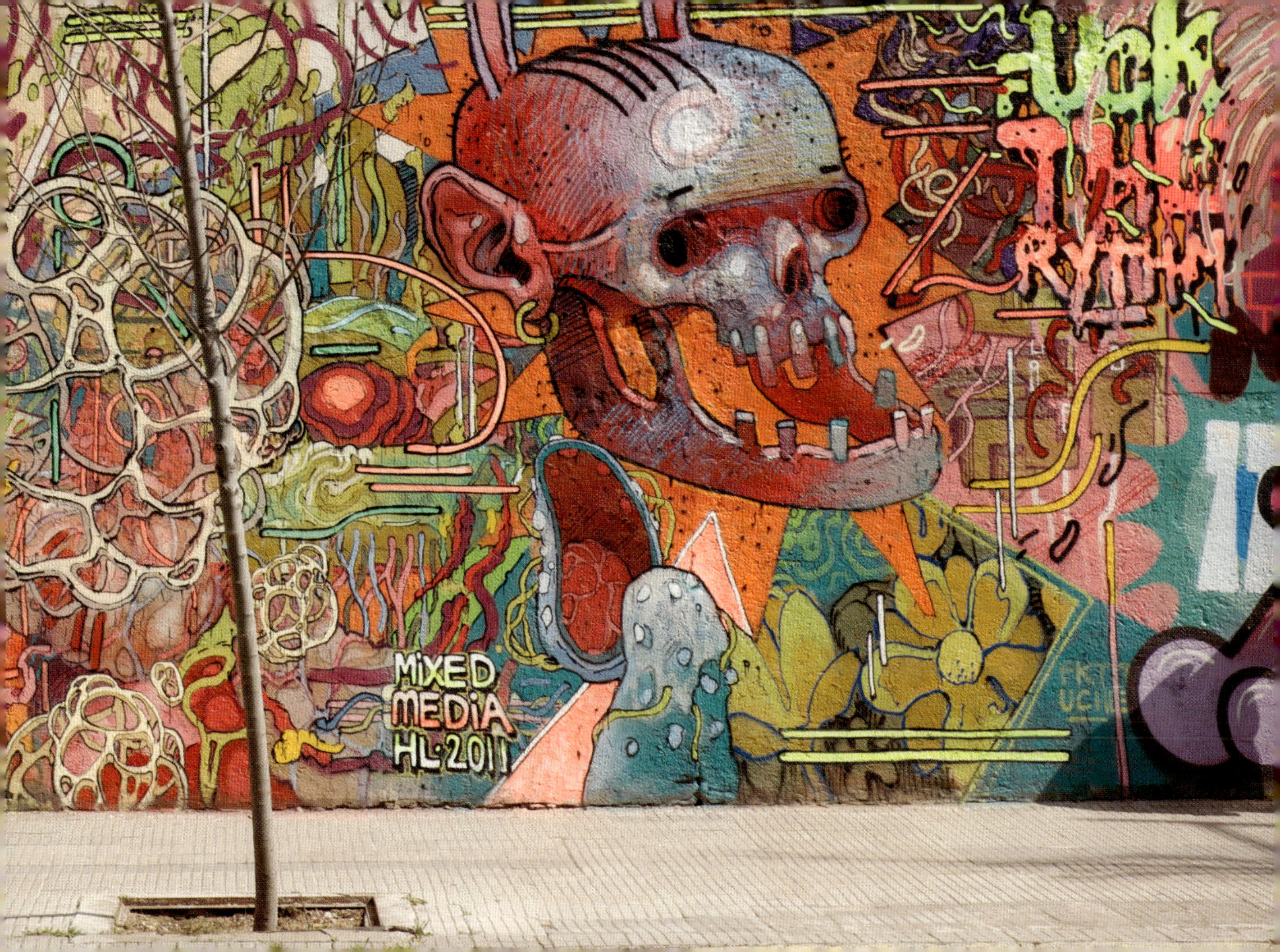
MiXED
MEDiA
HL·2011

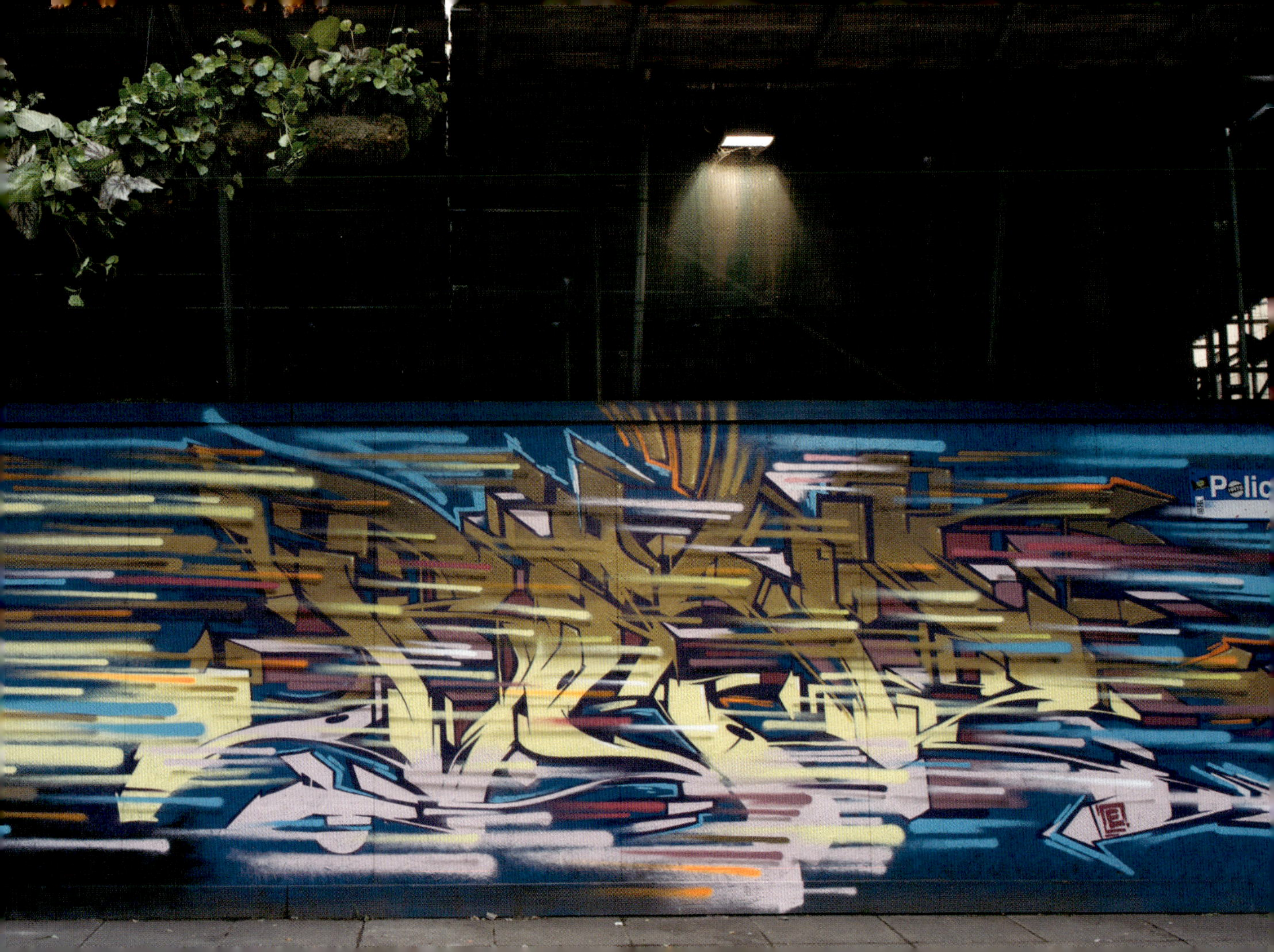
Polic

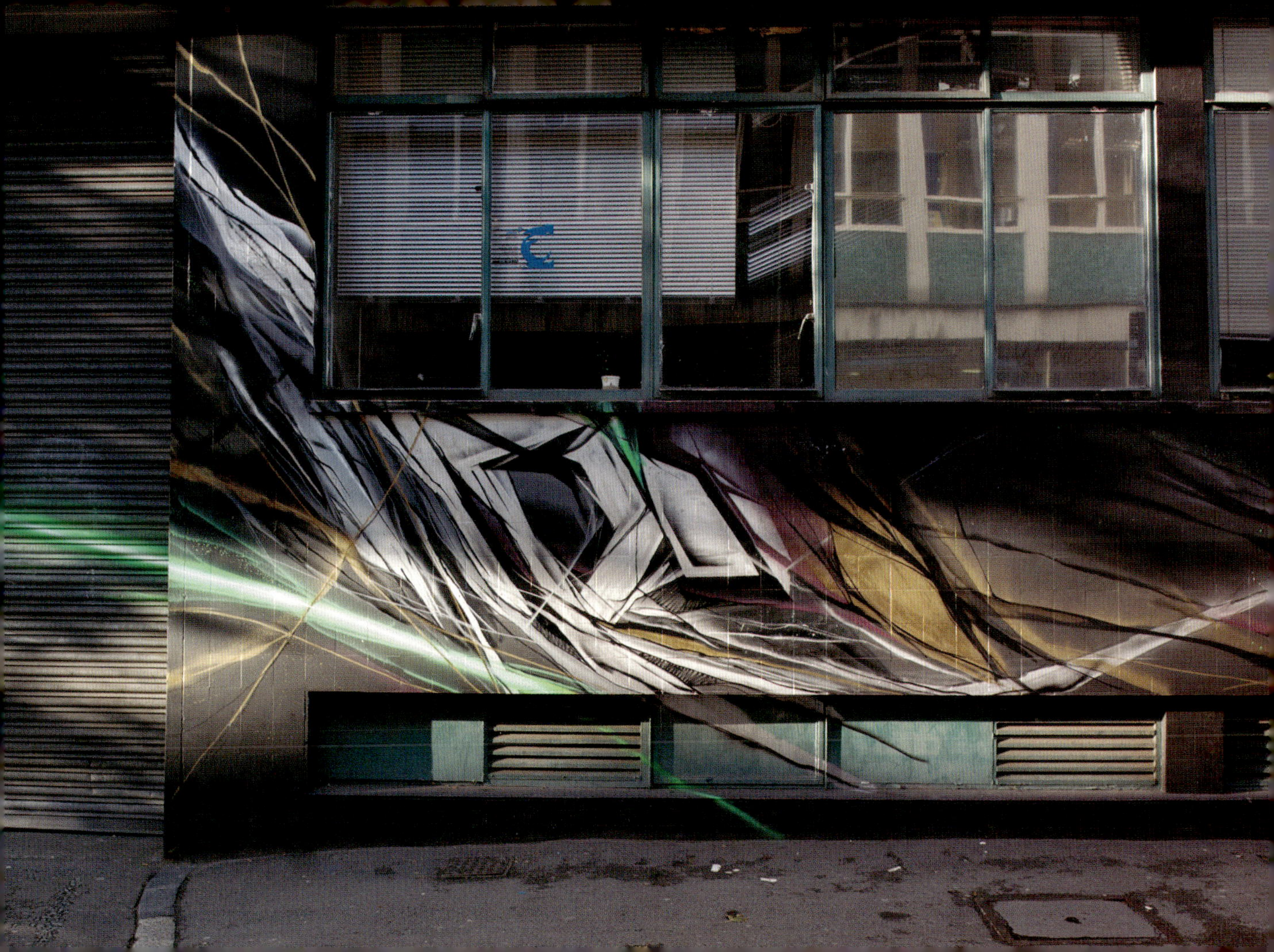

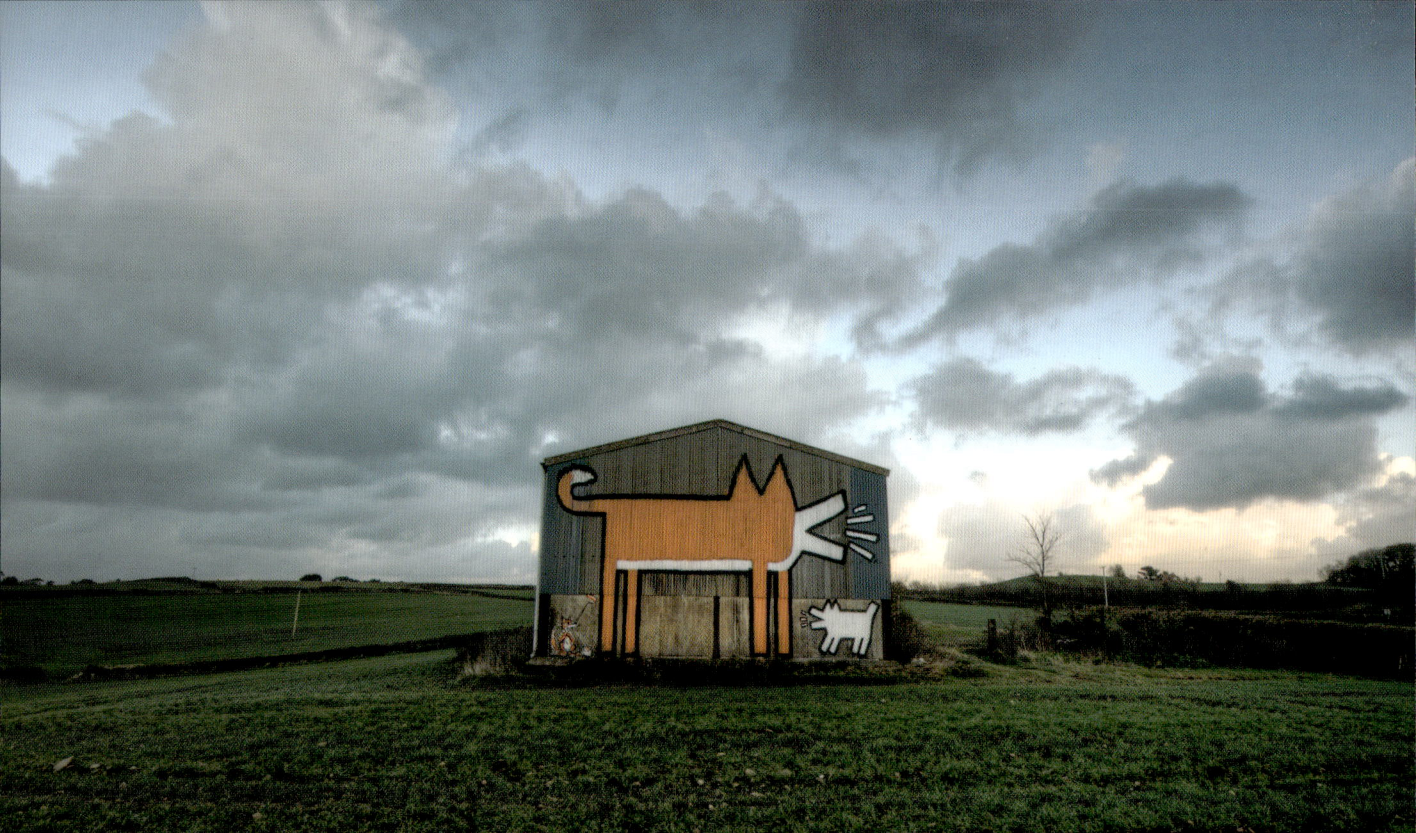

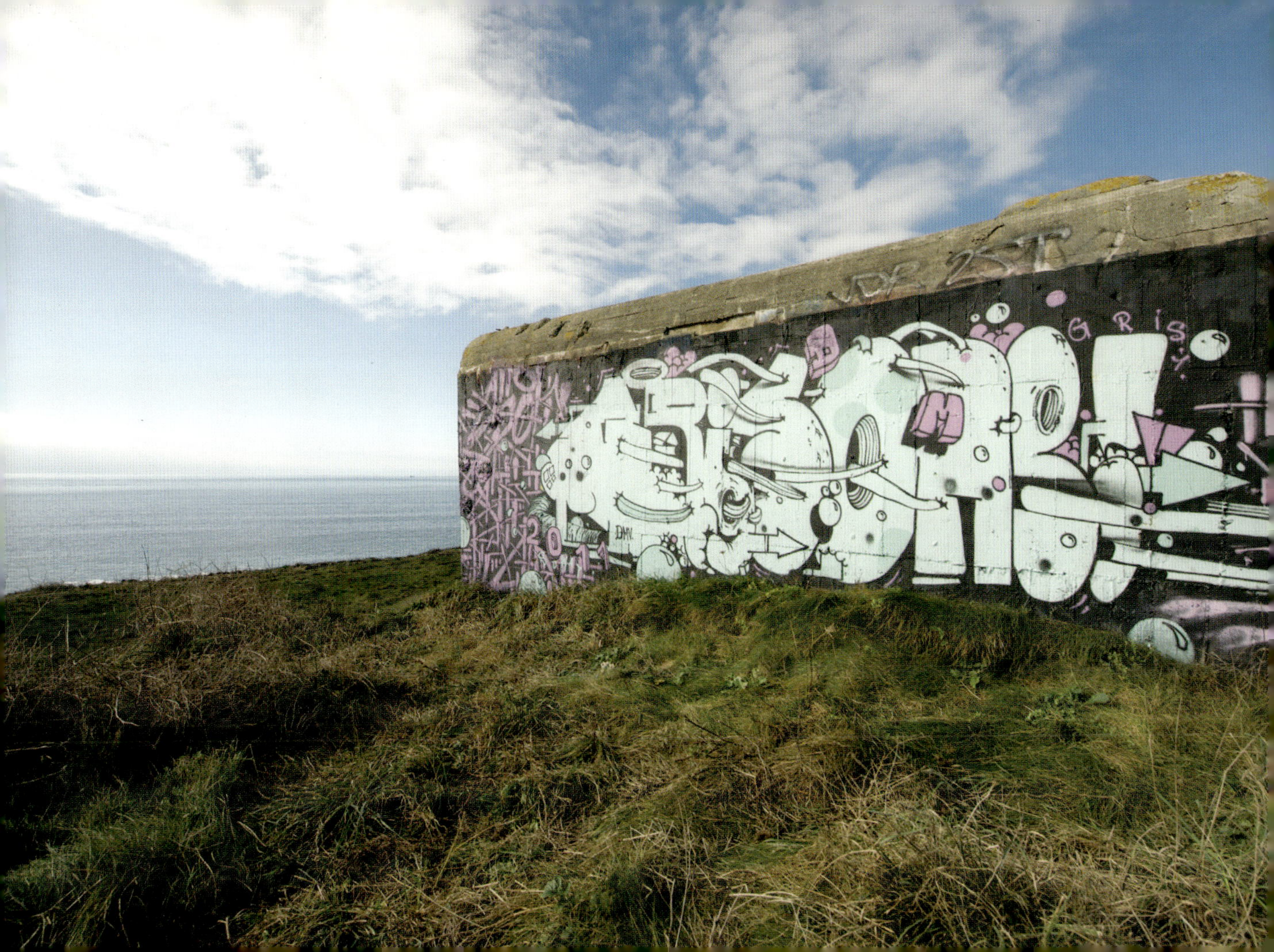

Abandoned places are great; virgin walls, undistracting huge white pages where you can do what you want and say what you want.

RESTO1981

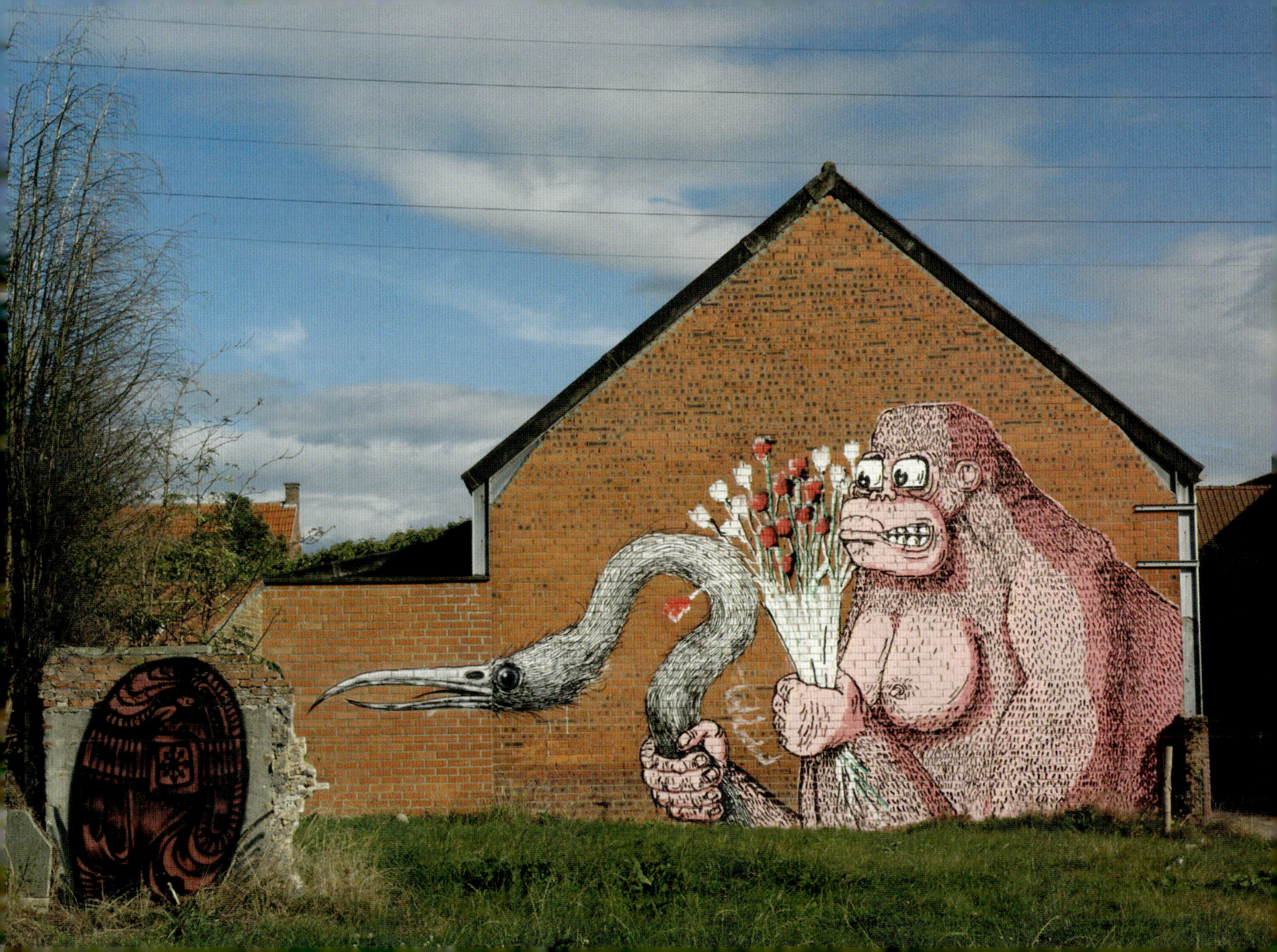

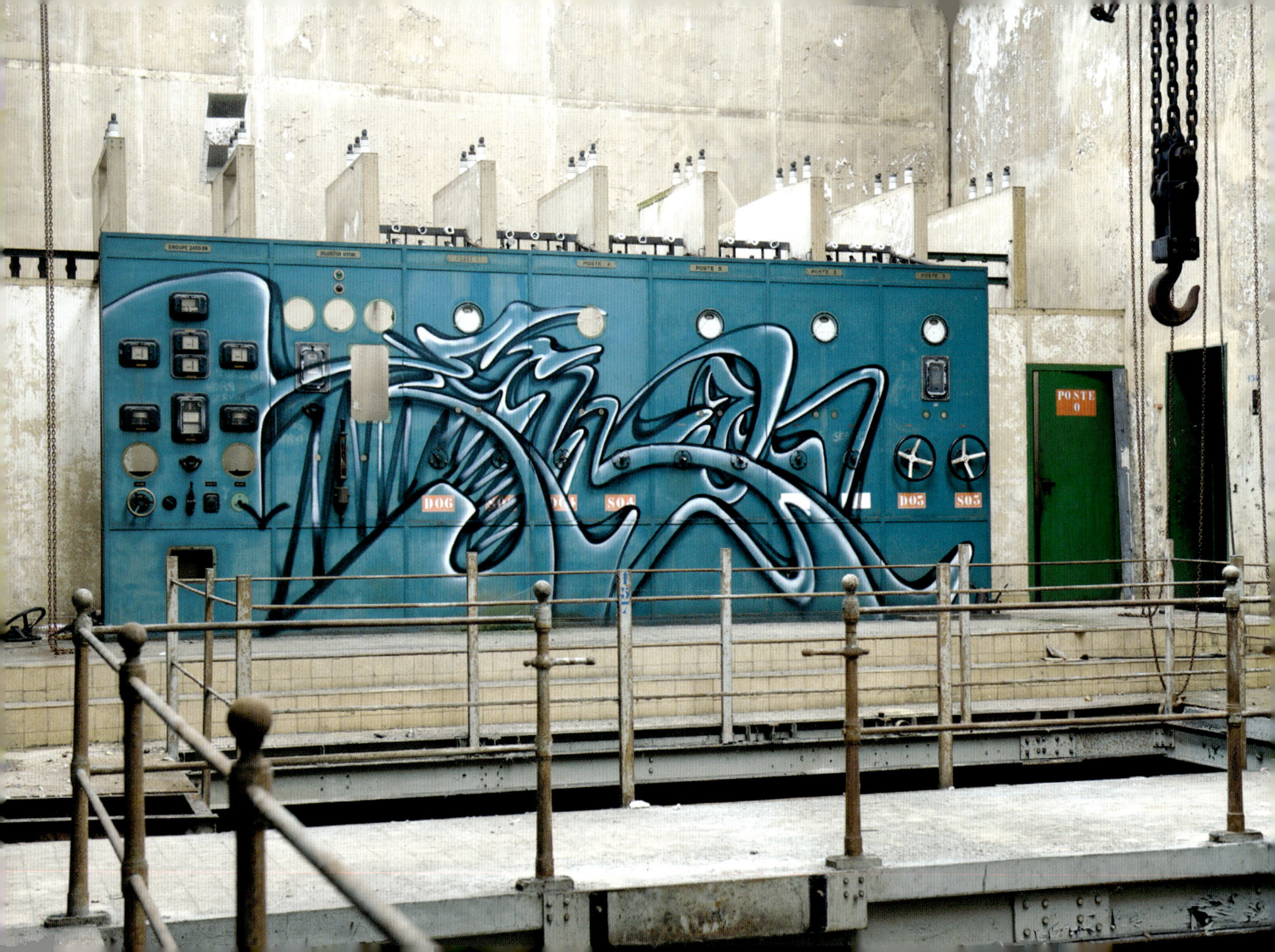
D06
S04
D05
S05
POSTE
0

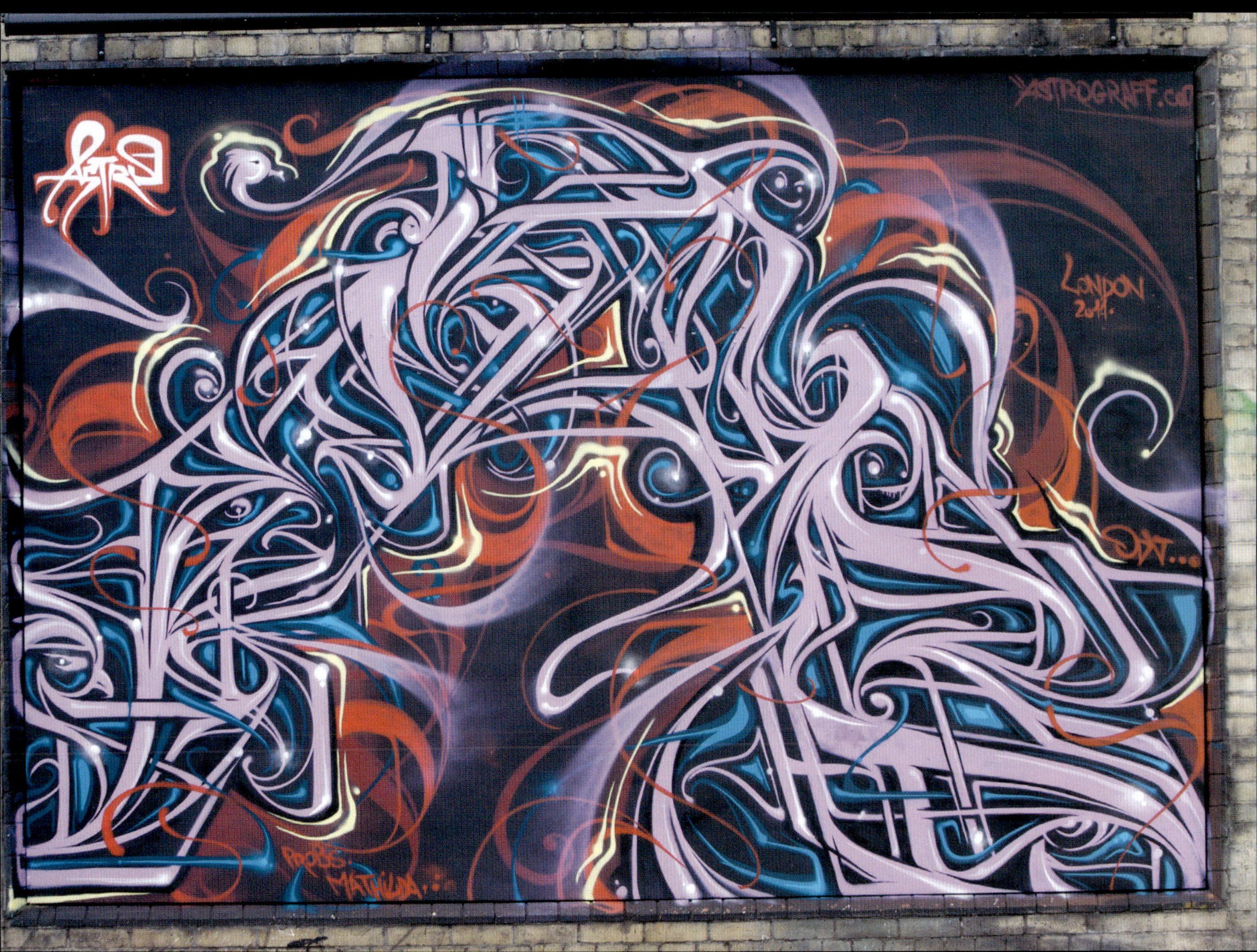
LONDON
2014.

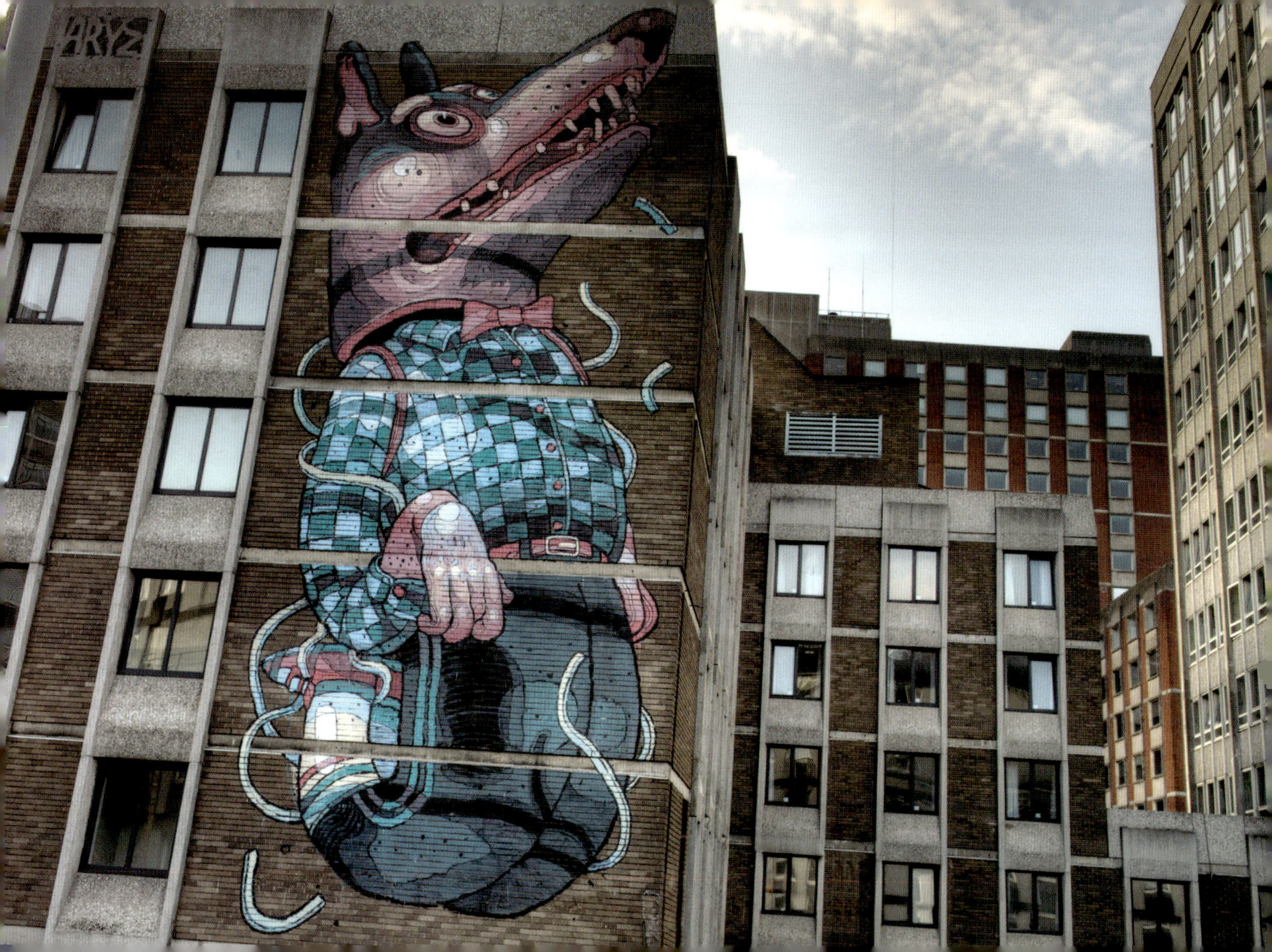
ARYZ

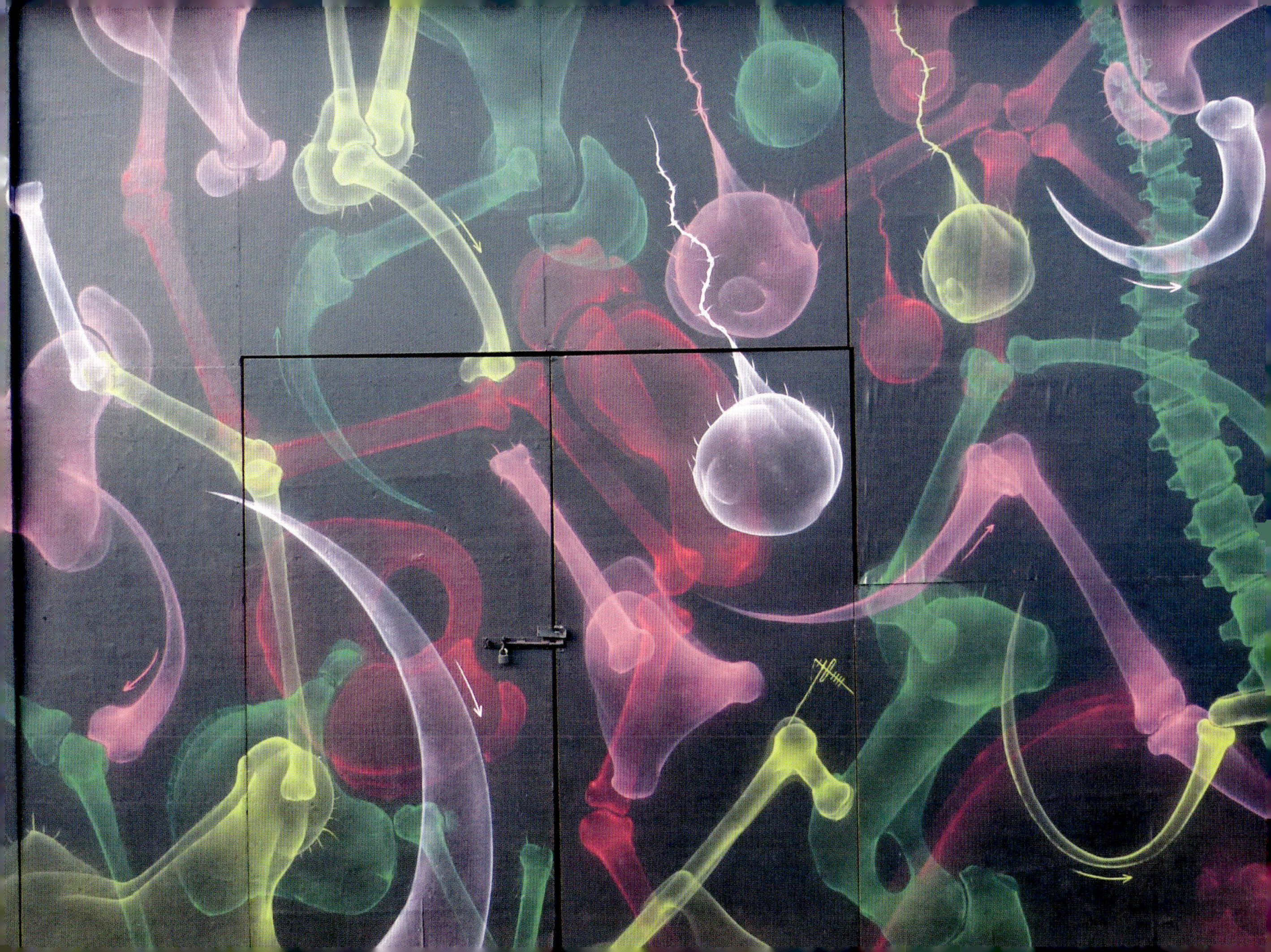

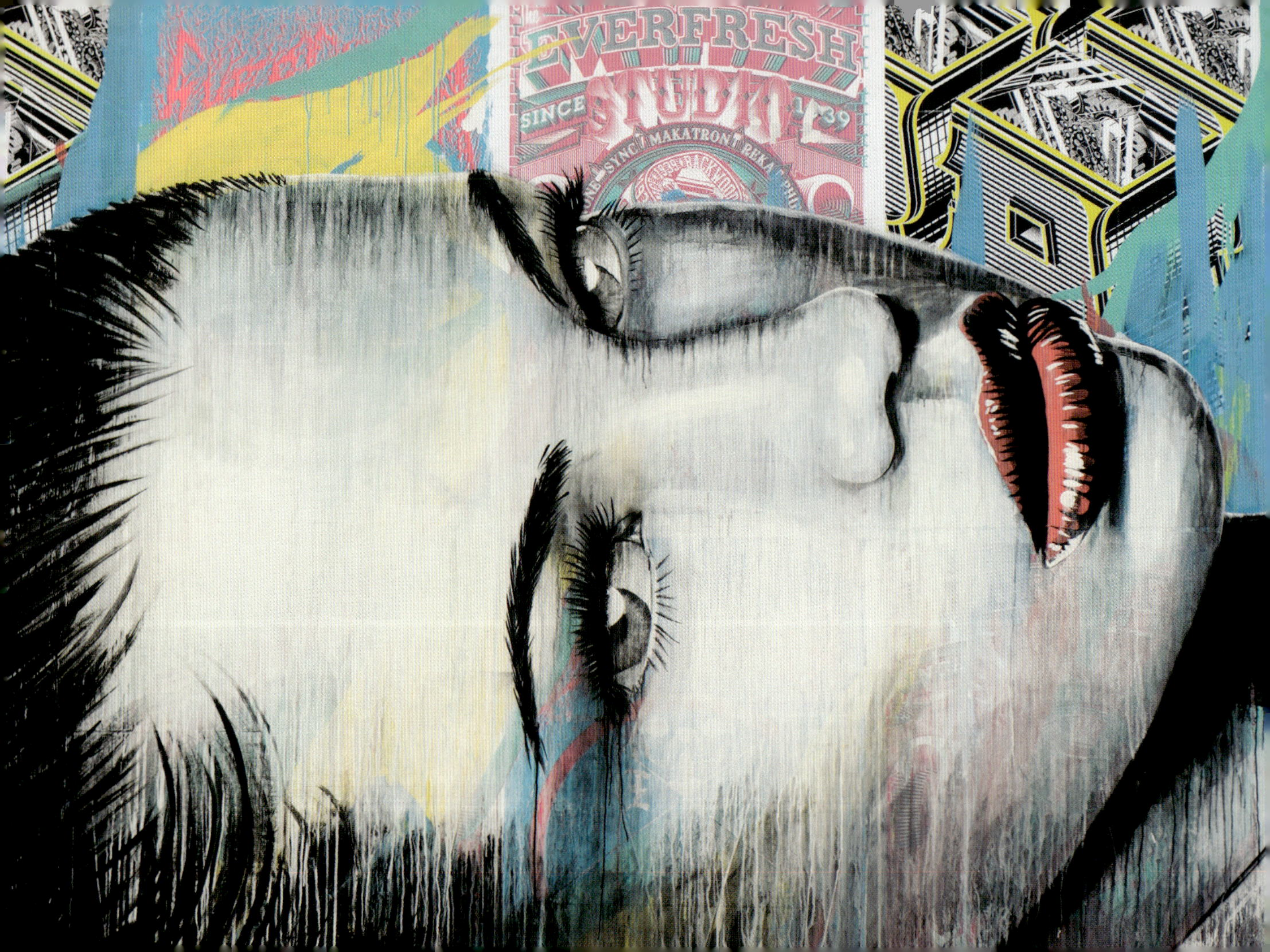
EVERFRESH
SINCE
SYNC
MAKATRON
REKA

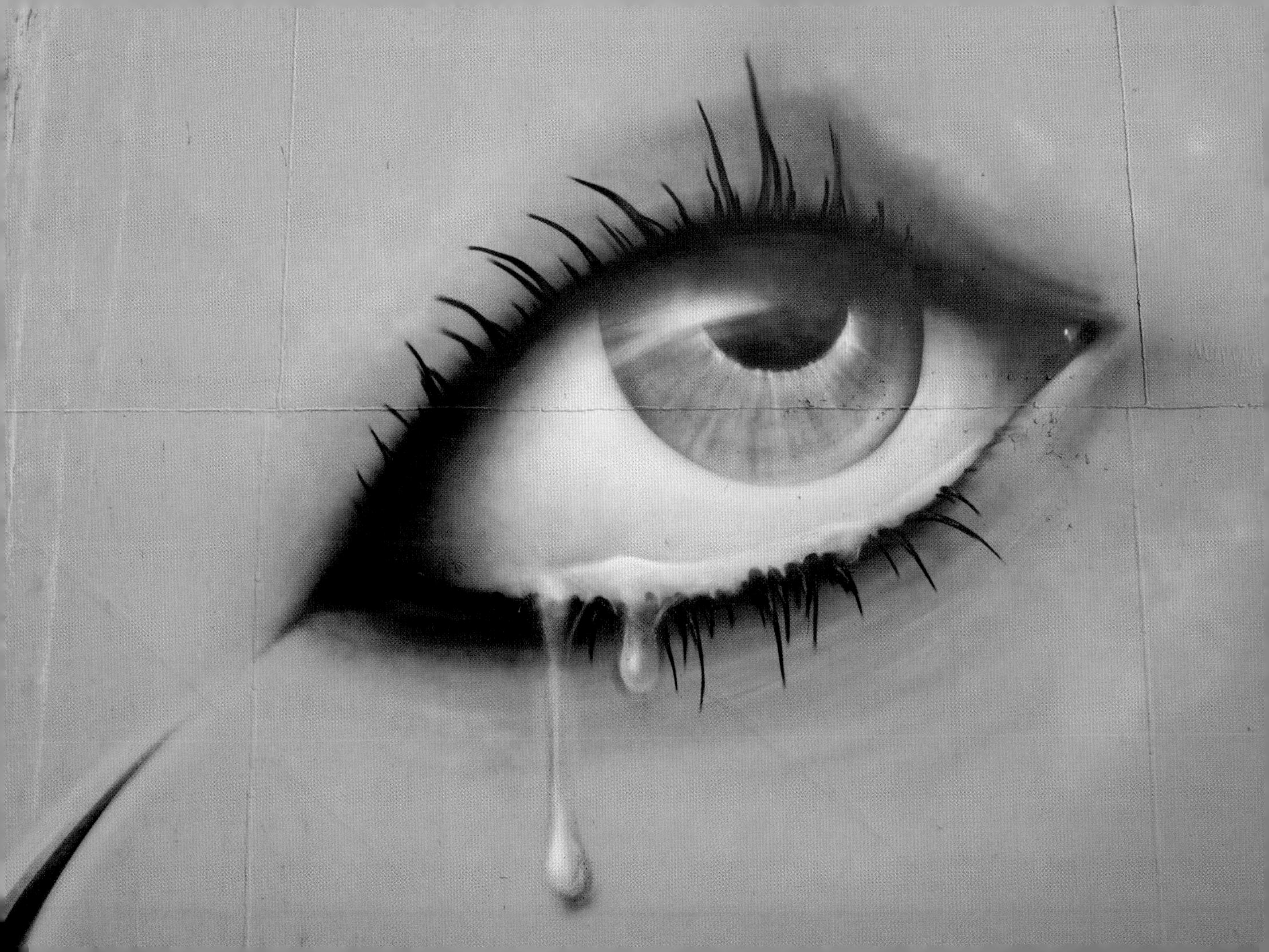

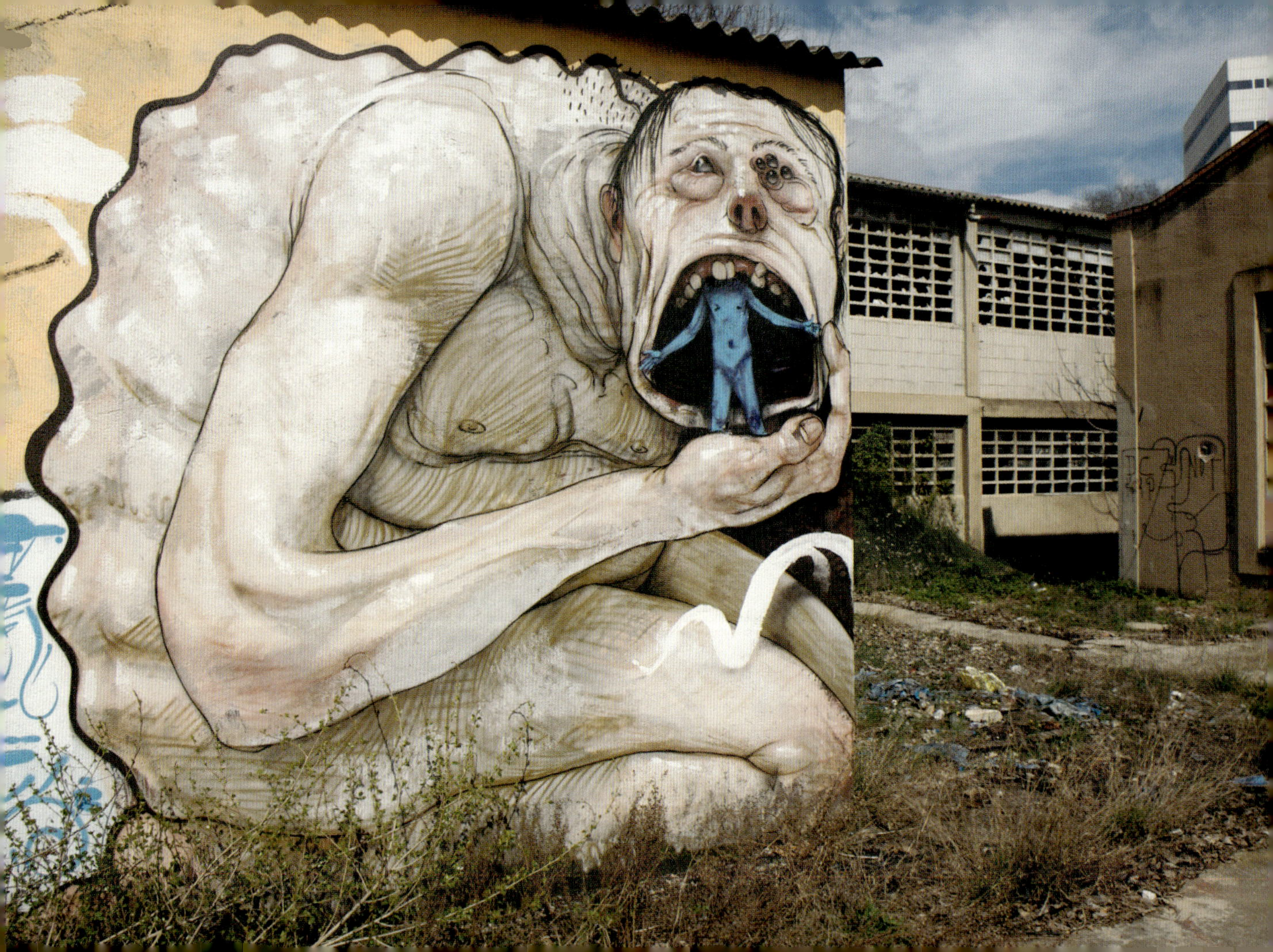

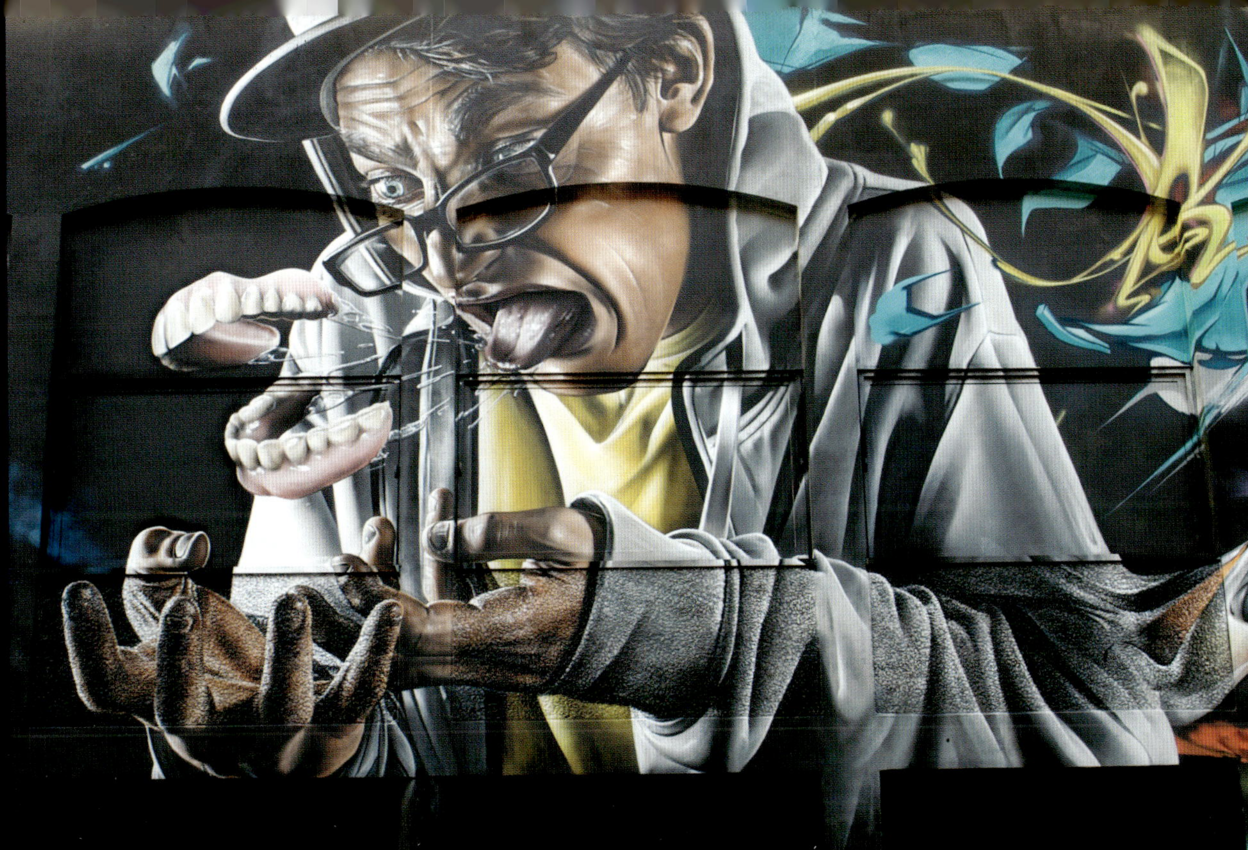

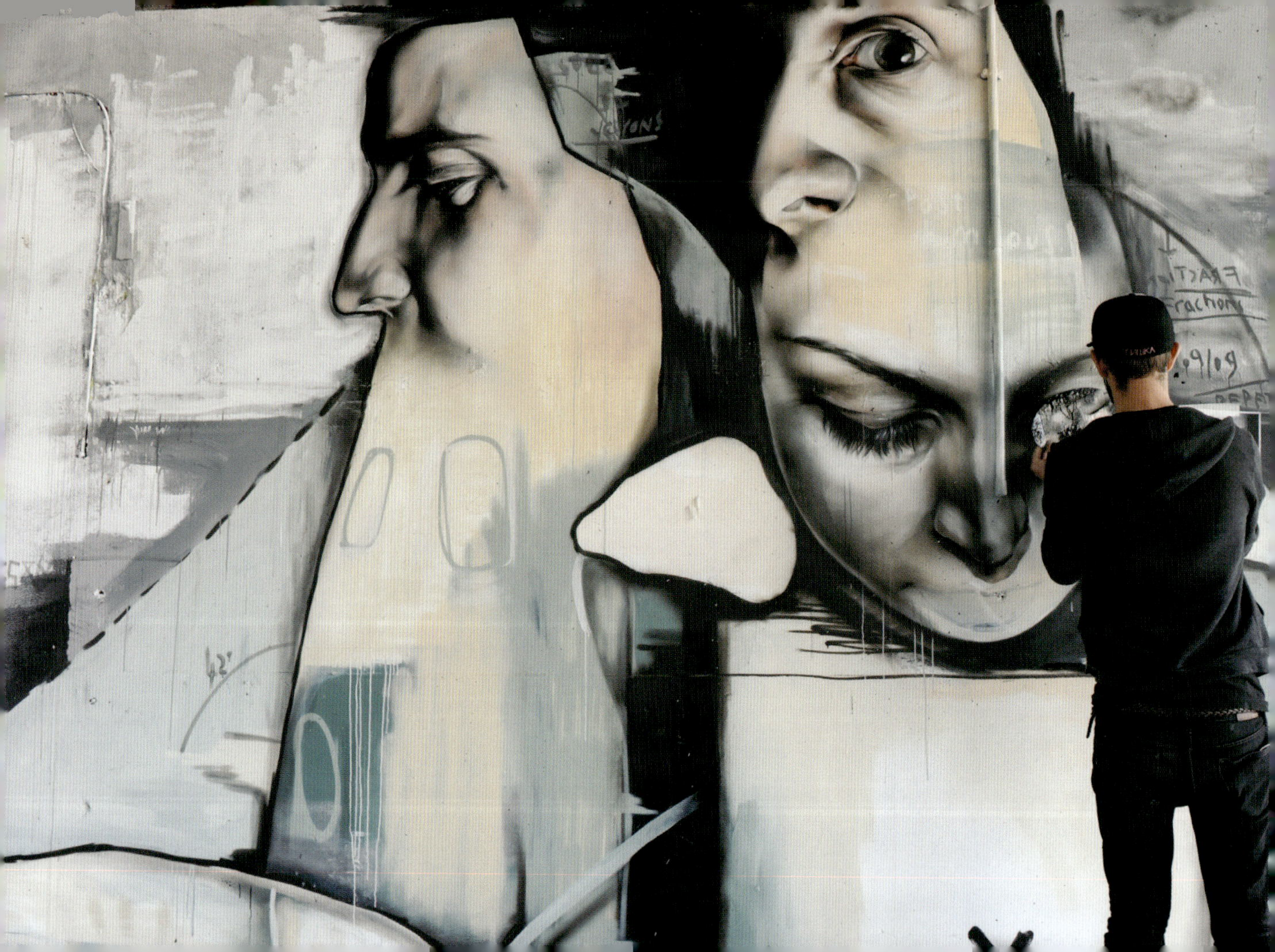

Painting in the streets for us doesnt seem alien at all, it's what we've always done. Coming from a graffiti background we do it to paint on a large scale, to have no restrains of a canvas, we can make it flow with the surroundings to mean something to the people who live there. Also walls have stood the test time, they have seen and heard a lot of things. I think that shows with some walls, within their colour and texture, it's just something you can't get with a canvas.

BEST EVER

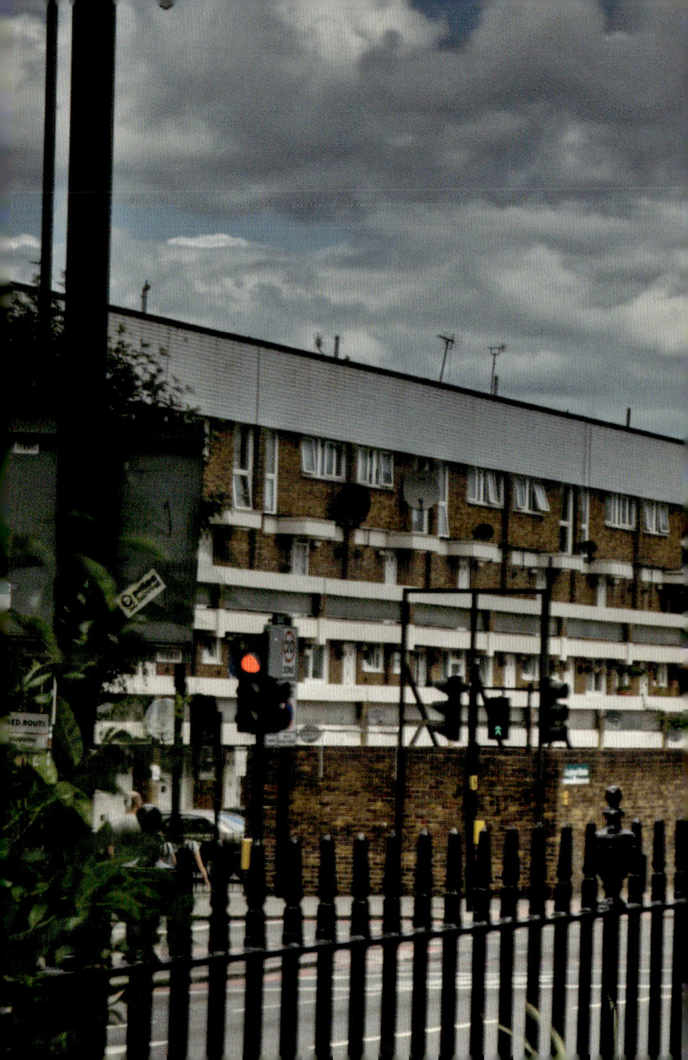

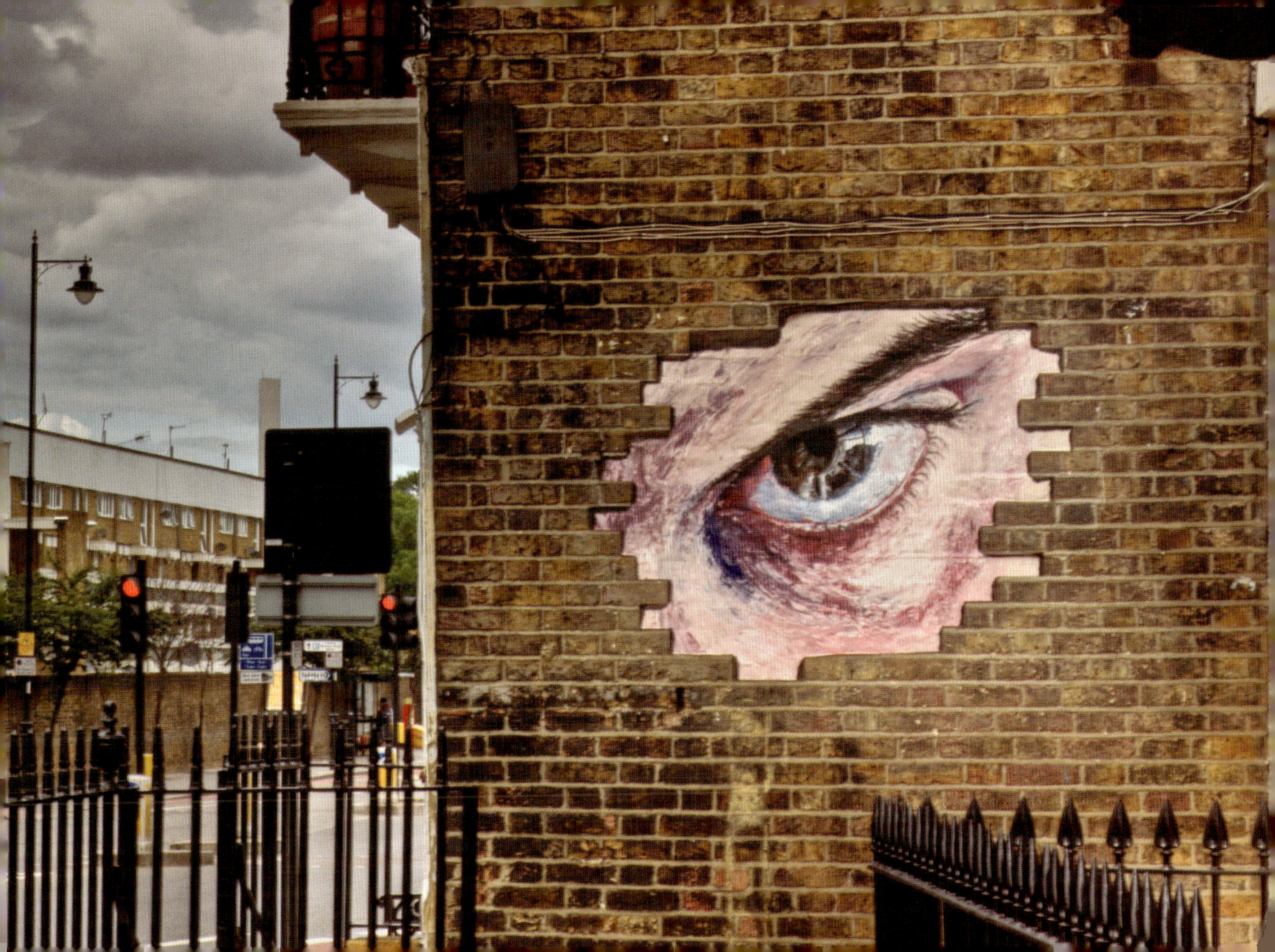

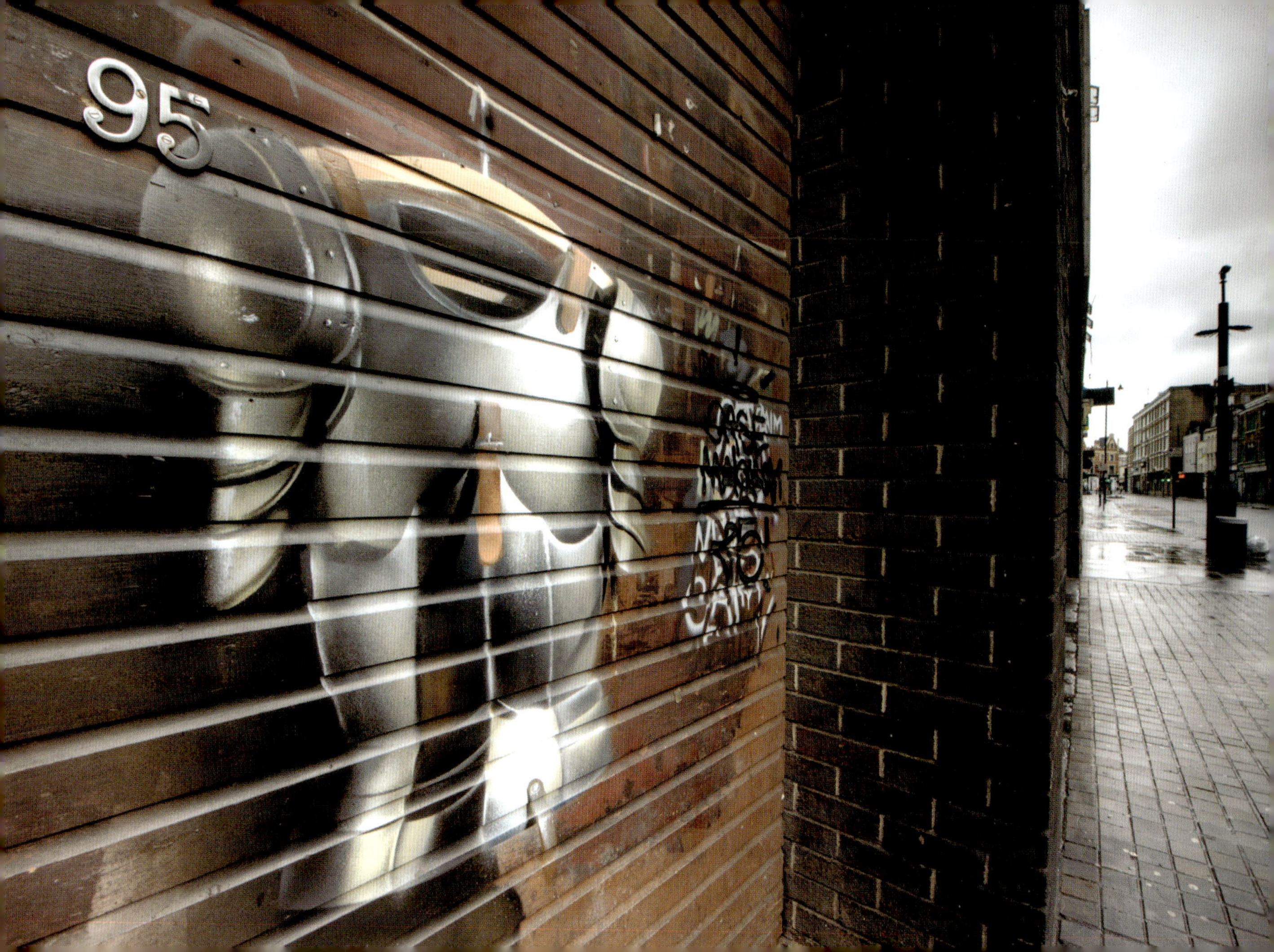
95

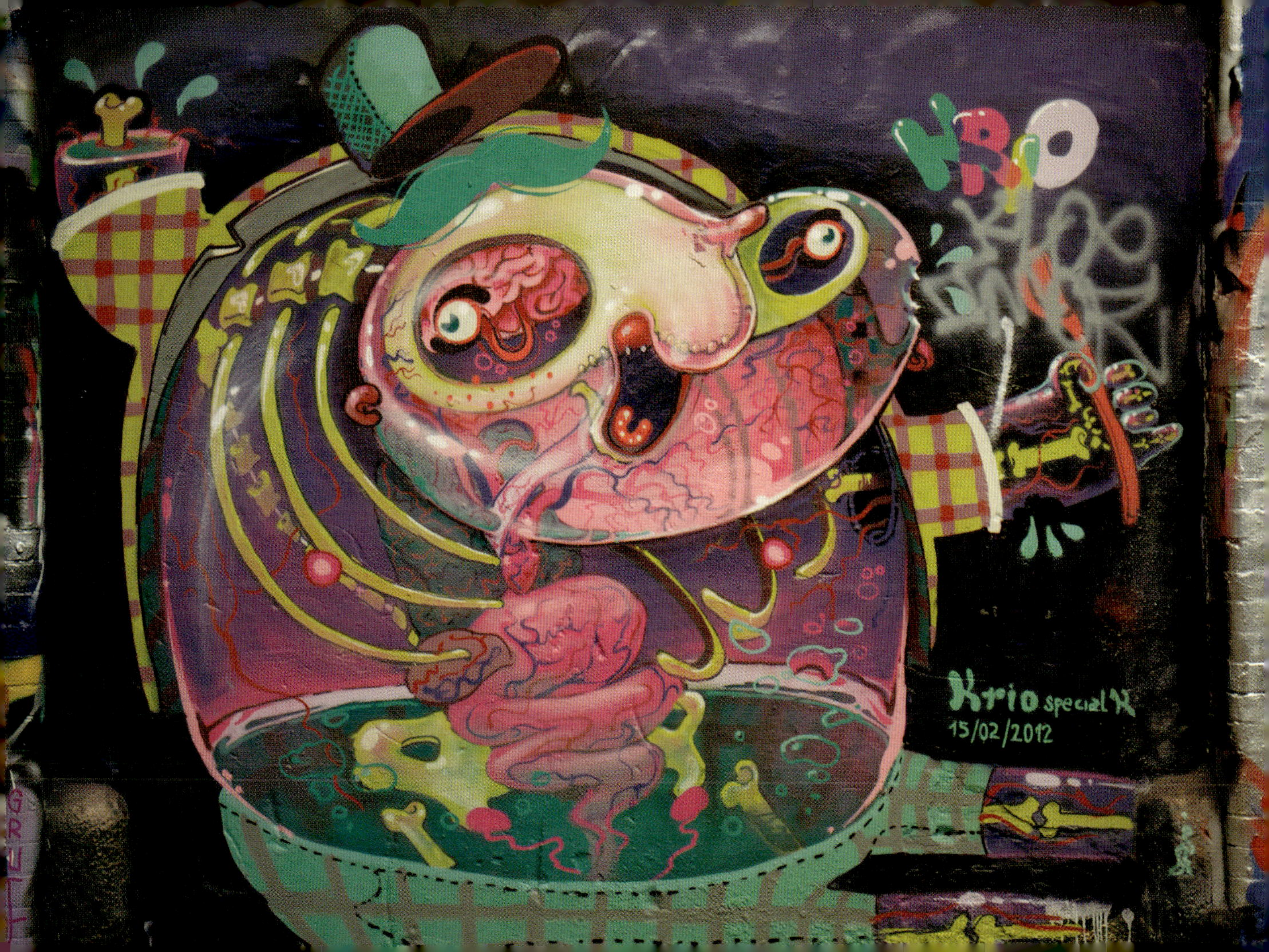
KRIO
Krio special H
15/02/2012

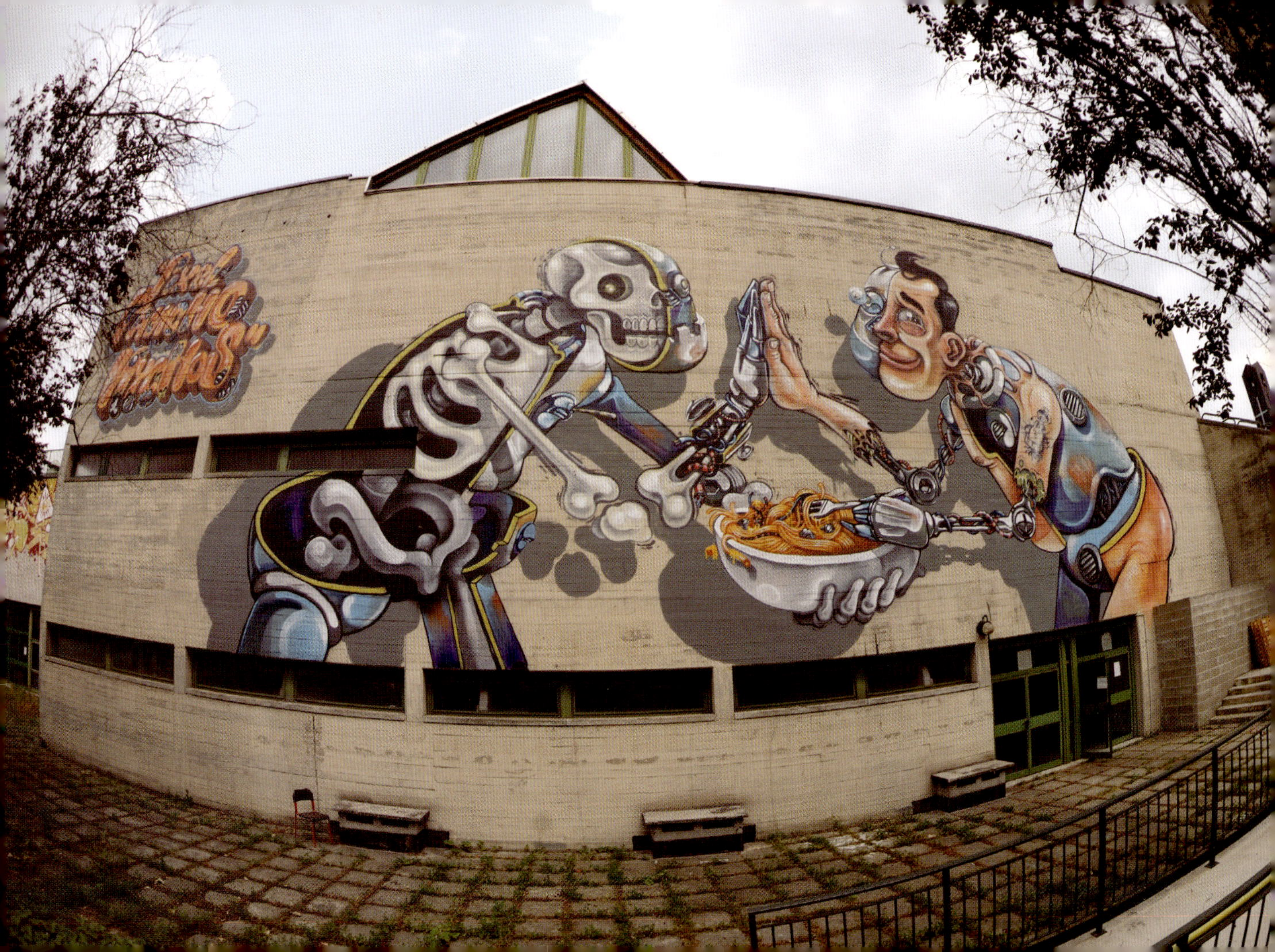

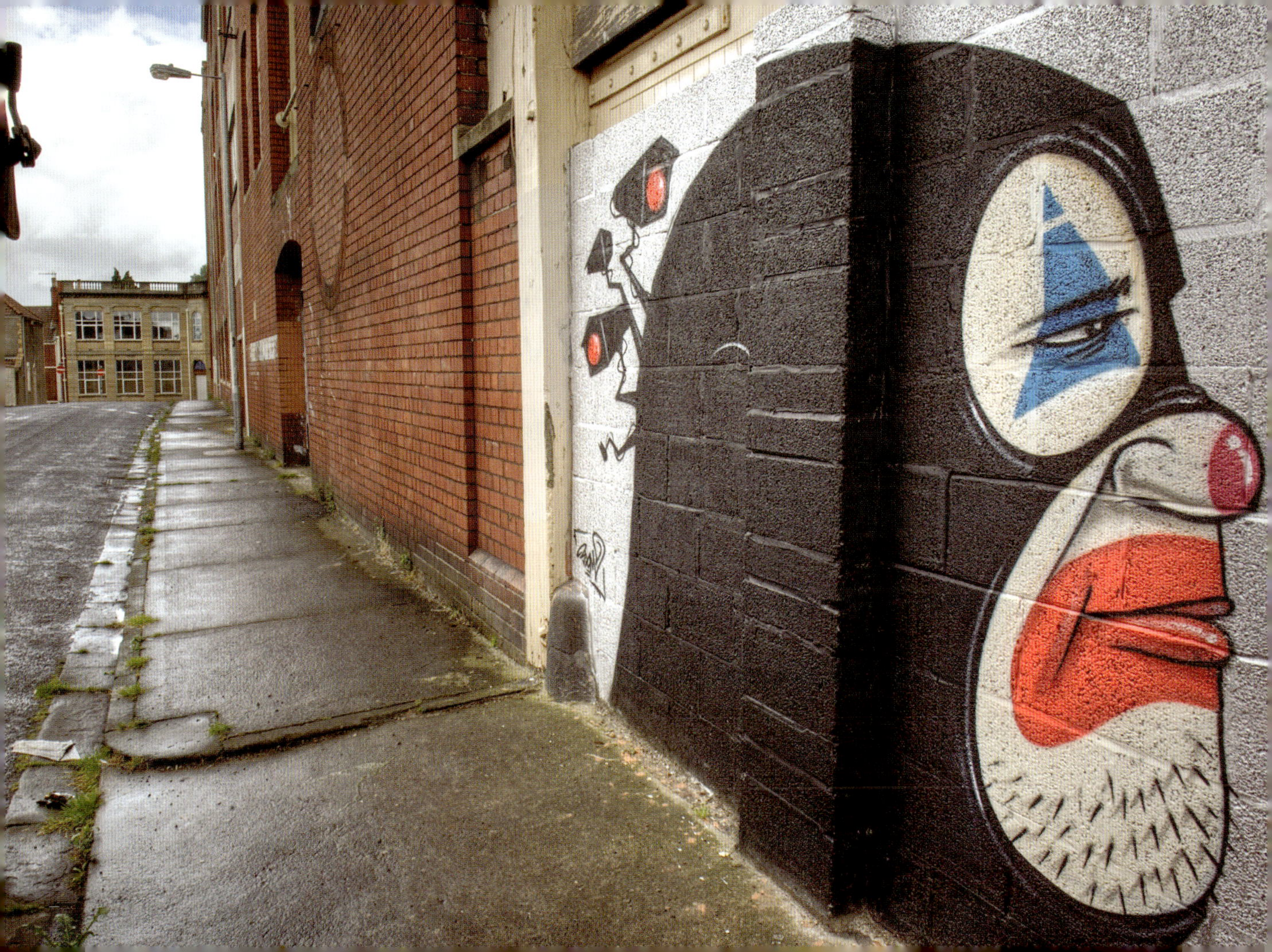

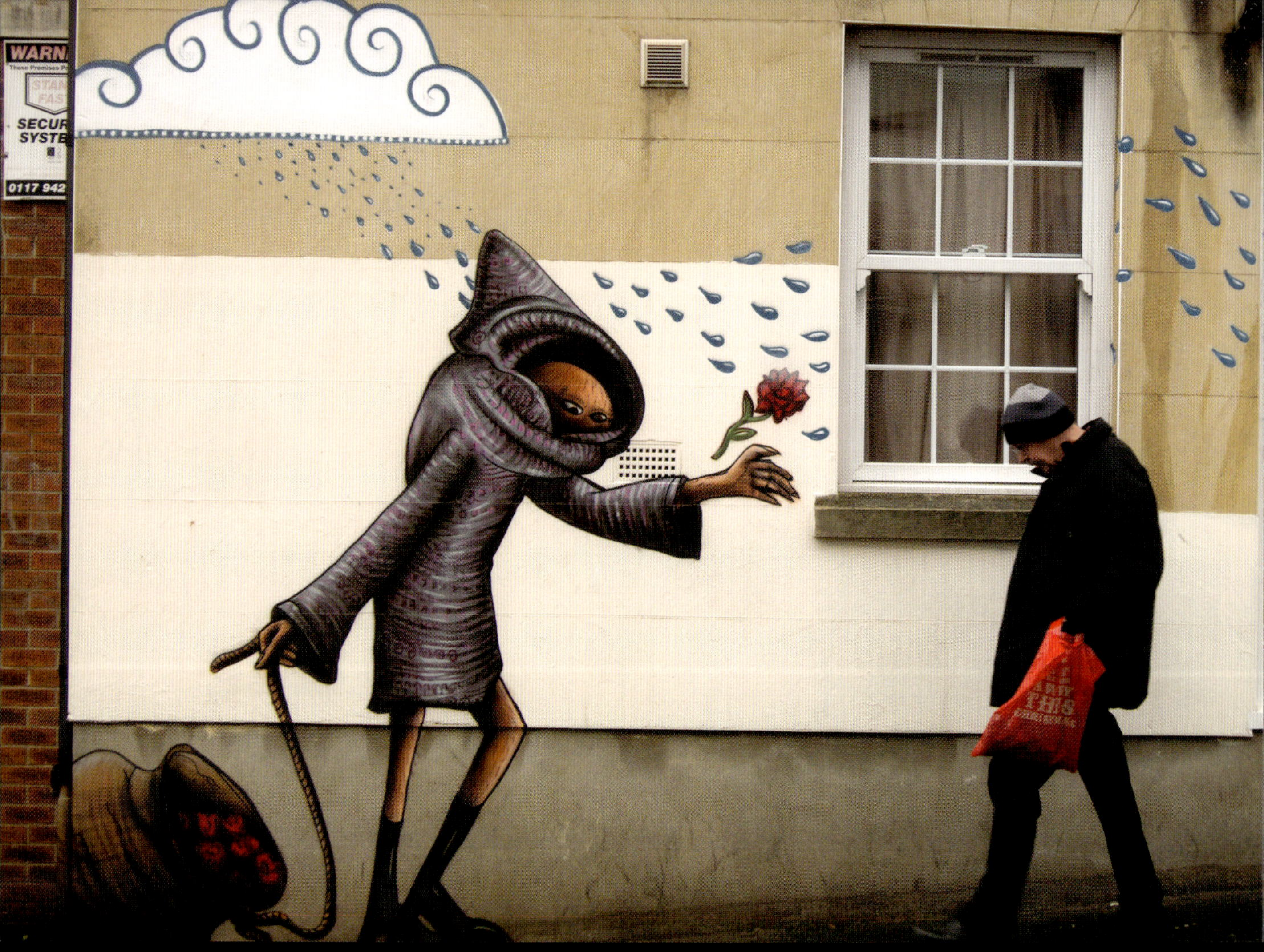
WARN
SECUR
SYSTE
0117 942
THIS

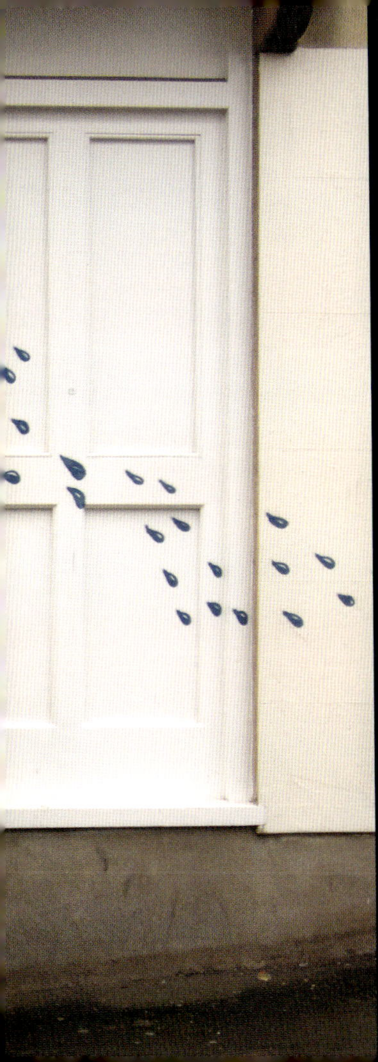

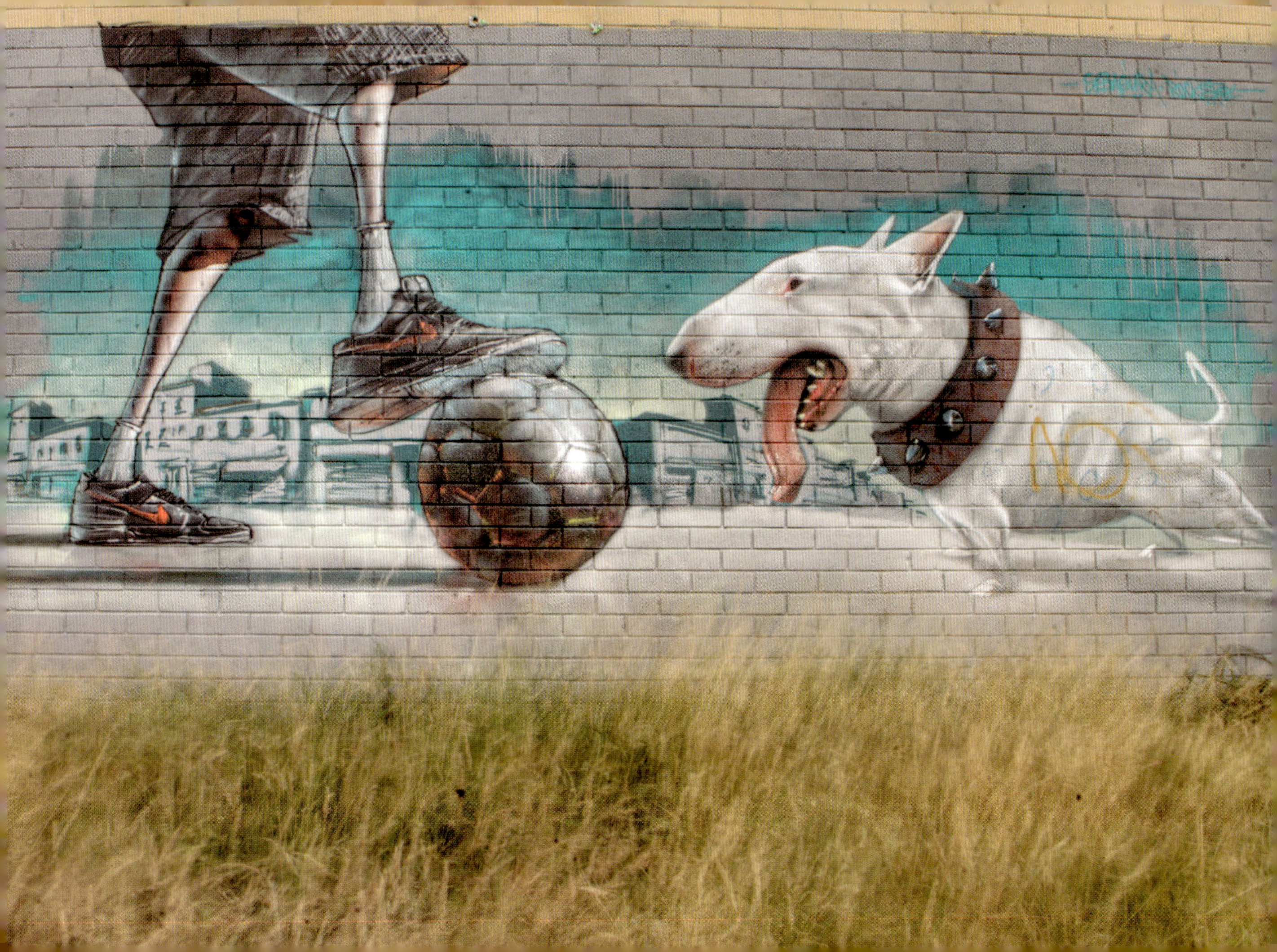
NO

I paint the streets because it's nice to paint in the public eye from time to time, rather than being hidden away at some graffiti spot or derelict factory. Introducing graffiti and street art to the public is still a new thing and an ongoing process. It's always a pleasure to see the public enjoy the work and to change their opinions about it.

ROCKET01

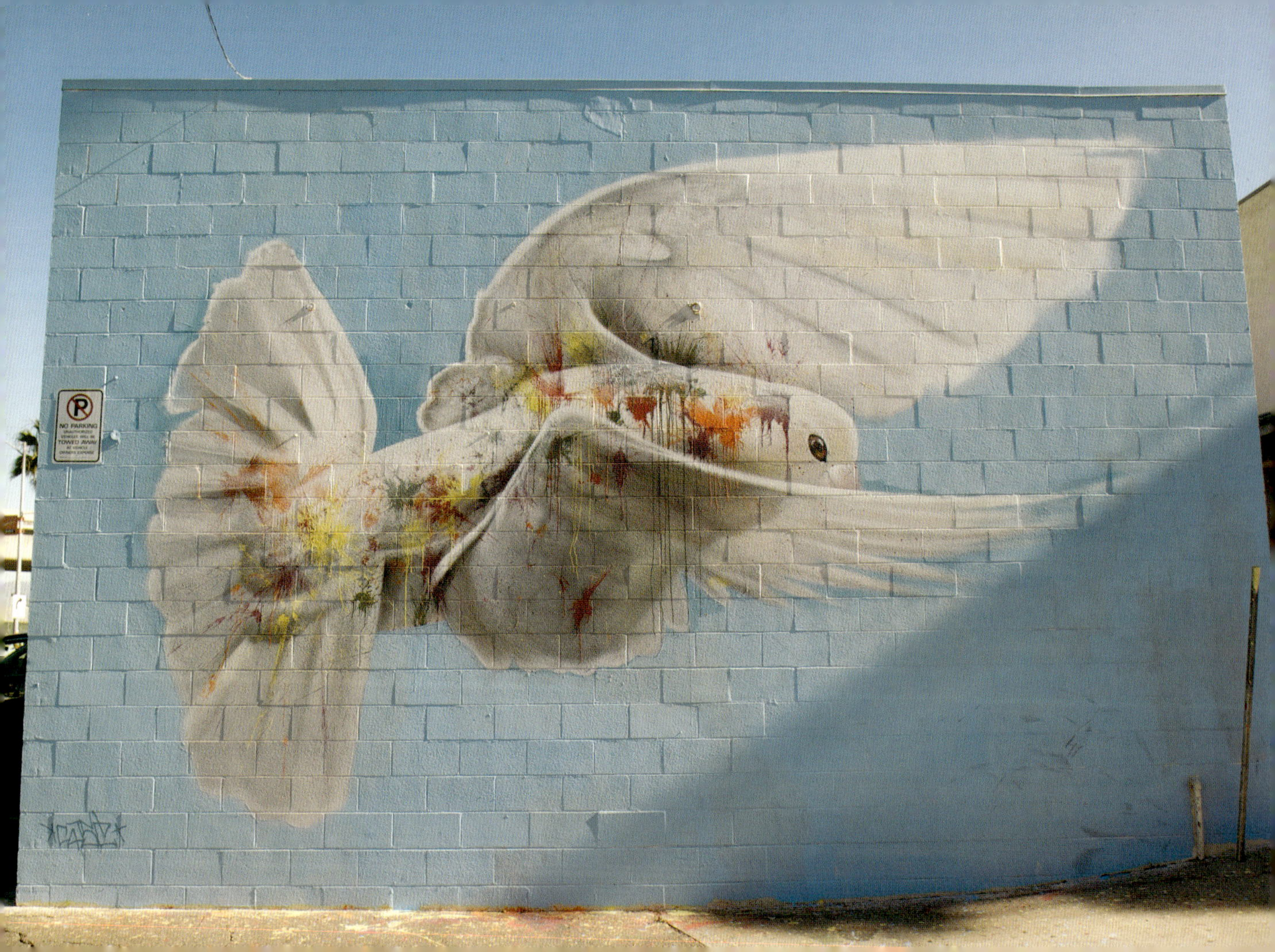
NO PARKING
TOWED AWAY

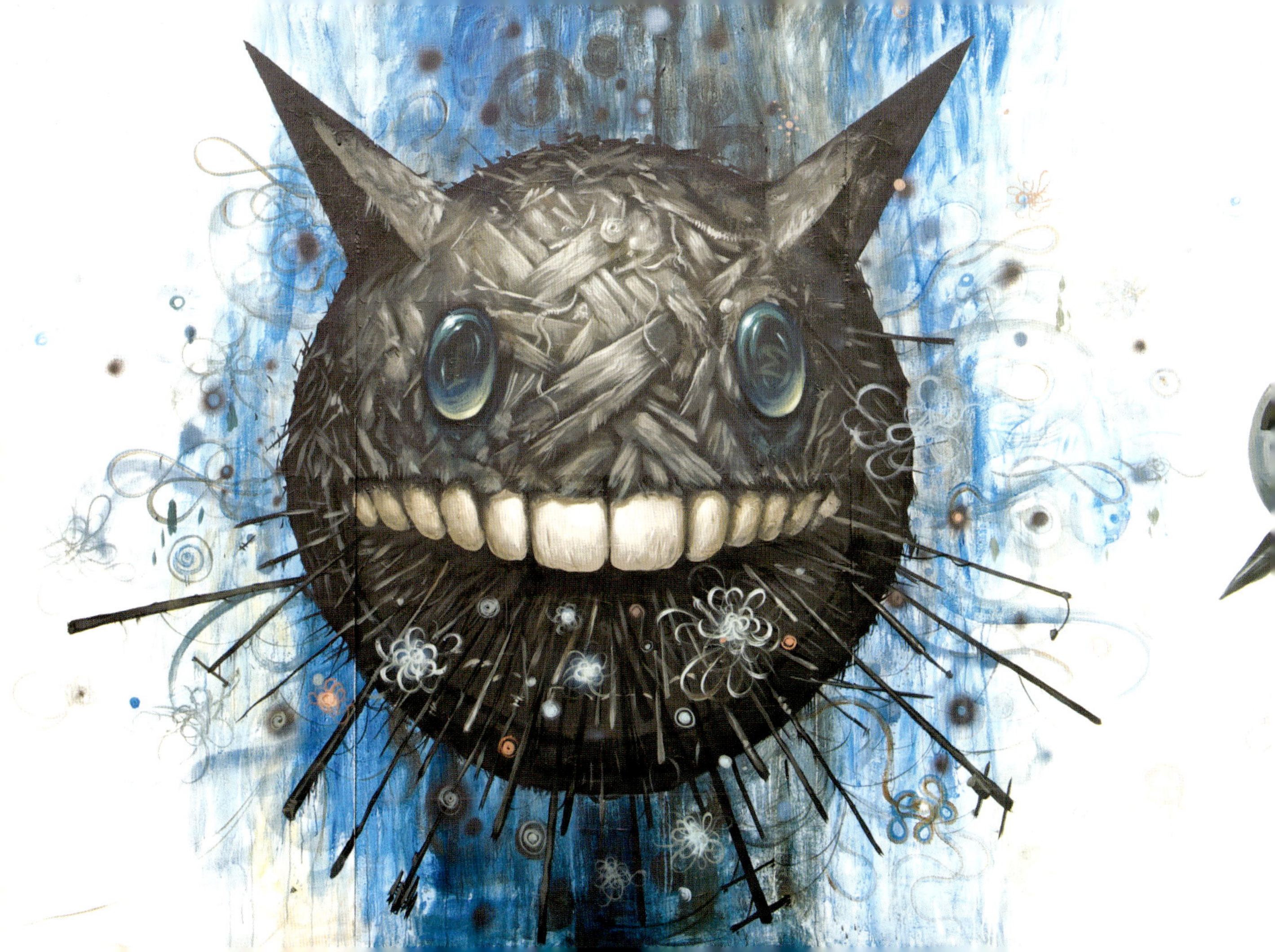

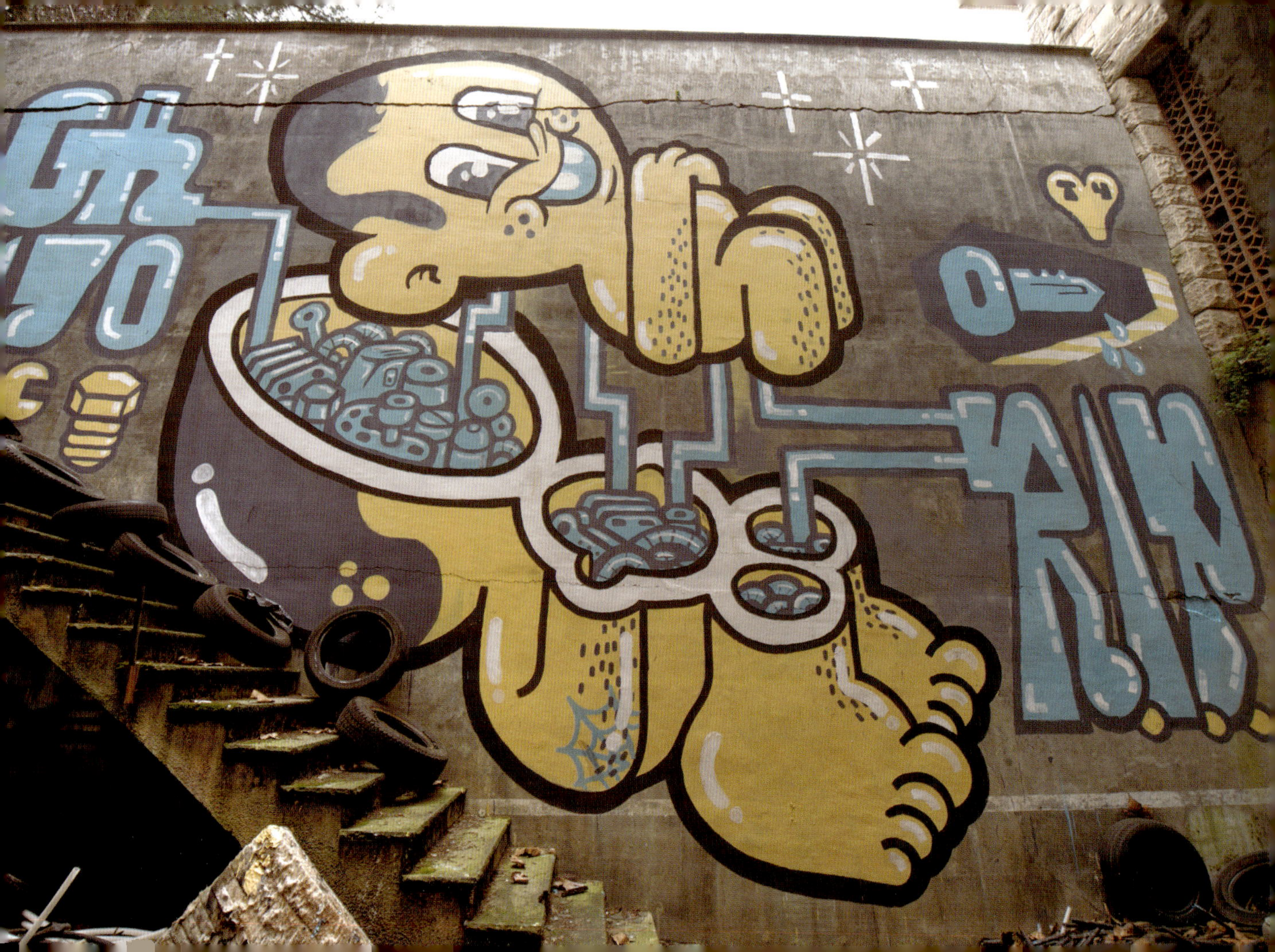

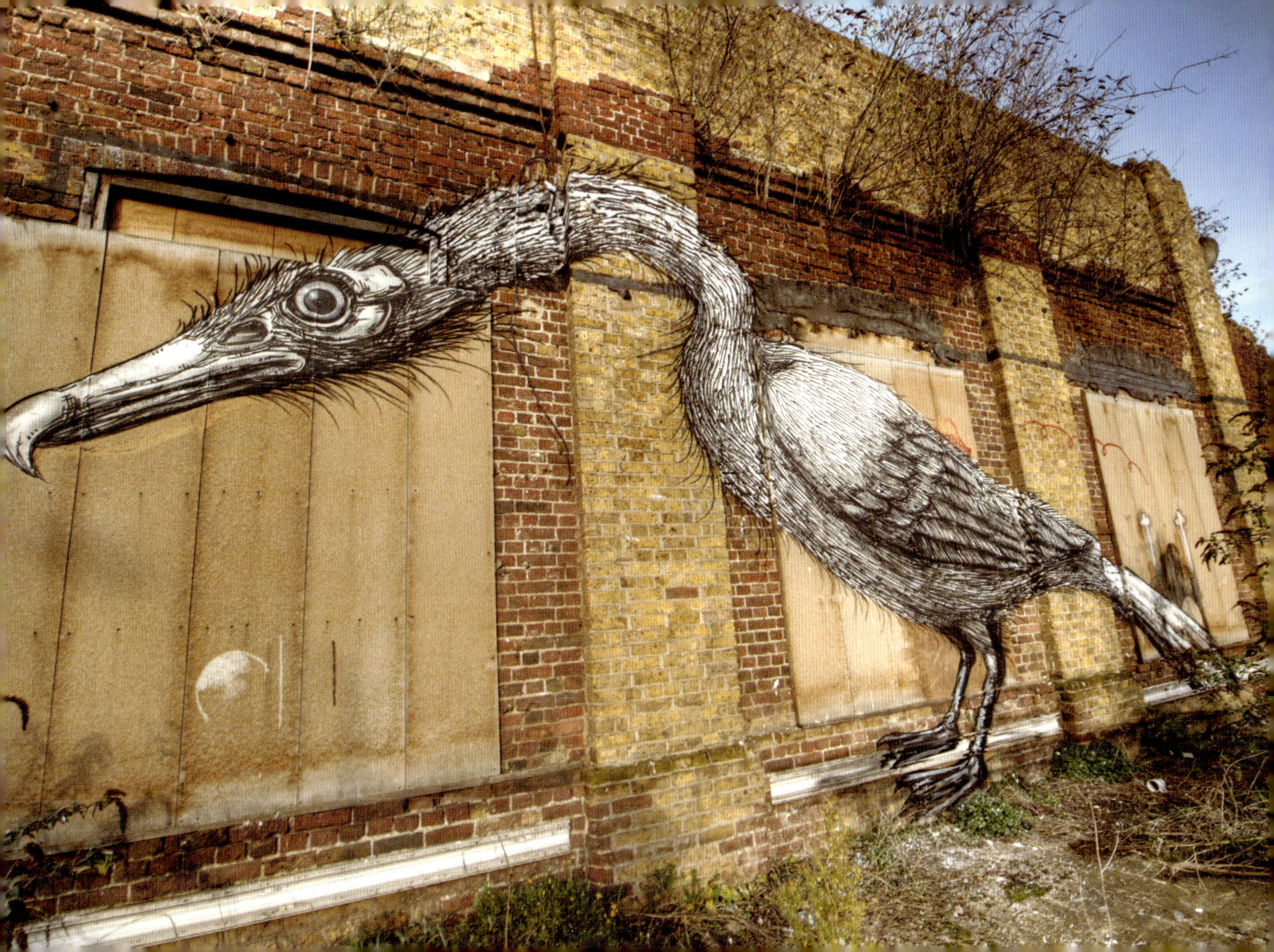

ARTISTS

6 Centina and James Kalinda / 8 Eine / 11 La Mouche / 12 Kikx / 14 Case / 17 Burning Candy / 18 La Mouche / 19 Cosmo / 21 Sickboy / 22 Mode 2 / 23 Mr Wany / 24 Cheo / 25 Bue & Roa / 26 Rabodiga & Sweet Toof / 28 Tom Hine / 30 Aryz & RIPO / 32 Charlie Isoe / 35 Burning Candy / 33 El Mac / 37 Aryz / 38 Sea / 40 Aryz / 43 Sea / 44 Aryz / 47 Sea / 49 Vilks / 50 James Kalinda / 52 James Kalinda / 53 C215 / 54 Jade / 55 DMV / 56 Leake Street / 57 Jade / 58 Sweet Toof & Paul Insect / 59 Aryz / 60 Roa / 61 Rensone / 62 Pixel Pancho / 64 Nychos / 65 Revert & Amigo / 66 Unknown / 67 T-Kid & Alex / 68 Unknown / 69 Nychos / 70 Alice / 72 Aryz / 73 Aryz / 74 Aryz / 75 Aryz / 77 Aryz / 78 Aryz / 79 Eine / 80 Best Ever / 81 DeadLeg / 82 Ponk & Amour / 83 Burning Candy / 85 DMV / 86 C215 / 87 3Dom & Sepr / 88 Aryz / 89 Iemza / 90 Iemza / 91 Iemza / 92 DMV / 94 Le Paquebot / 95 Kowalski / 96 Bomk / 97 Penny / 98 REM / 99 How & Nosm / 100 Roa / 102 Sea & Kraser / 103 Sea & Vine / 104/105 Vilks / 106 Vibes, Probs, Nychos, Crome / 108 Pure Evil / 109 The Fantasmo / 110 The Mouarf / 112 Ben Slow / 113 System, Juice & Remi Rough / 114 Alice (Crimes of Minds) / 115 Alice / 116 Gris & Sowat (DMV) / 117 Craola / 118 Eine / 121 Faunagraphic / 122 Herakut & Case / 123 Finbarr & Morten Anderson (Crimes of Minds) / 124 La Mouche / 125 SHOK1 / 127 Malarky, Lucs & Kamba / 129 Phlegm / 130 Best Ever / 133 Phlegm / 135 Phlegm / 137 Replete / 138 BC, Temp32 / 139 Burning Candy / 140 DMV (Crimes of Minds) / 142 Roa / 143 Roa / 144 Roa / 145 Rocket01 / 147 Sowat & Gris (DMV) / 149 Stinkfish / 151 El Mac & Retna / 152 Rocket01 / 153 Rocket01 / 154 El Mac & Retna / 157 Herakut / 158 El Mac & Retna / 159 Solo One / 160 Roa / 162 Zadok / 163 Herakut / 164 La Mouche / 165 DMV / 166 Roa / 168 Herakut / 169 Herakut / 170 Dran (DMV) / 171 SheOne / 172 Ghetto Farceur / 173 Bonzai / 175 C215 / 176 Brusk / 177 Brusk Sketch / 179 Best Ever & Obey / 180 RTeam / 181 Liliwenn / 182 Jago, Xenz & Will Barras / 183 Ghetto Farceur & Bonzai / 184 Probs / 185 Boxi / 186 Roa / 187 Bleach / 188 Jeff Soto / 189 Jeff Soto / 190 Lovenskate / 191 RUN / 192 Sares & Demo / 193 Voyder & 3Dom / 194/195 Mixed Media / 196 Sea / 198 Jesus Rocks / 199 Ghetto Farceur / 200 Phlegm / 201 Roa / 202 Aryz / 205 Burning Candy / 206 Aryz / 207 Aryz / 208 Phlegm / 210 Roa / 211 Roa / 213 Aryz / 214 Burning Candy / 215 Nychos / 217 Sea / 219 Ghetto Farceur & Bonzai / 220 Roa / 221 Snik / 223 Mixed Media / 224 Wow123 / 225 Revert / 226 Mau Mau / 227 Sowat & Gris (DMV) / 229 Yen, Roa, Resto & Santos / 230 Ecloz / 231 Astro / 232 Aryz / 233 SHOK1 / 234 Rone / 235 Steaz & Wacks / 236 Kikx / 237 Smug One / 238 Best Ever / 241 Unknown / 242 Case / 243 Krio special K / 244 Nychos & Pixel Pancho / 245 3Dom / 246 Phlegm / 248 Rocket01 / 250 Case / 251 Jeff Soto / 252 Grito / 253 Roa / 255 Aislap / 256 Unknown Vandal

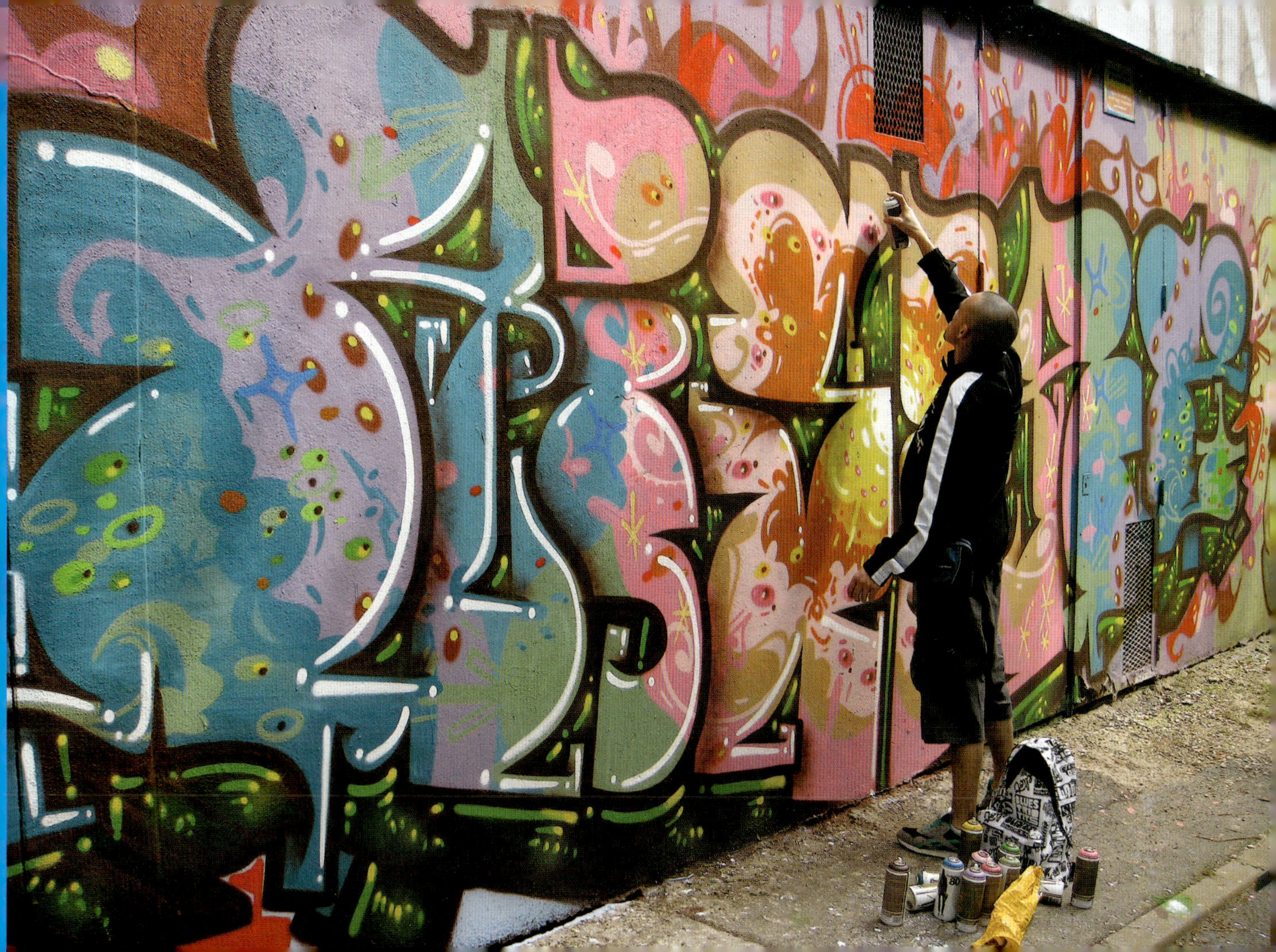

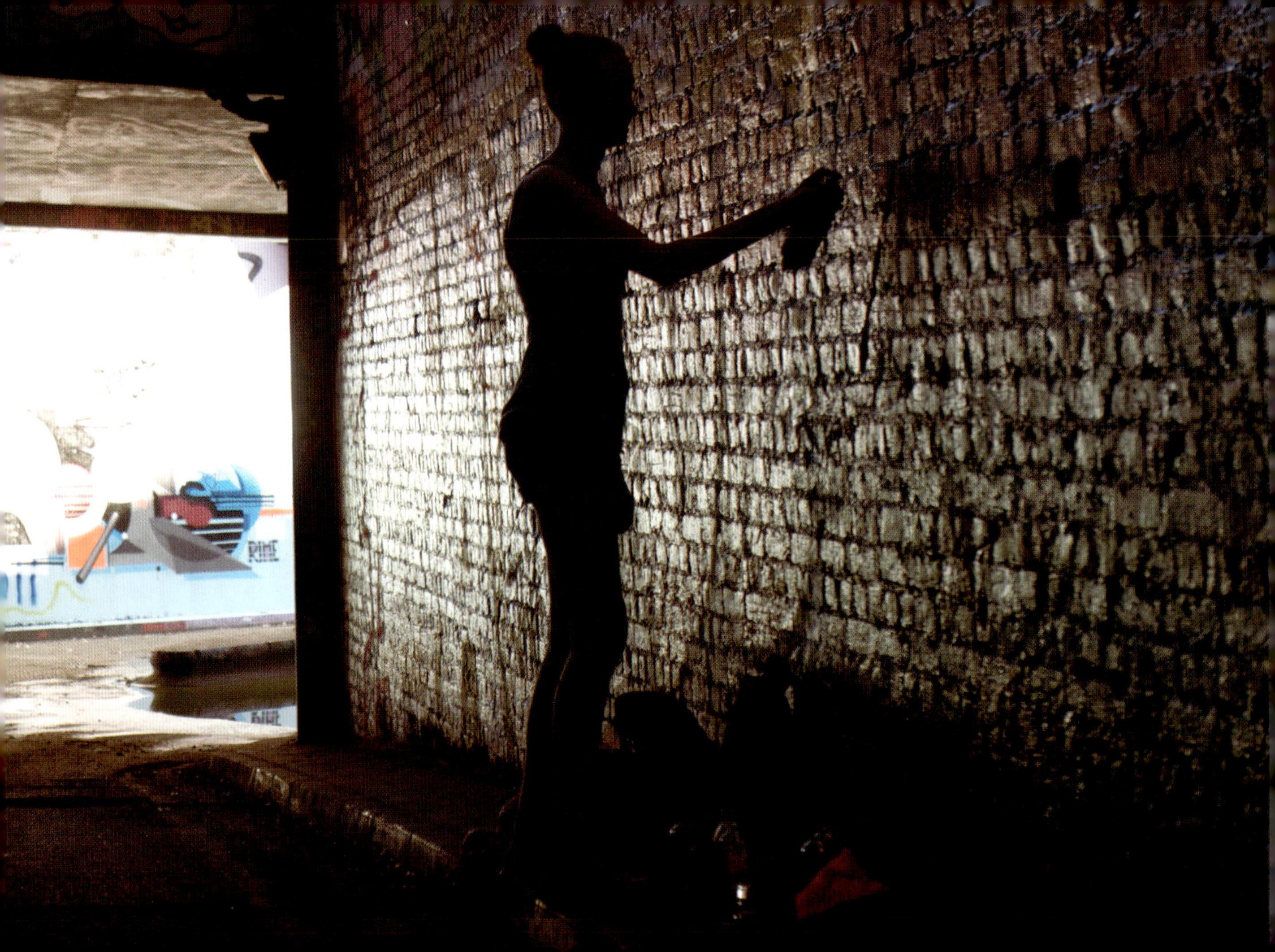